# INFANT CRYING
Theoretical and Research Perspectives

Written by 8-year-old Alyssa to her 5-year-old sister, Sarah

# INFANT CRYING
Theoretical and Research Perspectives

Edited by

## Barry M. Lester
and

## C. F. Zachariah Boukydis

The Children's Hospital and
Harvard Medical School
Boston, Massachusetts

PLENUM PRESS • NEW YORK AND LONDON

Library of Congress Cataloging in Publication Data

Main entry under title:

Infant crying.

Includes bibliographies and index.
1. Crying. 2. Infant psychology. 3. Crying—Research. 4. Interpersonal communication in children. I. Lester, Barry M. II. Boukydis, C. F. Zachariah. [DNLM: 1. Communication—in infancy & childhood. 2. Crying—in infancy & childhood. 3. Language Development. WS 105.5.E5 I43]
BF720.C78I54   1985                          155.4′22                          84-26414
ISBN 0-306-41775-8

© 1985 Plenum Press, New York
A Division of Plenum Publishing Corporation
233 Spring Street, New York, N.Y. 10013

Printed in the United States of America

To our fathers, Norman C. Lester and A. Charles Boukydis, and to
John Lind, one of the fathers of cry research.

# Contributors

MARTIN BAX, Community Paediatric Research Unit, St. Mary's Hospital Medical School, London, England

LOIS BLACK, Department of Psychology, Syracuse University, Syracuse, New York

C. F. ZACHARIAH BOUKYDIS, Department of Medicine, Harvard Medical School, and Department of Pediatrics, The Children's Hospital, Boston, Massachusetts

T. BERRY BRAZELTON, Division of Child Development, The Children's Hospital, and Department of Pediatrics, Harvard Medical School, Boston, Massachusetts

JENNIFER S. BUCHWALD, Department of Physiology, Brain Research Institute and Mental Retardation Research Center, School of Medicine, University of California at Los Angeles, Los Angeles, California

RAYMOND H. COLTON, Department of Otolaryngology and Communication Science, College of Medicine, Upstate Medical Center, State University of New York, Syracuse, New York

MICHAEL J. CORWIN, Department of Pediatrics, Boston University School of Medicine, and Department of Pediatrics, Boston City Hospital, Boston, Massachusetts

WILBERTA L. DONOVAN, Infant Development Laboratory, Waisman Center on Mental Retardation and Human Development and Department of Pediatrics, University of Wisconsin, Madison, Wisconsin

ANN FRODI, Department of Psychology, University of Rochester, Rochester, New York

JOHN GLEASON, Department of Psychology, Syracuse University, Syracuse, New York

HOWARD L. GOLUB, Pediatric Diagnostic Service Institute, Cambridge, Massachusetts

ANNA-LIISA JÄRVENPÄÄ, Department of Neonatology, Children's Hospital, University of Helsinki, Helsinki, Finland

LEWIS A. LEAVITT, Infant Development Laboratory, Waisman Center on Mental Retardation and Human Development and Department of Pediatrics, University of Wisconsin, Madison, Wisconsin

BARRY M. LESTER, Harvard Medical School and Division of Child Development, The Children's Hospital, Boston, Massachusetts

PHILIP LIEBERMAN, Department of Linguistics, Brown University, Providence, Rhode Island

JOHN LIND, late of the II Department of Pediatrics, Children's Hospital, University of Helsinki, Helsinki, Finland

KATARINA MICHELSSON, II Department of Pediatrics, Children's Hospital, University of Helsinki, Helsinki, Finland

ANN D. MURRAY, High Risk Infant Development Laboratory, Boys Town National Institute for Communication Disorders in Children, Omaha, Nebraska

THOMAS MURRY, Audiology and Speech Pathology Service, Veterans Administration Medical Center, San Diego, California

JOHN D. NEWMAN, Laboratory of Comparative Ethology, National Institute of Child Health and Human Development, National Institutes of Health, Bethesda, Maryland

PETER F. OSTWALD, Department of Psychiatry, Langley Porter Psychiatric Institute, School of Medicine, University of California at San Francisco, San Francisco, California

CARL SHIPLEY, Department of Physiology, Brain Research Institute and Mental Retardation Research Center, School of Medicine, University of California at Los Angeles, Los Angeles, California

ALFRED STEINSCHNEIDER, American SIDS Institute, Atlanta, Georgia

CARL-JOHAN THODÉN, II Department of Pediatrics, Children's Hospital, University of Helsinki, Helsinki, Finland

OLE WASZ-HÖCKERT, II Department of Pediatrics, Children's Hospital, University of Helsinki, Helsinki, Finland

PETER H. WOLFF, Department of Psychiatry, The Children's Hospital, Boston, Massachusetts

PHILIP SANFORD ZESKIND, Department of Psychology, Virginia Polytechnic Institute and State University, Blacksburg, Virginia

# Foreword

The cries of infants and children are familiar to essentially all adults, and we all have our own common sense notions of the meanings of various cries at each age level. As is often the case, in the study of various aspects of human behavior we often investigate what seems self-evident to the general public. For example, if an infant cries, he or she needs atttention; if the cry is different than usual, he or she is sick; and when we are upset by other matters, children's crying can be very annoying. As a pediatric clinician often faced with discussing with parents their concerns or lack of them with respect to their children's crying, these usual commonsense interpretations were frequently inadequate. As this book illustrates, when we investigate such everyday behaviors as children's crying and adults' responses to crying, the nature of the problem becomes surprisingly complex.

As a pediatrician working in the newborn nursery early in my career, I knew from pediatric textbooks and from nursery nurses, that newborn infants with high, piercing cries were often abnormal. In order to teach this interesting phenomenon to others and to understand under what circumstances it occurred, I found I needed to know what constituted a high-pitched cry or even a normal cry, for that matter, and how often this occurred with sick infants. Certainly I saw sick infants who did not have high-pitched cries, but I still wondered if their cries were deviant in some other way. Fortunately, several investigators in the past 25 years and many more in the past 10 years have pursued this problem.

As might be expected, the number of parameters used to define cries has escalated with improving analyzing techniques. At first, investigators studied the cries of infants with known neurological problems, then the cries of infants who were only at known risk for a neurological problem, and now infants considered to have had normal pregnancies and deliveries who might nevertheless have suffered some neurological problem. Thus the possibilities for clinical application have expanded. The chapters in this book on the cries of newborns and young infants amply illustrate the evolution of these important studies, which I think have great promise.

In clinical pediatrics, I also discovered that how and when infants' and children's cries were responded to depended as much on the characteristics of the listener as on the characteristics of the cry. While one might superficially think that all adults would give attention to an infant who cried and also become annoyed when the crying was excessive or strident, I was surprised at the many exceptions to this general wisdom. I followed the development of an infant who cried frequently and prolongedly in the early months of life, whose mother surprised me by her lack of complaints and her true devotion to this child. She expressed her happiness with this infant because she needed her so much. At the other extreme was the mother of a quiet, competent infant who cried very little, whose mother seemed disappointed, saying that this baby did not seem to need her. These extreme cases reflect the mothers' perceptions of their roles and what they attribute to their infants. Several chapters of this book address these important issues. I think this area of research is just getting started and is greatly enhanced by the studies of cry characteristics.

We are always limited in our interpretations of the precise role of the nervous system in the particular human behaviors we are studying. We, therefore, need animal models that will permit experimentation with the nervous system's controls over vocal output and reception, and such studies have been included in this book.

This is the first book that includes studies of the characteristics of infants' and children's normal and abnormal cries, the reasons for varying adult responses, and animal models that might provide further insight into these important subjects. It is an important contribution to this relatively new and exciting field.

ARTHUR H. PARMELEE
Los Angeles, California

# Acknowledgments

We would like to thank Joel Hoffman, Kate Neff, and Gaye Hoffman for their help in preparing and editing the manuscripts for this book.

# Contents

## CHAPTER 3

Howard L. Golub and Michael J. Corwin

## CHAPTER 4

Ole Wasz-Höckert, Katarina Michelsson, and John Lind

CHAPTER 5

Sound Spectrographic Cry Analysis of Pain Cry in
Prematures ................................................  105
*Carl-Johan Thodén, Anna-Liisa Järvenpää, and Katarina Michelsson*

CHAPTER 6

The Newborn Infant Cry: Its Potential Implications for
Development and SIDS ..................................... 119
*Raymond H. Colton, Alfred Steinschneider, Lois Black,
and John Gleason*

CHAPTER 7

The Communicative and Diagnostic Significance of
Infant Sounds ........................................... 139
*Peter F. Ostwald and Thomas Murry*

CHAPTER 8

A Developmental Perspective of Infant Crying .............. 159
*Philip Sanford Zeskind*

CHAPTER 9

Perception of Infant Crying as an Interpersonal Event ....... 187
*C. F. Zachariah Boukydis*

CHAPTER 10

# CHAPTER 16

# CHAPTER 17

# 1

# Introduction
## There's More to Crying Than Meets the Ear

BARRY M. LESTER

## 1. INTRODUCTION

Like a miracle of modern medicine, this book is both premature and overdue. It is premature because, despite many years of programmatic research and numerous published articles on infant crying, we know surprisingly little about the topic. This is probably more of a testimonial to the complexity of the phenomenon than anything else. That complexity is reflected throughout this volume and in other citations. Physiologically, crying involves the central and autonomic control of arousal/inhibitory mechanisms and the coordination of cardiorespiratory activity and the laryngeal musculature. Crying is a behavior; in fact, it is a sequence of behavior patterns that is part of the larger behavioral repertoire of the infant. And for the neonate and young infant, crying is the primary mode of expressing and communicating basic needs and events. It is a social behavior that has powerful effects on the parent–infant relationship, and it elicits strong emotions in parents. The cry is also an acoustical event that not only affects caregivers but also contains information about the functioning of the infant's nervous system. Finally, as a form of communication, crying is the beginning of vocalization and may have implications for the development of speech and language.

BARRY M. LESTER • Harvard Medical School and Division of Child Development, The Children's Hospital, Boston, Massachusetts 02115.

You can perhaps see now why this volume is also overdue—this vast array of information has not heretofore been brought together; this is the first full volume entirely devoted to crying in infancy. The disciplines represented by the international group of contributors include developmental psychology, pediatrics, neurology, engineering, speech, physiology, comparative psychology, and psychiatry. It is somewhat curious that, with all of this work, crying is only given a cursory glance in the developmental literature. In the *Handbook of Infant Development* (Osofsky, 1979), there are two entries under *cry* in the index, and in the *Handbook of Developmental Psychology* (Wolman, 1982), crying does not even appear in the index. Perhaps this is because this work has never before been brought together and has not been considered in a developmental framework.

There have been substantial advances in the field during the past few years, due, in part, to increased collaboration among investigators from different disciplines. The groundwork was laid in the 1960s by a Scandinavian team working first in Stockholm, then in Helsinki, resulting in two monographs, *Newborn Infant Cry* (Lind, 1965) and *The Infant Cry: A Spectrographic and Auditory Analysis* (Wasz-Höckert, Lind, Vuorenkoski, Partanen, & Valanne, 1968), and by the writings of Wolff, Prechtl, and Brazelton. Throughout this work, crying was defined as a distinct behavioral state through which basic sensations such as hunger and pain are expressed and as a normal developmental phenomenon. Sound spectrographic studies revealed acoustical properties of the cry that opened the door to using the cry for medical diagnosis.

In the last decade, the second generation of cry researchers has built upon this foundation, and it is a pleasure to have contributors from both generations included in this volume. The building and the advances that we have made have been aided by high speed computer technology and the interdisciplinary impact mentioned before. As a result, the signal processing and analysis of the cry is greatly improved, as is our understanding of the physiological and anatomical basis of cry production (see Chapter 3).

The study of crying from a normal developmental perspective has had a number of implications for the understanding of normal and abnormal developmental processes. Some of the acoustic features, such as increases in the fundamental frequency, which were thought to only characterize brain-damaged or very sick infants, we now know are also found in infants with less severe trauma (preterm infants and growth-retarded infants, infants with pre- and perinatal obstetric complications), no trauma (temperamentally difficult infants), or infants for whom there may be no other (as yet) identified sign such as those who later succumb to sudden infant death syndrome (SIDS) (see Chapters 3, 4, 5, 6, and

8; as well as Lester, 1984; Lester & Zeskind, 1982). These findings have several implications. One is that no single measure such as average fundamental frequency is likely to discriminate normal from abnormal infants; variability in the fundamental frequency, combinations of acoustic features, and an understanding of the context (age, state, eliciting stimulus) in which the cry is recorded will probably be necessary to identify pathology. Second, some acoustic features may be more of a general statement about the functional status or organization of the nervous system than a specific indicator of disease, lesion, or structural defect in the nervous system. It may be, for example, that changes in cry acoustics that have been found in temperamentally difficult or colicky infants are due to contemporaneous reorganizational changes in the nervous system such as those that have been described by Emde, Gaensbauer, and Harmon (1976). Third, removing the cry strictly from the domain of pathology or pathophysiology *expands* the possibilities for medical diagnosis.

There are three clinical situations in which the cry should prove useful for medical diagnosis. The first is where the cry is used to support differential diagnosis as in, for example, asphyxia, hyperbilirubinemia, or cerebral insult. There are usually other clinical signs, even though the cry may have drawn attention to the infant in the first place and the diagnosis is confirmed by follow-up laboratory or neurological work-up. The second category is the infant at risk. This large, catch-all category refers to infants who have experienced some trauma (for example, prematurity) known to be associated with later mental or motor handicap. Although many of these infants develop normally, a significant proportion do not; yet we do not have methods to determine which infants are truly headed for handicap, so that appropriate treatment or early intervention programs could be developed to alleviate or attenuate the problem.

At-risk infants show a wide range of individual differences in cry acoustics that as a group differ from normal infants and that might provide clues about their prognosis (see Chapters 4 and 5). There is evidence, for example, that neonatal cry patterns in preterm infants relate to mental performance in the second year of life (Lester, 1984). Many birth-asphyxiated infants do not actually sustain permanent brain damage, and this information may be contained in the cry (Michelsson, Sirvio, & Wasz-Höckert, 1977). As the jeopardized infant begins the recovery process, changes in the cry to patterns typical of normal infants could signify a normal developmental trajectory.

The third situation in which the cry may have diagnostic utility is where there are not other presenting clinical indicators except the unusual cry. Other signs may be more subtle or not yet known. In the case of SIDS, a link with the cry has been suggested (see Chapters 3 and 6). This may be due to the relationship between crying and respiratory activity and the role of neural input from the vagus nerve that could reveal brain stem involvement (Lester, 1984).

Another major advance in cry research, also aided by a normal developmental perspective, has been the burgeoning of cry perception studies—how adults feel about and respond to different infant cry patterns (see Chapters 8, 9, 10, 11, and 12). Cry perception studies provide an important adjunct to, and cross-validation of, acoustic analyses by showing the acoustical dimensions along which adults differentiate within the realm of normal infant cries and between the cries of normal and abnormal infants. They actually help in the selection of acoustic variables. It was statements from parents, such as "The cry is hard to read and understand, arrythmic," that led us to look at measures of variability such as how rapidly the fundamental frequency was changing. By manipulating cry acoustics with audiotape recordings and having adults rate cry tapes, one could determine the acoustic features that adults use to discriminate among cries; for example, hunger versus pain cries. Further, cry perception studies provide insights into the processes of the developing parent–infant relationship in several ways. The fact that the cries of some infants or certain groups of infants are perceived differently from others shows the effect of the infant on the caregiving environment. Infants at risk are communicating a specific messge when their cry is perceived by adults as sick and urgent, which may actually facilitate their care (see Chapter 8). How adults perceive the cry is thought by some to be an estimate of parenting behavior (see Chapter 12). For example, mothers who have abused their infants tend to have more negative reactions to infant cries. Cry perception studies provide information about both members of the interactive dyad—how the cry is perceived, along which acoustic dimensions, the nature of the message received by the adult, how the adult feels about the cry (parents who perceive a cry as aversive may also be making a statement about the infant), and the effects of the cry on adult physiological arousal systems (cardiac and electrodermal) (see Chapters 9, 11, and 12).

The notion that how adults perceive infant cries might relate to parenting behavior is intriguing because it has clinical as well as theoretical implications. The next step is to connect empirically the three cornerstones of this concept: measured cry acoustics, adult cry perception, and measured adult behavior. In particular, how does perception translate into action, or, phenomenologically, how are experiences felt, then perceived (see Chapter 9)? Obviously, most adults do not perpetuate negative feelings directly on their babies; if so, child abuse would be more common. The perception of a cry as negative does not neces-sarily imply negative parenting; yet for some adults it does, and it is critical to know under what circumstances (e.g., personality, stress, and socioeconomic factors) this holds true. Correlating measured cry acous-tics with adult cry perception is one way of separating what is heard from what is perceived.

The complexity of these dynamics is illustrated by the following examples. Infants with pre- and perinatal complications have cries that show elevations in fundamental frequency and these cries are perceived as sick and urgent as well as aversive and distressing. Yet adults report that their caretaking would be more structured, presumably because they recognize the jeopardized state of the infant (see Chapter 8). Cries of temperamentally difficult infants are perceived as more negative and physiologically more arousing (see Chapter 9). Physiological arousal to crying and negative perceptions of the infant are also associated with child abuse (see Chapter 12). In one study, the cries of preterm infants were perceived as *less* negative than term infant cries (Friedman, Zahn-Waxler, & Radke-Yarrow, 1982). In another study, overall increases in the fundamental frequency and the variability of the fundamental fre-quency in the cries of preterm infants were correlated with higher syn-chrony in mother–infant interaction, which in turn predicted higher mental performance (Lester, 1984). Lester, Garcia-Coll, Valcarcel, and Hoffman, (1984) found that the cries of growth-retarded infants, which showed a higher fundamental frequency and other unusual features, were perceived more negatively by nonteenage mothers but less nega-tively (in fact, toward the positive end of each dimension) by teenage mothers. Teenage mothers also had difficulties feeding their growth-retarded infants, who also showed more deviant Brazelton scale scores. In this situation, it appeared that the less negative perceptions of the infant cries by the teenage mothers was a denial of the difficult nature of their infants.

It is clear from these studies that adults do not respond uniformly to the cries of infants. The dynamics that cause mothers to perceive deviant cries as more positive could involve denial mechanisms that provide a necessary psychological barrier that could lead to optimal or nonoptimal parenting, depending on the psychological makeup and living conditions of the parents. Parenting behavior is likely to be dif-ferent for a middle-class family of a preterm infant than a lower-class teenager with a malnourished infant. Similarly, perceiving a cry as neg-ative may facilitate child care in some situations, especially where the infant is perceived as in need of special handling and the parents are emotionally equipped to provide the appropriate care. For other parents, negative feelings are acted out directly or indirectly with consequences ranging from more transient difficulties in the parent–infant relationship to failures such as abuse and neglect. Thus, no single acoustic property of the cry or pattern of parental perception leads to interactive failure; the interaction between these factors might place some dyads at risk.

One of the threads woven throughout the fabric of our discussion so far is that the cry is part of the infant's communicative system. It should be obvious by now that through the cry messages are being transmitted by the infant, received and processed by the caregiving environment, which returns feedback to the infant. Because the development of speech and language is the major accomplishment in the development of communication, it is attractive to think how infant crying may relate to the ontogeny of speech and language (see Chapter 2). One approach to this question is represented in this volume by the chapters on vocalization in primates (Chapter 14) and kittens (Chapter 13). A phylogenetic case is made for using animal models to better understand the evolutionary and neural origins of early infant vocalizations. One has to be struck by the similarity in structure and function of vocal patterns across species; human infant cries and kitten cries show remarkably similar acoustic patterns. Also, the qualitative aspects of adult speech—so-called prosodic or suprasegmental features—in contrast to the segmented or grammar and syntax aspect, are precisely what constitute human infant cries and nonhuman vocalizations. Infant cries and nonhuman vocalizations contain the same features as adult human speech, which leads one to wonder if segmented features develop from suprasegmented features, and, if so, how.

One possibility is through the development of social interaction, specifically the rhythmic structure of social interaction. It has long been recognized that interaction rhythms, nonverbal and verbal, form the basis for communication. Whereas crying and language may be directly related through the development of vocalization, crying may have indirect effects on language as well through the effect of the cry on the mother–infant interaction. In a study mentioned earlier (Lester, 1984), acoustic cry measures in the neonate (prosodic features, if you will) were correlated with the rhythmic structures of infant–mother face-to-face interactions at 3 months of age; specifically with the coherence between maternal and infant cycles of affective displays, a measure of synchrony in the interaction. Synchrony scores were in turn related to 18-month Bayley mental scores. We also found that dyadic interaction in term infant–mother pairs was more synchronous than in preterm infant–mother pairs, with preterms also showing lower Bayley scores.

It seems reasonable that early parent–infant interaction patterns are established around the management of major issues such as crying, feeding, and sleeping. Crying is also an opportunity for positive social interaction; when successfully managed, the parent is doubly rewarded, the crying stops, and playful interactions can occur. Moreover, crying is the young infant's primary means of communication; hence, it is the sound of the cry that parents listen to to determine what the infant needs. Parents tune into this channel, learn to understand what their infant is trying to say (how to read their baby) through the rhythm and other qualities of the cry, and establish the foundation of a communications system. Parents learn to modulate and manage their infant's crying by supplying verbal and nonverbal feedback, which in itself is rhythmic, establishing early cycles of social interaction. In soothing an infant, we introduce cadence and patterning in our voices; we use rocking, walking, music, sucking on a pacifier—all forms of rhythmic stimulation that establish the temporal patterning of social interaction. Temporal patterning provides a structure for the infant to organize cognitive and affective expressions and learn rules of communication such as turn taking. It is thought that symbolic functions later used in language are formed through the expectancies and structure provided by temporal patterning (e.g., Stern, Beebe, Jaffe, & Bennett, 1977).

Our discussion so far has focused on crying in the neonatal period; little is known about crying in older infants and children (see Chapter 16). For example, anatomical and physiological changes by the end of the second month of life enable the infant to begin to gain voluntary control over vocalization (see Chapter 2). What started out as a reflexive-like response now has an added volitional sounding dimension (see Chapter 9). Parents say, "He's okay, he's just crying because he wants attention," or "That's his spoiled cry." It may be that the voluntary control over crying provides experience that facilitates the infant's control over noncry vocalizations, such as gurgling, cooing, and babbling, that lead to later language. These developmental changes in crying and how they relate to noncry vocalizations have not been studied; yet they are all part of the infant's expanding vocal repertoire.

This goes back to a statement made earlier in this chapter, that there is really no theory of crying or understanding of how crying fits into the larger framework of development. Yet crying is a critically important clinical issue, probably the most common problem parents have with their infant during the first months of life. Brazelton (see Chapter 15) discusses crying as a normal developmental process from a clinical pediatric perspective.

Some of the issues raised in these introductory remarks are elaborated by Wolff in the epilogue of this volume. He provides a valuable critique of this volume and, by extension, of the field of infant cry. The next section of this introduction is a preliminary sketch of a theory, and it is the reason why I called this an introductory essay. My hope is that it will stimulate others to broaden our theoretical and empirical understanding of crying and help in the clinical management of crying.

## 2. SOME THEORETICAL SPECULATIONS

### 2.1. Crying and States of Arousal

We begin with the definitional property of crying as the highest state of arousal on the continuum from sleep to wakefulness. In the neonate, there is an intrinsic sleep/wakefulness cycle as well as a more primitive, basic rest/activity cycle (BRAC), and these are controlled by independent biological rhythms (Berg & Berg, 1979). Initially, these cycles are probably regulated at the brain stem level with forebrain mechanisms coming into play in the control of the sleep/wakefulness cycle during the first months of life as the infant becomes more aware of the environment. In the neonate, crying often signifies the onset of wakefulness as part of the sleep/wake cycle and usually leads to feeding. In most newborns, the state transitions are from sleep to crying, and although some infants do stop crying by themselves, in most cases it is the caretaker who intervenes to lower the arousal. With maturation, the wakefulness part of the cycle becomes more differentiated as alert states become interspersed between sleeping and crying. The state transitions are now from sleep to alert to crying, the periods of alertness increase in frequency and duration, and some infants cry rarely or not at all as part of this cyclical variation.

I have talked about crying as an adaptive function, and in the present context the function is usually to ensure feeding. *On demand* is such an apt phrase. Crying may decrease as part of this cycle as the caretaker anticipates or regularizes feeding, thereby intervening before or shortly after crying begins. In Latin American Indian cultures, for example, infants are carried on their mothers' backs and rarely cry because mothers can tell by the baby's movements that it is time for a feeding.

The increasing alertness and decreasing crying as part of the sleep/wakefulness cycle suggests that there may be a balanced exchange between crying and attention; as an awake state of arousal, crying is the other side of attention. The change from sleep/cry to sleep/alert/cry necessitates the development of control mechanisms to modulate arousal. The infant must increase arousal more gradually, in smaller increments, to maintain states of attention for longer periods. What starts out almost as an all or none or on/off system expands into a complex balance of differentiated levels of arousal that are biologically adaptive as they increase opportunities for the infant to interact with the environment more selectively and organize cognitive and affective experience. This is, however, initially a delicate balance. States of alertness and attention are at first fleeting and fragile. To maintain an alert state is difficult; to respond also to environmental input is more difficult. When this balance is upset, so is the infant, and crying is often the result; it is the infant's way of saying help.

The balanced exchange I spoke of is now apparent. Physiological regulation is the primary task of the neonate. As the newborn adjusts to the demands of the postnatal environment and physiological processes become stabilized, other maturational forces come into play to facilitate growth and development, such as the emergence of alertness and attention. Behavior contributes to physiological regulation, and crying plays an important role in the behavioral regulation of physiological processes. Crying affects physiology directly by increasing pulmonary capacity. The muscular activity that accompanies crying generates heat and contributes to thermoregulation. As we have already seen, crying also has indirect effects on physiological regulation by signaling the caretaker that the baby is stressed, hungry, in pain, sick, and so forth, and is in need of attention. As a result, the physiological process in question is attended. The interplay between these direct and indirect effects has been illustrated by Woodson (1983). Cold exposure leads to crying that generates heat and improves thermoregulation. At the same time, crying elicits warm physical contact from the caregiver, which again contributes to thermoregulation. By extending this vignette to include the cessation of crying and the elicitation of alertness and social interaction, we can see the reciprocal relationship between crying and alertness and how crying serves to regulate input from the environment. Alertness promotes stimulus intake, and crying leads to stimulus rejection, much like the defensive response described by Sokolov (1963). Crying is a loud and clear sign of stress that internal or external requirements are not being met and is adaptive by leading to the resolution of these demands. These requirements can be due to too little *or* too much, for example, overstimulation or understimulation. From this perspective, crying is part of a regulatory system in which the interplay of behavioral and physiological processes function to maintain homeostatic balance, regulate the duration of alertness and attention, and elicit caretaking when internal or external demands are not met. In this regulatory system, crying is the infant's first line of defense—the early warning sign, actually the spokesperson for the defense. It is a loud and clear and relatively economical way of showing distress and protecting more vital internal physiological functions.

One of the advantages of considering crying in this fashion is that it helps to explain more of the variation in crying. If crying is part of the regulatory system, some changes in the cry may be due to changes in the system, rather than indications of specific needs of the infant. Periods of crying for no apparent reason, often called colic, may be related to systemic changes in central nervous system (CNS) maturation. When parents say, "I can't understand what he wants, he just cries," they are probably correct. In these situations, crying is not communicating a specific need; it is a sign that the system is disorganized or overwhelmed. Colic will be discussed later, and obviously the key clinical questions are how to know when there really is nothing wrong and what to do when there is. The point here is to consider systemic changes in the regulatory system that in this sense are actually healthy, despite the difficulty parents may have in coping with certain patterns of crying. Infants who cannot stop crying or who cry very frequently or those who hardly cry or do not cry at all are possible examples of these systemic changes that may be maturationally based. We do not often think about not crying as a negative signal except in the inital pediatric evaluation of the newborn where crying is part of the Apgar assessment. There are lethargic, unresponsive babies who rarely cry, and when they do, it is weak and pathetic sounding. We see this problem in older infants in cases of malnutrition and neglect but also in some newborns. We have observed that very young preterm infants and asphyxiated infants often do not cry at first, and when they do, it is a sign of recovery. We often hear parents of preterms tell us how important it is to hear their babies cry; it lets them know he or she is really there—a human being. Friedman, Zahn-Walker, and Radke-Yarrow (1982) found that parents rated some preterm infant cries as more positive (e.g., more pleasing and less urgent) than full-term infant cries. Crying takes energy that the very sick or tiny preterm may not be able to expend. The ability to cry is a statement of the robustness of the infant. But there may also be a maturational side that is revealed by the preterm; how the onset and development of crying changes in sick and healthy preterm infants as they approach term age might reveal maturational factors in the development of their regulatory system. We have observed young preterms (especially below 32 weeks) who seem to make cry efforts. They build up as if to cry but do not; others look as if they are crying, but there is no vocalization; it is as if the coordination between breathing and phonation is not yet achieved. Thus, the context in which crying occurs and the expectations we have about crying will influence how we understand and interpret variations in patterns of crying.

## 2.2. Crying and the Development of Inhibition

If crying is part of an arousal-regulation system, it seems reasonable to explore how mechanisms that mediate arousal provide a better understanding of crying. Consider again the basic sleep/wakefulness cycle and what is involved in the regulation of state behavior. The primary task is how to balance excitation and inhibition; excitation increases arousal from lower to higher states, and inhibition enables the infant to maintain certain states or return from a higher to a lower state of arousal. The balance between excitation and inhibition keeps infants asleep or in an alert state; through inhibitory mechanisms arousal is lowered from crying to alertness or sleep. This characterization of crying and arousal may be taken as a more general property of development in infancy that provides a broader developmental perspective on crying and behavioral development. The infant's physiological organization can be viewed as a developing control system in which the basic task of infancy is to balance excitation and inhibition. Excitation is the developmentally more immature function as regards the hierarchical organization of the nervous system, in that excitation is produced by diffuse and generalized sympathetic nervous system activity. By contrast, inhibition is more localized, is parasympathetically mediated, and is a more advanced nervous system function. Arousal is controlled by increased inhibition. The inability to cry must be seen as a more fundamental CNS defect than too much crying. This is probably why measures of latency to respond have proved useful in reflecting nervous system involvement in cry (e.g., Karelitz & Fisichelli, 1962) as well as other response systems.

The balance between excitation and inhibition enables the infant to regulate physiological and behavioral processes. There is a constant interplay between endogenous and exogenous demands as the system seeks to maintain homeostasis.

The notion of homeostasis is used here as an active, dynamic concept and includes behavioral as well as physiological mechanisms. The importance of homeostasis as a dynamic concept is that it includes change as well as stability. We often equate homeostasis with stability or status quo, as if the goal is not to change. Homeostasis is constant change, but it is keeping the change in balance so as not to jeopardize vital processes; it is controlled change, or stability in the face of change. The constant dialectic between stability and change enables the infant both to maintain basic organizational structure and processes but also to grow, adapt, and develop.

Homeostasis allows for organizational stability and adaptive change. Crying as the behavioral regulation of physiological processes restores homeostasis and is followed by developmentally adaptive processes of alertness, attention, and social interaction. The development of inhibition emerges as a primary behavioral achievement during the neonatal period. Built on the substrate of physiological homeostasis, behavioral inhibition develops to enable the infant to regulate arousal, increasing opportunities for attentional states and social and cognitive stimulation. The task of the young infant is control of physiological processes through homeostatic mechanisms and of behavior through inhibition.

In crying, tension of the laryngeal musculature controls acoustic features of the cry sound (see Chapter 3). A neural model of cry production has been described elsewhere (Lester, 1984) based on vagal control of tension of the laryngeal muscles. Both neural facilitory and inhibitory mechanisms control vocal fold activity. Additional vagal input from the autonomic nervous system also supplies parasympathetic fibers that affect the respiratory influence on crying. Cry production is viewed as a complex, dynamic feedback system; it is specifically a system operating under feedback control—a closed loop system. One feedback loop involves proprioceptive feedback of the laryngeal muscles that contain both efferent and afferent neurons. A second feedback loop is through vagal parasympathetic pathways in which crying is modulated by autonomic homeostatic mechanisms.

The acceptance of the role of inhibition and control at both a basic nervous system and behavioral level leads to an understanding of the development of crying in infancy and has implications for the clinical management of crying. Crying is a heightened (the highest) state of arousal produced by nervous system excitation triggered by some form of biological threat that may involve basic physiological processes, such as hunger, pain, sickness, or insult, or individual differences in threshold for stimulation. Crying is modulated and development facilitated by control mechanisms that enable the infant to maintain noncrying (e.g., alert) states. The switch from the on/off sleep/cry/sleep cycle to the more differentiated sleep/alert/cry/alert/sleep cycle reflects the increasing role of inhibitory mechanisms. These mechanisms develop through the interplay of maturation and experience; inhibition is a property of the nervous system, but control of behavioral processes is modified by environmental input. The substrate of control is neurologically based (it will be argued later, through endogenous oscillating mechanisms), and it involves learning.

There is a wide constitutional variation in the behavioral control system; witness the range of individual differences in neonatal behavior, particularly with respect to the range and regulation of state behavior. Newborns differ along dimensions such as how many states are available. Some infants are hard to wake up and immediately cry; then if left alone return immediately to sleep, whereas others waken more gradually, some immediately, and they may or may not become alert, although they usually do cry. How rapidly and regularly states change and if the changes are smooth or abrupt depend on inhibitory control mechanisms, as does the ability to stop crying. The cessation of crying can be mediated through endogenous or exogenous means or a combination of both. Some infants stop crying simply when left alone (a very popular type of infant). There infants have well-developed inhibitory mechanisms that lower arousal without external input and often maintain a prolonged alert state and are attentive and interactive following the cessation of the cry. There are also infants who stop crying when left alone for other reasons; these are infants who have a lower tolerance level or threshold for stimulation. This can occur within the realm of normal behavior or can be a sign of hypersensitivity. Distinguishing among these various types of infants will depend upon how the rest of the infant's behavior relates to the pattern of crying. For example, hypersensitive babies often cannot tolerate much stimulation at all; maintaining an alert state is especially difficult, and one has the feeling that these infants want to be left alone. Many infants, of course, require caretaking to stop crying, but, again, there is a wide range of responsivity. For some babies, talking to them or mild restraint of their arms is all that is necessary; others need to be swaddled, picked up, held, or rocked. Notice, however, that virtually all of our techniques for soothing involve some form of containment, which is inhibition of motor activity. The caretaker provides the inhibition that lowers arousal. Consolability or soothability involves inhibition on the part of the infant or from the caretaker. Inhibitory control mechanisms also mediate other soothing techniques, such as rocking, vestibular stimulation, and music, and the like. To see how this works, we turn to rhythmic properties of the nervous system.

## 2.3. Crying and Endogenous Oscillators

Inhibition and, more accurately, the balance between excitation and inhibition or approach/withdrawal is, as we have seen, a basic property of the nervous system, and it enables the infant to regulate input from the environment through crying and other behavioral systems. In many control systems, including autonomic homeostatic functions such as cardiac and respiratory activity, this balance is partially maintained by oscillating timing mechanisms or biological rhythms. Temporal patterning is fundamental to biological systems and has been demonstrated in infant behaviors such as sucking, motility, social interaction, and sleep/wake and BRAC cycles as well as physiological functions such as EEG and cardiorespiratory activity. It has been suggested that there are rhythmical patterns in the cry, but this has not yet been quantitiatively demonstrated. Stratton (1982) reported a 40-minute cycle of vocal activity as part of the first extended sleep of newborns, although there were no periods of sustained crying.

In current work with Zachariah Boukydis and Joel Hoffman, we are using spectral analysis to study the rhythmicity in crying and cardiac and respiratory activity. Figure 1 shows periodicities in the fundamental frequency ($F_0$) of the cry in a newborn infant. A fast Fourier (FFT) routine was first used to plot the fundamental frequency of the cry over time. A second FFT was then computed on the $F_0$ over time data to reveal

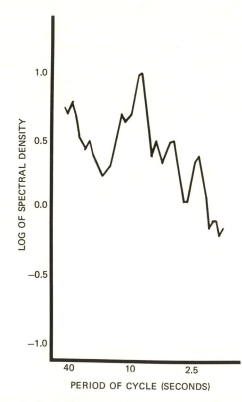

*Figure 1.* Periodicities in the fundamental frequency of the cry of a healthy term newborn infant. The fast Fourier transform was applied to the fundamental frequency computed in successive 50 msec blocks of time. This plot shows the spectrum of the fundamental frequency with a major peak having an 8 to 10 second cycle.

periodicities in $F_0$ as shown in the figure. The major peak is in the middle of the spectrum showing an 8–10 second rhythm in the cry. Other investigators have reported similar rhythms in cardiac and respiratory activity that are thought to be controlled by the same supramedullary oscillator (DeHaan, Patrick, Chess, & Jaco, 1977; Hathorn, 1979). It has been experimentally shown in dogs that the 8–10 second rhythm in cardiac activity is due to parasympathetic input. It may be that the homeostatic function of crying and cardiorespiratory activity is controlled by central neural oscillating mechanisms that control parasympathetic, particularly vagal, input. The functional significance of this 8–10 second rhythm may be to synchronize or coordinate crying and cardiorespiratory activity. Cardiorespiratory activity must adapt itself to crying as well as to other rhythmic activities such as sucking. Stratton (1982) has proposed that ontogenesis is marked by a shift from relaxation-type to pendulum-type oscillations. The pendulum oscillation is sinusoid in shape and is characterized by minimal energy exchange. Relaxation oscillations are sawtooth in shape, efficient, and more energy is transferred. They are more flexible, more easily entrained or synchronized by a forcing oscillation, and may be advantageous in early development. Neonatal functions such as respiration, heart beat, and crying fit the characteristics of relaxation oscillation. By being responsive to fluctuating demands, there is a considerable biological advantage in early development as these systems have the ability to synchronize with a wider range of periodicities.

There are grounds for proposing that endogenous oscillating or timing mechanisms are at the base of the development of behavioral control systems in infants. Control systems that oscillate around a mean as in relaxation oscillators, rather than trying to maintain a fixed level, as in pendulum oscillators, provide advantages for the integration of internal physiological processes and behavioral regulation through interaction with the caregiving environment (Stratton, 1982). The interplay of maturation and experience is suggested as biological rhythms synchronize internal homeostatic adjustments and provide the flexibility that enables the young infant to coordinate interrelated functions such as crying and cardiac and respiratory activity at a time when resources and functional capacities are more limited and adaptability to both internal and external demands is more critical. At this earlier developmental level, exchange of energy, although less efficient, provides for a more robust adaptable system that can regulate environmental input as part of the process of energy transfer.

Learning plays a critical role in the development of control systems by providing a temporal structure and expectancies that help the infant organize experience and by the regularity of behavior patterns that makes the infant more predictable, hence easier to take care of by caregivers. Endogenous pacemakers, self-sustaining oscillators that synchronize other rhythms, in the infant provide the substrate for the development of control systems by assuring homeostatic and behavioral regulation and regulating input from the environment. Crying as a behavioral control system functions as a mediator or thermostat between physiological and environmental demands. This mediation is accomplished by the presence of biological rhythms that underlie crying, link crying with physiological activity, and signal the needs and status of the infant to the caregiving environment.

Cries that are rhythmic are easier for parents to understand and make the infant more predictable. Crying rhythms can occur in three modes. Long-term periodicities may be evident in when or how often the infant cries, as part of sleep/wake cycles or diurnal variations. The best illustration of the latter is the often quoted parental complaint of infants who invariably cry between 5:00 and 7:00 P.M.—the dinner hour, when parents typically come home, the household is rushed, and the infant becomes irritable. Shorter periodicities are evident within the cry itself, as in the regularity of phonation. More accurately, cry phonation occurs during the expiratory phase of the respiratory cycle. We detect a pain cry because of the unusually long respiratory phase that upsets the normal cycle.

Even shorter periodicities are found in the pitch of the cry. The vocal cords oscillate to produce the cry, and the frequency of vocal cord oscillation is the fundamental frequency as neural control of the vocal cords (e.g., vagal input) changes. Periodicities in the fundamental frequency over time can be expected under normal conditions of vagal input. A constantly varying tension on the laryngeal musculature should produce inherent cycles in the pitch of the cry as the vocal cords oscillate around a mean, again describing a relaxation/oscillation system. Once these normal frequencies were known, one could then hypothesize durations that could indicate defects in neural control. For example, in some clinical conditions such as cri-du-chat or Down's syndrome, the cry is described as flat and monotonous. Changes in laryngeal tension due to vagal input would alter the variability in pitch by producing step function/like sudden increases in the fundamental frequency, resulting in higher amplitude and slower periodicities in the fundamental frequencies. To the extent that the cry signal becomes truly flat, there would be a loss of variability and perhaps rhythmicity. Although most studies have focused on the fundamental frequency and harmonics of the cry as measures of neurophysiological function, it is suggested here that the rhythmic structure of the cry is an independent dimension that may explain why low-pitched cries can also occur in abnormal infants. It is also worth noting that the two syndromes mentioned previously, cri-du-chat and Down's syndrome, are related genetic trisomy conditions and that there are also nongenetic syndromes in which the cry is characterized by lack of variability. This could suggest that the neural mechanisms controlling the rhythmic structure of the cry are different from those controlling the fundamental frequency component of the cry; the former may reveal more central involvement than the latter, perhaps at the level of the endogenous oscillating system itself.

Finally, if absence of rhythmicity is indicative of malfunction, so might be extremely high frequency or rapid oscillations in the pitch of the cry. A constantly fluttering cry, extreme vibrato, probably indicates more peripheral instability of vagal input. One way that biological systems respond to stress is to operate within narrower limits; it is more efficient, that is, less energy is lost, for short-term functioning. Breathing, for example, becomes faster, with less amplitude and higher frequency when infants are presented with more aversive stimuli. We also know that ontogenetically, high frequency rhythms such as neuronal discharge appear before low-frequency rhythms such as BRAC cycles. Postnatally, the 4-hour sleep rhythm appears before the 24-hour rhythm, faster EEG waves appear before slower ones, heart rate averages about 120 beats per minute (bpm) in the newborn and slows to about 60 in the adult, and so forth. Within the operation of individual systems, rhythms start out faster and slow to their encoded biological level. Once a level of normal functioning has been established, increases in frequency represent a return to more immature stages as a way of conserving energy, a primitive response to stress. Thus, an increase in the frequency of the fundamental frequency (i.e., more rapid oscillations in pitch) is most likely due to increased neural input, a kind of neurological rigidity as the system operates with more narrow limits to maintain homeostatic balance in the face of stress.

## 2.4. Developmental Changes in Crying

If crying in general is thought of as loss of inhibitory control related to physiological processes, it is likely that physiological changes that affect behavioral control systems could lower the threshold for the onset of crying. Perhaps periods in development characterized by major shifts or upheavals in physiological development lower the threshold for arousal, and particularly when accompanied by emotional stress, crying becomes more common.

There is a wide range of individual variation in the quality of infant cries, in how often and for how long a crying episode lasts, in the time of day, and the reasons for crying. Temperamental differences in infants are responsible for some of these variations. Also, infants cry for different reasons at different ages; the functional significance of crying changes with age. The school-aged child's crying because he or she does not want to go to school is a different situation from the toddler having a tantrum or the 3-week-old with colic.

In the first few weeks of life, crying has a reflexive-like quality and is most likely tied to the regulation of physiological homeostasis as the neonate is balancing internal with external demands. As physiological processes stabilize, periods of alertness and attention increase, which places additional demands on regulatory functions. Crying can occur in response to too much stimulation, when the system becomes overloaded due to external stimulation. Crying is a normal mechanism for discharging energy or tension (Brazelton, 1962; Chapter 15 in this volume), and the need for tension reduction is especially acute at times of major developmental upheavals and shifts. Periods of so-called unexplained fussiness and sudden increases in crying that occur in the first few months (Bernal, 1972; Brazelton, 1962; Emde et al., 1976; Rebelsky & Black, 1972) are probably related to maturational changes in brain structure and shifts in the organization of the CNS that occur between 3 and 12 weeks of age (Emde et al., 1976). These periods may function to promote time between the infant and the caregiver that provides opportunities for social stimulation. Fussiness can also serve to interrupt social interaction when the infant is overstimulated. Although colic is a distinct behavioral syndrome that can be distinguished from excessive crying in general, it is probably an extension of the increased crying that normally occurs over the first 3 months. Colic is probably a result of changes in the nervous system that accompany this early biobehavioral shift, but why some infants develop colic and others do not, if some infants are predisposed to colic, are important research areas.

Not only does the quantity of crying change over the first few months but so does the quality. As the infant gains more voluntary control over vocalization due to physiological and anatomical changes that occur around 1 to 2 months (see Chapter 2), crying becomes more differentiated. Mothers talk about the angry cry and the cry for attention as distinct from the hunger and pain cries, as there seems to be a more deliberate eliciting and expressive quality to crying. In the first few months we see a change from crying as a response to strictly physiological demands, to crying as part of the development of affective expression and emotions. Toward the end of the first year (7–9 months), there is a second biobehavioral shift characterized by major cognitive and affective changes that are also thought to reflect CNS reorganization, and crying now occurs for additional reasons. One is fear, most commonly fear of strangers and fear of separation from the caretaker, which can start to be a problem especially at bedtime. Also, increasing cognitive skills such as active memory generate uncertainty that can lead to crying as infants try to assimilate unfamiliar events (Kagan, 1982). Crying also occurs in response to frustration during play with objects and as the infant becomes more mobile and explores more of the environment. The frustration may be due to the build up of tension, so that an explosion of crying out of frustration or anger may be serving a tension-reduction function.

Periods of fussiness often precede the acquisition of a new skill or attainment of a new developmental stage due to the tension and apprehension that are part of the natural process of growth. In the 2-year-old, tantrums are often due to frustration and help reduce tension. The period between 17 and 24 months is also an important time of maturational change in the nervous system and in cognitive gains such as acquisition of symbolic function and signs of self-awareness. Emotions are very strong at this time as infants want to remain infants but also want to be separate. This struggle for autonomy as self-awareness increases is also a source of anxiety. We see crying in response to fear of failure as infants begin to internalize standards and develop a sense of right and wrong (Kagan, 1982). The infant's understanding of rules becomes an issue when parents set limits that the infant rejects but also wants. The start of school is another time when increases in crying are often reported. This, too, is a time of major maturational change, the so-called 5 to 7 shift (White, 1965) in which new cognitive abilities emerge, such as conservation, and the child's thinking is described as adultlike. Certainly, adolescents are thought of as more emotional due to the dramatic physiological changes that accompany that period of development.

What is characteristic of each of these periods—early infancy (7–9 months), toddler, school age, adolescence—is that maturational changes are accompanied by upheavals or sudden shifts in behavioral functioning that are usually thought of as major cognitive and affective gains, as a result of which the organism is qualitatively different. It is assumed that these developmental gains are due to changes in the nervous system; yet there may be another side to these gains, that is, there may be changes in emotionality as behavioral control systems become temporarily disorganized during these periods of rapid physiological changes. These changes produce stress to which control systems adapt by operating within more narrow limits. This lowers the threshold for arousal, making it easier to trigger crying. It would seem as if there were a loss of control in the individual infant or child. This is, of course, how parents describe temper tantrums: "Anything will set him off."

Also, notice how the functional significance of crying does change at these ages. In the 2-month-old, it is unexplained, or the infant wants attention; at 7 to 9 months, it is wariness, fear of strangers, of separation; at 2 years, the issues are around autonomy and independence; at 5 to 7 years, it is often associated with school; and in adolescents there is a general emotionality with crying often associated with guilt. It is suggested that because of the stress produced by major maturational changes, behavioral control systems are less stable and less flexible. The threshold for loss of inhibition is lowered; thus crying is more easily elicited. External or internal events that at other times would not necessarily result in crying do at these periods because of less tolerance in inhibitory control systems. It is also being suggested that these periods of disorganization occur in the service of cognitive and social gains. The elements or threads of the structural units of behavior become unraveled as part of the process of forming new structures. How often have we described infants who become fussy for a few days prior to the acquisition of a new skill? These increases in emotional lability and irritability are part of the process of change, a consequence of the homeostatic imbalance necessary for cognitive and affective development.

As with adults, it is often the case with infants that crying seems to be an emotional release that serves to discharge tension. And, like adults for whom crying is often cathartic, infants seem to feel better after crying and are often more responsive after they get "it" out of their system. We have repeatedly had the experience during the behavioral examination of neonates that many infants need to cry for a sustained period before they can be handled in a quiet alert state to elicit social interactive and attentional behavior. It is likely that during periods of CNS reorganization, there is an increase in tension due to stress as the demands on homeostatic processes are increased by endogenous and exogenous stimulation. The release of energy and reduction in tension provided by crying enables the infant to reestablish homeostatic balance and process information from the environment. The unraveling of existing structures and increased demands on homeostatic adjustments are sources of energy that work in a dialectical fashion. This energy can become a motivational force for the reorganization of cognitive and affective structures, but there can also be a surplus that creates tension that is discharged through crying. When there is too much tension, the system is stuck—overloaded—and there is no flexibility or room to move, leaving only frustration. With crying, the excess tension is released, homeostatic balance is restored, and change is possible. Thus, although crying may serve to reduce tension in many situations, during periods of biobehavioral shifts, this process is likely to occur more often.

## 2.5. Clinical Considerations

Colic is probably related to this process. Its occurrence overlaps with the first period of CNS reorganization at around 3 to 12 weeks (Emde *et al.*, 1976). Some of the unexplained or excessive crying described previously may be mistakenly labeled as colic. The reason it is mistaken is that colic is associated with additional symptoms, including muscular hypotonia and tension in the abdomen, that is why gastrointestinal causes are often attributed to colic. However, it may be that as a result of changes in the nervous system that accompany early maturational changes, some infants are more likely to develop colic than others. It used to be thought that colic was caused by hypotonus, a congenital imbalance of the autonomic nervous system, or vagotonia, in which minimal stimuli led to fussing and irritability (Eppinger & Hess, 1915). A further neurophysiological link between crying and gastrointestinal activity is provided by current theorizing about the role of the vagus in mediating cry activity through input to the larynx (Lester, 1984) because one of the other branches of the vagus terminates in the stomach.

Colic probably has multiple causes, and it is important to distinguish between the infant with colic and the difficult or irritable infant. The latter may be more of a temperamental problem, whereas the infant who develops colic may have gastrointestinal problems as well that trigger an underlying nervous system reaction to extreme irritability. For some infants, colic may be a consequence of physiological changes in the nervous system that lower the threshold for arousal anyway, and in colic, this normal process is exaggerated with gastrointestinal involvement. There may also be infants who are predisposed to develop colic and those with an imbalance in the autonomic nervous system who from birth are hypersensitive and irritable. Colic is also triggered by maturational changes in the nervous system. We have observed several cases of the latter in which infants who were extremely irritable during the first few days of life developed clinically defined colic at about 1 month of age.

Parenting or emotional causes are also thought to contribute to colic and infant difficultness, and there are many ways in which crying can become a psychodynamic issue between infants and parents. An infant who cries a lot can be a real stress on the family. Irritable and colicky infants are difficult to soothe, they reject the breast or bottle, the quality and amount of crying elicits angry feelings in the parents, and the caretaking of the baby may suffer. Handling of the baby can become less consistent and effective; parents feel rejected and may reject the baby in turn. Parents feel helpless because there is nothing they can do to stop their infant from crying, and they feel that it is their fault or that they are bad parents because they cannot figure out why their baby is crying and how to stop it. Guilt feelings are also generated because they feel they have done something wrong; they also feel guilty for the anger and hostility they feel toward their infant. This can result in a negative feedback cycle as infant behavior that is perceived as aversive by the parents causes nonoptimal caretaking that has negative consequences for the infant. This cycle can lead to interactive failure and ultimately child abuse and is an example of how the infant contributes to his or her own caretaking. It is critical for parents to realize that the problem is in the baby, not them. The crying is not their fault; it is a normal characteristic of their particular infant, almost like his or her hair color, but unlike hair color, it arouses strong emotions. Thus, it is just as critical to help parents acknowledge the negative feelings they experience toward the baby, to help them realize that most people also react similarly to incessant crying, and that there may be a quality to their infant's cry that is particularly negative sounding. These feelings and the guilt that goes with them need to be legitimized. It is helpful to parents to realize that their feelings do not make them bad parents, nor do their feelings mean they will act them out on the infant.

## 2.6. Parental Perceptions and Feelings

Parental perceptions and feelings about the sound of the cry also need to be considered. Differences in the acoustic properties of the cry are perceived along dimensions that reflect how adults feel about the status of the infant (e.g., sick), what kind of caretaking the infant needs, and how the sound makes them feel (see Chapters 8 and 9). This information can be very useful clinically because through acoustic analysis one can validate or not validate the parental perception. Confirmation by acoustic analysis of the perception that the infant's cry is high pitched and that there is something wrong with the baby, for example, could first of all lead to further work-up or referral to determine if there is a medical problem. A mother of a preterm infant in one of our studies knew that her baby was in trouble because the cry had changed, and although rebuffed by her pediatrician, her insistence made it possible for the baby to be seen, and anemia was diagnosed. Second, confirmation of the acoustics of the cry serves the important function of helping to legitimize the parent's perceptions. They can be shown *why* they are hearing what they are hearing, that what they are hearing is real, and that it is an inherent part of the baby and not something they made up or caused.

Disconfirmation of a parent's perception can point to other directions for clinical intervention; it may suggest that the basis of the perception is not readily apparent in the cry sound and that the issue may be more parent based than infant based. In other words, acoustic analysis can be a means to help identify infant-based issues from parent-based issues, which can then lead to appropriate clinical management.

In many cases, of course, these issues become more complicated, and problems about crying can become the basis for later psychodynamic or psychosomatic problems between infant and parents. We have seen how crying involves control from the infant and also from the parent in terms of the management of crying—parents need to control their baby's crying. Control can, however, become a problem in the parent-infant relationship. We often think of the separation/individuation process in the second year of life; however, it may be that these issues start earlier, particularly around the management of crying. The infant is learning self-control as he or she learns to inhibit arousal and control crying, but he or she also may need to cry to release tension. Parents want to stop the crying and intervene, but the baby also needs to learn to control his or her own crying. The control the infant is learning with help from the parents can become externalized and develop into psychodynamic issues that no longer relate to crying. These issues can become played out in other areas, such as feeding, sleeping, or perhaps tantrums in the second year of life. Unsuccessful coping with crying and resolution of issues around crying (such as feelings of inadequacy and guilt mentioned before) can spill over into other areas where parents and infants have to negotiate limits, where both infants and parents seek to maintain control. Crying is really the first test for parents—the first real demand from the infant, the first time or issue around which the parent is faced with saying no or placing limits, the first issue around which the parent feels angry because of something the baby did, and the first stress and challenge around successful child rearing. Thus, crying is likely to bring up many of the problems that parents will have to face throughout child rearing and particularly those that are issues for the parents themselves. Crying becomes a microcosm for psychodynamic aspects of the parent–infant relationship, and when unsuccessfully resolved, it can be transferred to other areas where control can be prominent, such as feeding, sleeping, and tantrums. In this sense, it can be a cause or symptom of problems in the parent–infant relationship.

## 2.7. Crying and Soothability

The clinical management of crying naturally involves soothing, and there are vast individual differences in what quiets an infant. Some infants can self-quiet or need little intervention from the environment. Most infants, however, do need input from the environment, and it may be useful to consider the nature of that input and how it works. Quieting an infant involves lowering the infant's level of arousal. Said in another way, it is the inhibition of arousal that enables the infant to regain control. Soothing stimulates the inhibitory control system and facilitates homeostatic regulation. I speculated earlier that this control system was based in the rhythmic structure of the nervous system, that endogenous oscillating mechanisms provide the substrate for the regulation of physiological homeostatic processes and the integration of behavioral and physiological processes that provide opportunities for the infant to learn adaptive control. I also pointed out how behavioral periodicities make the infant more predictable, hence facilitating infant–caregiver interaction. It should therefore come as no surprise to realize that most of our effective soothing techniques involve the provision of rhythmic stimulation; the inhibition of arousal is stimulated by rhythmic input from the environment—music, singing, swings, clocks, rocking, sucking, and the like. Rhythmic stimulation is not the only kind of input that lowers arousal, but it is the dimension that underlies most soothing procedures. A pacifier, for example, is effective because it stimulates the sucking response that is incompatible with crying, but sucking is also rhythmic. The rhythmic nature of sucking serves an organizing function for the infant's behavior and helps homeostatic regulation. It has long been known that the provision of rhythmic stimulation is soothing to infants, and it may be that the effectiveness of environmental rhythms is due to their effect on endogenous oscillating pacemakers. If endogenous timing mechanisms maintain homeostasis as well as organize experience from the environment, it seems reasonable that rhythmic variations in the environment could entrain these endogenous mechanisms and help to organize infant behavior by lowering arousal. Endogenous rhythms organize input from the environment if this input is itself rhythmic and oscillates at similar frequencies (or multiples of frequencies) to endogenous rhythms. Therefore, endogenous rhythms could be entrained or synchronized to exogenous stimulation. This entrainment would lower arousal by stimulating inhibitory mechanisms, for example, through proprioceptive feedback systems, thus increasing behavioral control.

Behavioral control systems can be strengthened and arousal lowered by direct motoric inhibition such as swaddling, activating inhibition by eliciting a competing system such as sucking, and by rhythmic stimulation that facilitates behavioral regulation as internal and external rhythms become synchronized. Of course, most soothing techniques employ various combinations of these methods; we often swaddle and rock or swaddle, put the infant upright on the shoulder, pat his or her back rhythmically, and perhaps jiggle the baby all at the same time. Most often, the more aroused or out of control the infant is, the more combinations of techniques there are that are employed. Also, note how intervention can be described along a continuum from external distal, such as music, to external proximal, such as talking to the infant face to face, using degrees of tactile containment ranging from gentle restraint to swaddling and holding, to stimulating internal systems that override crying, such as vestibular (upright) positioning and sucking. The most powerful combination and therefore useful intervention that is used with the most difficult infants seems to be when rhythmic stimulation is combined with the stimulation of a competing system. Many parents use swings to calm a very irritable infant. The swinging motion stimulates the vestibular system, the infant's eyes open to maintain equilibrium, and the back-and-forth motion provides a rhythmic structure. Note, too, that sucking, probably the most effective method, provides the stimulation of an overriding rhythmic system. In other words, consoling is more effective as we move closer to internal oscillating systems; music stimulates these mechanisms indirectly, whereas sucking directly elicits endogenous rhythmic mechanisms.

Finally, in terms of the clinical management of crying, one must realize that the long-term goal is to help the infant learn to control arousal. The immediate goal is, of course, to stop the crying, but at the same time we want the behavioral regulation to come increasingly from the infant, with less and less environmental input. Thus, gimmicks such as swings can be used as teaching devices to help the infant learn how to lower arousal, but the infant must be weaned or provided with alternative strategies so as not to become completely dependent on external stimulation. Consoling aids of various strengths (rocking to music) can be employed but gradually withdrawn, while at the same time providing reinforcement to the baby for maintaining a calm state. The danger is not weaning infants from consoling techniques with the result that their own behavioral regulatory abilities may not develop optimally and overdependence on the parents may create the kind of psychodynamic issues in the parent–infant relationship that I discussed earlier.

This essay has touched on a number of areas, some empirically based, others quite speculative, and I have taken the opportunity afforded by editorial license to sketch out some preliminary thoughts. The chapters that follow provide a comprehensive view of the field of infant cry. It is hoped that this first volume that brings together the empirical work in the field will stimulate others so that future volumes on infant crying can boast an even richer empirical and theoretical base. It is also hoped that the material in this book will give clinicians a better understanding of crying and help them help the families they serve.

## 3. REFERENCES

Berg, W. K., & Berg, K. M. Psychophysiological development in infancy: State, sensory function and attention. In J. Osofsky (Ed.), *Handbook of infant development*. New York: Wiley, 1979.

Bernal, J. Crying during the first ten days of life and maternal responses. *Developmental Medicine and Child Neurology*, 1972, *14*, 362–372.

Brazelton, T. B. Crying in infancy. *Pediatrics*, 1962, *29*, 579–588.

DeHaan, R., Patrick, J., Chess, G., & Jaco, N. Definition of sleep state in the newborn infant by heart rate analysis. *American Journal of Obstetrics & Gynecology*, 1977, *127*, 753–758.

Emde, R. N., Gaensbauer, T. J., & Harmon, R. J. Emotional expression in infancy: A biobehavioral study. *Psychological Issues*, 1976, *10*, Monograph 37.

Eppinger, H., & Hess, E. Vagotonia. *Nervous Mental Disease Monograph Series 20*. New York, 1915.

Friedman, S. L., Zahn-Waxler, C., & Radke-Yarrow, M. Perceptions of cries of full-term and preterm infants. *Infant Behavior and Development*, 1982, *5*, 161–173.

Hathorn, M. K. S. The rate and depth of breathing in newborn infants in different sleep states. *Journal of Physiology*, 1979, *243*, 101–113.

Kagan, J. Canalization of early psychological development. *Pediatrics*, 1982, *70*, 474–483.

Karelitz, S., & Fisichelli, V. The cry thresholds of normal infants and those with brain damage. *Journal of Pediatrics*, 1962, *61*, 679–685.

Lester, B. M. A biosocial model of infant crying. In L. P. Lipsitt (Ed.), *Advances in infancy research*. New York: Academic Press, 1984.

Lester, B. M., & Zeskind, P. S. A biobehavioral perspective on crying in infancy. In H. E. Fitzgerald, B. M. Lester, & M. W. Yogman (Eds.), *Theory and research in behavioral pediatrics* (Vol. 1). New York: Plenum Press, 1982.

Lester, B. M., Carcia-Coll, C., Valcercel, M., & Hoffman, J. Acoustic analyses and teenage versus older mothers' perceptions of the cries of growth retarded and normally grown infants. Manuscript in preparation, 1984.

Lind, J. (Ed.). Newborn infant cry. *Acta Pediatrica Scandinavica* (Suppl. 163), 1965.

Michelsson, K., Sirvio, P., & Wasz-Höckert, O. Pain cry in full-term asphyxiated newborn infants correlated with late findings. *Acta Paediatrica Scandinavica*, 1977, *66*, 611–616.

Osofsky, J. *Handbook of infant development*. New York: Wiley, 1979.

Rebelsky, F., & Black, R. Crying in infancy. *Journal of Genetic Psychology*, 1972, *121*, 49–57.

Sokolov, E. N. *Perception and the conditioned reflex*. New York: Macmillan, 1963.

Stern, D., Beebe, B., Jaffe, J., & Bennett, S. The infant's stimulus world during social interaction: A study of caregiver behavior with particular reference to repetition and timing. In H. P. Schaffer (Ed.), *Studies in mother–infant interaction*. New York: Academic Press, 1977.

Stratton, P. (Ed.). *Psychobiology of the human neonate*. New York: Wiley, 1982.

Wasz-Höckert, O., Lind, J., Vuorenkoski, V., Partanen, T., & Valanne, E. The infant cry. A spectrographic and auditory analysis. *Clinics in Developmental Medicine, 29*. Lavenham, Suffolk: Spastics International Medical Publications, 1968.

White, S. Evidence for a hierarchical arrangement of learning processes. In L. P. Lipsitt & C. K. Spiker, *Advances in child behavior and development* (Vol. 2). New York: Academic Press, 1965.

Wolman, B. (Ed.). *Handbook of developmental psychology*. Englewood Cliffs, N.J.: Prentice-Hall, 1982.

Woodson, R. Newborn behavior and transition to extrauterine life. *Infant Behavior and Development*, 1983, *6*, 139–144.

# 2

# The Physiology of Cry and Speech in Relation to Linguistic Behavior

PHILIP LIEBERMAN

The study of the linguistic behavior of human infants addresses one of the central questions of human biology and evolution: To what extent does human linguistic ability follow from innate, species-specific biological mechanisms? The research of the past 30 years has demonstrated that human speech is an integral part of human linguistic ability. The premise that I will develop in this chapter is that many of the linguistically salient aspects of human speech begin to develop and can be seen in the vocal behavior of infants. These data indicate to me that the biological substrate of human speech involves an interplay between biological mechanisms that have other vegetative functions and neural and anatomical mechanisms that appear to have evolved primarily for their role in facilitating human vocal communication. These data thus refute Chomsky's theory that human linguistic ability follows from the presence of a unique, species-specific "language organ" that yields linguistic behavior disjoint from other aspects of human cognitive behavior or the social communications of other animals.

PHILIP LIEBERMAN • Department of Linguistics, Brown University, Providence, Rhode Island 02912.

## 1.   HUMAN SPEECH AND HUMAN LANGUAGE

The production and perception of human speech has been studied using quantitative methods since the early part of the 19th century. Two general features of human speech have been isolated without which human language in the form that we know would be impossible. The "segmental" aspect of human speech used to be thought of as a trivial component of human linguistic ability. It was thought that any sounds could serve as "phonemes" to make up words of all human languages (Simpson, 1966). Simpson's position, which is typical of that of many scholars, is that any sounds that are discernible could be used to set up a code that would do to signal meaningful words. In a sense Simpson is correct. English, for example, makes use of a set of 26 letters in its orthography that can be related to phonemic sound sequences that constitute words. Words like *pin* and *bin* thus differ minimally by one phoneme or letter. A speaker of English has to learn how to produce all the phonemic sequences that can constitute the words of English. However, nonspeech sounds like the dots and dashes of Morse code or the noises that spoons and plates make when they are hit against a wall can also be used to set up a linguistic code. Telegraphers and prisoners, respectively, have used these nonspeech sounds to communicate in a linguistic mode. The difference between these systems and speech is that the rate at which we can transmit information using the sounds of speech is at least two times faster than that using any nonspeech sound. Human speech production and perception involves the "encoding" and "decoding" of phonemic distinctions that are collapsed into syllable-sized units. The acoustic cues that signal the sounds /k/, /ae/, and /t/ of the word *cat* are, for example, distributed throughout the word. We transmit these syllable-sized encoded segments at a rate of about 5 to 7 segments a second. The phonemes that make up syllables are perceptually resolved by the human neural decoding system to achieve the phonemic transmission rates of 15 to 20 units per second (Liberman, Cooper, Shankweiler, & Studdert-Kennedy, 1967). The encoding–decoding process is necessary because the constraints of the human auditory system would otherwise limit sound communication rates to the 5 to 7 unit-per-second rate at which syllables are transmitted (Miller, 1956).

It is simple to demonstrate the relative speed of human speech versus other auditory signals. If one takes a pencil and taps it against a table and asks someone else to count the number of taps that he or she can hear, it soon is apparent that people cannot count more than seven or so taps per second. One can readily determine the number of phonemic distinctions that occur per second of speech by tape-recording someone talking fast. The number of phonemic distinctions per second will exceed 20 per second. Because the fusion frequency of the auditory system is about 15 events per second, it is obvious that our perceptual response cannot map onto a string of independent phonemes that are strung together like "beads on a string." Recent experimental data on the perception of speech by human infants (e.g., Eimas, 1974; Morse, 1974) is consistent with the hypothesis that we are equipped from birth with genetically transmitted neural "mechanisms" that structure the "phonemic" perception of speech.

The "suprasegmental" aspects of human speech have received less attention in recent studies of the development of human speech in relation to human language. The intonation, stress, and general "melody" of speech constitute suprasegmental components of speech. Although these aspects of speech are among the first that develop in human infants (Lewis, 1936), we still have much to learn concerning the biological bases and the development and the linguistic function of these aspects of human speech. The acoustic parameters of the fundamental frequency of phonation and the amplitude of the speech signal and its timing all are relevant to the perception of the suprasegmental or "prosodic" features of human speech. Some of the linguistic functions of the prosodic features of human speech were explicitly noted since at least the 13th century. The instructions for the chanting of church music that can be found in old manuscripts, for example, recognize the "terminal" cues that segment the flow of speech into sentences and major syntactic units (Hadding-Koch, 1961). The role of intonation in segmenting the flow of speech into sentencelike units for syntactic analysis has been demonstrated in many independent linguistic, phonetic, acoustic, and psychoacoustic studies (e.g., Armstrong & Ward, 1926; Atkinson, 1973; Lieberman, 1967; Pike, 1945; Trager & Smith, 1951; Tseng, 1981). It is impossible to arrive at the meaning of a sentence unless one knows what words go together. One can test this hypothesis by simply taking a newspaper and moving the sentence beginning and ending punctuation over one word to the right. The result usually is incomprehensible because the "wrong" words have been grouped together. This segmenting function of intonation is its paramount *linguistic* function. Intonation can also transmit the attitude of the speaker with respect to the linguistic message that is transmitted by means of the words and rule-governed syntax of the language (Pike, 1945). However, this function is secondary to signaling the segments of speech to which we must apply the "rules" of our internal representation of our knowledge. In brief, without sentences we cannot have human language.

## 2. THE BREATH GROUP

The *breath group* is the primary element that people use to segment the flow of speech into sentence like units. The breath group is organized about vegetative constraints of respiration and the physiology of the lungs and larynx. Its primary elements can be seen in the initial cries of newborn infants and follow from the articulatory and respiratory maneuvers that are necessary to sustain life. Its full linguistic expression, however, involves behavioral patterns that are not present at birth, that is, a complex pattern of articulatory control that involves reference to the probable length of a sentence *before* a sound is uttered and linguistically motivated "overrides" of the central and peripheral chemoreceptors that otherwise mediate respiration.

I will start with a discussion of the acoustic parameters and articulatory and respiratory maneuvers that we can characterize as a breath group. In Figure 1, I have sketched a schematic diagram of the human

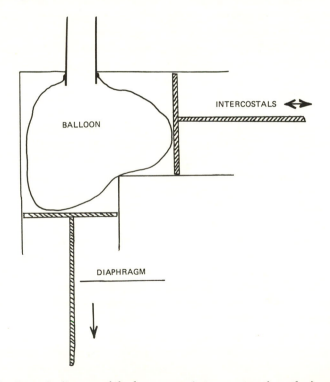

*Figure 1.* A schematic diagram of the human respiratory system from the larynx down.

respiratory system from the larynx down. This sketch, which does not seek to represent the actual anatomy of the human respiratory system, however, is a functionally accurate model for the aspects of respiratory control that are germane to our enquiry. The model has only one lung, but the points that are relevant for one lung will be relevant for both lungs. Note the lung "balloon" in the model and the three plungers that are attached to the side wall and bottom wall of the pleural chamber. The human respiratory system functions in an odd manner that reflects the fact that lungs evolved from the swim bladders of fish (Darwin, 1859; Negus, 1949). The swim bladders in phylogenetically advanced fish are internal sacks into which a fish can pump air that has been filtered out of the water by the fish's gills. The swim bladders are elastic so that they can expand or contract to take up the volume of air that the fish needs to balance its weight against displaced water at a given depth. Air-breathing animals retained the elastic sacks, which were connected to the outside atmosphere and filled by expanding the pleural space. Inspiration in human beings thus takes place when we expand the volume of the pleural space by moving the diaphragm downward or the rib cage outward. The plunger labeled *diaphragm* can exert force downward to expand the pleural space. The plunger labeled *intercostals* can also move outward to expand the pleural volume. The pressure inside the sealed pleural space will fall as the volume increases because the product of the volume and pressure is equal to a constant. Because the inside of the lung balloon is open to the outside air, the lung balloon will expand as the pleural air pressure falls. The constant atmospheric air pressure will be manifested against the inside of the lung balloon as it stretches. As the lung balloon expands and stretches, two things happen. Air flows into the lung, and energy is stored in the elastic walls of the lung balloon.

The lungs thus store energy that powers the *expiratory* phase of respiration during inspiration. If one thinks of a rubber balloon, it is clear that one stores energy when one blows up the balloon. The energy that one stores in the *elastic* balloon will force air out of the balloon when one releases one's hold on its open end. The intercostal and abdominal muscles can also squeeze inward on the pleural space and contribute power for the expiration of air. The plungers that schematize these muscle groups in Figure 1 thus point inward for the abdominals and inward and outward for the intercostals. The intercostals in adultlike *Homo sapiens* can function both as inspiratory and expiratory muscles. The main force that powers the expiratory phase of respiration, however, is the *elastic recoil* force of the lungs, that is, the elasticity of the lung "balloon." The difficulty that people have, for example, in breathing when they suffer from emphysema follows from the lungs' losing their elasticity.

Figure 2 shows the lung volume functions and air pressure developed in the lungs that occurs during normal, quiet respiration in an adult human being (Lieberman, 1967). Note that the inspiratory and expiratory phases of respiration have almost the same duration. Inspiration is marked by air flowing into the lungs so the lung volume increases; expiration is manifested in the lung volume plot as a fall in the volume. Note that the alveolar air pressure, the air pressure in the lungs, gradually falls during expiration. This follows from the gradual decrease in the elastic recoil force that is, of course, greatest when the lungs are distended and that falls as the lung volume decreases. The rubber balloon analogy again is useful in thinking about this effect. If one blows up a balloon and releases it, it will fly about quite fast at first when it is distended and the air pressure inside is highest. As the rubber balloon's volume decreases, the internal air pressure will fall, and it will fly slower and slower.

Figure 3 shows lung volume and air pressure functions for a speaker during the production of a sentence. Note the contrast with Figure 2. The duration of expiration is now long; it is keyed to the length of the sentence. The air pressure function, moreover, is relatively level

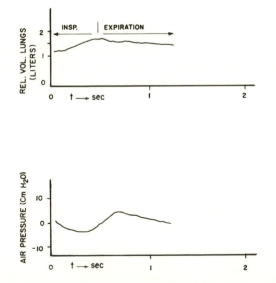

*Figure 2.* Lung volume functions and air pressure developed in the lungs over time during normal quiet respiration in an adult human being.

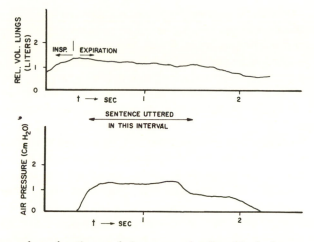

*Figure 3.* Lung volume functions and air pressure developed in the lungs over time for a speaker during the production of a sentence.

throughout the expiration. Human speakers typically produce speech using a relatively steady alveolar air pressure that ranges from about 8 to 10 cm of $H_2O$. (Bouhuys, 1974; Draper, Ladefoged, & Whitteridge, 1960; Lieberman, 1967; Lieberman, 1968). They maintain this relatively steady air pressure function throughout the length of the expiration. The length of the expiration and the depth of the inspiration that precedes an expiration are keyed to the length of the one sentence or sentencelike unit of speech that they are *going* to produce. Figure 4 shows lung volume functions for a speaker reciting a poem (Lieberman & Lieberman, 1973). Note that the length of the expiratory phase of respiration varies. It is determined by the line structure of the poem. Note too that

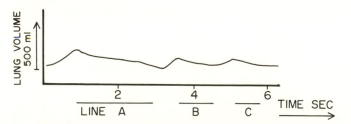

*Figure 4.* Lung volume functions over time for a speaker reciting a poem. The expirations that correspond to the successive lines A, B, and C of the poem are marked. Note that each poetic line corresponds to an expiration; note that the magnitude of inspiration immediately before each expiration (the height of the curve) is keyed to the length of the line that follows. The speaker is taking more air into his lungs before the production of a longer line.

a "deeper," that is, a greater inspiration occurs when the speaker is going to produce a longer expiration. The speaker thus "preprograms" his or her respiratory activity in terms of the structure of the poem. He or she takes in more air before he or she starts on a long expiration. The speaker thus must have some knowledge of the duration of the utterance that he or she is about to produce before a single sound is uttered. The psychological reality of the sentence thus is apparent at this level of observation.

The preprogramming requirement is, however, more complex than simply taking more air into one's lungs before a longer expiration. The sketch in Figure 5 is germane to a discussion of the maneuvers that people continually make when they talk, play wind instruments, or sing. The interrupted line represents the aveolar air pressure that would result if the elastic recoil (ER) function were the only force that the speaker brings into play. The solid line represents the steady alveolar air pressure that the speaker actually produces. The cross-hatched area to the left represents the "excess" pressure generated by the elastic lung recoil that

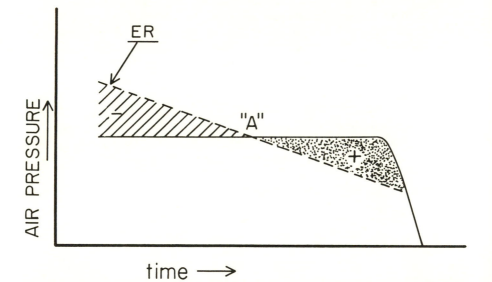

*Figure 5.* The interplay between muscle forces and elastic recoil involved in producing a steady subglottal air pressure function over a long utterance. The dashed line, ER, represents the falling air pressure function that would result as an unimpeded consequence of the gradual deflation of the lungs. The cross-hatched area to the left ( − ) signifies the work of the inspiratory muscles that the speaker uses in opposition to the elastic recoil force. At point A the speaker has to switch to his expiratory muscles, the stippled area ( + ) to supplement the elastic recoil force.

the speaker must counter when he or she takes a large volume into his or her lungs at the start of a long expiration. "Excess" air pressure is countered by pulling outward on the rib cage with the intercostal muscles. The intercostal "hold-back" muscle function has to be adjusted to the initial depth of the inspiration and has to decrease gradually as the lung volume decreases. When the air pressure developed by the elastic recoil matches the "desired air pressure" at point "A," the speaker has to supplement the elastic recoil force with the "expiratory" component of the intercostals and the abdominal muscles. The programming is thus complex and must change from one utterance to the next as the length of the sentence that the speaker intends to produce changes (Draper, Ladefoged, & Whitteridge, 1960). At the end of the expiration, the alveolar air pressure falls rapidly. This follows from the speaker's opening his or her larynx for inspiration and simultaneously starting to the transition to the negative air alveolar air pressure that is necessary for inspiration.

## 3.  NEWBORN INFANTS

Newborn infants can effect only some of the respiratory and articulatory maneuvers that I have discussed. The data of Truby, Bosma, and Lind (1965), Stark, Rose, and McLagen (1975), and Langlois, Baken, and Wilder (1980) all show a pattern of respiratory activity in which the expiratory phase is about five times longer than the inspiratory phase. Newborn infants appear to generate an initial positive alveolar air pressure by means of abdominal contraction about 100 msec before the onset of phonation. There is also an abrupt decrease in alveolar air pressure at the end of phonation as the infant goes into the inspiratory phase of respiration (Truby et al., 1965, p. 73). The flow rate of air and associated changes in lung volume function are small during phonation (Truby et al., 1965; Langlois et al., 1980). The low flow rate undoubtedly is a consequence of the high impedance that the glottis places in the airway during phonation. The flow rate during the sustained phonation is also low for adult speakers (Klatt, Stevens, & Mead, 1968). No precise measures of the alveolar air pressure exist for newborn infants during cry production. The intraesophageal air pressure data of Truby et al. (1965) can be used to estimate alveolar air pressure following the method outlined in Lieberman (1968). This method involves knowing exactly when the transitions from inspiration to expiration, and vice versa, occur. Calculations derived from the data of Truby et al. (1965, pp. 77–79, Figure 2) indicate that the alveolar air pressure function is probably quite steady after the initial 100 msec buildup before the onset of phonation. Simultaneous air flow and intraesophageal air pressure traces are not presented in Truby *et al.* (1965), but the pattern of respiratory events for the infants whose cries are analyzed in that study by means of spirograms and intraesophageal air pressure recordings is fairly stereotyped. The regulation of alveolar air pressure in newborn infants appears to involve the infant's supplementing the elastic recoil force to generate a pressure that is sufficient to overcome the impedance presented by the glottis in phonatory position; abdominal contraction usually leads the expiratory phase and probably generates the positive subglottal air pressure that precedes phonation (Langlois *et al.*, 1980, p. 73; Truby *et al.*, 1965, p. 73).

Three aspects of the intonation pattern of normal human newborn cry are similar to the patterns that adult speakers usually use.

1. The duration of the expiratory phase is usually longer than that of the inspiratory phase and can vary in duration. The cry patterns noted in Truby *et al.* (1965) had expiratory phases whose durations varied over a 2:1 range.

2. The alveolar air pressure function rapidly rises prior to the onset of phonation and then falls rapidly at the end of phonation as the infant enters the inspiratory phase of phonation. Phonation occurs until the end of expiration. The abrupt shift in the alveolar air pressure function at the end of phonation thus reflects a basic vegetative constraint. A negative air pressure is necessary for inspiration. Because the infant must maintain a positive air pressure during expiration, abrupt transition must take place at the end on the expiratory cycle coincident with phonation. Numerous studies (Atkinson, 1973; Lieberman, 1967; Lieberman, Knudsen, & Mead 1969; Ohala, 1970; Shipp, Doherty, & Morrissey, 1979) have found that, on the average, the rate of change of fundamental frequency ($F_0$) with respect to air pressure is approximately 10 Hz/cm $H_2O$. Thus, all things being equal, $F_0$ will fall at the end of an expiration. If the larynx does not maintain its phonatory configuration until the end of phonation but instead begins to open toward its inspiratory position, the terminal fall in $F_0$ will be enhanced as the laryngeal muscles relax (Atkinson, 1973; Van den Berg, 1962).

Most traditional perceptually based phonetic theories (e.g., Armstrong & Ward, 1926; Pike, 1945; Trager & Smith, 1951) and many instrumental studies (Atkinson, 1973; Hadding-Koch, 1961; Landahl, 1980; Lieberman, 1967; Tseng, 1981; Vanderslice & Ladefoged, 1972) agree insofar as a falling $F_0$ and amplitude contour forms the *terminal* of a breath group. The terminal intonation contour whose acoustic correlates are a falling $F_0$ and amplitude thus is the cue that signals the end of a declarative sentence or phrase in most human languages (Lieberman, 1967). This signal follows from the vegetative constraints of respiration. It reflects the biological necessity of a transition in alveolar air pressure from the positive air pressure of expiration to the negative air pressure of inspiration.

3. The third aspect wherein the newborn cry pattern's intonation is similar to the adult pattern is that the $F_0$ contour tends to be almost level in the nonterminal portion of the breath group. About 70% of the $F_0$ contours noted in the spectrograms in Truby *et al.* (1965) and the corpus that formed the data base sampled in Lieberman, Crelin, & Klatt, (1972) had a relatively steady nonterminal $F_0$ contour. The other cry patterns involved either gross perturbations of the $F_0$ pattern where the infant blew his vocal cords apart because of excessive subglottal air pressure relative to medial compression (Van den Berg, 1962) or exhibited other patterns of $F_0$ variation. What was not noted was the steady "declination" that some recent studies claim is the "base form" for intonation (Maeda, 1976; Pierrehumbert, 1979; Sorenson & Cooper, 1980). The declination theory claims that a general fall in $F_0$ throughout the breath group characterizes the intonation contours of most languages. According to Pierrehumbert (1979), this hypothetical gradual fall in $F_0$ follows from some as-yet unknown, basic property of speech production that should be manifested in the initial utterances of infants and children. The intonation pattern of newborn cry does not show a consistent $F_0$ declination that fits any version of the declination theory. Different versions of the declination theory characterize the hypothetical $F_0$ fall in different ways. None of these variations of the declination theory is, however, consistent with data derived from the discourse of adult speakers of American English or Chinese (Tseng, 1981). The data that Maeda (1976) discusses in his version of the declination theory do not match his hypothesis.

## 4. THE DEVELOPMENT OF SENTENCE INTONATION

There is one crucial difference between the intonation signals that newborn infants produce and those typical of older human speakers. Newborn infants cannot regulate subglottal air pressure by a "hold-back" intercostal muscle gesture. The hold-back, that is, inspiratory function of the intercostal muscles, is a mechanical consequence of the fact that the ribs are angled downward and outward from the spine in human beings after the age of about 3 months. At birth, the ribs in newborn infants are almost perpendicular to the spine. Newborn infants thus inherently cannot effect a steady subglottal air pressure by working against the air pressure generated by the elastic recoil of the lungs. The control of subglottal air pressure during long expirations requires a hold-back function because the elastic recoil pressure at the start of the expiration will exceed the level of 8 to 10 cm $H_2O$ that is normally used during speech. Newborn infants can generate the air pressure functions that occur in short breath groups because the air pressure that results from the elastic recoil is quite low, in the order of 2 cm $H_2O$. Newborn infants can supplement this pressure with their abdominal muscles to generate the subglottal air pressures necessary for phonation. They, however, cannot regulate air pressure during long breath groups because the increased lung volume generates a subglottal air pressure function that is initially too high. Although adult speakers tend to produce short breath groups that again involve the simpler pressure regulation scheme of the newborn infant (Froscher, 1978), they can also produce very long breath groups. Human infants begin to produce long episodes of phonation after their third month of life when their rib cages have restructured toward the adult configuration (Langlois *et al.*, 1980).

## 5. LEARNING TO CONTROL INTONATION

The regulatory patterns that are involved in generating the air pressure functions typical of speech are quite complex even for the relatively "simple" situation that occurs when we produce short breath groups and do not have to program an intercostal hold-back function. The elastic recoil function still must be supplemented by the precisely coordinated activity of the "expiratory" intercostal and abdominal muscles. The diaphragm does not seem to enter into the control pattern during speech production, singing, or when we play wind instruments (Bouhuys, 1974). It is striking that newborn infants do as well as they do, and it is reasonable to hypothesize an innately determined mechanism that has evolved to regulate subglottal air pressure during phonation. The presence of such an innate mechanism would not be surprising because the larynx clearly has evolved to facilitate the production of sound at the expense of respiratory efficiency (Negus, 1949). The restructuring of the anatomy of the rib cage in infants between birth and age 3 months again is not surprising. There are other parallel changes in the anatomy of the supralaryngeal airways. The larynx in newborn humans is positioned close to the base of the skull (Crelin, 1969; Negus, 1949). The high position of the larynx in newborn infants is similar to its position in other animals and allows the newborn human to form a patent, that is, sealed, airway from the nose to the lungs. The newborn infant can move his or her larynx upward into the nasopharynx. The soft palate and epiglottis effect a double seal, and liquids can flow around the relatively small larynx into the esophagus while air moves through the nose through the larynx and trachea into the lungs (Laitman, Crelin, & Conlogue, 1977). There is no possibility of choking by having food lodge into the larynx as is the case for adultlike human beings. The anatomy of the upper airways in newborn infants is "matched" to a neural control system—newborn infants are obligate nose breathers. They normally will not breathe through their mouths even when their noses are blocked. The larynx descends in infants, and by 3 months of age it migrates down in the pharynx to the point where it no longer can form a sealed airway from the nose (George, 1978; Laitman *et al.*, 1977). The neural control system that regulates breathing restructures at this point to allow mouth breathing. The restructuring of the neural regulatory system can be understood in the light of the Darwinian process of natural selection. After age 3 months there no longer is a selective advantage for obligate nose breathing because the larynx is too low to form a sealed airway. Foreign bodies thus could lodge in the larynx whether or not infants were breathing through their noses. There, however, would be a selective advantage in being able to breathe through the mouth if one's nose were blocked. It is most unlikely that infants "learn" to mouth breathe at age 3 months. It is also unlikely that they "learn" to regulate subglottal air pressure during cry production or speech.

## 6. OVERRIDING THE VEGETATIVE REGULATORY SYSTEM

There are a number of layered feedback mechanisms that monitor breathing in humans and other animals to ensure that the respiratory system meets the physiologic demands of both normal and strenuous activities. Mechanical stretch receptors in the lung tissue feed afferent signals back via the vagus, or tenth cranial nerve, to the brain. The vagus nerve is composed of both efferent and afferent pathways to and from the larynx, pharynx, esophagus, stomach, and heart. These stretch receptors monitor the degree of inflation of the lungs and activate a control system that limits the depth, that is, magnitude of inspiration. Herring and Breuer first proposed this feedback control system over 100 years ago. Recent data derived from experiments with cats and human beings show that it may function to limit the depth of inspiration in strenuous activity, but its importance in regulating normal breathing is not clear (Bouhuys, 1974). There are, however, two additional "layers" of feedback control that make use of "chemoreceptors" that monitor the levels of dissolved $CO_2$ (carbon dioxide) and oxygen and the pH (the degree of acidity or alkalinity) of our blood and cerebrospinal fluid. These feedback mechanisms are basic in that they sustain the ventilatory conditions that are necessary to sustain life. They probably are "layered" to maintain redundancy in the life support system. However, we routinely override these regulatory systems when we talk, sing, or play wind instruments.

The two layers of chemoreceptor-actuated feedback are "central" and "peripheral" with respect to the brain. The central chemoreceptors are located near the ventrolateral surface of the medulla, or "spinal bulb," of the brain. The medulla is continuous with the spinal cord and is one of the "primitive" parts of the brain. The chemoreceptors are located in a part of the medulla that is relatively far from the traditional "respiratory centers" that regulate respiration. They monitor the $CO_2$ and pH of both the cerebrospinal fluid and the blood that perfuses the medulla. Peripheral chemoreceptors are located in two places: in the carotid bodies, near the bifurcation of the common carotid artery in the neck and in the aortic bodies, near the arch of the aorta. The aorta is the main artery that carries oxygenated blood from the heart. The peripheral chemoreceptors monitor pH and oxygen in the arterial blood (Bouhuys, 1974).

The central and peripheral chemoreceptor feedback system acts rapidly to make small changes in respiration. The central feedback system operates slowly, but it can effect large changes in respiration. When healthy people breathe low concentrations of $CO_2$ in air (3–7%), their breathing rate, the depth of their breathing, and the volume of air that passes through their respiratory system per minute all increase. The chemoreceptors are quite sensitive. They, for example, initiate increased respiratory activity when one breathes in a closed room with a number of other people because the oxygen content of the "stale" room air is lower than it should be. The chemoreceptor system feedback systems can operate rapidly; when one is breathing stale air, a single breath of pure oxygen will lead to a temporary reduction of ventilation (Dejours, 1963).

## 7. SPEECH PRODUCTION AND RESPIRATORY REGULATION

Despite these redundant regulatory systems, human beings typically override the control pattern that prevails during quiet respiration when they talk. When one breathes room air and talks, ventilation per minute increases during speech. The ventilation rate can become quite high when one produces high flow sounds like /h/ (Klatt *et al.*, 1968). A significant decrease from normal blood $CO_2$ levels thus can occur during sustained speech during normal activity levels (Dejours, 1963). In contrast, when it is necessary to transfer more air through the lungs to meet basic vegetative constraints, for example, during strenuous activities, speech production decreases in the flow rate. Though speakers in some cases adapt patterns of respiration that maintain optimum air transfer with flow rates compatible with intelligible speech, they usually give priority to the flow rates that are necessary for speech production and override the regulatory mechanisms.

It again is unlikely that the ability to override these basic vegetative regulatory mechanisms is "learned" in the normal sense of that word. However, we do not know when infants begin to act in this mode, or whether exposure to an environment in which they hear people talking is necessary to "trigger" genetically transmitted patterns of linguistic behavior. The generally poor quality of the intonation of deaf speakers suggests that some exposure to speech is necessary.

## 8. IMITATING INTONATION

By 3 months of age, infants imitate the detailed intonation contours that they hear. Sander (1981), for example, presents data of a 3-month-old boy imitating the intonation contours that his mother produces over a 5-minute interchange of "conversation" between the infant and his German-speaking mother. The infant imitates the absolute values of his mother's $F_0$ contour, tracking her $F_0$ modulation. The process of imitation of intonation appears to start quite early in life. Acoustic analysis of a "conversation" between a Japanese-speaking mother and her 6-week-old infant son shows that the mother appears to initiate the exchange by imitating the intonation of a sound that her son produces (Lieberman, 1984). The infant then responds by imitating the next sound that his mother produces. Infants, by these procedures, may "learn" that it is appropriate to imitate speech sounds. There, of course, may be a genetically transmitted tendency for children to imitate sounds and for mothers to acculturate their children to the imitation of speech. However, whether or not there are any innate mechanisms that are specifically "designed" to facilitate the imitation of speech sounds, it is evident that infants begin to imitate the intonation contours that occur in their native language at a very early age. These instrumental data are consistent with the traditional, oft-repeated claim that children acquire the characteristic intonation patterns of their native language in the first year of life (Lewis, 1936).

## 9. STUDY OF LINGUISTIC "BASE FORMS"

The study of the acquisition of intonation by infants can yield some insight into the nature of the "base form" of intonation. It is obvious that children learn to speak without any formal instruction. It is likely, as many linguists and psychologists have proposed, that there may be some innate mechanisms in human beings that facilitate the acquisition of speech and language and enable children to filter out the linguistically salient aspects of speech and language from the various other sounds, speech errors, and the like, that they encounter as they grow up. Whether there exists a specialized "language-acquisition device" or some general cognitive facility that structures other aspects of the intellectual and communicative development of children is an open question (Lenneberg, 1967; Lieberman, 1984). However, we do not have to resolve the issue of whether language acquisition in children rests on a language-specific neural ability or not to make use of the fact that children *do* somehow manage to extract the linguistically salient aspects of speech from the "noise" that they encounter in life. Jakobson (1940) thus proposed that the sequence in which children acquired the distinctive speech

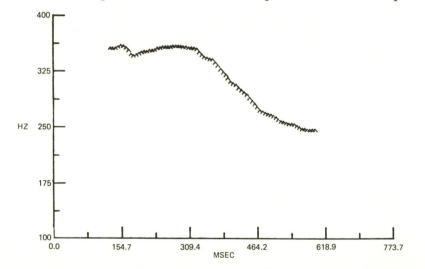

*Figure 6.* Fundamental frequency (F$_0$) contour of a 70-week-old girl for the word *sour.*

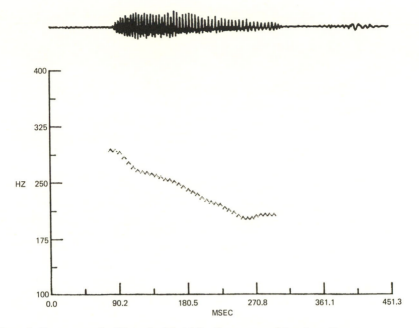

*Figure 7.* F$_0$ contour of a 70-week-old girl for the one-word "sentence" *man.*

contrasts of their first native language yields an insight into the linguistic hierarchy of the speech code. A long-term study at Brown University has followed the development of speech in normal infants from birth to ages that range from 3 to 4 years. One aspect of this study involves the acoustic and linguistic analysis of the intonation contours that children use in their initial one-word utterances. Landahl (1980, 1982) in these studies shows that the F$_0$ contours of these one-word utterances are quite similar to the contours that adult speakers of American English usually use to segment speech into meaningful sentences.

Acoustic analyses of the intonation of declarative sentences of American English show that the linguistically salient acoustic cue that usually delimits the scope of a sentence is a breath group *terminal* abrupt fall in F$_0$ accompanied by a concomitant fall in the amplitude of the speech signal (Atkinson, 1973; Lieberman, 1967; Vanderslice & Ladefoged, 1972). In Figures 6, 7, and 8, F$_0$ contours of some of the first one-word utterances of a 70-week-old girl are presented (Landahl, 1980). The F$_0$ contour was derived using an autocorrelation program on a PDP 11-34 computer after the speech signals were sampled at a rate of 20,000 samples per second with 11-bit quantization. The computer program is

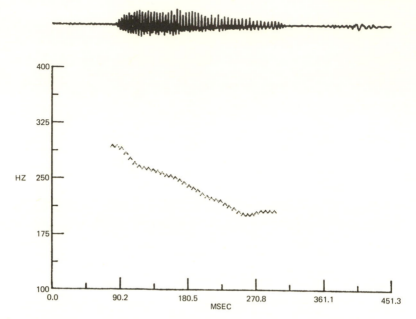

*Figure 8.* F$_0$ contour of a 70-week-old girl for the word *here*.

accurate to within 3 to 5 Hz in the absence of gross errors that can occur if the signal level is too low. The parameters that enter into the auto-correlation program can be adjusted to eliminate errors as the algorithm's output is monitored. The system thus makes use of the computer oper-ator as an interactive "component" to recognize certain classes of errors and make appropriate corrections.

The ordinate in these figures is the F$_0$ scale, and the abcissa is time in msec. Note that the F$_0$ contour in Figure 6 that corresponds to the word *sour* initially is level and then falls. In Figure 7, the F$_0$ that occurred for the one-word "sentence" *man* is presented. Note that there again is a terminal F$_0$ fall; the nonterminal F$_0$ contour is again relatively flat after an initial rise. In Figure 8, the F$_0$ contour for the utterance *here* shows a gradual fall throughout the breath group. Figure 8 shows a "declination" or fall throughout the breath group; the other two samples do not. The one-word utterances analyzed in Landahl (1982) that are derived from the spontaneous speech of three children show that declination does not typically characterize these utterances. The most general acoustic cue is a terminal fall in F$_0$. Thus, if the general claim of Jakobson (1940) is correct and children acquire the base form for the intonation of Amer-ican English, these data show that it does not consist of a "declination."

The $F_0$ contours of these one-word utterances do appear to be typical of those of adult speakers of American English. Figure 9 shows the $F_0$ contour that was derived for an adult male speaker when he produced the sentence "Good, which one?" in normal discourse (Lieberman & Tseng, 1980). Note that the peaks in $F_0$ at times 50 and 260 msec have the same absolute value, contrary to the claims of declination theorists (Pierrehumbert, 1979; Sorenson & Cooper, 1980). The terminal fall at 640 msec ends at a lower value than the initial $F_0$ "valley" at 120 msec as the declination theory of Maeda (1976) claims, but this relation also would hold for breath group theories (Atkinson, 1973; Lieberman, 1967; Vanderslice & Ladefoged, 1972) because the terminal fall is, by definition, supposed to have a lower value than a nonterminal $F_0$. Figure 10 shows that $F_0$ contour that this same speaker produced when he uttered the sentence "Remember, we talked about the alternative solution." There is an $F_0$ prominence on the word *remember* that yields the percept of *stress* or *prominence* on this word (Fry, 1958; Lieberman, 1960).

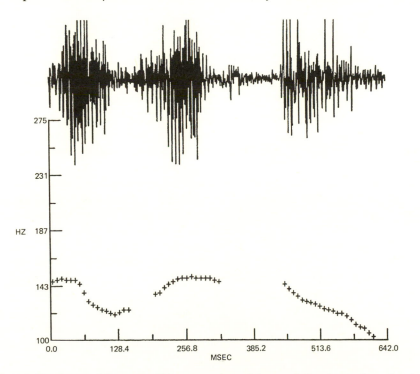

*Figure 9.* Fundamental frequency ($F_0$) contour derived for an adult male speaker when he produced the sentence "Good, which one?" in normal speech.

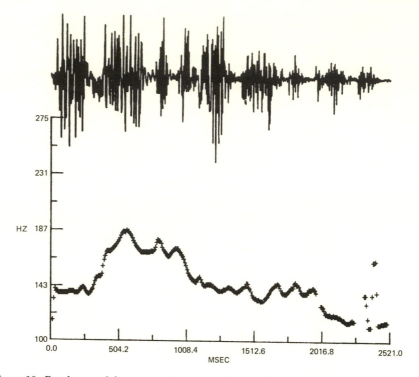

*Figure 10.* Fundamental frequency ($F_0$) contour derived for the speaker used in Figure 9 when he spoke the sentence "Remember, we talked about the alternative solution."

Neither the $F_0$ "peaks" nor "valleys," however, show a general "declination" if we discount this initial peak. The nonterminal portions of the breath groups do show a consistent fall in $F_0$ for some speakers, but the effect does not occur consistently for all speakers of English (Lieberman, 1967) or Chinese (Tseng, 1981). No theory of the linguistic sentence-segmenting function of intonation can, at present, account for all of the $F_0$ contours that actually occur in normal discourse (Tseng, 1981).

The communicative function of level versus falling nonterminal $F_0$ contours is not clear. Pike (1945), in his comprehensive phonetic study of the intonation of American English, attempted to show that different intonation contours conveyed particular attitudes of the speaker. Pike, however, concluded that the attitudinal value of the intonation contour was not independent of the lexical content of the words of a sentence. Umeda (1979), who has studied a large corpus of $F_0$ contours of sentences uttered in the course of sustained discourse, suggests that $F_0$

"declination" may be a discourse effect that serves to introduce a "new" topic in a conversation. Umeda's data show that an initial $F_0$ peak, like that in Figure 10, serves as an acoustic "paragraph" marker in discourse. Umeda also notes that some speakers continually make use of this acoustic cue in virtually all of their sentences. The declination theory makes too strong a claim about the form of the nonterminal $F_0$ contour of the breath group. Some of the data cited in support of the declination theory are misleading: If $F_0$ contours that are essentially level are averaged with ones that do fall, the average is bound to be a contour that will fall. The claim of the declination theory that all $F_0$ contours must fall is clearly wrong. The $F_0$ contour in Figure 11 from Landahl (1982), for example, shows the $F_0$ contour of the same child whose one-word utterances were plotted in Figures 6, 7, and 8. The child at a later stage of language acquisition is producing the sentence "Can I take another man?" Note the absence of any $F_0$ declination, whether it is measured with respect to the peaks or valleys of the nonterminal $F_0$ contour.

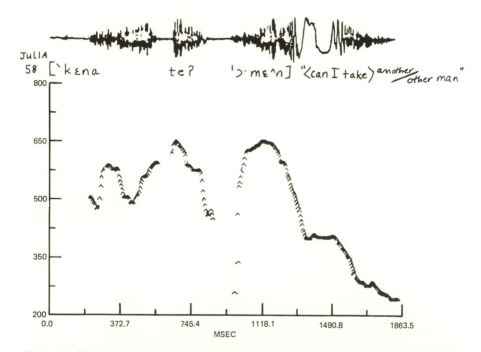

*Figure 11.* Fundamental frequency ($F_0$) contour derived for the speaker who supplied the data used in Figures 6–8 at a later stage of language acquisition in producing the sentence "Can I take another man?". (Courtesy K. Landahl, 1982.)

## 10. THE RANGE OF FUNDAMENTAL FREQUENCY VARIATION

The analysis of the utterances of infants with respect to the $F_0$ variation (Keating & Buhr, 1978) shows that we have also underestimated the range of variation of actual discourse. The $F_0$ of noncry vocalizations varied from 25 Hz to 2750 Hz in one 36-week-old child who used the cry, modal, and falsetto registers of phonation (Van den Berg, 1962). The range of $F_0$ was somewhat more constrained in 16-week-old children; their $F_0$s ranged from 15 to 1440 Hz.

## 11. DURATION AS A CUE TO SENTENCE SEGMENTATION

Analysis of the speech of adult speakers of English shows that the duration of the word or syllable that occurs in breath group final position is longer than it otherwise would be (Klatt, 1976). The data of Kubaska and Keating (1982) show that children appear to learn to make this distinction as they progress from one-word to multiword utterances. The strategy that the children appear to follow involves their shortening the durations of words that are produced in the nonterminal portion of the breath group.

## 12. VOWEL PRODUCTION

The anatomy of the supralaryngeal vocal tract of human infants at birth is similar to that of nonhuman primates (Bosma, 1975; George, 1978; Laitman, Heimbuch, & Crelin, 1978; Lieberman & Crelin, 1971; Lieberman et al., 1972). Human infants do not initially produce vowels like /i/, /u/, and /a/. (Buhr, 1980; George, 1978; Lieberman et al., 1972; Stark et al., 1975). Though the neural control for speech production may not be well developed at birth, the anatomy of the supralaryngeal vocal tract in itself is a limiting factor until it restructures at about the age of 3 months. Studies in which the supralaryngeal vocal tract that is typical for newborn infants is modeled using a computer-implemented simulation show that it is inherently impossible to produce these vowels (Lieberman, 1975; Lieberman & Crelin, 1971; Lieberman et al., 1972). The tongue in the human newborn is long and thin and is positioned entirely within the oral cavity. The newborn's tongue does not have the almost circular shape of the adult human tongue (Nearey, 1978). This difference in tongue shape, which follows from the high position of the newborn's larynx that I noted earlier, makes it impossible for newborns to produce the supralaryngeal vocal-tract-area functions that are necessary to produce these sounds (Fant, 1960; Stevens & House, 1955).

Goldstein (1980) in her computer-implemented modeling study claims that the newborn vocal tract can produce these vowels. The hypothetical newborn vocal tract on which Goldstein bases this claim, however, bears little relation to the actual supralaryngeal vocal tract of newborn infants that have been described in a number of anatomic and radiographic studies (Bosma, 1975; George, 1978; Grosmangin, 1979; Laitman et al., 1977, 1978; Lieberman & Crelin, 1971; Negus, 1949). Goldstein did not base her newborn vocal tract on data derived from newborn infants. The key parameters that she uses to estimate the shape of the tongue and the relation of the oral cavity to the pharynx are derived from King's (1978) data for 3-month-old infants. Her hypothetical newborn vocal tract is essentially that of a 3-month-old infant because she does not take account of the profound restructuring of the basicranium and mandible that occurs between birth and 3 months.

Acoustic analyses are consistent with the results of modeling studies (with Goldstein's, 1980, "newborn" vocal tract assigned to its correct 3-month-old status). The data of George (1978) and Buhr (1980) thus show that the vowels /i/, /u/, and /a/ first appear in the phonetic inventory of infants at age 3 months. The vowels that infants produce during their first year of life during "babbling" gradually appear to approximate the vowel space of English for children raised in this linguistic environment. Figures 12 and 13 show the first and second formant frequencies of the sounds identified as English vowels for an infant at ages 66 and 147 weeks, respectively. These data were derived from recordings made at 2-week intervals while the child "conversed" with its mother (Lieberman, 1980). Formant frequency data for vowels show that the child's approximation to the "well-formed" vowel space of English gradually improves while the child enters the phonological stage of language acquisition.

The study of speech production in the phonologic stage removes some of the uncertainty that necessarily attends our interpretation of the child's behavior during babbling. We can be somewhat more certain about the relation between the sounds that a child is producing and the sounds that he or she hears in the phonologic stage. Olmsted (1971) thus discovered that children had better success in producing the phonetic equivalents of the words that their mothers used when the consonants of these words were ones that are more readily identified under conditions of noise (Miller & Nicely, 1955). Olmsted (1971) concludes that children acquire these phonetic contrasts by means of the general

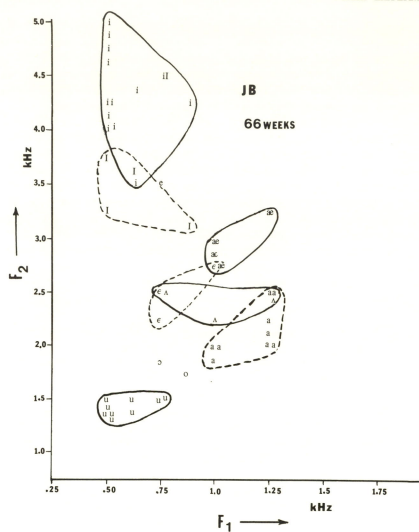

*Figure 12.* First and second formant frequencies of the sounds identified as English vowels for another infant at age 66 weeks.

cognitive process of imitation. The data regarding the imitation of intonation that were noted earlier are consistent with Olmsted's imitation hypothesis as are the vowel data of Lieberman (1980). The child's delineation of the vowel space of English becomes a better and better approximation to that of the adult speakers as the child grows. However, there is a second factor that necessarily enters into the "imitation" of formant frequency patterns by infants and children. A child cannot imitate the

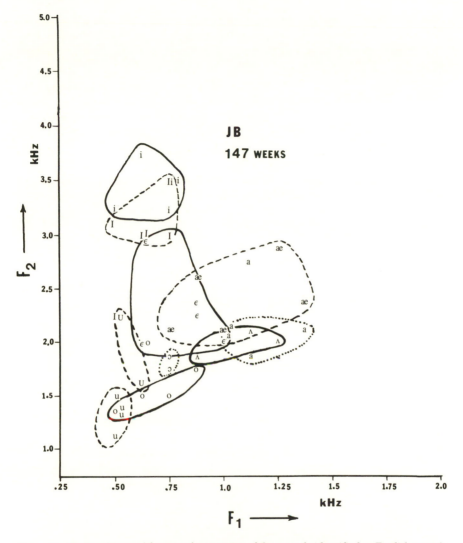

*Figure 13.* First and second formant frequencies of the sounds identified as English vowels for the infant who supplied the data in Figure 12, at age 147 weeks.

absolute values of the formant frequency patterns that he or she hears from his or her parents, or from older children. The supralaryngeal vocal tract of a young child is shorter than any normal adult's (Goldstein, 1980); the child's formant frequencies necessarily are higher in frequency.

The child's formant frequency patterns are always frequency scaled in terms of the adult exemplars that the child hears. In order to "imitate" the speech sounds of the adult language, a child must first form an equivalence class between his or her productions and the adult exemplars. In the early stages of word acquisition, it is frequently the case that adults do not recognize the child's attempt to produce a word until several weeks have passed in which the child gradually produces better approximations to the phonological pattern of the intended word (Landahl, 1982). Children thus must monitor their own attempts at speech and try to approximate the adult system. The only way in which they can do this is by first establishing a frequency-scaled equivalence class between their own productions and the adult exemplars. The process of "formant frequency normalization" is a necessary element in the perception of human speech (Nearey, 1978). The vowel productions of children in the early phonologic stage and the antecedent speech behavior of infants is consistent with the presence of an innately determined neural mechanism that effects vocal tract normalization of speech signals.

## 13. CONCLUDING COMMENTS

The acoustic and linguistic analysis of cry and speech production in infants and young children demonstrates that human linguistic behavior is structured by physiologic mechanisms. Some of these mechanisms appear to be primarily adapted for vegetative, nonlinguistic functions. In this sense, human linguistic ability follows from our general biological endowment. Other aspects of speech production that are manifested quite early in an infant's life appear to involve physiologic mechanisms that are adapted for communication. The biological bases of human linguistic ability thus involves a mosaic that, like other aspects of human behavior, reflects the course of hominid evolution in that it involves mechanisms that occur in other animals and certain specializations that characterize hominids.

## 14. REFERENCES

Armstrong, L. E., & Ward, I. C. *Handbook of English intonation*. Leipzig and Berlin: B. G. Teubner, 1926.

Atkinson, J. R. *Aspects of intonation in speech: Implications from an experimental study of fundamental frequency*. Doctoral dissertation, University of Connecticut, 1973.

Bosma, J. F. Anatomic and physiologic development of the speech apparatus. In D. B. Towers (Ed.), *Human communication and its disorders*. New York: Raven, 1975.

Bouhuys, A. *Breathing*. New York: Grune & Stratton, 1974.

Buhr, R. D. The emergence of vowels in an infant. *Journal of Speech and Hearing Research*, 1980, 23, 75–94.

Crelin, E. S. *Anatomy of the newborn: An atlas*. Philadelphia: Lea and Febiger, 1969.

Darwin, C. *On the origin of species* (Facsimile ed.). London: Atheneum, 1859.

Dejours, P. Control of respiration by arterial chemoreceptors. *Annals of the New York Academy of Science*, 1963, 109, 682–695.

Draper, M. H., Ladefoged, P., & Whitteridge, D. Expiratory pressures and air flow during speech. *British Medical Journal*, 1960, 1, 1837–1843.

Eimas, P. D. Auditory and linguistic processing of cues for place of articulation by infants. *Perception and Psychophysics*, 1974, 16, 513–521.

Fant, G. *Acoustic theory of speech production*. The Hague: Mouton, 1960.

Froscher, M. M. *The effects of respiratory function of sense-group duration*. Doctoral dissertation, Columbia University, 1978.

Fry, D. B. Experiments in the perception of stress. *Language and Speech*, 1958, 1, 125–152.

George, S. L. A longitudinal and cross-sectional analysis of the growth of the post-natal cranial base angle. *American Journal of Physical Anthropology*, 1978, 49, 171–178.

Goldstein, U. G. *An articulatory model for the vocal tracts of growing children*. Unpublished doctoral dissertation, Massachusetts Institute of Technology, 1980.

Grosmangin, C. Base du crâne et pharynx dans leurs rapports avec l'appareil du langage articule. *Mémoires de Laboratoire D'Anatomie de la Faculté de Médecine de Paris*, 40, 1979.

Hadding-Koch, K. *Acoustic-phonetic studies in the intonation of southern Swedish*. Lund: C. W. K. Gleerup, 1961.

Jakobson, R. Kindersprache, Aphasie und allgemeine Lautgesetze. In *Selected writings*. The Hague: Mouton, 1940.

Keating, P., & Buhr, R. Fundamental frequency in the speech of infants and children. *Journal of the Acoustical Society of America*, 1978, 63, 567–571.

King, E. W. A roentgenographic study of pharyngeal growth. *Angle Orthodontist*, 1978, 63, 567–571.

Klatt, D. Linguistic uses of segmental duration in English: Acoustic and perceptual evidence. *Journal of the Acoustical Society of America*, 1976, 59, 1208–1221.

Klatt, D. H., Stevens, K. N., & Mead, J. Studies of articulatory activity and airflow during speech. *Annals of the New York Academy of Sciences*, 1968, 155, 42–54.

Kubaska, C., & Keating, P. Word duration in early child speech. *Journal of Speech and Hearing Research*, 1981, 24, 614–621.

Laitman, J. T., Crelin, E. S., & Conlogue, G. J. The function of the epiglottis in monkey and man. *Yale Journal of Biology and Medicine*, 1977, 50, 43–48.

Laitman, J. A., Heimbuch, R. C., & Crelin, E. S. Developmental change in a basicranial line and its relationship to the upper respiratory systems in living primates. *American Journal of Anatomy*, 1978, 152, 467–482.

Landahl, K. Language-universal aspects of intonation in children's first sentences. *Journal of the Acoustic Society of America*, 1980, 67, 563.

Landahl, K. *The onset of structural discourse: A developmental study of the acquisition of language*. Doctoral dissertation, Brown University, 1982.

Langlois, A., Baken, R. J., & Wilder, C. N. Pre-speech respiratory behavior during the first year of life. In T. Murry & J. Murry (Eds.), *Infant communication: Cry and early speech*. Houston: College Hill Press, 1980.

Lenneberg, E. H. *Biological foundations of language*. New York: Wiley, 1967.

Lewis, M. M. *Infant speech: A study of the beginnings of language*. New York: Harcourt Brace, 1936.

Liberman, A. M., Cooper, F. S., Shankweiler, D. P., & Studdert-Kennedy, M. Perception of the speech code. *Psychological Review*, 1967, 74, 431–461.

Lieberman, M. R., & Lieberman, P. Olson's "projective verse" and the use of breath control as a structural element. *Language and Style*, 1973, 5, 287–298.

Lieberman, P. Some acoustic correlates of word stress in American-English. *Journal of the Acoustical Society of America*, 1960, 33, 451–454.

Lieberman, P. *Intonation, perception and language*. Cambridge, Mass.: M.I.T. Press, 1967.

Lieberman, P. Direct comparison of subglottal and esophageal pressure during speech. *Journal of the Acoustical Society of America*, 1968, *43*, 1157–1164.

Lieberman, P. *On the origins of language: An introduction to the evolution of human speech*. New York: Macmillan, 1975.

Lieberman, P. On the development of vowel production in young children. In G. H. Yeni-Komshian, J. F. Kavanagh, & C. A. Ferguson (Eds.), *Child phonology: Production*. (Vol. 1). New York: Academic Press, 1980.

Lieberman, P. *The biology and evolution of language*. Cambridge, Mass.: Harvard University Press, 1984.

Lieberman, P., & Crelin, E. S. On the speech of Neanderthal Man. *Linguistic Inquiry*, 1971, *2*, 203–222.

Lieberman, P., & Tseng, C. Y. On the fall of the declination theory: Breathing groups versus "declination" as the base form for intonation. *Journal of the Acoustical Society of America* (Suppl. 1), 1980.

Lieberman, P., Knudsen, R., & Mead, J. Determination of the rate of change of fundamental frequency with respect to the sub-glottal air pressure during sustained phonation. *Journal of the Acoustical Society of America*, 1969, *45*, 1537–1543.

Lieberman, P., Crelin, E. S., & Klatt, D. H. Phonetic ability and related anatomy of the newborn, adult human, Neanderthal Man, and the chimpanzees. *American Anthropologist*, 1972, *74*, 287–307.

Maeda, S. *A characterization of American English intonation*. Unpublished doctoral dissertation, Massachusetts Institute of Technology, 1976.

Miller, G. A. The magical number seven, plus or minus two: Some limits on our capacity for processing information. *Psychological Review*, 1956, *63*, 81–97.

Miller, G. A., & Nicely, P. E. An analysis of perceptual confusions among some English consonants. *Journal of the Acoustical Society of America*, 1955, *27*, 338–352.

Morse, P. A. Infant speech perception: A preliminary model and review of the literature. In R. L. Schiefelbush & L. L. Lloyd, (Eds.), *Language perspectives—acquisition, retardation, and intervention*. Baltimore: University Park Press, 1974.

Nearey, T. *Phonetic features for vowels*. Bloomington: Indiana University Linguistics Club, 1978.

Negus, V. E. *The comparative anatomy and physiology of the larynx*. New York: Hafner Press, 1949.

Ohala, J. Aspects of the control and production of speech. *UCLA Working Papers in Phonetics* *15*, 1970.

Olmsted, D. L. *Out of the mouth of babes*. The Hague: Mouton, 1971.

Pierrehumbert, J. The perception of fundamental frequency declination. *Journal of the Acoustical Society of America*, 1979, *66*, 363–369.

Pike, K. L. *The intonation of American-English*. Ann Arbor: University of Michigan, 1945.

Rabson, S., Lieberman, P., & Ryalls, J. *Imitation of intonation by Japanese speaking infants*. Manuscript in preparation.

Sandner, L. W. Communication with a three-month-old baby. *Proceedings of the Thirteenth Annual Child Language Research Forum*, Stanford University, 1981.

Shipp, T., Doherty, E. T., & Morrissey, T. Predicting vocal frequency from selected physiologic measures. *Journal of Acoustical Society of America*, 1979, *66*, 678–684.

Simpson, G. G. The biological nature of man. *Science*, 1966, *152*, 472–478.

Sorenson, J. M., & Cooper, W. E. Syntactic coding of fundamental frequency in speech production. In R. A. Cole (Ed.), *Perception and production of fluent speech*. Hillside, N.J.: Erlbaum, 1980.

Stark, R. E., Rose, S. N., & McLagen, M. Features of infant sounds: The first eight weeks of life. *Journal of Child Language*, 1975, *2*, 202–221.

Stevens, K. N., & House, A. S. Development of a quantitative description of vowel articulation. *Journal of the Acoustical Society of America*, 1955, *27*, 484–493.

Trager, G. L., & Smith, H. L. *Outline of English structure*. Norman, Ok.: Battenburg, 1951.

Truby, H. M., Bosma, J. F., & Lind, J. *Newborn infant cry*. Upsala: Almquist and Wiksell, 1965.

Tseng, C. Y. *An acoustic phonetic study on tones in Mandarin Chinese*. Unpublished doctoral dissertation, Brown University, 1981.

Van den Berg, J. Modern research in experimental phoniatrics. *Folia Phoniatrica*, 1962, *14*, 18–149.

Vanderslice, R., & Ladefoged, P. Binary suprasegmental features and transformational word-accentuation rules. *Language*, 1972, *48*(4), 819–838.

# 3

# A Physioacoustic Model of the Infant Cry

HOWARD L. GOLUB and MICHAEL J. CORWIN

## 1. INTRODUCTION

The infant cry is the result of the complex interaction between many anatomic structures and physiologic mechanisms. These interactions involve the central nervous system, respiratory system, peripheral nervous system, and a variety of muscles.

Physicians have long been aware that infants with certain diseases (meningitis, cri du chat, etc.) have distinctive cries. Since the early 1960s, Scandinavian researchers have utilized the sound spectrogram to correlate acoustical data with a variety of pathologic conditions. These studies have determined normal ranges for a number of spectrographically measurable acoustical features. When the cries of normal infants were compared to those with known medical problems, significant cry abnormalities were found in infants with such problems as low birth weight and birth asphyxia (Michelsson, 1971), hyperbilirubinemia (Wasz-Höckert, Koivisto, Vuorenkoski, Partanen, & Lind, 1971), meningitis (Michelsson, Sirvio, & Wasz-Höckert, 1977b), cleft palate (Michelsson, Sirvio, Koivisto, Sovijarvi, & Wasz-Höckert, 1975), Down's syndrome (Lind, Vuorenkoski, Rosberg, Partanen, & Wasz-Höckert, 1970), cri-du-chat

HOWARD L. GOLUB • Pediatric Diagnostic Service Institute, Cambridge, Massachusetts 02142.    MICHAEL J. CORWIN • Department of Pediatrics,    Boston University School of Medicine, and Department of Pediatrics, Boston City Hospital, Boston, Massachusetts 02118.

syndrome (Vuorenkoski, Lind, Partanen, Lejeune, Lafourcade, & Wasz-Höckert, 1966), and many others.

Despite this 20-year Scandinavian experience, clinicians in the United States appear unaware of the potential applications of infant cry analysis. There are several factors that may have contributed to cry analysis being underutilized in clinical practice. First, no conceptual model of cry production existed whereby one could correlate the cry output with specific pathologic conditions. Secondly, spectrographic analysis has several disadvantages that make widespread use difficult. The physical limitations of the spectrogram include poor dynamic range, often inadequate frequency resolution, and limited ability to analyze a large number of cries quickly. Perhaps a more important consideration is that physicians generally lack the expertise necessary to interpret the complex light and dark lines of the spectrogram easily and therefore may be reluctant to use this technique. Finally, no prospective studies with long-term follow-up have been done to determine the predictive value of specific cry abnormalities when discovered on routine cry analysis.

In an attempt to address the issues just discussed, we have developed a new approach to cry analysis that utilizes a conceptual model of infant cry production and a computer-based signal processing system that enable the observer to relate closely the acoustic properties of the cry to the infant producing the cry. In this chapter we will begin by defining terms with which the reader may be unfamiliar. This is followed by a description of the physioacoustic model of cry production. Finally, we will describe the various cry analysis techniques, review some of the studies that have utilized these techniques, and discuss the potential medical applications of infant cry analysis.

## 2. DEFINITIONS

This section is not meant to serve as a comprehensive acoustical dictionary. We have attempted to give simple definitions for terms with which the reader is likely to be unfamiliar and for common terms that have a specific definition in the context of this chapter.

- *Fundamental frequency* ($F_0$): A physical characteristic of all periodic wave forms. It is measured in cycles per second or hertz (Hz) and refers to the number of times a complex wave form repeats itself in one second.
- *Harmonic:* A multiple of the fundamental frequency. For example, if the fundamental frequency is 100 Hz, then the first harmonic

would be 200 Hz, the second 300 Hz, the third 400 Hz, and so forth.

- *Pure tone:* A periodic wave form containing a single frequency.
- *Complex tone:* A periodic wave form whose shape is determined by the fundamental frequency and by the relative amplitude of its harmonics.
- *Fourier analysis:* A mathematical process that allows one to determine the amplitude of each of the harmonics that make up a complex tone.
- *Frequency spectrum:* The frequency content of a signal. This can be graphed as magnitude versus frequency by doing Fourier analysis.
- *Resonance frequencies:* Input frequencies at which a system will respond with maximal amplitude. These frequencies are a physical property of the system.
- *Formant frequencies:* The resonance frequencies of the vocal tract. They are referred to as first formant ($F_1$), second formant ($F_2$), and so forth. Formant frequencies are usually independent of the fundamental frequency and its harmonics.
- *Pitch:* The subjective property of a sound that allows one to order the sound on a scale ranging from "low" to "high." Its unit is the mel. Pitch is not a physical property of the sound but rather a human judgment that is primarily dependent on the fundamental frequency but also is affected by the other component frequencies and the sound intensity.
- *Band width:* A specified range of frequencies.
- *Octave:* A band width in which the highest frequency is double the lowest frequency. For example, 100–200 Hz or 800–1600 Hz would each be equal to one octave.
- *Band pass filter:* An acoustic filter that only allows passage of frequencies within a particular band width.
- *Time domain:* A representation of a signal that plots amplitude versus time.
- *Frequency domain:* A representation of a signal that plots magnitude versus frequency.
- *Cry unit:* The sound that results during the passage of air past the vocal folds during a single inspiratory/expiratory cycle.
- *Cry:* The total sound response to a specific stimulus. This may contain many cry units.
- *Cry type or mode:* One of four types of acoustic output an infant may exhibit during a cry unit. (See phonation, hyperphonation, dysphonation, and inspiratory phonation.)

- *Phonation:* A segment of a cry unit that is periodic and typically has a fundamental frequency from 250 to 700 Hz.
- *Hyperphonation:* A segment of a cry unit that is periodic and typically has a fundamental frequency from 1000 to 2000 Hz.
- *Dysphonation:* A segment of a cry unit that is not periodic.
- *Inspiratory phonation:* Any sound produced during inspiration.

## 3. PHYSIOACOUSTIC MODEL

### 3.1. Overview

A simplified view of our cry production model (Golub, 1979) is shown in Figure 1.

The model divides cry production into four parts. The first part is the subglottal (respiratory) system that is responsible for developing the pressure (Ps[t]) below the glottis necessary for driving the vocal fold source. The second part is the sound source located at the larynx. The sound source may be described mathematically, in the frequency domain, as either a periodic source (S[f]) or a turbulence noise source (N[f]). These sources may operate alone, or more frequently, simultaneously. Both acoustic sources originate at the vocal folds. The periodic source results from vibration of the folds. The turbulence noise is most likely produced by the turbulence created by forcing air through a small opening left by incomplete closure of the vocal folds. Rothenberg (1974) has shown that adults exhibit the same kind of aspiration noise, to a lesser degree, during vowel production. The third source of cry production is the vocal and nasal tracts located above the larynx. This part of the cry production system is an acoustic filter that has a transfer function (T[f]) whose characteristics change with the shape and length of the vocal and nasal tracts and the degree of nasal coupling. The fourth part of the cry production system is the radiation characteristic (R[f]) that describes the filtering of the sound between the mouth of the infant and the microphone located some distance (d) away.

The frequency spectra of idealized periodic (S[f]) and turbulence (N[f]) sources, the vocal tract transfer function (T[f]), and the radiation characteristic (R[f]) are shown in Figures 2A–2D. The frequency spectrum of the output sound can now be constructed by multiplying the spectra of each of these three parts, keeping in mind that the amplitude of the sound is directly related to the subglottal pressure (Ps[t]). This calculated spectrum of the idealized output is shown in Figure 2E.

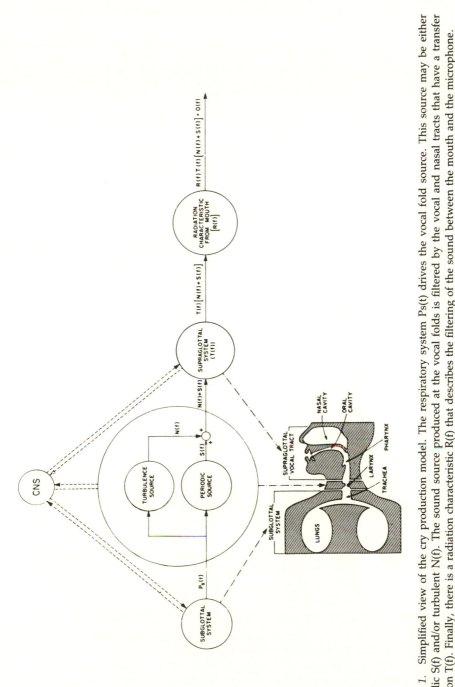

*Figure 1.* Simplified view of the cry production model. The respiratory system Ps(t) drives the vocal fold source. This source may be either periodic S(f) and/or turbulent N(f). The sound source produced at the vocal folds is filtered by the vocal and nasal tracts that have a transfer function T(f). Finally, there is a radiation characteristic R(f) that describes the filtering of the sound between the mouth and the microphone.

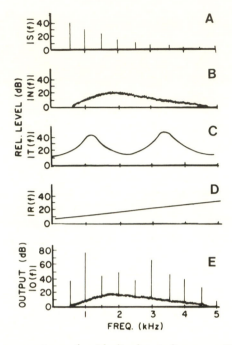

*Figure 2.* (A) Frequency spectrum of an idealized periodic source; (B) frequency spectrum of an idealized turbulence source; (C) frequency spectrum of an idealized vocal tract transfer function; (D) frequency spectrum of an idealized radiation characteristic; and (E) calculated spectrum of an idealized output, which is constructed by multiplying the spectra shown in the figure.

Figure 3 shows an overall conceptualization of the organization of the infant's central nervous system (CNS). The model assumes that muscle control is accomplished within three levels of central nervous system processing, which we call upper, middle, and lower processors. The upper processor is involved in choosing and modulating the state of action of the child and is probably where the more complex feedback from external and internal factors is collected and acted upon. Of course, during the neonatal period, this higher processor may be relatively immature and "conscious" control infrequent. As a result, at this stage of maturation, many activities occur in a "reflexlike" manner.

It is assumed that all vegetative states such as swallowing, coughing, respiration, bowel movements, and crying are within the middle processor. The stimuli that help the upper processor to choose the appropriate vegetative state include hunger, pain, hypoxemia, or hypercapnia, and a full bladder. An important assumption, therefore, is that the neonatal cry is very much like other actions present at birth that are stimulated by survival pressures. The causes of crying are less complex for

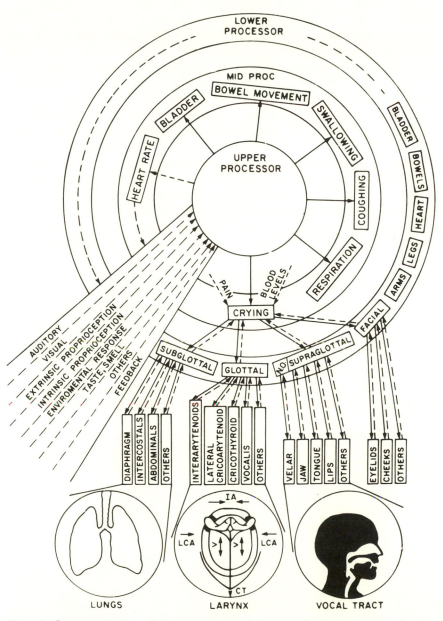

*Figure 3.* Conceptualization of the organization of the control of the infant cry, showing the proposed upper, middle, and lower processors.

newborns than those for older infants. As the nervous system matures and the child's environment becomes more complicated, the cry may no longer be assumed to be "reflexlike" but may often be the result of volitional activity.

The initiation of each of the previously mentioned vegetative states, in response to a stimulus, must result in the control of a large number of muscles. Some of these muscle groups are shown in Figure 3. Most likely, there exists some sort of "coordinative structure" that makes it unnecessary for higher processors to exert control of each individual muscle within a muscle group. For example, swallowing involves a well-defined control sequence that is kept relatively constant from one swallow to the next. Upper processor control of each muscle involved in swallowing would be quite inefficient, and a more reasonable hypothesis would be that following the stimulus for swallowing the upper processor triggers the "swallow box" in the middle processor, and then the lower processor acts to control the muscular movements involved in swallowing.

The newborn cry is envisioned as resembling the same type of process as the vegetative states shown in Figure 3. Following the cry stimulus, the upper and/or middle processors for cry production trigger the lower processor control of the relevant muscle groups.

Based on these muscle control hypotheses, we assume that each of the three muscle groups important for cry production are controlled independently. Consequently, the parameters that each are responsible for are likely to vary independently. Secondly, if we can pinpoint differences in the cry as caused by subglottal (respiratory), glottal (laryngeal), or supraglottal malfunctions, then we will be able to correlate the acoustic abnormality with specific physiological or anatomical abnormalities.

In summary, the mathematical formulation of the acoustic theory initially developed for adult speech production (Fant, 1960; Flanagan, 1972; Stevens, 1964) may be applied, with the preceding assumptions, to infant cry production. This mathematical formulation

$$\text{Output} = \text{Source} \times \text{Filter}$$

illustrated in Figures 2A–E is used as a guide for the interpretation of the dynamic aspects of the source-filter linear system as it relates to the infant cry.

It is apparent from the preceding discussion that there are basically two components to the model of cry production: an acoustical component that specifies how sound is generated at the larynx and in the airways above the larynx and a physiological component that specifies how the configuration and movements of the respiratory, laryngeal, and supralaryngeal structures are controlled.

## 3.2. Acoustical Component of the Model

Utilizing the spectrogram, Truby and Lind (1965) have described three cry types: phonation = basic; cry hyperphonation = shift; and dysphonation = turbulence. In the case of our model, we have assumed that the sound source is at the larynx, and that the three cry types previously described represent different modes of vibration of the vocal folds. In phonation, the vocal folds vibrate fully at an $F_0$ range of approximately 250–700 Hz. Hyperphonation results from a "falsetto" like vibration pattern of the vocal folds with an $F_0$ range of about 1000–2000 Hz. Presumably, only a thin portion of the vocal ligament is involved in this mode. Finally, dysphonation contains both a periodic and aperiodic sound source and occurs when turbulence noise is generated at the vocal folds. This turbulence noise, however, is modulated by vocal fold vibration. At our present state of knowledge of the mechanisms of laryngeal mechanics of infants, it is not possible to explain the details of these three modes of laryngeal operation. Based on observation of a large number of infant cries, and studies done by others on adults and animals, it is simply postulated that these three modes of vibration can occur during the expiratory cry.

The filtering of the source by the vocal tract introduces several spectral peaks or formants into the sound output. The positions of these formants depends upon the shape of the vocal tract. The formant structure is influenced by acoustic coupling to the nasal tract if the velopharyngeal port is open. For a vocal tract length of about 8 cm (the average vocal tract length for a term newborn; see Goldstein, 1979) and for a roughly uniform vocal tract cross-sectional area, acoustic theory (Stevens, 1964) predicts that formants occur at about 1100 Hz and 3300 Hz. If there is a substantial velopharyngeal opening, then theoretical analysis predicts an additional spectral peak in the frequency range of 2–3 kHz, with the possibility of some small shifts in the position of the other formants.

If the cross-sectional area of the vocal tract deviates from a roughly uniform shape or if the length of the vocal tract is different from 8 cm, then the formants would be expected to shift from the values of 1100 Hz and 3300 Hz. In particular, if the pharyngeal region is narrowed, then acoustic theory predicts an upward shift of the formants.

The fundamental frequency of vocal fold vibration and indeed the mode of operation of the vocal folds depend upon the subglottal pressure and the adjustment of the intrinsic laryngeal musculature. Increased subglottal pressure would be expected to result in a higher $F_0$; however, $F_0$ may also be influenced by contraction of the cricothyroid muscle (Van den Berg, 1965).

A cry sequence for an infant usually consists of a series of relatively long expiratory cries separated by brief inspiratory intervals. It is not unreasonable to expect that the durations of the units within the cry sequence and the time intervals between cry units are dependent on the state of the infant's respiratory system. For example, a diminished vital capacity resulting in a relatively small tidal volume, would be expected to produce short and lower intensity cry units (Golub, 1980).

## 3.3. Physiological Component of the Model

The physiological component of the model is based on the hypothesis that newborns tend to control the tension in their muscles in a noncontinuous fashion. This assumption is based in the overall view of the organization of the infant's central nervous system as illustrated in Figure 3. If we start with this assumption as the basis for a production model, then describing the various acoustic events becomes a much easier task. For example, one can now explain the three cry types described spectrographically by Truby and Lind (1965). The large differences in the acoustics between these three cry types can be explained by changes in the relative tensions (high or low) of just two or three laryngeal muscles (Golub, 1979). These changes would be analogous to register shifts in adult speech (Van den Berg, 1965).

The distinction between constant tension and constant control should be made, especially when describing the action of the larger muscle systems (e.g., respiratory system). For example, evidence from measurements made on the acoustics and subglottal pressure during the cry (Truby & Lind, 1965) indicates that the tensions of the larger respiratory muscles do indeed change somewhat continuously during the expiratory phase. In the case of these larger muscles, the continuous, relatively slow tension changes probably occur due to peripheral state changes of the muscles rather than continuous variation in the control of these muscles. The most important of these state changes can be described by the length-tension-loading aspects of the particular muscles of the system. The resulting muscle tensions are not only a function of higher level control, which is probably quantal in nature, but also of the particular length-loading characteristics of the muscle at the onset of the control. The smaller laryngeal muscles have smaller peripheral state changes, and the tensions developed would not be expected to vary considerably during the course of any particular kind of phonation.

The muscle control hypotheses previously described are used to help direct our choice of acoustical features so they will accurately reflect the physiology of the infant. For example, we have stated before that the three cry types described by Truby and Lind (1965) may represent different modes of sound production analogous to register shifts in adult speech. If we make this assumption, then it is clear that the acoustical features one measures will vary with the particular mode of sound production. In fact, one would expect that a different range of normal acoustical features could be defined for each mode of sound production. This implies that meaningful cry analysis requires an assessment of what the mode of sound production was at the time of recording. In fact, previous spectrographic data (Truby & Lind, 1965) have shown that the maxium $F_0$ in phonation rarely exceeds 550 to 600 Hz; however, a maximum $F_0$ of 1500 to 1600 Hz is not unusual in hyperphonation.

In summary, the model of cry production can provide guidance for the selection of the acoustical features that are most likely to reflect the anatomy and physiology of the infant accurately.

## 4. CRY ANALYSIS TECHNIQUES

In the first part of this chapter we described the physioacoustic model of cry production that forms the basis for our approach to infant cry analysis. The purpose of our model is to help us to understand the relationship between specific acoustical features of the cry sound and the anatomical and physiological characteristics of the infant. This understanding is crucial if we wish to investigate the medical applications of infant cry analysis. However, it is not enough to be able to identify the important features; one must also be able to extract the features in an accurate and efficient way. Part 4 of this chapter will review the techniques that have been developed for the extraction of acoustical data, and we will discuss how recent advances in computer-aided signal-processing techniques have dramatically improved our ability to obtain acoustical information.

### 4.1. Auditory Analysis

The most readily available means for cry analysis is the human ear. Over the years, various technological advances have increased our ability to assess the infant cry by listening. It is instructive to review briefly the reports that have examined the value of diagnostic listening.

The art of diagnostic listening was described in ancient times by Hippocrates. The art, however, was essentially ignored until 1855 when Charles Darwin treated the topic of infant crying and screaming quite comprehensively, using photographs and drawings to illustrate various expressions of emotion. Flatau and Gutzmann (1906) used a graphophone to record infant vocalizations. They listened to the cry recordings of 30 neonates and noted 3 infants with higher pitched phonations. In 1936, Lewis used the International Phonetic Alphabet (IPA) for the first time in an attempt to describe infant vocalizations. Fairbanks (1942) listened to gramophone records to study the frequency characteristics of the "hunger wails" of one infant over a period of 9 months.

Wasz-Höckert, Partanen, Vuorenkoski, and Valanne (1964) have found from tape recordings that hunger, pain, pleasure, and birth cries can be identified auditorily. Valanne, Vuorenkoski, Partanen, Lind, and Wasz-Höckert (1967) found that mothers can recognize the vocalizations of their own infants. This finding was supported by work by Formby (1967). Massengill (1968) found that speech clinicians were not able to recognize the grade of nasality or the type of crying of infants with cleft palate. Partanen, Wasz-Höckert, Vuorenkoski, Theorell, Valanne, and Lind (1967) demonstrated that the pain cries of healthy infants could be differentiated from the cries of sick babies with one of the following diagnoses: neonatal asphyxia, neonatal brain damage, neonatal hyperbilirubinemia, and Down's syndrome. It was shown that after a training period of approximately 2 hours 82 pediatricians could diagnose normal versus pathological cries very accurately and differentially diagnose the specific pathology somewhat less accurately.

The preceding studies demonstrate that medical information can be obtained from listening to cries. This method of analysis is readily available and can be improved with experience and training. However, it is clear that auditory analysis provides only a fraction of the information contained in the cry signal and that more sophisticated techniques might give more significant diagnostic information.

## 4.2.  Time Domain Analysis

Time domain information is obtained from devices that graph sound magnitude versus time on a paper strip chart. Fisichelli and Karelitz (1963), Fisichelli, Karelitz, Eichbauer, and Rosenfeld (1961), and Karelitz and Fisichelli (1962) used such a device to examine infant cries. They found that infants with diffuse brain damage require a greater stimulus to produce 1 minute of crying (1962) and that the mean latency period between pain stimulus and onset of crying was significantly longer for abnormal infants (2.6 sec) compared to healthy infants (1.6 sec) (1963).

A direct writing oscillograph was a time domain device used by Lind, Wasz-Höckert, Vuorenkoski, and Valanne (1965) to study the time course of the durations and latencies of different kinds of crying. They found that the initial phonations of a cry record are more irregular than those that appear once the infant is fully aroused. After this arousal, a gradual reduction in time and intensity of the cry units occurs until the baby stops crying.

Wolff (1967, 1969) measured inspiratory as well as expiratory phonations and revealed duration differences between "hungry, mad pain-produced, and teased crying" in 4-day-old infants. His data also indicate that in pain-produced cries, the cry units (one expiratory phonation) are longer in the beginning of the cry record than at the end.

The preceding studies illustrate that useful (though limited) information can be obtained utilizing time domain instruments. This technique has the advantage of being relatively easy to operate, and it is inexpensive, reliable, and easy to inspect visually. However, there are also many problems with this method of analysis. There is signal distortion due to pen inertia and paper speed variation that results in poor frequency response. Manual measurement of features is open to human error and is a rather tedious process. Finally, the magnitude information shown is, in reality, an average measurement over a short time interval. This interval is fixed in the wiring of the apparatus and is thus inflexible and liable to lose important information.

## 4.3. Frequency Domain Analysis

Devices performing frequency domain analysis allow one to obtain a coarse representation of the frequency spectrum characteristics of a sound. They utilize a bank of band pass filters. These filters only allow input of a specified frequency range, measure the average magnitude in that range, and give a visual display of the relative magnitude. One can then compare the relative magnitude of a series of frequency ranges. The band pass filters are either one-third or one-half of an octave in width.

Ostwald, Freedman, and Kurtz (1962) used the half octave band analyzer to examine the cries from 32 twins. They determined that the variability in pitch measurements and temporal characteristics between the cries of twins could be explained by differences in "weight, size, physical development and vigor of the children recorded." Ostwald *et al.* concluded that it was these "other factors" that determined the characteristics of the cries and that heredity did not play a major role. Later, Ostwald (1963) used half-octave analysis to analyze the cry of a normal neonate and found the fundamental frequency to be between 425 and 600 Hz.

As implied by the name, these devices only give information about the relative magnitude of various frequency ranges. They do not give timing information. In addition, the band pass filters use a relatively large and inflexible band width. This makes the frequency information obtained of limited value. However, as illustrated by the work of Ostwald, some useful informtion is obtainable with this method of sound analysis.

## 4.4. Spectrographic Analysis

The sound spectrograph produces a permanent visual record showing the distribution of energy in both frequency and time. It was originally developed at the Bell Laboratories in the late 1940s. Its main goal was to aid the deaf by presenting a visual display of speech. It did not achieve this goal because of the complexity of the speech signal as well as the limitations of the spectrograph itself. However, since it was presented in 1946, it has been a very useful and important device in many areas of signal processing. These areas include adult speech, animal and bird sounds, music, and infant cries.

Over the past 20 years, most studies of the infant cry have utilized the sound spectrogram. Scandinavian research headed by O. Wasz-Höckert and J. Lind has particularly advanced our understanding of the infant cry. They have defined spectrographically based cry parameters that can be grouped into two general categories: durational features and fundamental frequency features. A short description of these spectrographic features follows.

### 4.4.1. Durational Features

- *Latency period:* The time between the pain stimulus applied to the child and the onset of the cry sound. The onset of crying was defined as the first phonation lasting more than .5 seconds.
- *Duration:* This feature is measured from the onset of the cry to the end of the signal and consists of the total vocalizations occurring during a single expiration or inspiration. The boundaries were determined by the point on the spectrogram where the sound "seems" to end.

- *Second pause:* The time interval between the end of the signal and the following inspiration.

### 4.4.2. Fundamental Frequency Features

- *Maximum pitch:* The highest measurable point of the fundamental frequency seen on the spectrogram.
- *Minimum pitch:* The lowest measurable point in the $F_0$ contour seen on the spectrogram.
- *Pitch of shift:* Frequency after a rapid increase in the $F_0$ seen on the spectrogram.
- *Glottal roll or vocal fry:* Unperiodic phonation of the vocal folds usually occurring at the end of an expiratory phonation when the signal becomes very weak and $F_0$ becomes very low.
- *Vibrato:* Defined to occur when there are at least four rapid up-and-down movements of $F_0$.
- *Melody type:* Either falling, rising/falling, rising, falling/rising, or flat.
- *Continuity:* A measure of whether the cry was entirely voiced, partly voiced, or voiceless.
- *Double harmonic break:* A simultaneous parallel series of harmonics in between the harmonics of the fundamental frequency.
- *Biphonation:* An apparent double series of harmonics of two fundamental frequencies. Unlike double harmonic break, these two series seem to be independent of each other.
- *Gliding:* A very rapid up and/or down movement of $F_0$, usually of short duration.
- *Noise concentration:* High energy peak at 2000–2300 Hz, found both in voiced and voiceless signals; this attribute is clearly audible.
- *Furcation:* Term used to denote a "split" in the $F_0$ where a relatively strong cry signal suddenly breaks into a series of weaker ones, each one of which has its own $F_0$ contour. It is seen mainly in pathological cries.
- *Glottal plosives:* Sudden release of pressure at the vocal folds producing an impulsive expiratory sound.

Many investigators have examined the correlation between abnormal ranges of spectrographically obtained cry features and particular medical problems.

Spectrographic studies were carried out for infants with oropharyngeal anomalies (Lind *et al.*, 1965; Massengill, 1968; Michelsson *et al.*, 1975); asphyxia neonatorum (Michelsson, 1971; Michelsson *et al.*, 1977a;

Wasz-Höckert, Lind, Vuroenkoski, Partanen, & Valanne, 1968); symp-
tomless low birth weight (Michelsson, 1971); herpes encephalitis and
congenital hypothyroidism (Michelsson & Sirvio, 1975, 1976); hyperbilirubinemia (Wasz-Höckert *et al.*, 1971); various forms of brain damage
(Fisichelli & Karelitz, 1963; Karelitz & Fisichelli, 1962; Lind *et al.*, 1965;
Michelsson *et al.*, 1977b; Wasz-Höckert *et al.*, 1968); malnourished infants
(Lester, 1976); genetic defects (Fisichelli, Coxe, Rosenfeld, Haber, Davis,
& Karelitz, 1966; Lind, 1965; Lind *et al.*, 1970; Ostwald, Peltzman, Green-
berg, & Meyer, 1970; Vuorenkoski *et al.*, 1966; Wasz-Höckert *et al.*, 1968);
sudden infant death syndrome (SIDS) (Colton & Steinschneider, 1981;
Stark & Nathanson, 1972); and mixed syndromes (Ostwald, Phipps, &
Fox, 1968; Wasz-Höckert *et al.*, 1968).

The spectrographic parameter ranges for some of the pathologies
studied by the Swedish group are as follows:

- *Brain damage from severe oxygen deficiency after birth, or meningitis
  or hydrocephalus:* The cry becomes more high-pitched and the melody type changes to more rising, falling-rising and flat types. The
  fundamental frequency becomes more unstable, too. Both gliding
  and biphonation occur. The cry duration of the phonation can
  change and the cry becomes either very short or unusually long.
- *Jaundice:* Usually furcation is present.
- *Brain infection from herpes virus:* Noise concentration has been found
  but not with infants with severe oxygen deficiency or brain
  damage.
- *Hypothyroidism:* The $F_0$ is lower than normal, but otherwise the
  spectrogram resembles that seen in the crying of healthy neonates.
- *Non-asphyxiated low birth weight:* No significant differences were
  found.
- *Premature neonate:* There were increases in minimum and maximum pitch, maximum pitch of shift, as well as the occurrences
  of biphonation and glides.
- *Peripheral respiratory distress:* The investigators reported an increase
  in the duration of the cry and the total crying period and an
  increase in the maximum $F_0$ as well as occurrence of biphonation.
- *Central respiratory distress:* There was a change in the duration of
  the cry (increase for full terms, decrease for prematures) and in
  the minimum and maximum pitch as well as the occurrence of
  biphonation and incidence of rising, falling/rising and flat types
  of melody patterns.

Obviously, the spectrogram has been a useful tool for the advance-
ment of our understanding of infant cry analysis. It is relatively inexpensive and is a good way to "visualize" acoustic signals. However, it

has several limitations that hinder its widespread use in medicine. First, there are the physical limitations of the analysis. The spectrogram has a poor dynamic range and often inadequate frequency resolution. In addition, the spectrogram requires visual inspection of the output for interpretation. Extracting acoustical information spectrographically is a long and tedious process that requires much expertise. As a result, it is not possible to analyze a large sample of cries quickly and accurately.

## 4.5. Computer-Based Signal Processing

All of the analysis systems described previously give useful acoustical information. However, as we have noted, they have significant limitations. The most important of these limitations is that the extraction of the acoustical information is a difficult and tedious process. We have developed an automated computer-based system that can extract the relevant acoustical information in a matter of minutes. Computer analysis allows more accurate determination of the acoustical information and also allows extraction of information that would otherwise be unobtainable.

The analysis procedure consists of five major steps: (1) recording of the cry; (2) obtaining the parameters of fundamental frequency, formants and amplitude versus time; (3) sampling the complex $F_0$ contours in order to facilitate the development of $F_0$ features; (4) developing a number of features from the parameters and samples by procedures that include averaging within-cry modes and calculation of probability of being in any mode at any point in the cry; and (5) conglomerating relevant features into a set of "diagnostic tests."

An overview of these steps is given later. The requirements for the tape-recording system include a relatively flat (3 dB 100–5000 Hz) frequency response, a dynamic range of 40 to 45 dB, and a signal to noise ratio of approximately 20 to 25.

The recordings are processed to obtain the parameters of amplitude, fundamental frequency, and formant frequencies. Regions in which the three laryngeal modes (phonation, hyperphonation, and dysphonation) occur are marked as well as the occurrence of glottal stops and inspiratory phonations.

From the amplitude contours, formant tracks, and fundamental frequency contours, features are extracted at appropriate times in order to allow reconstruction of the contour or track with a minimum of lost information. Timing and amplitude data are obtained from each of the first eight cry units and detailed formant frequency, and $F_0$ data are extracted from the first two cries in each sequence. These features specify certain attributes of the $F_0$ contour for phonation and for hyperphonation (e.g., average $F_0$, maximum $F_0$, and final $F_0$), certain attributes of the formant contours, classification of phonation types in each cry, and so forth. In the present analysis system, there are 88 such features.

Basically, the selection of features is guided by our understanding of the relation between acoustic properties of the cry and the physiological and anatomical characteristics of the infant that are likely to influence the cry.

The final analysis stage utilizes the 88 features to determine the outcome of specific cry tests. This stage essentially entails the conglomeration of those features that best represent the specific test of interest. For example, the features included in the test we call *Glottal Instability* (GI) are all measures of whether or not the infant is capable of maintaining an acoustically stable laryngeal configuration. Another example is the test we call *Abnormal Respiratory Effort* (ARE) that measures the ability of the baby to sustain the required respiratory function for the pain-induced cry. Those important features that do not readily lend themselves to conglomeration with other features will stand alone (such as *T01*, which is the duration between the pain stimulus and onset of the cry). Eight cry tests are used at present. They include GI, ARE, and *T01* as described before. In addition, each subject's cry is tested for the occurrence of a rising slope of $F_0$ at the end of a phonation or hyperphonation (RHS), a high $F_0$ during phonation (HPP), crying only in the hyperphonation mode (HONLY), an abnormally short or long cry (SCLC), and for a cry consistent with a constriction in the vocal tract (CVT).

In summary, each cry is analyzed by deriving 88 cry features. One can then assess each feature individually or group features into appropriate tests. Grouping of features into tests is based on the model of cry production.

A computer-based signal-processing system is utilized for all data extraction. This system allows complete analysis of a cry in 5 to 10 minutes and is entirely automatic. The computer is able to control the tape recorder, so that one can merely insert a tape, tell the computer what time to start the analysis, and then return later to examine the results.

## 5. PRELIMINARY STUDIES

Using the principles described previously we carried out a pilot study (Golub & Corwin, 1982) designed to refine our techniques for cry recording and analysis, to obtain data on the properties of normal infants, and to test the ability of the cry model to predict specific pathologies based on analysis of the cry. This study evaluated the cries of 87 infants who were assigned to one of four groups. Group 1 contained 55 apparently healthy term infants. No infant in this group had a history of birth asphyxia, jaundice, respiratory disease, or abnormal physical findings. Group 2 consisted of 17 infants who had either multiple or severe abnormalities. Severe abnormalities included respiratory problems (hyaline membrane disease, transient tachypnea of the newborn and bronchopulmonary dysplasia), apnea, bradycardia and low Apgar scores. The associated abnormalities were prematurity, jaundice, hypoglycemia, and electrolyte disturbances. Group 3 was made up of 12 infants who were normal except for a serum bilirubin concentration of 10 to 20 mg per 100 ml on the second or third day of life. Group 4 was made up of 3 infants. Two of these infants subsequently died of presumed sudden infant death syndrome. The third was a child whose sibling had recurrent apnea.

Cry recordings were made in a private examining room where there was a minimum of background noise. A SONY model TC-104AV portable tape recorder was used, and the microphone was held 15 cm from the infant's mouth. The infants were awake and were positioned supine and flat in an open crib. They were not crying at the time of the cry stimulus. The cry stimulus consisted of a heel stick performed at the time of routine blood studies. Cry analysis was accomplished by utilizing the automated cry analysis system described previously.

Forty-five of 55 normal infants had none of the eight abnormal cry tests; 10 of 55 had one, and no infant had more than one abnormal test. In contrast, among the 17 infants with multiple or severe abnormalities (Group 2), all the infants had at least one abnormal pattern, and 14 of 17 had two or more. We also looked separately at those infants with respiratory diseases. The cry model predicts that these infants will have the cry features indicating an abnormal respiratory effort (ARE). Ten of 12 infants with respiratory problems exhibited ARE, whereas only 4 of 77 subjects without respiratory problems showed this pattern.

Cry analysis of the Group 3 infants showed that 11 of 12 of these infants whose only problem was a moderate elevation in serum bilirubin showed the cry abnormality Glottal Instability (GI). In addition, there were 12 infants in the group with multiple abnormalities (Group 2) who also had moderate elevation in their serum bilirubin concentration (defined for this group as infants who required phototherapy but did not receive an exchange transfusion).

Twenty-two of the 24 jaundiced infants showed abnormal GI, whereas only 8 of 63 without clinical jaundice showed this cry test. These findings were surprising; we do not know if this abnormality is persitent, and we can only speculate as to the etiology of $F_0$ from the GI. However, previous studies utilizing spectrographic methods (Wasz-Höckert *et al.*, 1971) have found similar abnormalities in infants with very high levels of serum bilirubin. It has been suggested that the cry changes may reflect involvement of the central nervous system. Whatever the etiology, it appears that these cry changes may be a marker for some pathologic process in infants with presumably safe levels of serum bilirubin.

The last group (Group 4) included three infants; two subsequently died of presumed SIDS; the third was an infant whose sibling had recurrent apnea. Cry analysis of the Group 4 infants showed that all three infants had cries indicative of a constriction in the vocal tract (CVT). No other abnormality was found in the cry of these infants, and no other infants showed the CVT cry test.

It is of interest that an anatomic or functional constriction in the pharyx has been postulated as a related factor in at least some sudden infant deaths. Stark and Nathanson (1972) analyzed the spontaneous cry of a normal 4-day-old infant who died unexpectedly at 6 months of age. Based on cry analysis, they reached the conclusion that the infant had a constriction of the vocal tract. Felman, Loughlin, Leftridge, and Cassisi (1979) used fluroscopy to study nine infants who exhibited sleep-related upper airway obstruction but who were asymptomatic while awake. They showed a constriction in the hypopharynx of these infants consistent with the cry patterns shown in the Group 4 infants. Unpublished studies from our own laboratory have examined the cry changes caused by a pharyngeal constriction using a computer-produced representation of the anatomy of the vocal tract. This computer simulation had the identical cry characteristics found in Group 4 infants. If there is indeed a group of infants with either a functional or anatomical constriction in the pharynx causing a predisposition for sudden death, then cry analysis may become an important screening test for identifying these infants.

The preceding results indicate great promise for cry analysis to become a useful medical tool. Two findings, in particular, suggest areas for further investigation. First, as stated before, our finding of CVT only in the subjects in Group 4 suggests that studies should be performed correlating cry abnormalities with eventual risk for sudden death. The second important finding was that GI was found with increased frequency in infants with safe levels of serum bilirubin. Bilirubin is a well-recognized central nervous system toxin. Previous studies have suggested that relatively low levels of serum bilirubin might result in subtle central nervous system damage (Boggs, Hardy, & Frazier, 1967). We suggest that studies correlating serum bilirubin with serial cry recordings and long-term developmental follow-up be done to determine if cry analysis would be useful for the identification of at-risk infants.

## 6. CONCLUSIONS

The long-range goal of our work is to demonstrate the value of cry analysis for determining the medical status of an infant. In this chapter, we have described a model of cry production that enables us to correlate medical abnormalities with acoustical measurements. This cry model may allow us to identify disease processes reliably that effect the cry production system in a consistent manner. These disorders include respiratory problems, structural defects of the vocal cords or vocal tract, muscular abnormalities, and abnormalities of the peripheral and central nervous systems. Specifically, previous work has suggested that the results of cry analysis may be abnormal in infants with various forms of brain damage (Karelitz & Fisichelli, 1962; Lind et al. 1965); chromosomal abnormalities (Michelsson, Tuppurainen, & Aula, 1980); respiratory problems (Golub & Corwin, 1982); increased risk for the sudden infant death syndrome (Colton & Steinschneider, 1981; Golub & Corwin, 1982; Stark & Nathanson, 1972); and infants at risk for postnatal problems secondary to prenatal and perinatal complications such as prematurity, low birth weight, and undernutrition (Zeskind & Lester, 1978). The fact that abnormal cries have been documented in many apparently healthy but at-risk infants has led Lester and Zeskind (1978) to argue that, on the one hand, the severity of clinical signs of brain damage make cry analysis superfluous and, on the other, that in the absence of other clinical signs one could not reliably distinguish a brain-damaged infant from a healthy baby with prenatal and perinatal complications. We agree that isolated cry abnormalities may represent transient nonspecific indicators of stress. However, further studies are still required to determine if a group of infants can be identified in whom there is no obvious clinical evidence of brain damage but whose cry analysis will accurately place them at increased risk for poor developmental outcome. In addition, if an infant does have obvious clinical evidence of brain damage, it is possible that cry analysis may be useful for making a prediction concerning prognosis. Only after prospective studies are performed that include serial cry analysis and long-term developmental follow-up will we be able to determine the true value of cry analysis for the assessment of potential developmental disabilities.

Cry analysis, if proven to be reliable, is particularly well suited to its proposed role as a newborn screening test. It is noninvasive, and, by utilizing the automated analysis system, it can be efficiently and economically performed on large numbers of infants without significantly disrupting normal hospital procedures. We are now beginning the prospective long-term follow-up studies necessary to evaluate the efficiency and accuracy of cry analysis as a newborn screening test. These studies will examine the cry abnormalities found in a wide range of medical problems, but in particular, those found in infants with increased risk for either developmental disabilities or sudden death. We are hopeful that one day, in addition to the screening blood tests currently in use, all newborn babies will routinely be screened via cry analysis for a variety of medical problems.

## 7.  REFERENCES

Boggs, T., Hardy, J., & Frazier, T. Correlation of neonatal serum total bilirubin concentration and developmental status at age 8 months. *Journal of Pediatrics*, 1973, *54*, 319.

Colton, R. H., & Steinschneider, A. The cry characteristics of an infant who died of the Sudden Infant Death syndrome. *Journal of Speech and Hearing Disorders*, 1981, *46*, 359–363.

Darwin, C. *The expression of emotion in man and animals.* New York: Philosophical Library, 1855.

Fairbanks, G. An acoustical study of the pitch of infant hunger wails. *Child Development*, 1942, *13*, 227.

Fant, G. *Acoustic theory of speech production.* The Hague: Mouton, 1960.

Felman, A. H., Loughlin, G. M., Leftridge, C. A., & Cassisi, N. J. Upper airway obstruction during sleep in children. *American Journal of Radiology*, 1979, *133*, 213–216.

Fisichelli, V. R., & Karelitz, S. The cry latencies of normal infants and those with brain damage. *Journal of Pediatrics*, 1963, *62*, 724.

Fisichelli, V. R., Karelitz, S., Eichbauer, J., & Rosenfeld, L. S. Volume-unit-graphs: Their production and applicability in studies of infant cries. *Journal of Psychology*, 1961, *52*, 423.

Fisichelli, V. R., Coxe, M., Rosenfeld, R., Haber, A., Davis, J., & Karelitz, S. The phonetic content of the cries of normal infants and those with brain damage. *Journal of Psychology*, 1966, *64*, 119.

Flanagan, J. L. *Speech analysis synthesis and perception* (2nd ed.): New York: Springer-Verlag, 1972.

Flatau, T. S., & Gutzmann, H. Die Stimme des Säuglings. *Archiv für Laryngologie und Rhinologie*, 1906, *18*, 139.

Formby, D. Maternal recognition of infant's cry. *Developmental Medicine and Child Neurology*, 1967, *9*, 293.

Goldstein, U. Modeling children's vocal tracts. In J. J. Wolf & D. H. Klatt (Eds.), *Speech Communication Papers Presented at the 97th Meeting of the Acoustical Society of America.* Cambridge, Mass.: Acoustical Society of America, 1979.

Golub, H. L. A physioacoustic model of the infant cry and its use for medical diagnosis and prognosis. In J. J. Wolf & D. H. Klatt (Eds.), *Speech Communication Papers Presented at the 97th Meeting of the Acoustical Society of America*. Cambridge, Mass.: Acoustical Society of America, 1979.

Golub, H. L. *A physioacoustic model of infant cry production*. Unpublished doctoral dissertation, Massachusetts Institute of Technology, Cambridge, Mass., 1980.

Golub, H. L., & Corwin, M. J. Infant cry a clue to diagnosis. *Pediatrics*, 1982, *69*, 197.

Karelitz, S., & Fisichelli, V. R. The cry thresholds of normal infants and those with brain damage. *Journal of Pediatrics*, 1962, *61*, 679.

Lester, B. M. Spectrum analysis of the cry sounds of well nourished and malnourished infants. *Child Development*, 1976, *47*, 237–241.

Lester, B. M., & Zeskind, P. Brazelton scale and physical size correlates of neonatal cry features. *Infant Behaviour and Development*, 1978, *1*, 393–402.

Lind, J. (Ed.). Newborn infant cry. *Acta Paediatria Scandinavica*, 1965, *163*. (Suppl.)

Lind, J., Wasz-Höckert, O., Vuorenkoski, V., & Valanne, E. The vocalization of a newborn brain-damaged child. *Annales Paediatriae Fenniae*, 1965, *11*, 32.

Lind, J. Vuorenkoski, V., Rosberg, G., Partanen, T., & Wasz-Höckert, O. Spectrographic analysis of vocal response to pain stimuli in infants with Down's syndrome. *Developmental Medicine and Child Neurology*, 1970, *12*, 478–486.

Massengill, R. M. Cry characteristic in cleft-palate newborns. *Journal of the Acoustical Society of America*, 1968, *45*, 782.

Michelsson, K. Cry analyses of symptomless low birth weight neonates and of asphyxiated newborn infants. *Acta Paediatrica Scandinavica*, 1971, *19*, 309–315.

Michelsson, K., & Sirvio, P. Cry analysis in herpes encephalitis. In *Proceedings of the 5th Scandinavian Congress in Perinatal Medicine, 1975*. Stockholm: Almquist & Wilksell, 1975.

Michelsson, K., & Sirvio, P. Cry analysis in congenital hypothyroidism. *Folia Phoniatrica*, 1976, *28*, 40–47.

Michelsson, K., Sirvio, P., Koivisto, M., Sovijarvi, A., & Wasz-Höckert, O. Spectrographic analysis of pain cry in neonates with cleft palate. *Biology of the Neonate*, 1975, *26*, 353–358.

Michelsson, K., Sirvio, P. & Wasz-Höckert, O., Pain cry in full term asphyxiated newborn infants correlated with late findings. *Acta Paediatrica Scandinavica*, 1977, *66*, 611. (a)

Michelsson, K., Sirvio, P., & Wasz-Höckert, O. Sound spectrographic cry analysis of infants with bacterial meningitis. *Developmental Medicine and Child Neurology*, 1977, *19*, 309–315. (b)

Michelsson, K., Tuppurainen, N., & Auld P. Cry analysis of infants with karyotype abnormality. *Neuropediatrics*, 1980, *11*, 365–376.

Ostwald, P. F. *Soundmaking—The acoustic communication of emotion*. Springfield, Ill.: Charles C. Thomas, 1963.

Ostwald, P. F., Feedman, D. G., Kurtz, J. H. Vocalizations on infant twins. *Folia Phoniatrica*, 1962, *14*, 37.

Ostwald, P. F., Phipps, R., & Fox, S. Diagnostic use of infant cry? *Biology of the Neonate*, 1968, *13*, 68–82.

Ostwald, P. F., Peltzman, P., Greenberg, M., & Meyer, J. Cries of a trisomy 13-15 infant. *Developmental Medicine and Child Neurology*, 1970, *12*, 472.

Partanen, T. J., Wasz-Höckert, O., Vuorenkoski, V., Theorell, K., Valanne, E., & Lind, J. Auditory identification of pain cry signals of young infants in pathological conditions and in sound spectrographic basis. *Annales Pediatriae Fenniae*, 1967, *13*, 56–63.

Rothenberg, M. Glottal noise during speech. *Speech Transmission Laboratory Quarterly Progess and Status Report,* 1974, pp. 2–3.

Stark, R. E., & Nathanson, S. N. Unusual features of cry in an infant dying suddenly and unexpectedly. In J. F. Bosma & J. Showacre (Eds.), *Development of upper respiratory anatomy and function: Implication for SIDS.* Washington, D.C.: U.S. Department of Health, Education and Welfare, 1972.

Stevens, K. N. Acoustical aspects of speech production. In W. O. Fenn & H. Rahn (Eds.), *Handbook of physiology: A critical comprehensive presentation of physiological knowledge and concepts. Section 3: Respiration.* (Vol. 1). Washington, D.C.: American Physiological Society, 1964.

Truby, H. M., & Lind, J. Cry sounds of the newborn infant. In J. Lind (Ed.), *Newborn infant cry. Acta Paediatrica Scandinavica,* 1965, *163.* (Suppl.)

Valanne, E. H., Vuorenkoski, V., Partanen, T. J., Lind, J., Wasz-Höckert, O. The ability of human mothers to identify the hunger cry signals of their newborn infants during the lying-in period. *Experientia,* 1967, *23,* 1.

Van den Berg, J. Sound production in isolated human larynxes. *Annals of the New York Academy of Sciences: Sound Production in Man* 1965, *155,* 18–27.

Vuorenkoski, V., Lind, J., Partanen, T. J., Lejeune, J., Lafourcade, J., & Wasz-Höckert, O. Spectrographic analysis of cries from children with maladie du cri-du-chat. *Annales Paediatriae Fenniae,* 1966, *12,* 174.

Wasz-Höckert, O., Partanen, T., Vuorenkoski, V., & Valanne, E. The identification of some specific meanings in the newborn and infant vocalization. *Experientia,* 1964, *20,* 154.

Wasz-Höckert, O., Lind, J., Vuorenkoski, V., Partanen, T., & Valanne, E. *The infant cry: A spectrographic and auditory analysis.* London: Heinemann, 1968.

Wasz-Höckert, O., Koivisto, M., Vuorenkoski, V., Partanen, T., & Lind, J. Spectrographic analysis of pain cry in hyperbilirubinemia. *Biology of the Neonate,* 1971, *17,* 260–271.

Wolff, P. H. The role of biological rhythms in early psychological development. *Bulletin of the Menninger Clinic,* 1967, *31,* 197.

Wolff, P. H. The natural history of crying and other vocalizations in early infancy. In B. M. Foss (Ed.), *Determinants of infant behavior* (Vol. 4). London: Methuen, 1969.

Zeskind, P. S., & Lester, B. M. Acoustic features and auditory perception of the cries of newborns with prenatal and perinatal complications. *Child Development,* 1978, *49,* 580–589.

# 4

# Twenty-Five Years of Scandinavian Cry Research

OLE WASZ-HÖCKERT, KATARINA MICHELSSON,
and JOHN LIND

## 1. SCANDINAVIAN CRY RESEARCH

### 1.1. Cry Studies in Scandinavia

The study of crying can be dealt with from many different perspectives: anatomical, physiological, psychological, phonetic, and pediatric. During the last two decades, the cry has also been an important factor in studies of mother–child interaction.

The first studies on infant cries were from the end of the last century. They were mainly based on auditory identification of the cry and its characteristics. Progress in cry research was maintained by the development of equipment for permanent recording of sound, from the graphophone and the gramophone almost a hundred years ago, to the development of tape recorders in the 1920s and the sound spectrograph

OLE WASZ-HÖCKERT, KATARINA MICHELSSON, and the late JOHN LIND • II Department of Pediatrics, Children's Hospital, University of Helsinki, SF-00290 Helsinki 29, Finland. Financial support has been received from the Sigrid Juselius Foundation, the Finnish Medical Academy, and Finska Lakaresallskapet, Finland, and the National Institutes of Health of the United States.

in the 1940s. Now in the 1980s, computer analysis of various cry characteristics might become the most profitable mode to develop cry research for different disciplines.

As many other pediatricians before, one of the authors (Wasz-Höckert) had also been interested in the cry of newborns. Cries were demonstrated at the International Pediatric Congress in Montreal, 1959, by Karelitz from a tape with normal and Down's syndrome babies. By systematically employing the sound spectrographic method, cry research became an objective science in Finland in 1960. Through the research methods used in biology, Wasz-Höckert became familiar with the sonograph used at the Institute of Phonetics at the University of Helsinki. The first preliminary report by the original members of the cry research group was published in 1962 (Wasz-Höckert, Vuorenkoski, Valanne, & Michelsson). Another of the first reports (Wasz-Höckert, Valanne, Vuorenkoski, Michelsson, & Sovijarvi, 1963) dealt with four types of infant vocalization: the first birth cry, the hunger cry, the pain cry, and the pleasure cry. We found that these cry types could be distinguished from each other both auditorily and by means of sound spectrography (Wasz-Höckert, Partanen, Vuorenkoski, Valanne, & Michelsson, 1964a).

Another research group was founded in Stockholm to study the relationship between physiology and infant crying. The results were reported in the monograph *Newborn Infant Cry*, edited by Lind (1965).

In 1963, the research group headed by Wasz-Höckert joined the Lind group, and several cooperative research projects were reported. During the years of cry cooperation between Helsinki and Stockholm, the cry samples were mainly collected in Helsinki by Michelsson. The spectrograms were, however, made by Vuorenkoski in Stockholm at the Royal Technical Institute.

When we started with sound spectrographic cry analysis, no nomenclature existed of how and what to measure from the infant cries. In this respect, almost all the definitions and the nomenclature of the cry attributes had to be developed by the research group.

For several years, Scandinavian cry research was performed in three cities: Helsinki, Oulu, and Stockholm. Since 1972, the cry research laboratory in Helsinki has been the most active, enjoying the cooperation of visiting active scientists, such as Raes from Belgium, Makoi from Hungary, Fridman from Argentina, and Schukova and Syutkina from the USSR.

For the last 10 years we have mainly been interested in sound spectrographic cry analysis of infants with various diseases in the newborn period. Cry analysis can be an additional tool in the clinical diagnosis  .

of newborn infants. We have, therefore, analyzed cries of children with diseases that affect the central nervous system in order to evaluate in which respect these cries differ from the crying of healthy infants. Systematic analysis of the cries in various diseases in the newborn period have been performed. The first cry analyses were made on infants with chromosomal abnormalities (Vuorenkoski, Lind, Partanen, Lejeune, Lafourcade, & Wasz-Höckert, 1966). Also, infants with metabolic diseases such as hyperbilirubinemia and hypoglycemia have been analyzed (Koivisto, Michelsson, Sirvio, & Wasz-Höckert, 1974; Wasz-Höckert, Koivisto, Vuorenkoski, & Lind, 1971). Additionally, we have samples of cries of infants with diseases affecting the central nervous system, such as asphyxia (Michelsson, 1971; Michelsson, Sirvio, & Wasz-Höckert, 1977a) and meningitis (Michelsson, Sirvio, & Wasz-Höckert, 1977b). We have also studied cries of infants with disorders of the larynx and oral tract, such as cleft palate (Michelsson, Sirvio, Koivisto, Sovijarvi, & Wasz-Höckert, 1975), laryngitis and laryngeal malformation (Raes, Michelsson, & Despontin, 1980). It has been proved that the cry in laryngeal disorders differs significantly from cries obtained from infants with cerebral diseases (Raes, Michelsson, Dehaen, & Despontin, 1982). Additionally, we have noted that certain cry attributes, which are seldom seen in cries of healthy infants, occur more often in cries of infants with diseases involving the central nervous system (Michelsson *et al.*, 1977a, b).

## 1.2. Auditory Identification of Cry Types

Wasz-Höckert *et al.* (1964a) showed that the four basic cry types—birth, hunger, pain, and pleasure—could be identified auditorily. We investigated this with a tape with 24 selected short cry samples. It was found that the cries were recognized best by adults who had had previous experience with infant cries, such as nurses on pediatric wards and midwives. It was also found that training increased the ability to recognize different kinds of cries (Wasz-Höckert, Partanen, Vuorenkoski, Valanne, & Michelsson, 1964b). Valanne, Vuorenkoski, Partanen, Lind, and Wasz-Höckert (1967) found that mothers could recognize the cry of their own infant after they had listened to the cry of their own baby only once.

Partanen, Wasz-Höckert, Vuorenkoski, Theorell, Valanne, and Lind (1967) found that cries of sick infants could be distinguished auditorily from cries of healthy infants. The tape used in this research included cries of infants with asphyxia, brain damage, hyperbilirubinemia, and Down's syndrome. Training improved the ability to recognize the cries.

## 1.3. The Cry Analyzer

One of the results of the Finnish–Swedish cry research cooperation was the Cry Analyzer, which was manufactured by Special Instruments, Sweden, and constructed by a team consisting of Vuorenkoski, Kaunisto, Tjernlund, and Vesa (1971). It was originally intended for everyday use in clinical neonatal wards. The approach was to develop a screening device to collect cry samples from all babies on a newborn ward. A more detailed sound spectrographic analysis would be then done on cries of infants that differed from the normal.

The Cry Analyzer measures the number of cries with a pitch above and below 1000 Hz. The duration of the cry signals is also noted. Additionally, the frequency of heart and respiration rates can be measured. Objective evaluation of the analyser has indicated that the use in clinical practice is limited. Cries with a pitch over 1000 Hz with a duration of at least .4 sec in order to be registered are infrequent even in cries of sick infants.

## 1.4. Physiological Cry Studies

Investigations of the initiation of breathing in the newborn infant and also the cry motions and cry sounds were carried out at the Wenner-Gren Research Laboratory, Stockholm, by Truby, Bosma, and Lind in 1959–1965.

Normal newborn infants, 0 to 12 days old (gestational age 34 to 43 weeks), were, after pain stimulation (pinch), studied by the combined methods of cineradiography of the upper airways and sound spectrography and spirography or esophageal pressure recordings (Truby & Lind, 1965). The cry act that comprises intricate motor activity involving the upper respiratory tract was analyzed and correlated with the simultaneously registered cry sounds—the acoustic manifestations of the complex motor performances. The cry sound recording and analysis was considered useful in the clinical examination of the neonate. Permanent acoustic recording of the cry sound, which is similar to heart sound, could conceivably become a standard feature of the clinical record.

The cineradiographic studies of the cry motions (Bosma, Truby, & Lind, 1965) demonstrated that the cry actions of the pharynx and the oral cavity are relatively slow and incompletely integrated with the laryngeal action. Further, the integration is less complete in less mature infants. With increasing development, the whole organization of functioning is progressively integrated so that the discrepancies in coordination of respiratory motions of the larynx, pharynx, and thorax in infants are no longer discernible.

The study of the relation of cry sound to respiration (Bosma *et al.*, 1965) demonstrated a consistently similar pattern of respiratory volume displacement associated with the separate cry cycles in spite of the variations in intrathoracic pressure. This precise coordination between body wall compression and laryngeal valving is another of the remarkable motor achievements identified with cry.

## 1.5. Cry and Mother–Child Interaction

Improved standards of health among today's mothers have changed the nature of the service provided in maternity hospitals. Increased time has been devoted to psychological aspects of the care of "the newborn family." These developments have made possible a more individual care of the newborn. One precondition to carry out this individualized care is that one understands what the baby is trying to say when he or she cries. Parents are those who will best understand the needs of the neonate. Therefore, the introduction of "rooming in" right from birth meant a great improvement because in rooming-in wards babies cried less than half as often as babies in wards with no rooming-in facilities (Mooney & Lind, 1969).

The promotion of breast feeding has been important. Many investigations have demonstrated the medical and psychological benefits of breast feeding. The effect of infant cries on the breasts of the mother has been studied using thermography (Vuorenkoski, Wasz-Höckert, Koivisto, & Lind, 1969). It was found that cries rapidly increased the skin temperature over the breasts and that maximal skin temperature was reached within 3 to 5 minutes prior to feeding. The cries prepare the breasts, in a sense, for feeding.

## 1.6. Baby Carriers Increase the Contact between Parents and Children

In the fragile transition period after birth, it is important that every effort be made to make everything run as smoothly as possible. The baby must get used to a whole new way of life and to his or her parents. The parents must get used to the baby, learn to be parents, and become familiar with each other in this new role as parents. As a kind of extension of the intimate relationship during pregnancy, parents in many non-Western cultures carry their babies. In these cultures, the infants cry much less than in the Western world, where the crying of the young infant is one of the most serious problems of the new family. In one study, a group of parents were given a baby carrier at the maternity hospital and instructed on how to use it. Seventy-four of 83 mothers thought that the baby carrier promoted good contact with the baby when interviewed 3 months after delivery, and 69 out of 79 reported that the baby stopped crying when placed in the baby carrier (Brzokoupil, Fohrer, Lind, & Stensland-Junker, 1973).

## 1.7. Singing—An Aid to Parental Attachment

Infant crying initiates the search for causes. If the newborn is fed, properly dressed, and comfortably placed in his or her bed, why might he or she still cry? The child is born into a new strange world. One of the greatest changes for him/her after birth must be the loss of the rhythms of maternal heart sounds, breathing, voice and movements, which characterized life so completely within the uterus.

The mother's heart sounds become the unborn child's constant companion during the fetal period and constitute an important part of the fetal environment. Thus, it seems natural to imitate sounds, which are suggestive of heart sounds and which can be recognized by the child after birth. These sounds have a calming effect, creating a sense of security and comfort (Murooka, Machida, Sasaki, Iwasa, & Matumoto, 1978; Salk, 1973). Earlier generations in the Western world recognized the significance of rhythms, and infants were put in cradles, rocked, and songs were sung for them in order to calm and please them.

Music and rhythm bring joy to the listener and help develop feelings of communion. The musical interplay between parent and child increases their sense of belonging to each other. The experiences that we share when we sing, play instruments, or listen to each other become cornerstones of a stable foundation on which to build the family future. At Karolinska Hospital in Stockholm, it has been demonstrated that singing of lullabies for the unborn baby is a part of preparation for parenthood (Lind, 1980).

## 2. SOUND SPECTROGRAPHY

### 2.1. The Cry Characteristics

The nomenclature used for different cry characteristics in sound spectrographic cry analysis of newborn and small infants will now be explained. More clear and detailed information of the various cry characteristics is available in monographs by Wasz-Höckert, Lind, Vuorenkoski, Partanen, and Valanne (1968) and Michelsson (1971). Sirvio and

Michelsson (1976) and Michelsson (1980) have made detailed reviews of the various cry parameters measured. When studying the existing international literature on cry analysis, it is obvious that the terms used for the definitions of specific cry characteristics should be uniform before the results from different research centers can be precisely compared. Standardized methods for international use are urgently needed.

The following cry characteristics on the basis of sound spectrography, using the narrow band filter, have been measured by our research group. Some of these cry characteristics can probably be omitted in the future as less important when comparing cries of healthy and sick infants. When starting with cry analysis, there was no nomenclature available for sound spectrograpic cry studies; therefore many of the definitions of the cry characteristics were developed in the 1960s.

Some differences exist in the phonations in a cry sequence after the pain stimulus. Therefore, we have mainly used only the first phonation after the pain stimulus when comparing cries of healthy and sick infants. Lately, we have also evaluated the cry characteristics in the second and third phonation after the stimulus (Thoden & Koivisto, 1980).

### 2.1.1. Latency

The latency period, that is, the time between the pain stimulus and the onset of crying, has been measured in several studies. The cry has mainly been elicited by a pinch of the infant's arm or a snap on the ear.

The latency time is dependent not only on the infant's disease but also on the time since the last feeding as well as the wakefulness of the child at the time of the cry recording. Differences might also occur if the child at the time of the pain stimulus is deeply asleep or awake. The mean latency in cries of healthy infants was 1.2 sec in the study by Thodén and Koivisto (1980).

Fisichelli and Karelitz (1966) used a rubber band apparatus for eliciting the cry. They found a mean latency of 2.6 sec for children with brain damage and 1.6 sec for a normal group. In a study by Lester (1976) and Lester and Zeskind (1978) the latency was 1.4 to 1.6 sec.

### 2.1.2. Duration of the Cries

The duration of the cry signal after the pain stimulus is the time from the onset of crying to the end of the last phonation before inspiration, independently of whether the signal is continuous or consists of several short phonations. In the measurement of the duration of the second and third signals, all crying occurring between two inspirations was included. In interrupted signals, the duration of the total vocalization and the time of pauses between the signals has not yet been studied by us or by other research groups.

The mean duration of pain cries in our studies of healthy infants has varied between 2.6 sec (Wasz-Höckert *et al.*, 1968) and 5.2 sec (Thodén & Koivisto, 1980). In the first studies, however, very short phonations before or after the main signal were excluded. This made the duration shorter. The duration of the phonations has been shorter in cries of sick infants, for instance, a mean of 1.7 sec in infants with meningitis (Michelsson *et al.*, 1977b).

In cry analysis of the duration by different authors, variations have been noted between 1.0 to 6.5 sec (Gleiss & Hohn, 1968; Lester, 1976; Lester & Zeskind, 1978; Prescott, 1975; Ringel & Kluppel, 1964). Variations in the definitions of the cry sequence that have been measured do exist.

### 2.1.3. Fundamental Frequency

From the fundamental frequency, we have measured the maximum and the minimum pitchs. The maximum pitch is the highest voiced point of the fundamental frequency ($F_0$), and the minimum pitch is the lowest voiced point. However, if rapid changes in the fundamental frequency (shifts) have occurred, they have been measured separately. In recent studies we have made measurements of the maximum of the fundamental frequency both excluding and including shifts.

The mean maximum pitch of the fundamental frequency has, in our studies, varied between 570 to 680 Hz and the mean minimum pitch between 330 to 420 Hz (Michelsson, 1971; Thodén & Koivisto, 1980; Wasz-Höckert *et al.*, 1968). Ostwald, Phibbs, and Fox (1968) reported a mean maximum pitch of 540 Hz. Other investigations have usually reported a mean value for pitch based on the mean frequency of the whole cry. These values have varied between 308 to 606 Hz (Flatau & Gutzmann, 1906; Kittel & Hecht, 1977; Lester, 1976).

The fundamental frequency has been higher in cries of infants with diseases involving the central nervous system (Michelsson *et al.*, 1977a, b; Michelsson, Raes, Thodén, & Wasz-Höckert, 1982).

### 2.1.4. Shift

Shifts occur in almost every third pain cry of healthy infants, mostly at the beginning of the signals. Shifts can also occur at the end of the phonations or in the middle when a kind of double shift is seen. The shift is usually more high pitched than the fundamental; a maximum pitch of 1000 to 2000 Hz of the shift is common. High-pitched shifts occur in pain cries of infants with central nervous system disturbances.

### 2.1.5.  The Melody Type

The melody type of the fundamental frequency has been classified as falling, rising/falling, rising, falling/rising, and flat. No melody type is detectable when the pitch is very unstable or voiceless. In cries of healthy newborn infants, both full-term and premature, the main melody type is falling or rising/falling. Especially rising and falling/rising types of melodies have been considered as pathological and are usually seen in cries of infants with central nervous system disorders (Michelsson *et al.*, 1977a, b; Michelsson, Raes, Thodén, & Wasz-Höckert, 1982). Flat signals are frequent in cries of infants with chromosomal abnormalities (Michelsson, Tuppurainen, & Aula, 1980).

Studies on the melody type are rare. Stark, Rose, and McLagen (1975) have reported on three types of pitch contour—flat, rise, and fall or a combination of these. Out of a total of 95 cries, they found a rising pitch in 11 signals and a falling pitch in 12 signals.

### 2.1.6.  Glottal Roll and Vibrato

The glottal roll, or vocal fry, is a sound with a very low-pitched fundamental frequency. Glottal roll seems to be relatively common at the end of the phonations in cries of healthy infants; it was noted in 18% to 73% of cries (Michelsson, 1971; Stark *et al.*, 1975; Thodén & Koivisto, 1980; Wasz-Höckert *et al.*, 1968). Sometimes the glottal roll is preceded by a vibrato, which also can occur alone. The glottal roll is less common in sick infants who often have shorter cry signals that end abruptly (Michelsson *et al.*, 1977b; Michelsson, Raes, Thodén, & Wasz-Höckert, 1982).

### 2.1.7.  Double Harmonic Break and Biphonation

The double harmonic break occurs on the sound spectrogram as parallel lines between the fundamental and its harmonics. The feature is not specific for any disease, and it occurs in 40 to 62% of pain cries of healthy infants (Wasz-Höckert *et al.*, 1968). On the contrary, biphonation is an important diagnostic feature when comparing cries of healthy and sick infants. This feature, which on the spectrogram is displayed as a double series of fundamental frequencies, does usually not occur in cries of healthy infants (Michelsson, 1971; Thodén & Koivisto, 1980). This feature has been present, especially in cries of infants with diseases that affect the central nervous system (Michelsson, 1971; Michelsson *et al.*, 1977a, b; Michelsson, Raes, Thodén, & Wasz-Höckert, 1982).

### 2.1.8. Glide

Glide is a very rapid change of the fundamental frequency of 600 Hz or more during a time of .1 sec. Glide has mainly been seen in crying of sick infants, and it also occurs in cries of symptomless prematures (Michelsson, 1971; Michelsson *et al.*, 1977a, b, Michelsson, Raes, Thodén, & Wasz-Höckert, 1982).

### 2.1.9. Other Cry Characteristics

In our cry studies we have determined if the signals are continuous or interrupted and if the cries are voiced, half voiced, or voiceless. Tonal pitch has, in some studies, been used to denote a rapid up-and-down movement of the fundamental frequency. Glottal plosives have been used to describe very short coughlike sounds. Furcation describes a split of the fundamental frequency into a series of fundamentals. This feature has been observed mainly in cries of infants with hyperbilirubinemia (Wasz-Höckert *et al.*, 1971). Noise concentration was introduced to denote a high energy peak at 2000 to 2500 Hz found in both voiced and voiceless parts of the signals. This feature has been observed especially in cries of infants with herpes virus encephalitis (Pettay, Donner, Michelsson, & Sirvio, 1977).

## 3. CRY IN NEWBORN INFANTS

### 3.1. Cry in Healthy Full-Term Infants

Analysis of pain cries from more than 300 healthy newborn infants has been analyzed by our research group (Michelsson, 1971; Wasz-Höckert *et al.*, 1963, 1964a, 1968). A recent study on normal infant crying by Thodén and Koivisto (1980) deals with a prospective analysis of cries of 38 infants from birth to 6 months of age and analyzes the first, second, and third phonation after the pain stimulus.

In all our cry studies on the pain cry of healthy full-term newborn infants, the mean maximum pitch of the fundamental frequency without shift has been about 650 Hz and the mean minimum pitch about 400 Hz. In 80% of the samples, the pain cry had a falling or rising/falling melody type with a stable pitch and a duration of approximately 2.5 sec. Shifts with a higher pitch occurred roughly in every third cry. The mean maximum pitch of shift was about 1200 Hz. The mean maximum pitch of the whole cry signal was about 800 Hz when the maximum pitch had been measured from the highest part of either the main fundamental frequency or the shift. The signals were voiced and continuous in about two-thirds of the cries. The occurrence of glottal roll was quite common, mainly at the end of the phonations. Vibrato occasionally preceded the glottal roll part. Biphonation, glide, furcation, and noise concentration were extremely rare in normal infant crying (Michelsson, 1971; Thodén & Koivisto, 1980; Wasz-Höckert et al., 1968).

When comparing cries of healthy and sick infants we have mainly used the pain cry and in most of the studies the first cry signal after the pain stimulus. In order to investigate possible differences and standardize the cry characteristics of the second and the third cry signal in pain-induced cries, Thodén and Koivisto (1980) did a study on cries of 38 children. They found that the three first cry signals after the pinch did not differ much from each other. There was no significant difference in the maximum and minimum pitchs of the fundamental frequency in the three signals analyzed. Shifts were, however, seen more often in the first cry signal, even if the difference was not statistically significant. Because of the more frequent occurrence of shifts, the maximum pitch, including shift, was somewhat higher in the first cry signal. The second and third signals were significantly shorter and more often continuous than was the first signal. Glottal roll and vibrato were more common in the first signal.

Hunger, birth, and pleasure cries were analyzed by Wasz-Höckert et al. (1968). In 148 hunger cries, the mean maximum pitch was 550 Hz and mean minimum pitch 390 Hz. Shifts occurred in only 2% of the cries. The melody type was falling or rising/falling in 80%. Glottal roll occurred in 24%.

In 77 first birth cries, the mean maximum pitch was 550 Hz and mean minimum pitch 450 Hz. Shifts occurred in 18%. The cries were of short duration, mean 1.1 sec.

Pleasure cries had a mean maximum pitch of 650 Hz and mean minimum pitch of 360 Hz; shifts were seen in 19%; glottal roll in 26%. Flat signals were more common, occurring 46% of the time.

Thodén and Koivisto (1980) made a prospective study of cries of infants at 1 and 5 days of age and at 3 and 6 months. The only significant differences in the first cry signals at the age of 1 day, 5 days, 3 months, and 6 months were that the signals were less often continuous at the age of 3 months and that vibrato was less common at the age of 6 months.

The results indicate that there are few changes in the cry characteristics from 1 day of life up to the age of 6 months. The results showed, however, that there were differences in the cry characteristics, depending on whether or not we had analyzed the first, the second, or the third signal after the pain stimulus. The first signal was longer, more often interrupted, and ended more often in glottal roll than the second and the third signals. The maximum pitch of shift and the maximum pitch of the cry signal, including shift, were more high pitched in the first cry signal when compared to the third one at the ages of 1 and 5 days. According to these differences, the number of cries in a cry sequence should be stated in cry analysis. In the second and the third cry signals, there were no significant differences in these cry characteristics.

Studies by other authors concerning cries of healthy infants have mainly dealt with the duration and pitch of the cries and are in agreement with our studies (Kittel & Hecht, 1977; Lester & Zeskind, 1978; Murry, Amundson, & Hollien, 1977; Ostwald et al., 1968; Prescott, 1975; Ringel & Kluppel, 1964).

## 3.2. Cry in Low-Birth-Weight Infants

The first cry study of low-birth-weight infants was by Michelsson (1971). The results showed that the cry of full-term infants who were small for gestational age did not differ considerably from the crying of full-term infants with normal birth weights. The cry results of the truly premature infants showed that the more premature the infant, the higher the fundamental frequency. The mean maximum pitch of the cry of prematures born at 35 to 37 weeks gestational age was 1010 Hz and of those born at 34 weeks or earlier, 1360 Hz. The mean minimum pitch was 480 Hz for the 35–37 gestational week group and 570 Hz. for the smaller prematures. Relatively large variations occurred in the fundamental frequencies in cries of very small prematures. These variations may be due to immaturity alone. However, pre- or perinatal complications might have changed the cry characteristics. In 1963–1967, when the cries were collected, attention was not paid to all complications affecting premature infants.

Cry analysis on prematures has been done by Thodén, Järvenpää, and Michelsson (1982) and Michelsson, Raes, Thodén, & Wasz-Höckert (1982). These results also showed that the more premature the infant was, the more the cry differed from the crying of healthy full-term infants. The cries were shorter and more high pitched.

The dominating melody type in cries of symptomless premature infants was falling or rising/falling, similar to that seen in the full-term controls. Both biphonation and glide occurred in cries of the prematures in 5% to 14% in the study by Michelsson (1971).

## 4. CRY IN VARIOUS DISEASES

### 4.1. Cry in Clinical Diagnostics

In order to evaluate how the cry changes in various diseases in newborn and small infants, systematic studies have been done to evaluate the sound spectrographic cry characteristics in sick infants. It has been found that it is not only the pitch but also other cry characteristics that change when the child is sick, and these changes are especially common in diseases in which the central nervous system is affected. Thus, cry analysis may be valuable in clinical diagnostics in order to evaluate whether the central nervous system is involved.

In a study by Michelsson, Raes, Thodén, & Wasz-Höckert (1982), the cries of 200 consecutive cases admitted to the newborn ward at the Children's Hospital were analyzed blindly. The results showed that the cries of infants with metabolic and neurological disturbances were more abnormal than cries of infants who were at the ward for observation or who had heart or lung diseases. The following cry characteristics were found to be useful in diagnosis when central nervous system involvement was expected: the maximum and minimum of the fundamental frequency increased, rising and falling/rising melody types became more common, and so did the occurrence of biphonation and glide.

### 4.2. Cry in Chromosomal Abnormalities

Our first study on cries of infants with chromosomal abnormalities was by Vuorenkoski et al. (1966), who analyzed the cries of infants with deletion of chromosome no. 5, the cri-du-chat syndrome. A general pitch of 860 Hz in 44 cries of 8 children was noted. Additionally, it was found that a flat melody type occurred in 36% and a rising melody type in 23% of the samples.

Michelsson et al. (1980) found approximately the same value of the fundamental frequency in two infants with cri-du-chat syndrome. Flat melody types were common. Luchsinger, Dubois, Vassella, Joss, Gloor, and Wiesmann (1967) and Bauer (1968) have also found that children with the cri-du-chat syndrome have cries with a pitch of 600 to 1000 Hz.

Lind, Vuorenkoski, Rosberg, Partanen, and Wasz-Höckert (1970) analyzed 120 cry samples of 30 infants with Down's syndrome, 0 to 8 months old. The vocalizations were often of long duration with a mean of 4.5 sec. The mean maximum pitch was 510 Hz, and the mean minimum pitch was 270 Hz. This was significantly less than in healthy controls. A flat melody type occurred in 63% of the cry samples.

Michelsson *et al.* (1980) have analyzed cry samples of 14 infants with various chromosomal abnormalities. In infants with 13- and 18-trisomy, the cries were, as in Down's syndrome, low pitched and monotonous whereas the cries were more high pitched in infants with abnormalities of chomosomes nos. 4 or 5. No biphonation was seen in the cries of the chromosomal abnormalities, and glide appeared only in 1 of the 135 cry samples studied.

We have found that the cry analysis is useful in clinical pediatrics when chromosomal abnormalities are expected. A cry analysis can give some guidance while waiting for the chromosomal estimation that takes several weeks.

## 4.3. Cry in Infants with Endocrine Disturbances

The cry in congenital hypothyroidism, studied in 40 cries of 4 infants by Michelsson and Sirvio (1976), was of lower pitch than usually seen in cries of healthy infants. The mean maximum pitch was 470 Hz and the mean minimum pitch 270 Hz. A low number of shifts, 7%, and a frequent occurrence of glottal roll, 57%, at the end of the phonations accentuated the audible impression of a hoarse low-pitched cry. The hoarse cry seems to be present for several months. Vuorenkoski, Vuorenkoski, and Anttolainen (1973) showed that even at the age of 8 months, a child who suffered from congenital hypothyroidism did not have any cries with a pitch above 1000 Hz.

## 4.4. Cries in Infants with Diseases and Malformations of the Orolaryngeal Tract

Sound spectrographic analysis of infants with cleft palate was reported by Michelsson *et al.* (1975); 52 cries from 13 infants with cleft palate were analyzed. When compared to cries of healthy neonates of the same age, no differences were observed with respect to the fundamental frequency. The mean maximum pitch was 710 Hz, the mean minimum pitch 360 Hz, and the melody type was falling or rising/falling in 88% of the cry samples. Glide occurred in 10% of cleft palate infants' cries. Biphonation was not seen.

Several cry characteristics that we have, according to our cry studies, connected with disturbances of the central nervous system were not seen in the cries of cleft palate infants. In studies by Raes *et al.* (1980) and Raes, Michelsson, Dehaeu, and Despontín (1982), these results were confirmed.

These cry results have clinical implications, especially when newborn infants are concerned. When the cry is audibly different, sound spectrography of the cries can reveal whether the cry characteristics have changed because of laryngeal or cerebral diseases.

## 4.5.   Cry in Infants with Metabolic Disturbances

The cry of infants with neonatal hyperbilirubinemia was reported by Wasz-Höckert *et al.* (1971). The most abnormal cry signals were selected from 45 infants with hyperbilirubinemia. Both the maximum and minimum pitchs of the fundamental frequency were highly increased. The mean maximum pitch was 2120 Hz, and the mean minimum pitch was 960 Hz. Biphonation was common in 49% of the samples, as was furcation, in 42% of the samples. Furcation has been seen more commonly in pain cries of infants with hyperbilirubinemia than in cries of infants with any other disease.

Wasz-Höckert *et al.* (1971) noted also that the cries of some children with hyperbilirubinemia changed already 1 to 2 days prior to increased serum bilirubin values. The cry analysis method can thus enable early treatment with phototherapy or blood exchange.

A preliminary report on the crying of newborn infants with low blood sugar—hypoglycemia—was reported by Koivisto *et al.* (1974). Hypoglycemic infants with clinical symptoms are more likely to develop irreversible brain damage than those without symptoms (Koivisto, Blanco-Sequeiros, & Krause, 1972). Cry analysis can be one criterion in deciding which treatment is needed. In cries of 15 full-term infants with hypoglycemia and clinical symptoms, a mean maximum pitch of 1600 Hz was noted, with the highest part of the fundamental most often at the beginning of the cry signals. Vibrato and biphonation were seen in about two-thirds of the cries. Glides occurred in 3 of the 17 cries studied.

Cries of newborn infants to diabetic mothers have been studied by Thodén and Michelsson (1984). The mean maximum pitch, including shift, in cries of these infants was 1480 Hz. An interesting fact was that the pitch was still higher when the child also had hypoglycemia or hyperbilirubinemia, or both simultaneously. The maximum pitch rose to 1520 Hz (hypoglycemia), 1790 Hz (hyperbilirubinemia), and 1980 Hz (both). The minimum pitch was higher when the child had hypoglycemia, hyperbilirubinemia, or both. The study shows that both hyperbilirubinemia and hypoglycemia change the cry characteristics in the newborn period.

The results of cry analysis of infants with hyperbilirubinemia were confirmed by Michelsson, Raes, Thodén, and Wasz-Höckert (1982). These results showed that the cry characteristics changed whether the child was born full-term or premature.

## 4.6. Crying in Newborn Infants with Asphyxia

Michelsson (1971) collected cries from 250 asphyxiated infants during the first 3 days of life. All infants were born with Apgar scores of 7 or less at 1 or 5 minutes of age. The children were divided into two groups, depending on whether the child suffered from respiratory distresss (peripheral aphyxia) or had neurological symptoms in the newborn period (central asphyxia). The cry characteristics were compared to the crying of 50 healthy full-term and 75 premature infants, depending on whether the neonate with asphyxia was full term or premature. In both gestational-age groups, the cry was more abnormal in 125 children with central asphyxia than in 80 children with peripheral asphyxia. The cry was, however, different in both groups from a normal series of 50 infants. The mean maximum pitch, including shift, was 1460 Hz in the full-term neonates with central asphyxia, 1000 Hz in peripheral asphyxia, and 650 Hz in controls (Michelsson & Wasz-Höckert, 1980). Prematures with central asphyxia had a mean maximum pitch of 1950 Hz, including shift; the mean in peripheral asphyxia was 1610 Hz, and in symptomless prematures, 1520 Hz. Michelsson (1971) showed that biphonation occurred in more than 20% and glide in more than 10% of the samples of infants with asphyxia. Rising and falling/rising types of melody occurred in more than 30% of the signals. These changes in the cry characteristics were more marked the more severely the newborn had suffered from asphyxia.

The changes in cry characteristics in newborn infants with asphyxia were so obvious that we have a good reason to use the cry analysis as an additional tool in neonatal neurological examination. Michelsson (1971) found that if the cries became normal in a few days after asphyxia, the child was more likely to recover without neurological sequelae than if the cry characteristics remained abnormal during the hospitalization period. The prognostic value of cry analysis in asphyxia was confirmed in a follow-up study by Michelsson et al. (1977a). The results showed that infants who at later checkup were found to be neurologically damaged had had more abnormal cries in the newborn period.

Syutkina, Michelsson, and Sirvio (1982) have, in animal studies, experimentally confirmed that asphyxia produces changes in the sounds produced. The study analyzed the utterances of Wistar rats in which asphyxia was experimentally caused by clamping the umbilical cord 2 to 4 days before birth. The cord was clamped until the fetal heart rate dropped to 50, which took about 15 to 20 minutes. Antenatal hypoxia was found to produce a significant increase of maximum pitch and decrease in the duration of the phonations. The mean maximum pitch was 4140 Hz in 61 pain-induced utterances of asphyxiated rats and 2890 Hz in 34 utterances of control rats.

## 4.7. Crying in Diseases of the Central Nervous System

The cry of 14 infants with bacterial meningitis was studied by Michelsson et al. (1977b). The cries of the 0–6-month-old infants were higher pitched, with a mean maximum pitch of 750 Hz in the 110 cries studied. The mean minimum pitch was 560 Hz. Rising and falling/rising melody types were more common (24%) than in control babies. Biphonation (49%) and glide (11%) occurred more frequently. Infants who at later checkup had neurological sequelae had more abnormal cry characteristics at the time of the disease. The results indicate that cry analysis has not only diagnostic but also prognostic value when analyzing cries of infants with meningitis.

In cries of infants with herpes simplex virus encephalitis (Pettay et al., 1977), noise concentration occurred at the frequency region of 2000 to 3000 Hz. We have, therefore, used the cry analysis in clinical diagnostics when herpes encephalitis has been suspected. The cries were more high pitched. Both biphonation and glide were more common than in healthy controls.

A study on crying in children with hydrocephalus was done by Michelsson, Kaskinen, Aulanko, and Rinne (1984). The cry analysis of 248 cries—4 cries from each of 62 infants—were analyzed. The mean maximum pitch without shift was 750 Hz and the mean minimum pitch 430 Hz. When the infants with hydrocephalus were separated into groups according to etiology, the only significant difference in the maximum pitch when compared to controls was noted in infants who had congenital hydrocephalus present at birth. Flat types of melody were common, regardless of the cause of hydrocephalus. Biphonation occurred in 14% and glide in 8% in the whole material.

The cry results show that the cry is different from normal crying in diseases of the central nervous system. Biphonation was more common in meningitis than in encephalitis and hydrocephalus. Noise concentration occurred in herpes encephalitis. All groups of children had more high-pitched cries than controls. In infants with congenital abnormalities, such as Down's syndrome (Wasz-Höckert *et al.*, 1971), hypothyroidism (Michelsson & Sirvio, 1976), and congenitial syphilis (Kittel & Hecht, 1977), the cry was low pitched. Thus, it is obvious that the results of cry analysis are different in children with acquired and congenital disorders of the central nervous system.

### 4.8. Cries in Malnutrition

Cries of children with severe malnutrition were studied by Juntunen, Sirvio, and Michelsson (1978). In infants suffering from kwashiorkor, the cry characteristics did not differ from normal crying. The children often recover without sequelae. In marasmus, children can suffer from irreversible organic brain dysfunction (Stock & Smyth, 1967), and the cry is very high pitched and monotonous. The mean maximum pitch in the marasmic children was 1340 Hz; the mean minimum pitch 730 Hz.

### 4.9. Cry in Malformation Syndromes

In three cases with Krabbe's disease, the cry characteristics were analyzed and showed a higher mean maximum pitch (1120 Hz) and mean minimum pitch (590 Hz) than in controls (Thodén & Michelsson, 1979). Rising and falling/rising types of melody were seen significantly more often (27%) in the cries of these infants.

### 4.10. Cry in Twin Pairs

A study on cries in twins has been finished by Michelsson and Rinne (1984). The results showed that the cries in twin pairs who were both healthy were more equal than the cries in twin pairs in which one was healthy and the other was diseased. The study also confirmed previous results that the cries are more abnormal the more premature the infant is.

We have analyzed 90 cries from two pairs of Siamese twins (Michelsson, Raes, & Thodén, 1982). The results showed that the cries of the conjoined twins fell well into normal limits for crying. Cry features of a set of quadruplets was reported by Thodén, Raes, and Michelsson (1979).

## 5. SUMMARY

Scandinavian cry research has been ongoing since 1960. The first cry studies concerned both auditory identification and sound spectrographic analysis of various cry characteristics.

Lately, the main purpose of our cry research has been to show that cry analysis is an additional aid in making diagnoses in clinical pediatrics, especially in the newborn period and in diseases that have affected the central nervous system. For this purpose, systematic sound spectrographic analyses have been done on cries of newborn and small infants with various diseases.

When a child is sick and the cry changes from normal to abnormal, it can be caused by diseases or malformations affecting the central nervous system, the lungs or the larynx, or the oral cavities. We have, therefore, investigated by sound spectrogaphy, in which diseases the cry is similar to and in which diseases the cry is different from the crying of healthy infants. We have additionally evaluated whether there are some cry features that are specific for certain disorders. We believe that any method that can be useful for clinical assessment in the newborn period is valuable and should be developed further.

Classical pediatric textbooks have associated a high-pitched shrill cry with diseases affecting the central nervous system. We have proved that not only the pitch changes in diseases affecting the central nervous system but also other cry characteristics, such as the melody type and the occurrence of biphonation and glide. The cry signals have been more abnormal in severely sick infants. Cry analysis has been helpful not only in clinical diagnostics but also in estimating prognosis in diseases that have affected the central nervous system.

## 6. REFERENCES

Bauer, H. Phonatrischer Beitrag zum Cri-du-Chat Syndrom. *HNO: Wegweiser für die Facharztliche Praxis*, 1968, *6*, 185–187.

Bosma, J. R., Truby, H. M., & Lind, J. Cry motions of the newborn infant. *Acta Paediatrica Scandinavica*, 1965, *163*, 61–92.

Brzokoupil, K., Fohrer, U., Lind, J., & Stensland-Junker, K. A study of the importance of a Japanese carrier for the communicative developments of infants. *Acta Paediatrica Scandinavica*, 1973, *65* (Suppl. 236).

Fisichelli, V. R., & Karelitz, S. The cry latencies of normal infants and those with brain damage. *Journal of Psychology*, 1966, *64*, 119–126.

Flatau, T. S., & Gutzmann, H. Die Stimme des Säuglings. *Archiv für Laryngologie und Rhinologie*, 1906, *18*, 139–151.

Gleiss, J., & Hohn, W. Das Verhalten beim Schreien nach konstanter Schmertzreizung atemgesunder und atemgestorter Neugeborenen. *Deutsche Zeitschrift für Nervenheilkunde*, 1968, *194*, 311–317.

Juntunen, K., Sirvio, P., & Michelsson, K. Cry analysis of infants with severe malnutrition. *European Journal of Pediatrics*, 1978, *128*, 241–246.

Kittel, G., & Hecht, L. Der erste Schrei—Frequenzanalytische Untersuchungen. *Sprache— Stimme—Gehor*, 1977, *1*, 151–155.

Koivisto, M., Blanco-Sequeiros, M., & Krause, U. Neonatal symptomatic and asymptomatic hypoglycemia: A follow-up study of 151 children. *Developmental Medicine and Child Neurology*, 1972, *14*, 603–614.

Koivisto, M., Michelsson, K., Sirvio, P., & Wasz-Höckert, O. Spectrographic analysis of pain cry of hypoglycemia in newborn infants. *XIV International Congress of Pediatrics*, 1974, *1*, 250.

Lester, B. M. Spectrum analysis of the cry sounds of well nourished and malnourished infants. *Child Development*, 1976, *47*, 237–241.

Lester, B M., & Zeskind, P. Brazelton scale and physical size correlates of neonatal cry features. *Infant Behaviour and Development*, 1978, *1*,393–402.

Lind, J. (Ed.). Newborn infant cry. *Acta Paediatrica Scandinavica*, 1965, 1–132 (Suppl. 163).

Lind, J. Music and the small human being. *Acta Paediatrica Scandinavica*, 1980, *69*, 129.

Lind, J. Vuorenkoski, V., Rosberg, G., Partanen, T. J., & Wasz-Höckert, O. Spectrographic analysis of vocal response to pain stimuli in infants with Down's syndrome. *Developmental Medicine and Child Neurology*, 1970, *12*, 478–486.

Luchsinger, R., Dubois, C., Vassella, F., Joss, E., Gloor, R., & Wiesmann, U. Spektralanalyse des "Miauens" bei Cri-du-Chat Syndrom. *Folia Phoniatrica*, 1967, *19*, 27–33.

Michelsson, K. Cry analysis of symptomless low birth weight neonates and of asphyxiated newborn infants. *Acta Paediatrica Scandinavica*, 1971, *216*, 1–45. (Whole Supplement)

Michelsson, K. Cry characteristics in sound spectrographic cry analysis. In T. Murry & J. Murry (Eds.), *Infant communication: Cry and early speech.* Houston: College Hill Press, 1980.

Michelsson, K., & Rinne, A. *Cry in twin pairs.* Unpublished manuscript, 1984.

Michelsson, K., & Sirvio, P. Cry analysis in congenital hypothyroidism. *Folia Phoniatrica*, 1976, *26*, 40–47.

Michelsson, K., & Wasz-Höckert, O. The value of cry analysis in neonatology and early infancy. In T. Murry & J. Murry (Eds.), *Infant communication: Cry and early speech.* Houston: College Hill Press, 1980.

Michelsson, K., Sirvio, P., Koivisto, M., Sovijarvi, A., & Wasz-Höckert, O. Spectrographic analysis of pain cry in neonates with cleft palate. *Biology of the Neonate*, 1975, *26*, 353–358.

Michelsson, K., Sirvio, P., & Wasz-Höckert, O. Pain cry in full-term asphyxiated newborn infants correlated with late findings. *Acta Paediatrica Scandinavica*, 1977, *66*, 611–616. (a)

Michelsson, K., Sirvio, P., & Wasz-Höckert, O. Sound spectrographic cry analysis of infants with bacterial meningitis. *Developmental Medicine and Child Neurology*, 1977, *19*, 309–315. (b)

Michelsson, K., Tuppurainen, N., & Aula, P. Sound spectrographic cry analysis of infants with karyotype abnormality. *Neuropediatrics*, 1980, *11*, 365–376.

Michelsson, K., Raes, J., Thodén, C. J., & Wasz-Höckert, O. Sound spectrographic cry analysis in neonatal diagnostics. An evaluative study. *Journal of Phonetics*, 1982, *10*, 79–80.

Michelsson, K., Raes, J., & Thodén, C. J. Cry analysis in two pairs of siamese twins. *Cry Research Newsletter*, 1982, 2, 4–8.

Michaelsson, K., Kaskinen, H., Aulanko, R., & Rinne, A. Sound spectrographic cry analysis of infants with hydrocephalus. *Acta Paediatrica Scandinavica*, 1984, 73, 65–68.

Mooney, B., & Lind, J. *Rooming-in babies cry less than half as often*. North Central Publishing Company, St. Paul, 1969.

Murooka, H., Machida, T., Sasaki, T., Iwasa, Y., & Matumoto, J. Relationship between neonates and intrauterine sound. *Asian Medical Journal*. Paper presented by Sankyo Co., Ltd., 1978.

Murry, T., Amundson, P., & Hollien, H. Acoustical characteristics of infant cries: Fundamental frequency. *Journal of Child Language*, 1977, 4, 321–328.

Ostwald, P. F., Phibbs, R., & Fox, S. Diagnostic use of infant cry. *Biology of the Neonate*, 1968, 13, 68–82.

Partanen, T., Wasz-Höckert, O., Vuorenkoski, V., Theorell, K., Valanne, E., & Lind, J. Auditory identification of pain cry signals of young infants in pathological conditions and its sound spectrographic basis. *Annales Paediatriae Fenniae*, 1967, 13, 56–63.

Pettay, O., Donner, M., Michelsson, K., & Sirvio, P. New aspects on the diagnosis of herpes simplex virus (HSV) infections in the newborn. *XV International Congress of Pediatrics*, 1977, 4, 235.

Prescott, R. Infant cry sound: developmental features. *Journal of the Acoustical Society of America*, 1975, 57, 1186–1191.

Raes, J., Michelsson, K., & Despontin, M. Spectrografische analyse van het geschrei van baby's met laryngeale aandoeningen. *Acta Otorhinolaryngologica Belgica*, 1980, 34, 224–237.

Raes, J., Michelsson, K., Dehaen, F., & Despontin, M. Cry analysis in infants with infections and congenital disorders of the larynx. *Journal of Pediatric Otorhinolaryngology*, 1982, 4, 156–169.

Ringel, R. L., & Kluppel, D. D. Neonatal crying: A normative study. *Folia Phoniatrica*, 1964, 16, 1–9.

Salk, L. The role of heart beat in the relations between mother and infant. *Scientific American*, 1973, 24, 228.

Sirvio, P., & Michelsson, K. Sound spectrographic cry analysis of newborn infants, normal and abnormal. *Folia Phoniatrica*, 1976, 28, 161–173.

Stark, R. E., Rose, S. N., & McLagen, M. Features of infant sounds: The first eight weeks of life. *Journal of Child Language*, 1975, 2, 205–221.

Stock, M. B., & Smyth, P. M. The effects of undernutrition during infancy on subsequent brain growth and intellectual development. *South African Medical Journal*, 1967, 41, 1027–1030.

Syutkina, E. V., Michelsson, K., & Sirvio, P. *Influence of antenatal hypoxia on the utterances of newborn rats*. (In Russian.) *Bulletin of Experimental Biology and Medicine*, 1982, 8, 25–27.

Thodén, C. J., & Koivisto, M. Acoustic analysis of the normal pain cry. In T. Murry & J. Murry (Eds.), *Infant communication: Cry and early speech*. Houston: College Hill Press, 1980.

Thodén, C. J., & Michelsson, K. Sound spectrographic cry analysis in Krabbe's disease. *Developmental Medicine and Child Neurology*, 1979, 21, 400–401.

Thodén, C. J., & Michelsson, K. Pain cry in infants born to diabetic mothers. *Developmental Medicine and Child Neurology*, 1984. (Accepted for publication.)

Thodén, C. J., Raes, J., & Michelsson, K. Cry features in a quadruplet. *Cry Research Newsletter*, 1979, *2*, 3–4.

Thodén, C. J., Järvenpää, A. L., & Michelsson, K. Sound spectrographic pain cry in prematures. In *Infant cry: Theoretical and research prospectives*. New York: Academic Press, 1982.

Truby, H. M., & Lind, J. Cry sounds of the newborn infant. *Acta Paediatrica Scandinavica*, 1965, 8–54 (Suppl. 163).

Valanne, E. H., Vuorenkoski, V., Partanen, T. J., Lind, J., & Wasz-Höckert, O. The ability of human mothers to identify hunger cry signals of their own newborn infants during the lying-in period. *Experientia*, 1967, *23*, 768.

Vuorenkoski, V., Lind, J., Partanen, T. J., Lejeune, J., Lafourcade, J., & Wasz-Höckert, O., Spectrographic analysis of cries from children with maladie du cri du chat. *Annales Paediatriae Fenniae*, 1966, *12*, 174–180.

Vuorenkoski, V., Wasz-Höckert, O., Koivisto, E., & Lind, J. The effect of cry stimulus on the temperature of the lactating breast of primipara: A thermographic study. *Experientia*, 1969, *25*, 1286-1287.

Vuorenkoski, V., Kaunisto, M., Tjernlund, P., & Vesa, L. Cry detector. Clinical applications of real time detection of some parameters in newborn infants. *XIII International Congress of Pediatrics*, 1971, *17*, 81–84.

Vuorenkoski, L., Vuorenkoski, V., & Anttolainen, I. Cry analysis in congenital hypothyroidism: An aid to diagnosis and clinical evaluation. *Acta Paediatrica Scandinavica*, 1973, 27–28 (Suppl. 236).

Wasz-Höckert, O., Vuorenkoski, V., Valanne, E., & Michelsson, K. Sound spectographic analysis of the infant cry. (In German.) *Experientia*, 1962, *18*, 583–586.

Wasz-Höckert, O., Valanne, E., Vuorenkoski, V., Michelsson, K., & Sovijarvi, A. Analysis of some types of vocalization in the newborn and in early infancy. *Annales Paediatriae Fenniae*, 1963, *9*, 1–10.

Wasz-Höckert, O., Partanen, T., Vuorenkoski, V., Valanne, E., & Michelsson, K. The identification of some specific meanings in infant vocalization. *Experientia*, 1964, *20*, 154–156. (a)

Wasz-Höckert, O., Partanen, T., Vuorenkoski, V., Valanne, E., & Michelsson, K. Effect of training on ability to identify preverbal vocalizations. *Developmental Medicine and Child Neurology*, 1964, *6*, 393–396. (b)

Wasz-Höckert, O., Lind, J., Vuorenkoski, V., Partanen, T., & Valanne, E. The infant cry. A spectrographic and auditory analysis. *Clinics in Developmental Medicine 29*. Lavenham, Suffolk: Spastics International Medical Publications, 1968.

Wasz-Höckert, O., Koivisto, M., Vuorenkoski, V., & Lind, J. Spectrographic analysis of pain cry in hyperbilirubinemia. *Biology of the Neonate*, 1971, *17*, 260–271.

# 5

# Sound Spectrographic Cry Analysis of Pain Cry in Prematures

CARL-JOHAN THODÉN, ANNA-LIISA JÄRVENPÄÄ,
and KATARINA MICHELSSON

## 1. INTRODUCTION

The literature on cry studies in the newborn contains few investigations dealing with the premature baby. Michelsson (1971) reported data on sound spectrographic cry analysis of 75 symptomless prematures. The results showed that the pain cry of the prematures differed in many respects from that of the term infant. The cry characteristics were found to be more dependent on the gestational age (GA) than the birth weight. The more premature the newborn baby was, the more different the cry was from that of full-term infants. The cries became more high pitched and shorter with decreasing gestational age. Biphonation and glide became more common.

Michelsson divided the premature infants into two groups: those born at 35 to 37 weeks gestational age (35 infants) and those born at 34

CARL-JOHAN THODÉN • II Department of Pediatrics, Children's Hospital, University of Helsinki, SF-00290 Helsinki 29, Finland. The study was supported by grants from the Sigrid Juselius Foundation and the Foundation for Pediatric Research, Finland.    ANNA-LIISA JÄRVENPÄÄ • Department of Neonatology, Children's Hospital, University of Helsinki, SF-00290 Helsinki 29, Finland.    KATARINA MICHELSSON • II Department of Pediatrics, Children's Hospital, University of Helsinki, SF-00290 Helsinki 29, Finland.

weeks, or earlier gestational age (40 infants). She reported in 1971 the median of the pitch values. Michelsson and Wasz-Höckert (1980) estimated the mean from the previous results. The mean maximum pitch for babies born at 35 to 37 GA was 1010 Hz without shift and 1450 Hz including shift; the corresponding values for the smallest prematures were 1360 Hz and 1590 Hz, respectively, and for 75 full-term controls 650 Hz and 810 Hz, respectively.

Tenold, Crowell, Jones, Daniel, McPherson, and Popper (1974) found a median of the fundamental frequency of 752 Hz in cries of five prematures compared to 518 Hz for nine full-term infants.

Cries of full-term infants who were small for gestational age were studied by Michelsson (1971). The cries were similar to full-term with proper birth weight. The mean maximum pitch for infants who were small for gestational age was 760 Hz. Lester and Zeskind (1978) found a mean fundamental frequency of 740 Hz for 12 full-term but under-weight infants.

Michelsson, Raes, Thodén, and Wasz-Höckert (1982) reported that the cries of 22 healthy prematures had a mean maximum pitch of 880 Hz, excluding shift, and 1160 Hz, including shift.

The cry characteristics of sick prematures have been studied by Michelsson (1971). She analyzed cries of 95 newborn prematures of whom 40 had respiratory diseases and 55 had neurological symptoms. Infants with respiratory distress had two or more of the following criteria: persistent respiratory rate over 60/min, intercostal and sternal retractions, expiratory grunting, or cyanosis, when breathing room air. All neonates with neurological symptoms were born with Apgar scores of 1 to 7 at 1 min, and in the majority of cases signs of intrauterine asphyxia were considered to be present because of changes in the fetal heart rate and discolored amniotic fluid. The results showed that the cries in both groups differed from cries of healthy controls. The most abnormal cries occurred in infants with neurological symptoms. The mean maximum pitch was 1730 Hz, excluding shift, and 1950 Hz, including shift. The cries were shorter, they had rising and falling/rising melody types, and biphonation and glide were more common than in symptomless prematures. The most abnormal cries occurred in infants who at later follow-up were found to be neurologically damaged. The prognostic significance of cry analysis in asphyxiated infants was confirmed in a study by Michelsson, Sirvio, and Wasz-Höckert (1977a).

Michelsson et al. (1982) found in cries of 21 prematures with cardiopulmonary disorders a mean maximum pitch of 1100 Hz without shift and in 14 infants with severe asphyxia and/or neurological symptoms a mean maximum pitch of 1540 Hz. Rising and falling/rising melody types were more common if the child had metabolic disturbances or neurological symptoms than if the child was healthy or had cardiopulmonary disturbances.

Thodén and Koivisto (1980) reported in a prospective study cry characteristics of 38 full-term healthy infants ages of 1 and 5 days and 3 and 6 months. The purpose of the study was to obtain new normative material. Since the previous, more extensive cry analysis by Wasz-Höckert, Lind, Vuorenkoski, Partanen, and Valanne (1968), new cry characteristics have been included in the measurements, and the measurement technique has changed slightly.

The aim of this study was to analyze the cry characteristics of healthy prematures at different gestational ages. We wanted to obtain normative material by which cries of prematures with various diseases could be compared. The cry analysis of the previous series by Michelsson (1971) had shown high-pitched cries in small prematures. We wanted to control for whether the cries occurring in small prematures were due to immaturity of the children or could have been caused by some pathological factors because the series by Michelsson was collected in 1963–1967 at which time less attention was paid to all factors, which could have changed the cry characteristics of newborn babies.

## 2. MATERIAL AND METHODS

The aim was to study the cry characteristics of healthy premature infants. The following selection criteria were used: weight appropriate for gestational age (Backstrom & Kauppinen, 1968) and no respiratory distress syndrome, or septic infection, severe hypoglycemia (blood-glucose $\leq$ 1.2 mmol/liter), hyperbilirubinemia requiring blood exchange transfusion, or neurological symptoms or signs, such as convulsions, hypotonia, hypertonia, or increased intracranial pressure. The gestational age was estimated by using the system developed by Dubowitz, Dubowitz, and Goldberg (1970).

The 69 infants included in the investigation were born between 31 and 36 weeks gestational age. The mean birth weight was 1820 g (range 1230–2170 g). The Apgar scores were 7 to 10 at 1 minute of age.

The cries were collected from the newborn infant on the first day of life and every week thereafter as long as the child stayed at the hospital. Thus, 285 cries were analyzed. Because the cries consisted of the first, second, and third cry signals, the number of cry signals totaled 772. The first cry signal denotes the phonated part of a cry between the pain stimulus and the first inspiration; the second signal is located between the first and second inspirations; and the third signal is located between the second and the third inspirations.

The pain cry was initiated by pinching the infant's ear lobe. The infants were awake at the moment of induction of the cry, that is, in Stage 3 or 4 as defined by Prechtl and Beintema (1964).

The cries were recorded on a Uher 4000 Report-L tape recorder or a Sony TC-55 cassette recorder. The cries were visualized as sonagrams using a Sona-Graph 7029 A (Kay Elemetrics, N.J.) provided with a narrow band filter. The sonagrams were analyzed according to the principles given by Sirvio and Michelsson (1976) and modified by Thodén and Koivisto (1980).

The following cry characteristics were analyzed from the sound spectrograms: latency and duration, occurrence of shift, maximum pitch, both including and excluding shift, minimum pitch, melody type, occurrence of voiced and continuous signals, biphonation, glide, double harmonic break, vibrato, glottal roll, glottal plosives, and furcation.

In the statistical measurements, the Wilcoxon test for two samples was used when comparing the continuous variables—duration and pitch—in the different groups. For the discrete variables the chi-square test was used.


## 3. RESULTS

The series of infants was divided into three groups, according to the gestational age (GA) at which the pain cry was recorded. The cries recorded at 31 to 33 weeks GA, 34 to 37 weeks GA, and 38 to 41 weeks GA were grouped together. The mean latency was 1.2 sec in the 31 to 33 GA group, 1.2 sec in the 34 to 37 GA group and 1.1 sec in the 38 to 41 GA group (see Table 1). There were no statistical differences between the groups on the latency data.

The duration of the cry signals at different gestational ages showed significant differences (see Table 1). The durations in all three signals were significantly shorter in the 31 to 33 GA group than in the 34 to 37 GA and the 38 to 41 GA groups. The values for the first signal were 2.6 sec, 4.0 sec, and 4.0 sec, respectively. In all gestational age groups it was found that the first cry signal was significantly longer than the second and the third ones.

The maximum pitch of the fundamental frequency, including shift, changed with increasing age (see Table 2). At 31 to 33 GA and 34 to 37 GA the means of the first signal were 1170 Hz and 1230 Hz, respectively. At the gestational age of 38 to 41 weeks, the mean maximum pitch of the first signal decreased to 890 Hz. In signals 2 and 3 the mean maximum

Table 1. The Durational Features (Sec) of the Cry in Prematures of 31–33, 34–37 and 38–41 Weeks GA

| Cry feature | 31–33 weeks GA | | 34–37 weeks GA | | 38–41 weeks GA | | weeks GA | p |
|---|---|---|---|---|---|---|---|---|
| | n | mean ± SD | n | mean ± SD | n | mean ± SD | | |
| Latency, sec | 45 | 1.2 ± 0.7 | 163 | 1.2 ± 0.6 | 75 | 1.1 ± 0.4 | NS | |
| Duration, sec | | | | | | | | |
| I signal | 45 | 2.6 ± 1.9 | 163 | 4.0 ± 1.9 | 75 | 4.0 ± 2.3 | 31–34 | < .001 |
| | | | | | | | 31–38 | < .001 |
| | | | | | | | 34–38 | NS |
| II signal | 43 | 1.3 ± 0.8 | 146 | 1.5 ± 0.7 | 70 | 1.7 ± 0.9 | 31–34 | < .001 |
| | | | | | | | 31–38 | < .001 |
| | | | | | | | 34–38 | NS |
| III signal | 42 | 1.0 ± 0.7 | 126 | 1.2 ± 0.6 | 60 | 1.4 ± 0.8 | 31–34 | < .05 |
| | | | | | | | 31–38 | < .01 |
| | | | | | | | 34–38 | NS |

*Table 2. The Pitch (Hz) of the Fundamental Frequency (Mean ± SD)*[a]

|  | 31–33 weeks GA | 34–37 weeks GA | 38–41 weeks GA | weeks GA | p |
|---|---|---|---|---|---|
| **Maximum pitch including shift** |  |  |  |  |  |
| I signal | 1170 ± 670 | 1230 ± 730 | 890 ± 610 | 31–34 | NS |
|  |  |  |  | 31–38 | < .01 |
|  |  |  |  | 34–38 | < .01 |
| II signal | 900 ± 510 | 850 ± 560 | 780 ± 570 | NS |  |
| III signal | 890 ± 540 | 780 ± 420 | 670 ± 350 | 31–34 | NS |
|  |  |  |  | 31–38 | < .05 |
|  |  |  |  | 34–38 | NS |
| **Maximum pitch excluding shift** |  |  |  |  |  |
| I signal | 990 ± 620 | 890 ± 530 | 750 ± 460 | 31–34 | NS |
|  |  |  |  | 31–38 | <. 05 |
|  |  |  |  | 34–38 | < .01 |
| II signal | 820 ± 440 | 750 ± 440 | 720 ± 490 | NS |  |
| III signal | 780 ± 450 | 710 ± 340 | 650 ± 350 | NS |  |
| **Minimum pitch** |  |  |  |  |  |
| I signal | 470 ± 290 | 370 ± 220 | 370 ± 290 | 31–34 | < .05 |
|  |  |  |  | 31–38 | < .05 |
|  |  |  |  | 34–38 | NS |
| II signal | 460 ± 260 | 390 ± 170 | 380 ± 180 | 31–34 | NS |
|  |  |  |  | 31–38 | < .05 |
|  |  |  |  | 34–38 | NS |
| III signal | 450 ± 160 | 430 ± 230 | 370 ± 160 | 31–34 | NS |
|  |  |  |  | 31–38 | < .05 |
|  |  |  |  | 34–38 | < .05 |

[a]The number of cries analyzed is the same as in Table 1.

pitch decreased from 900 Hz in the 31 to 33 GA group to 670 Hz in the 38 to 41 GA group.

Shifts were more common in the first cry signal in all gestational age groups. A statistically significant difference was noted in the 31 to 33 GA group between the first and the second signals ($p <$ .05) and in the 34 to 37 GA group between the first and the two other signals. Shifts occurred in the 31 to 33 GA group in 27% of the first, in 9% of the second, and in 17% of the third signals. The values for the 34 to 37 GA group were 34%, 14%, and 8%, respectively, and for the 38 to 41 GA group 15%, 7%, and 7%, respectively.

The maximum pitch was somewhat lower when the shifts were omitted from the calculations (see Table 2). A decrease in the mean of the fundamental was found with increasing gestational age; the difference was significant in the first signal. The highest pitch value, 990 Hz, occurred in the first signal in the 31 to 33 GA group and the lowest value, 650 Hz, in the third signal in the 38 to 41 GA group.

The minimum pitch of the cry signals at different gestational ages varied between 470 Hz and 370 Hz (see Table 2). The minimum pitch, 470 Hz, in the first signal at 31 to 33 GA was significantly higher than in the two other gestational age groups. There was also, in the second and the third signals noted, a lower mean minimum pitch with increasing gestational age. No significant differences were noted between the first, second, and third signals in any gestational age group.

The first signal was continuous in 64% to 78% of the cry signals (see Table 3). The second and third signals were continuous in more than 80% of the signals, except for the third signal at 31 to 33 GA, which showed 71% continuity. The differences were not significant between the gestational age groups. The second and the third signals were significantly more often continuous than the first signal at 34 to 37 and 38 to 41 GAs.

The majority of the signals were voiced; they were 81% to 100% in the different gestational age groups (Table 3). There were no significant differences in the first and third signals between the age groups. In the second signal, we noted significantly more voiced signals at 38 to 41 GA than at 31 to 33 and 34 to 37 GA ($p < .01$). At 34 to 37 GA, we noted that the second and the third signals were more often voiced than the first ones ($p < .001$).

The most common melody types were falling and rising/falling, which were seen in 91% to 98% of the signals (Table 3). Rising and falling/rising melody types occurred almost solely in the first signal, in 4% to 5%. Flat melody type was most common in the third signals, and it occurred in 2% to 5% of the cries. Cries with no melody type were rare. No significant differences were found between the gestational age groups or between the first, second, or third signals.

Vibrato occurred in about 50% of the first signals at all ages, in 30% of the second signals, and in 20% of the third signals. The differences according to signal number were significant.

Glottal roll was seen in about 20% of the first signals. The occurrence of glottal roll declined with increasing signal number and was significantly lower, below 5%, in the second and the third signals. Significant differences were seen between the first and the two other signals but not between the gestational age groups.

Glottal plosives occurred in less than 10% of the cry signals in all groups. No significant differences were seen.

Glide was found in 8% to 15% of the first signals and in 1% to 4% of the second and the third signals (Table 3). The differences between the age groups were not significant. Glide was significantly more common in the first signal than in the second and third ones.

*Table 3. Cry Characteristics in Premature Infants[a]*

| Cry characteristic | | Percentage of cry signals | | |
|---|---|---|---|---|
| | | 31–33 weeks GA | 34–37 weeks GA | 38–41 weeks GA |
| Voiced | I signal | 84.4 | 81.0 | 86.7 |
| | II signal | 86.0 | 95.9 | 100.0 |
| | III signal | 88.1 | 96.8 | 91.7 |
| Continuous | I signal | 77.8 | 65.0 | 64.0 |
| | II signal | 86.0 | 86.3 | 85.7 |
| | III signal | 71.4 | 86.5 | 80.0 |
| Occurrence of shift | I signal | 26.7 | 34.4 | 14.7 |
| | II signal | 9.3 | 13.7 | 7.1 |
| | III signal | 16.7 | 7.9 | 6.7 |
| Melody type | | | | |
| Falling or rising/failing | I signal | 93.3 | 92.6 | 90.7 |
| | II signal | 97.7 | 97.9 | 97.1 |
| | III signal | 90.5 | 92.9 | 96.7 |
| Rising of falling/rising | I signal | 4.4 | 4.3 | 5.3 |
| | II signal | 0.0 | 1.4 | 1.4 |
| | III signal | 2.4 | 1.6 | 0.0 |
| Flat | I signal | 2.3 | 1.2 | 1.3 |
| | II signal | 2.3 | 0.6 | 1.4 |
| | III signal | 4.8 | 4.0 | 1.7 |
| None | I signal | 0.0 | 1.8 | 2.6 |
| | II signal | 0.0 | 0.0 | 0.0 |
| | III signal | 2.4 | 1.6 | 1.7 |
| Biphonation | I signal | 0.0 | 1.8 | 1.3 |
| | II signal | 0.0 | 0.0 | 0.0 |
| | III signal | 0.0 | 0.0 | 0.0 |
| Glide | I signal | 11.1 | 14.7 | 8.0 |
| | II signal | 4.3 | 0.6 | 1.3 |
| | III signal | 2.1 | 0.6 | 1.3 |
| Double harmonic break | I signal | 22.2 | 17.8 | 25.3 |
| | II signal | 11.6 | 6.2 | 5.7 |
| | III signal | 4.8 | 7.1 | 5.0 |
| Glottal plosives | I signal | 2.2 | 6.7 | 9.3 |
| | II signal | 2.3 | 1.4 | 2.9 |
| | III signal | 4.8 | 1.6 | 0.0 |

[a]The number of cries analyzed is the same as in Table 1.

Biphonation occurred in 2% of the first signals at 34 to 37 GA and 1% in the 38 to 41 GA group. No biphonation was seen in the other cry signals. Furcation did not occur in any cry.

There were no significant differences in the occurrence of double harmonic break between the gestational age groups (Table 3). Double harmonic break occurred in 18% to 25% of the first signals and in 5%

to 12% of the second and the third signals. Double harmonic break was, at 31 to 33 GA, significantly more common in the first signals than in the third signals and in the first signals at 34 to 37 GA and 38 to 41 GA compared to the second and the third signals.

## 4. DISCUSSION

Michelsson (1971) found that the cry characteristics in prematures were more dependent on gestational age than birth weight. Furthermore, she noted that the cry of a premature baby, when the child had reached the age at which it should have been born, was similar to the cry of a baby born full term. Thus, the changes in the cry characteristics seemed to be independent of whether the child lived an intra- or extra-uterine life. According to these findings, we decided to group together all cries of prematures at the same gestational age irrespective of when they had been born.

Thodén and Koivisto (1980) have reported results on the pain cry of full-term healthy newborn infants. When the cries of the prematures were compared to cries of the full terms, it was noted that the latency time was stable and independent of gestational age. Thus, the latency could be an important feature when comparing cries of healthy and sick infants, as sick infants react slower to pain stimuli. Longer latencies have been found in children with brain damage (Fisichelli & Karelitz, 1963; Michelsson, 1971).

The duration of the signals lengthened with increasing gestational age. This is in concordance with the study by Chiswick and Milner (1976) who found that prematures had a smaller crying vital capacity.

The duration of the second and third signals was shorter than the first one in our cry analysis. This indicates that, when comparing the durational features of cries of different infants, the order of the cry signal in a cry sequence should be mentioned and should be the same. The duration of cries has varied between 1.5 to 6.4 sec depending on the study (Gleiss & Hohn, 1968; Lester & Zeskind, 1978; Ostwald, Phibbs, Fox, 1968; Ringel & Kluppel, 1964; Wolff, 1969; Zeskind & Lester, 1978). It is difficult to compare the duration values achieved by different authors because the measurement techniques have varied greatly.

There was an interesting change in the maximum pitch of the first signal with increasing gestational age. A sharp decline was noted in the mean of the maximum pitch when the prematures reached maturity, that is, the age when they should have been born. This change was seen in the maximum pitch, both when shifts were included and when they were excluded. Comparison of the present results with the cry material by Thodén and Koivisto (1980) of healthy full-term infants of 1 day of age revealed that the values of the maximum pitch of initially premature infants at 38 to 41 GA were somewhat more high pitched than those of the full-term infants. The differences were not significant. This was also true for the minimum pitch. Michelsson's (1971) value for the maximum pitch of prematures born at 34 GA or less was 1340 Hz, compared with our value of 990 Hz for the 31 to 33 GA group. The difference could be due to the fact that Michelsson included newborns with a lower gestational age in her group, but it may also indicate that our infants had fewer neonatal problems than were envisaged when Michelsson's material was collected in 1963–1967. Furthermore, there was a difference in the definition and measurement of shift that could account for the differences in the results (Michelsson, 1971; Thodén & Koivisto, 1980). In the 35 to 37 GA group, the mean value in the study by Michelsson (1971) was 1010 Hz, which did not differ considerably from 890 Hz for the 34 to 37 GA group. The occurrence of shift was in agreement with that of Michelsson (1971). However the 38 to 41 GA group showed considerably fewer shifts than the data from our study of healthy full-term infants (Thodén & Koivisto, 1980).

The cry of full-term infants with diseases affecting the central nervous system has been more high pitched than the cry in the healthy full-term infants (Michelsson, 1971; Michelsson et al. 1977a, b, 1982). The same has been found in prematures. The pitch that initially is more high pitched in symptomless prematures than in the healthy full-term has been still higher in sick prematures (Michelsson, 1971, Michelsson et al., 1982). Thus, both in the full-term and premature, changes occur in the cry characteristics when the child is sick.

The melody types and the voicing and continuity of the signals in the different age groups showed no differences when compared with the material for healthy full-term infants given by Thodén and Koivisto (1980) and the results for prematures given by Michelsson (1971). The dominating melody type in healthy newborns is falling or rising/falling. In prematures with metabolic disturbances and neurological symptoms, an increase of rising and falling/rising types of melodies has been found (Michelsson, 1971; Michelsson et al., 1982). The same types of changes have also occurred in full-terms with metabolic and neurological diseases (Michelsson, 1971; Michelsson et al., 1977a, b, 1982; Wasz-Höckert, Koivisto, Vuorenkoski, & Lind, 1971).

The incidence of vibrato and glottal roll were more common in the first than in the second and third cry signals. Glottal roll has been common in cries of healthy infants (Michelsson, 1971; Wasz-Höckert et al.,

1968) and less common in cries of sick infants, who have shorter cries that end abruptly (Michelsson *et al.*, 1977a, b, 1982). The decrease of glottal roll in cries of prematures in the second and third signals can be explained by the shorter duration of the second and third signals.

Biphonation among the prematures was of the same magnitude as in our normative material (Thodén & Koivisto, 1980). Michelsson (1971) reported biphonation in 5% in the less-than or equal-to 34 GA group and in 14% in the 35 to 37 GA group. In a series of healthy prematures (Michelsson *et al.*, 1982), biphonation occurred in 14%. In premature babies with asphyxia and neurological symptoms, the occurrence of biphonation rose to 31%.

In cry analysis of full-term infants (Michelsson *et al.*, 1982), biphonation has also occurred, especially in cries of infants with diseases affecting the central nervous system. Biphonation was noted in 34% of infants with asphyxia (Michelsson *et al.*, 1977a) and in 49% of infants with meningitis (Michelsson *et al.*, 1977b).

Glide has been associated as a cry characteristic occurring in cries of infants with diseases affecting the central nervous system (Michelsson *et al.*, 1977a, b, 1982). It has, however, also been present in cries of symptomless prematures (Michelsson, 1971; Michelsson *et al.*, 1982). In healthy prematures, however, when glide and biphonation occur, it is often together with a falling or rising/falling melody type. In cries of sick infants, a combination of both biphonation, glide, and a rising or falling/rising melody is more common.

It is well known that many of the biochemical and physiological functions of the premature infant differ from those of the term baby and that the maturation is correlated with gestational age. An interesting feature is the comparison of the maturation of the pain cry with that of the respiration and the sleep patterns of the premature infant. Parmelee, Stern, and Harris (1972) studied respiratory patterns in premature infants and found that regular respiration increased after 36 weeks gestation and that very little periodic breathing was seen after that age. After that age also, the percentage of quiet sleep increased, and the percentage of active sleep decreased. The proportions of the different sleep states reached those of a term infant at 40 weeks of gestation (Parmelee, Wenner, Akiyama, Schultz, & Stern, 1967). The decrease of the maximum pitch occurring between the 34 to 37 GA group and the 38 to 41 GA group in our study might be an indication of the same process of maturation seen in the respiratory and sleep patterns that also have correspondingly typical EEG patterns representing a maturation of the central nervous system. This points to a close connection between the maturity of the central nervous system and the pain cry.

## 5. SUMMARY

The cry analysis of premature infants showed that the cry signals were more high pitched the more premature the infant. The cry analysis indicated that the fundamental frequency of the pain cry decreased with increasing gestational age and also that the duration of the cry signals lengthened. It seemed as if the turning point in the change of the cry characteristics was about 38 GA when the differences with the pain cry of full-term infants disappeared. Thus, a maturation of the pain cry parallels the maturation of the premature infant. The results have important implications for the use of the pain cry. Because of the differences in cry characteristics according to gestational age, it is important to use gestational-age-matched normals when comparing cries of healthy and sick infants. The results also indicated that there were differences in the cries according to the order of the cry signal in a cry sequence.

## 6. REFERENCES

Backstrom, L., & Kauppinen, M. A. The fetal weight growth. *Journal of the Finnish Medical Association*, 1968, 23, 1553–1557.

Chiswick, M. L., & Milner, R. D. G. Crying vital capacity. Measurement of neonatal lung function. *Archives of Disease in Childhood*, 1976, 51, 22–27.

Dubowitz, L. M. S., Dubowitz, W., & Goldberg, C. Clinical assessment of gestational age in the newborn infant. *Journal of Pediatrics*, 1970, 77, 1–10.

Fisichelli, V. R., & Karelitz, S. The cry latencies of normal infants and those with brain damage. *Journal of Pediatrics*, 1963, 62, 724–734.

Gleiss, J., & Hohn, W. Das Verhalten beim Schreien nach konstanter Schmertzreizung atemgesunder und atemgestorter Neugeborenen. *Deutsche Zeitschrift für Nervenheilkunde*, 1968, 194, 311–317.

Lester, B. M., & Zeskind, P. S. Brazelton scale and physical correlates of neonatal cry features. *Infant Behavior and Development*, 1978, 1, 393–402.

Michelsson, K. Cry analysis of symptomless low birth weight neonates and of asphyxiated newborn infants. *Acta Paediatrica Scandinavica*, (Suppl. 216), 1971.

Michelsson, K., & Wasz-Höckert, O. The value of cry analysis in neonatology and early infancy. In T. Murry & J. Murry (Eds.), *Infant communication: Cry and early speech.* Houston: College Hill Press, 1980.

Michelsson, K., Sirvio, P., & Wasz-Höckert, O. Pain cry in full-term asphyxiated newborn infants correlated with late findings. *Acta Paediatrica Scandinavica*, 1977, 66, 611–616. (a)

Michelsson, K., Sirvio, P., & Wasz-Höckert, O. Sound spectrographic cry analysis of infants with bacterial meningitis. *Developmental Medicine and Child Neurology*, 1977, 19, 309–315. (b)

Michelsson, K., Raes, J., Thodén, C. J., & Wasz-Höckert, O. Sound spectrographic cry analysis in neonatal diagnostics. An evaluative study. *Journal of Phonetics*, 1982, 10, 79–88.

Ostwald, P. F., Phibbs, R., & Fox, S. Diagnostic use of infant cry. *Biology of the Neonate*, 1968, *13*, 68–82.

Parmelee, A. H., Wenner, W. H., Akiyama, Y., Schultz, M., & Stern, E. Sleep states in premature infants. *Developmental Medicine and Child Neurology*, 1967, *9*, 70–77.

Parmelee, A. H., Stern, E., & Harris, A. Maturation of respiration in prematures and young infants. *Neuropaediatrie*, 1972, *3*, 294–304.

Prechtl, H. F. R., & Beintema, D. *The neurological examination of the fullterm newborn infant*. London: Heinemann, 1964.

Ringel, R. L., & Kluppel, D. D. Neonatal crying: A normative study. *Folia Phoniatrica*, 1964, *16*, 1–9.

Sirvio, P., & Michelsson, K. Sound spectrographic cry analysis of normal and abnormal newborn infants. *Folia Phoniatrica*, 1976, *28*, 161–173.

Tenold, J. L., Crowell, D. H., Jones, R. H., Daniel, T. H., McPherson, D. F., & Popper, A. N. Cepstral and stationarity analyses of fullterm and premature infants' cries. *Journal of the Acoustical Society of America*, 1974, *56*, 975–980.

Thodén, C. J., & Koivisto, M. Acoustic analysis of the normal pain cry. In T. Murry & J. Murry (Eds.), *Infant communication: Cry and early speech*. Houston: College Hill Press, 1980.

Wasz-Höckert, O., Lind, J., Vuorenkoski, V., Partanen, T., & Valanne, E. The infant cry. A spectrographic and auditory analysis. *Clinics in Developmental Medicine 29*. Lavenham, Suffolk: Spastics International Medical Publications, 1968.

Wasz-Höckert, O., Koivisto, M. Vuorenkoski, V., & Lind, J. Spectrographic analysis of pain cry in hyperbilirubinemia. *Biology of the Neonate*, 1971, *17*, 260–271.

Wolff, P. H. The natural history of crying and other vocalizations in early infancy. In B. M. Foss (Ed.), *Determinants of infant behaviour IV*. London: Methuen, 1969.

Zeskind, P. S., & Lester, B. M. Acoustic features and auditory perceptions of the cries of newborns with prenatal and perinatal complications. *Child Development*, 1978, *49*, 580–589.

# 6

# The Newborn Infant Cry
## Its Potential Implications for Development and SIDS

RAYMOND H. COLTON, ALFRED STEINSCHNEIDER,
LOIS BLACK, and JOHN GLEASON

## 1. THE CRY AND HEALTH

Human speech is the manifestation of numerous fine motor acts that require precise control and timing. Even in the simplest act of sustaining a vowel, several major physiological systems (e.g., respiratory, auditory, neural) must be precisely coordinated if the speaker is to be successful in completing the act. Continuous speech production requires even more precise timing and dynamic movement. For example, the simple presence or absence of voicing (vibration of the vocal folds) is, itself, a motor gesture requiring precise timing. Without it, a /b/ sound would become a /p/ sound and a /p/ sound would become a /b/. From the very onset of life, human speech is a highly specialized, finely controlled and coordinated behavior requiring intact bodily functions for its proper production.

RAYMOND H. COLTON • Department of Otolaryngology and Communication Science, College of Medicine, Upstate Medical Center, State University of New York, Syracuse, New York 13210.    ALFRED STEINSCHNEIDER • American SIDS Institute, Atlanta, Georgia 30328.    LOIS BLACK and JOHN GLEASON • Department of Psychology, Syracuse University, Syracuse, New York 13210.    The research reported in this chapter was supported in part by contracts (N01-H0-5-2853 and N01-HD-9-2808) and a research grant (1-R01-HD-07460) from the National Institute of Child Health and Human Development.

Disordered speech production is often a reflection of a malfunctioning or deficient physiological system. For example, a hoarse voice may reflect (1) a pathological growth on one or both vocal folds; (2) a unilateral peripheral nerve paralysis; or (3) improper use of the voice (pathophysiology). Nasal speech may result from a (1) cleft palate; (2) short palate; or (3) inadequate velopharyngeal closure. Central neurological deficits may result in slurred articulation as in Parkinsonism or amyotropic lateral sclerosis (among only a few possibilities). Although the exact reason for the disordered speech may be unclear, any malfunction of the many systems required for speech and voice production could result in abnormal speech.

Infants do not possess the physiological and/or neurological maturity for many speech acts. The young infant's immature neurological system imposes some narrow limits on the motor control he or she can achieve with the respiratory, phonatory, or articulatory systems prerequisite for speech. Anatomical differences may further restrict the kinds of sounds or maneuvers the infant can engage in during the speech maturation process. Lieberman (1977) believes that the absence of certain sounds like /i/, /a/, and /u/ in the repertories of nonhuman primates and newborn infants "can be ascribed to the constraints of their supralaryngeal vocal tracts, as well as to the possible lack of neural control of their vocal apparatus" (p. 186). As the body grows and the neurological, phonatory, and respiratory systems mature, speech development accelerates until about the time when the child is 2 years of age and the first words are spoken. Production of the first words by an infant requires a high level of physical and intellectual development. Simple speech acts like crying, cooing, and babbling are also a reflection of the integrity of the speech motor control mechanisms, although they appear at an earlier stage in the infant's development (Lenneberg, 1967; Lester & Zeskind, 1978; Parmelee, 1962).

Phonation is, like speech, a complex integrated physiological act. The major phonatory act of young infants is the cry that may reflect the integrity of the respiratory, laryngeal, or neurological systems. It may also reflect a structural defect or the infant's emotional state. Thus, an infant's cry may be a symptom of a structural or physiological abnormality. That is not to say that the cry itself may be diagnostically significant, and, as Zeskind and Lester (1978) have demonstrated, be used to identify the etiology of a dysfunction. However, just as a hoarse adult voice may be associated with a number of different potential phonatory disorders, the cry of the infant may be associated with a number of different potential disorders also. Among young infants, the cry may be an important screening mechanism that can be used in the absence of, or prior to, more formal physiological testing.

The cry is a multifaceted acoustic event, and thus there are many acoustic variables one could study. If the cry reflects a disordered mechanism, then which of the acoustic cry variables are important to quantify in our effort to relate the cry to the underlying disorder? That question has been the impetus for much of the previous research on the human infant cry (e.g., chapters in Murry & Murry, 1980; also see Fisichelli & Karelitz, 1963; Karelitz & Fisichelli, 1969; Prechtl, Theorell, Gramsbergen, & Lind, 1969; Wasz-Höckert, Lind, Vuorenkoski, Partanen, & Valanne, 1968). Unfortunately, the optimum set of acoustic cry variables has not been found or at least reported in the literature. Thus, it remains for each investigator to define his or her own set of variables to relate to anatomical, physiological, or developmental indices. Perhaps the development of such a standardized set of variables may help resolve some of the puzzling and contradictory findings in the literature.

## 2. THE CRY AND SIDS

One area of infant health that has received considerable research and clinical attention in recent years is the sudden infant death syndrome, or SIDS.

Valdes-Dapena (1980) has reviewed much of the current research concerning the anatomical, physiological, and pathological characteristics of infants who died of SIDS in an attempt to shed some light on the possible physiological variables associated with this tragic event. Little information is available concerning the relationship of these physiological variables and the cry of SIDS infants. Naeye, Messmer, Specht, and Merritt (1976), in a retrospective study, reported that the parents of SIDS victims had noted that their children's cries sounded strange or different when compared to those of siblings or other infants. Stark and Nathanson (1975) reported some experimental data on the relationship between the cry and SIDS. They studied the cries of one male infant who died suddenly at 6 months of age and found the cries to be shorter and weaker when compared to the cries of four non-SIDS infants. In addition, a high proportion of the SIDS cries were associated with glottal voicing and a higher fundamental frequency ($F_0$) with many sudden pitch breaks or shifts.

Colton and Steinschneider (1981) have reported on the cry characteristics of a female SIDS infant who had died of SIDS at the age of 63 days. Fourteen cries were analyzed for their fundamental frequencies, sound pressure levels, center frequencies of the first three formants, as well as the energy in three frequency bands (50 Hz–4 kHz, 4–8 kHz, 8–16 kHz). The SIDS infant exhibited cries in which the fundamental frequency was lower, the duration longer, and the sound pressure levels (overall and in the frequency range from 50 to 4000 Hz) were greater than one standard deviation from the mean of a group of 124 normal control infants and 22 siblings of SIDS victims (normative data reported by Colton & Steinschneider, 1980).

It would appear that there are several differences among the acoustic cry characteristics of SIDS infants when they are compared to the cries of normal infants. In previous research (Colton & Steinschneider, 1981; Stark & Nathanson, 1975), the direction and magnitude of the differences is contradictory. Perhaps these results reflect the notion that there are multiple etiologies associated with SIDS. On the other hand, there may simply not be enough data on the cries of SIDS infants to allow more rigorous statistical testing. Quite simply, we do not know whether or not the cries of SIDS infants are normal or abnormal with respect to their acoustic characteristics.

On the practical side, because the relative incidence of SIDS is small (1–3 per 1000 live births, Valdes-Dapena, 1980), it would be necessary to study extremely large numbers of infants prospectively in order to obtain data on a sufficient number of SIDS cases for statistical purposes. There are, however, several groups of infants that have been identified as at increased risk for SIDS and that are available for study. Such at-risk infants may show several of the many neurological and physiological abnormalities that have been reported in SIDS infants but to a lesser degree. One such group is the siblings of SIDS infants (Froggatt, 1970). Some evidence for this line of reasoning was provided in an article by Colton and Steinschneider (1980) in which the cries of 22 siblings and 124 normal infants were studied. When compared to the normal group, the cries of the siblings exhibited lower fundamental frequencies and higher sound pressure levels in the spectral range from 4 to 8 kHz. The SIDS infant reported by Colton and Steinschneider (1981) also differed from the normal infants on the same acoustic cry measures in the same direction as the SIDS siblings but to a greater degree.

## 3. RESPIRATORY INSTABILITY, SIDS, AND BEHAVIORAL DEVELOPMENT

Subsequent to the hypothesis implicating prolonged sleep apnea as of possible etiologic significance in SIDS (Steinschneider, 1972), infants who have recurrent episodes of prolonged apnea have been identified and studied physiologically. In one such study, it was found that these infants differed from controls by demonstrating more frequent and longer apneic pauses during a nap when observed under controlled laboratory conditions (Steinschneider, 1977). As part of this study, summary measures of respiratory instability were examined that on the one hand incorporated the apneic episodes and on the other discriminated infants with prolonged sleep apnea from controls. A measure of respiratory instability was developed to accomplish these objectives—the PSA-4 score (see page 130 for a more complete definition).

Black, Steinschneider, and Sheehe (1978), utilizing the PSA-4 score to categorize neonates, found that infants with elevated PSA-4 scores (increased respiratory instability) in the first week of life compared to infants classified as demonstrating a low degree of respiratory instability had significantly lower mental and psychomotor development scores (Bayley Scales of Infant Development; Bayley, 1969) when assessed at approximately 9 months of age. In a follow-up study (Black, 1980), the negative effects of the elevated PSA-4 scores on development persisted. Two hypotheses were offered to account for these results. In one, it was suggested that infants with increased neonatal instability subsequently developed prolonged apneic episodes and cerebral anoxia. A second hypothesis considered the possibility that increased neonatal respiratory instability and lower developmental scores were both manifestations of the same underlying central nervous system (CNS) deficit. If this latter hypothesis is valid, the deficit may be sufficiently general in nature to influence the characteristics of neonatal cries.

## 4. PURPOSE OF THIS STUDY

A main purpose of the investigation to be reported in this chapter was to determine the acoustic characteristics of human infant cries recorded during the fourth week of life and to relate these findings to the results of a previous study of the acoustic characteristics of cries recorded during the first week of life (Colton & Steinschneider, 1980). A second purpose was to determine if infants with varying degrees of respiratory instability (low vs. high) exhibited differences in the acoustic characteristics of their cries. We also wished to evaluate the relationship between the cry and respiratory instability measured in the first and fourth weeks of life and developmental indices obtained at 9 months of age. Finally, we hoped that these data would help in our understanding of the processes and possible antecedent events that eventually leads to SIDS.

## 5. PROCEDURE

### 5.1. Infant Groups Studied

The cries of infants in three groups were recorded during the fourth week of life. These groups were (1) full-term infants; (2) premature infants (defined as weighing less than 2500 g); and (3) siblings of SIDS infants. All of these infants had been studied during their first week of life; a description of their cries was reported by Colton and Steinschneider (1980). Measures of neonatal respiratory instability and developmental data were also available for these infants. A summary of characteristics of these three infant groups is shown in Table 1. In all of the summary tables to follow, data will be presented on those infants whose complete set of first- and fourth-week cry data was available. Consequently, the number of subjects in each of the three groups is smaller than the number given in other reports (Black, 1980; Colton & Steinschneider, 1980) in which only the first- or fourth-week data were considered.

### 5.2. Method of Recording Cries

During and immediately after preparing the infant for the sleep study, the infant would emit many spontaneous cries. At these times, the infant was placed supine and about 9 inches away from a Teledyne

Table 1. Summary of Selected Background Variables of Three Infant Groups Whose Cries Were Recorded at 1 Week and 4 Weeks of Age

| Variable | Full-term | Premature | SIDS siblings |
|---|---|---|---|
| Number | 57 | 37 | 19 |
| Birth weight* | | | |
|   Mean | 3419.69  (N=54) | 2184.62 | 3448.11 |
|   SD | 463.79 | 287.86 | 560.94 |
| Years parental education | | | |
|   Mean | 26.58  (N=52) | 25.14  (N=35) | 25.37 |
|   SD | 4.66 | 4.06 | 4.47 |
| Gestational age* | | | |
|   Mean | 39.63  (N=56) | 36.11  (N=36) | 40.22  (N=18) |
|   SD | 1.72 | 5.24 | 1.31 |
| Sex | | | |
|   Males | 31 | 12 | 13 |
|   Females | 26 | 25 | 6 |
| Apgar Score | | | |
|   Mean | 8.29  (N=56) | 7.22  (N=36) | 8.61  (N=18) |
|   SD | 0.73 | 1.62 | 0.85 |

*Differences among the three groups are significant at the .05 level.

Electret microphone attached to the side of the crib. About 2 to 3 minutes of the crying was recorded on a Nakamichi 550 cassette tape recorder. The tape recorder was held in a state of readiness in case the infant should cry during the sleep period. On a few occasions, an infant would cry during the sleep period. On a few occasions, an infant did not cry sufficiently when handled prior to the nap. In these cases, he or she was recorded at the conclusion of the nap when once again, he or she was handled to remove the electrodes.

## 5.3. Analysis of Cries

The analysis of the cries was similar to the method reported by Colton and Steinschneider (1980) and will be reviewed here only briefly.

Five cry segments were analyzed for each infant (a cry segment was at least 500 msec long and separated by another cry segment by at least 100 msec). The following acoustic variables were analyzed:

1. Fundamental frequency ($F_0$ Hz)
2. Overall sound pressure level (dB)
3. Duration (sec)
4. Center frequency of the first formant ($F_1$ Hz)
5. Center frequency of the second formant ($F_2$ Hz)
6. Center frequency of the third formant ($F_3$ Hz)
7. Energy in the frequency range from 50 to 4000 Hz (dB)
8. Energy in the frequency range from 4000 to 8000 Hz (dB)
9. Energy in the frequency range from 8000 to 16000 Hz (dB)

Variable 1 ($F_0$) was measured from narrow band (45 Hz) spectrograms, whereas variables 3 through 6 were measured from wide band spectrograms (450 Hz). Variable 2 and variables 7 to 9 were analyzed using a General Radio 1523 Graphic Level recorder and, where appropriate, after low pass or band pass filtering.

## 5.4. Measures of Infant Development

The Neonatal Behavioral Assessment Scale (Brazelton, 1973) was administered in the hospital nursery within the first week of life. This scale provides for an evaluation of infant state, alertness, irritability, responsiveness to stimulation, reflexes, and habituation. Included within this scale is an assessment of the defensive maneuvers initiated in response to trigimenal stimulation. This scale includes neurological measures from Prechtl and Beintema (1964) and was designed to be used with full-term infants. However, these measures have been employed by Scarr-Salapatek and Williams (1973), among others, in the evaluation of prematurely born infants.

The Mental and Psychomotor scales of the Bayley Scales of Infant Development (Bayley, 1969) were administered at 9 months of age. These scales have been standardized on a nationwide sample.

## 6. RESULTS

The results of the analysis of the cries from the infants in the three groups during the first week of life have been reported elsewhere (Colton & Steinschneider, 1980). Where appropriate, however, these results will be included for purposes of comparison.

### 6.1. Intergroup Cry Comparisons

Table 2 presents a summary of the nine acoustic cry variables measured in the cries of infants in the three groups recorded during the first and fourth weeks of life.

Reviewing the data for the first-week cries presented in Table 2, the full-term infant group exhibits the highest average fundamental frequency followed by the premature group, whereas the SIDS siblings have the lowest average fundamental frequency. The $F_0$ differences among the three infant groups are not, however, statistically significant. The average duration of the cry is similar for all three infant groups.

Formants 1, 2, and 3 reflect the length and configuration of the infants' vocal tract (oral and pharyngeal cavities). In its most simple configuration (uniform cross-sectional area), the human vocal tract is considered to behave acoustically as a tube closed at one end (Fant, 1960; Stevens & House, 1961). From the results in Table 2, the average center frequency of the first formant (first resonance of the tube) is approximately 1600 Hz. This result, although not statistically significant, is somewhat higher than would be predicted from theory for a vocal tract length expected in the very young infants (about 8 cm). We believe that the higher than expected first formant reflects a greater amount of mouth opening than theoretically postulated. The acoustic effect of greater mouth opening is a rise in the frequency of the first formant with a lesser effect on the other formants (Fant, 1960). In general, the sibling group tended to show the highest $F_1$ center frequency.

The four remaining variables reflect the level of the cry either overall or in certain frequency bands. In all of these measures, the siblings

Table 2. Summary of Nine Acoustic Cry Variables Recorded at 1 Week and 4 Weeks of Age for Three Groups of Infants

| Cry variable | Full term (N=57) | | Premature (N=37) | | SIDS siblings (N=19) | |
|---|---|---|---|---|---|---|
| | First | Fourth | First | Fourth | First | Fourth |
| Fundamental frequency (Hz) | | | | | | |
| Mean | 507.18* | 490.79* | 499.89 | 519.54 | 465.16* | 503.32* |
| SD | 91.40 | 60.66 | 107.88 | 53.32 | 64.69 | 74.65 |
| Duration (sec) | | | | | | |
| Mean | 1.23* | 1.33* | 1.22 | 1.24 | 1.22 | 1.38 |
| SD | 0.31 | 0.35 | 0.37 | 0.36 | 0.38 | 0.36 |
| First formant center frequency (Hz) | | | | | | |
| Mean | 1638.19* | 1452.35* | 1635.00 | 1545.95 | 1683.74 | 1729.32 |
| SD | 360.55 | 445.18 | 391.25 | 417.93 | 407.59 | 403.59 |
| Second formant center frequency (Hz) | | | | | | |
| Mean | 3269.77* | 3003.05* | 3394.70 | 3278.32 | 3392.11 | 3368.79 |
| SD | 525.35 | 523.04 | 604.52 | 715.70 | 653.33 | 584.16 |
| Third formant center frequency (Hz) | | | | | | |
| Mean | 5352.96* | 4806.82* | 5633.27 | 5208.92 | 5311.84 | 5371.69 |
| SD | 753.87 | 794.84 | 1285.10 | 972.00 | 1094.29 | 863.14 |
| Overall sound pressure level (dB) | | | | | | |
| Mean | 73.69* | 79.25* | 72.39* | 79.32* | 76.41* | 79.79* |
| SD | 6.97 | 4.27 | 5.74 | 4.97 | 5.71 | 6.32 |
| Spectral Band Number (50–4000 Hz) (dB) | | | | | | |
| Mean | 72.75* | 78.21* | 71.56* | 77.85* | 74.91 | 78.26 |
| SD | 7.47 | 4.80 | 5.93 | 4.81 | 5.56 | 6.33 |
| Spectral Band Number 2 (4000–8000 Hz) (dB) | | | | | | |
| Mean | 63.26 | 62.62 | 64.43 | 62.63 | 69.48 | 63.00* |
| SD | 10.18 | 6.16 | 6.92 | 7.96 | 7.93 | 8.07 |
| Spectral Band Number 3 (8000–16000 Hz) (dB) | | | | | | |
| Mean | 45.03* | 52.74* | 45.99* | 53.33* | 48.42* | 53.02* |
| SD | 8.75 | 5.74 | 7.09 | 4.60 | 6.29 | 6.56 |

*The difference between first and fourth week statistically significant, $p \leq .05$.

exhibited the highest sound pressure level (SPL), with the premature infants second and full-term infants third. The only intergroup difference that was statistically significant, however, was in Spectral Band (SB) Number 2 (4000–8000 Hz). Note in Table 2 that the sibling group is 5 to 7 dB higher than the other groups.

Table 2 also shows the results of the analysis performed on the fourth-week cries. The fundamental frequency of the premature and sibling fourth-week cries is greater than the normal newborns; the differences were not, however, statistically significant. The duration of the fourth-week cries is longer for the full-term and sibling group than for the premature group. Again, the differences among the three infant groups were not statistically significant.

## 6.2. First-versus Fourth-Week Cry Comparisons

In comparison to the first-week cries, the average fundamental frequency of the normal newborns was lower than either of the two other infant groups. As shown in Table 2, the difference of $F_0$ between the first and fourth-week infant cries was not statistically significant.

The duration of the fourth-week cries was longer for the normal newborn and sibling groups when compared to the premature group. Only the first- and fourth-week cry duration of the normal newborns attained statistical significance.

With respect to the resonant characteristics of the vocal tracts of these infants, the center frequencies of the first three formants are highest for the sibling group. For this group, the difference between the first and fourth weeks was not statistically significant. Full-term infants had a slightly lower average $F_1$ center frequency than the other groups. The $F_2$ and $F_3$ center frequency differences among the three infant groups were statistically different. The premature and sibling groups had higher second and third formant frequencies when their cries were recorded at 4 weeks. The average frequency of the three formants in normal newborn cries was lower in the fourth week in comparison to the first week.

The overall sound pressure level as well as the level within spectral bands 1–3 are very similar for the three groups. Overall SPL as well as the level of the highest frequency band (SB No. 3) are greater in the fourth week when compared to the first-week data for all infant groups. These differences are statistically signficant. Furthermore, the variance associated with the fourth-week data is smaller than for the first-week data (except, interestingly, the SIDS siblings fourth-week cries). This result suggests that at 4 weeks of age the infants produced greater energy in their cries; much of this energy was in the higher frequencies (as indicated by the greater energy in SB No. 3) and exercised more control over the acoustic sound pressure level of their cries than at 1 week. This increased control of acoustic level may reflect the infant's increased physiological control, specifically over subglottal air pressure—the major determinant of vocal level in human phonation.

## 6.3. Derived Cry Variables

Inspection of the data in Table 2 reveals that much redundancy exists among the nine cry variables studied. In particular, there are high correlations among the three formant frequencies and the four measures of sound pressure level. In the attempt to reduce this redundancy, we submitted the first-week cry data to a Principal Components Factor Analysis with Varimax rotation. With this procedure, the number of significant cry variables was reduced; the results have been reported in Colton and Steinschneider (1980). A similar procedure was applied to the fourth-week cry data, and the results are shown in Table 3. Four factors were reported, and they accounted for 85% of the original variance among the nine cry measures. The most important factor is labeled a *Level* factor because of its high correlations with overall SPL and with the SPL in the three frequency bands (50–4000 Hz, 4000–8000 Hz, 8000–16000 Hz.) The second factor is called a *Resonance* factor because of its high correlations with the center frequencies of the first three formants. Presumably, this factor reflects the overall resonance characteristics of the infants' vocal tract. The remaining two factors, Fundamental Frequency and Duration, loaded only on their respective variables. Subsequent analysis of the cry data with respect to the physiological and developmental data used these four derived variables.

The results of the factor analyses conducted on the first-week and fourth-week cry data were very similar and suggest a similarity of factor structure in the two sets of data. That is, the acoustic cry factor important in the first-week cries are similar to those in the fourth-week cries.

A more formal comparison of the factor structure of the two sets of cry data was performed using the general method of matrix rotation known as Procrustes Rotation. The specific method used was that developed by Schonemann and Carroll (1970) and Lingoes and Schonemann (1974). In this approach, the elements of one matrix are dilated (or

Table 3. *Rotated Factor Pattern for Nine Acoustic Variables in the Fourth-Week Cries of Three Infant Groups*

| Cry variable | Factors | | | |
| --- | --- | --- | --- | --- |
| | Level | Resonance | $F_0$ | Duration |
| $F_0$ | −0.02 | 0.03 | 1.00 | −0.95 |
| Duration | −0.04 | 0.06 | −0.05 | 0.99 |
| F1 | 0.10 | 0.89 | 0.02 | 0.12 |
| F2 | 0.06 | 0.97 | 0.00 | 0.00 |
| F3 | 0.00 | 0.94 | 0.02 | −0.02 |
| Overall SPL | 0.95 | −0.01 | 0.04 | −0.01 |
| SB No. 1 | 0.92 | −0.05 | 0.01 | 0.06 |
| SB No. 2 | 0.92 | 0.06 | −0.06 | −0.06 |
| SB No. 3 | 0.83 | 0.19 | −0.03 | −0.06 |
| % Variance | 36.64 | 29.67 | 11.14 | 11.23 |

expanded) and/or the columns of the matrix interchanged and/or the entire matrix rotated so as to best approximate another matrix. A measure of fit between the two matrices, called $S$, is computed and is equivalent to 1-R squared. A Procrustes Rotation analysis of the first- and fourth-week cry factor structures resulted in an $S$ of .0327, suggesting that a high degree of redundancy exists between the factor structures of the cries obtained at these two time periods for all three infant groups studied.

## 7. THE CRY AND NEONATAL INSTABILITY

In the work reported here, measures of respiration, eye movement, and electroencephalogram (EEG) were obtained as each infant slept. Each infant was studied in an environmentally controlled room at a temperature of 90°F. Eye movement and EEG were recorded with standard electrodes and techniques, whereas respiration was sensed with a thermister bead taped below one nostril and a mercury strain gauge taped across the chest. After affixing these devices, the infant was allowed to sleep at least 1 hour.

In this study, the PSA-4 score was used as a measure of respiratory instability (Steinschneider, 1977). The PSA-4 score is defined as

$$PSA\text{-}4 = -2.695 + 0.607\,(MT) + 0.023\,(AR) + 0.042\,(AN) - 0.143\,(A/D)$$

where an apneic pause is defined as the cessation of breathing for at least 2 seconds and $MT$ is the mean duration of all apneic pauses; $AR$ is the percentage of REM epochs during which at least one apneic pause was initiated; $AN$ is the percentage of NREM epochs during which at least one apneic pause was initiated; and $A/D$ is $100 \times$ the summed duration of all apneic pauses divided by the duration of the sleep.

In this section, we will discuss the relationship between cry and the PSA-4 score. The principal statistical method used was multiple regression.

The results of the multiple regression analysis performed between the PSA-4 scores and the cry factors observed in the first week of life revealed no statistically significant relationships for any of the three infant groups. Thus, in the first week of life, respiratory instability in an infant is not reflected in the cry.

The results of the multiple regression analyses performed between fourth-week PSA-4 score and the cry factors are shown in Table 4. The only statistically significant result ($p < 0.05$) occurs in the sibling groups

*Table 4. Relationship between PSA-4 and Fourth-Week Cry Factors for 3 Infant Groups*

| Source | Slope estimate | t | p |
|---|---|---|---|
| Full term | | | |
| Intercept | −0.69 | −1.05 | 0.30 |
| $F_0$ | 0.00 | 0.51 | 0.61 |
| Duration | 0.00 | 1.16 | 0.25 |
| Level | 0.04 | 1.73 | 0.09 |
| Resonance | −0.05 | −1.91 | 0.06 |
| Premature | | | |
| Intercept | 1.19 | 1.16 | 0.26 |
| $F_0$ | 0.00 | −0.77 | 0.45 |
| Duration | 0.00 | −1.55 | 0.13 |
| Level | 0.00 | −0.17 | 0.88 |
| Resonance | 0.04 | 1.09 | 0.28 |
| SIDS siblings | | | |
| Intercept | 1.99 | 2.41 | 0.03 |
| $F_0$ | 0.00 | −0.67 | 0.51 |
| Duration | 0.00 | −2.37 | 0.03 |
| Level | −0.03 | −0.99 | 0.34 |
| Resonance | 0.02 | 0.42 | 0.68 |

where there is a significant inverse relationship between the duration of the cry and apnea, that is, the shorter the duration of the cry, the greater (more positive) the PSA-4 score and presumably the greater the respiratory instability during sleep.

## 8. THE CRY, NEONATAL BEHAVIOR, AND MENTAL AND PSYCHOMOTOR DEVELOPMENT

The data to be reported in this section should be considered preliminary inasmuch as the number of subjects is small and the number of tests conducted is large to permit more definitive conclusions, at least statistically. In view of the large number of statistical tests conducted and the relatively small numbers of infants, statistically significant chance results are probable among the data reported in Tables 5 and 6. In the discussion that follows, we will highlight those findings that are statistically significant and consistent either within a group or across the time periods studied.

In addition, although we assessed the relationship between the Brazelton scores, cry, and the Bayley Test given at 9 months of age, there were no statistically significant trends between the cry factors and the Brazelton even when the PSA-4 score was included in the analysis.

*Table 5. Relationship between MDI, PDI , and  MDI/PDI  Indices of the Bayley Test and 4 Cry Factors for Full-Term Infants' First-Week Cries[a]*

| Dependent variable | Cry factors | Slope estimate | t | p |
|---|---|---|---|---|
| MDI | $F_0$ | - 0.006 | −0.26 | 0.80 |
| | Duration | -11.138 | −1.98 | 0.05 |
| | Level | 0.388 | 0.63 | 0.53 |
| | Resonance | − 1.049 | −1.49 | 0.15 |
| PDI | $F_0$ | 0.043 | 1.21 | 0.24 |
| | Duration | − 2.577 | −0.33 | 0.74 |
| | Level | − 0.958 | −1.11 | 0.27 |
| | Resonance | 0.308 | 0.29 | 0.78 |
| MDI/PDI | $F_0$ | 0.056 | 0.97 | 0.34 |
| | Duration | − 7.664 | −0.53 | 0.60 |
| | Level | 0.113 | 0.08 | 0.94 |
| | Resonance | − 0.500 | −0.29 | 0.77 |

[a]$N = 54$.

The results of a multiple regression analysis performed between the Mental Development Index (MDI) and the Psychomotor Development Index (PDI) as well as a pooled MDI/PDI score of the Bayley Test are shown in Table 5. The results of a similar analysis performed on the fourth-week cry factors are shown in Table 6.

For the full-term infant group, there is a significant inverse relationship between the first-week and the fourth-week infant cry duration and MDI (Table 5). The same relationship attained statistical significance for the pooled MDI/PDI measure. This result suggests that longer cries are associated with lower MDI levels. With respect to this finding, Michelsson and Wasz-Höckert (1980) report that infants with some form of

*Table 6. Relationship between MDI, PDI, and MDI/PDI Indices of the Bayley Test and 4 Cry Factors for Full-Term Infants' Fourth-Week Cries[a]*

| Variable | Cry factors | Slope estimate | t | p |
|---|---|---|---|---|
| MDI | $F_0$ | − 0.007 | −0.24 | 0.82 |
| | Duration | − 9.687 | −2.00 | 0.05 |
| | Level | − 0.277 | −0.55 | 0.59 |
| | Resonance | 0.233 | 0.38 | 0.70 |
| PDI | $F_0$ | − 0.044 | −0.79 | 0.43 |
| | Duration | −14.568 | −1.88 | 0.07 |
| | Level | − 0.385 | -0.44 | 0.66 |
| | Resonance | 2.011 | 2.03 | 0.05 |
| MDI/PDI | $F_0$ | − 0.071 | −1.01 | 0.32 |
| | Duration | − 21.423 | -2.00 | 0.05 |
| | Level | 0.869 | −0.67 | 0.51 |
| | Resonance | 2.748 | 1.89 | 0.07 |

[a]$N = 54$.

brain damage or central nervous system dysfunction (especially infants with asphyxia) show greater cry durations than other normal or abnormal groups of infants. Although it is not necessarily true that low MDI scores are solely the result of central nervous system dysfunction or damage, it is possible that both cry duration and low MDI may be related to the same cause. No significant relationships were found between PDI or the pooled MDI/PDI scores and the four first-week cry factors.

The only significant relationship occurred between the Resonance cry factor and PDI in the fourth week. This relationship is not seen in the first-week cries and although high for the pooled MDI/PDI scores, it is statistically nonsignificant. Interpretation of this relationship is made difficult because little is known about the shape and length changes of the infant's vocal tract during a cry. However, it may reflect a full-term infant's psychomotor maturation and ability for control of some of the dynamic motions of his or her upper air way or oral cavity.

With respect to the premature infant group, there are no significant relationships between first-week cry factors and MDI although the first-week cry duration/PDI relationship is strong (Table 7).

There is a significant and positive relationship between the premature infant group's fourth-week cry sound pressure level and PDI (Table 8). Unlike the full-term infant, as the premature infant's psychomotor skills mature, he or she achieves greater control of the expiratory breath stream (see Langolis, Baken, & Wilder, 1960). Better respiratory control may result in stronger cries or cries that dynamically

Table 7. Relationship between MDI, PDI, and MDI/PDI Indices of the Bayley Test and 4 Cry Factors for Premature Infants' First-Week Cries[a]

| Variable | Cry factors | Slope estimate | $t$ | $p$ |
|----------|-------------|----------------|-----|-----|
| MDI | $F_0$ | 0.010 | 0.35 | 0.73 |
|  | Duration | 8.500 | 0.86 | 0.40 |
|  | Level | − 0.657 | − 0.72 | 0.47 |
|  | Resonance | − 0.644 | − 0.51 | 0.62 |
| PDI | $F_0$ | 0.006 | 0.19 | 0.85 |
|  | Duration | 16.779 | 1.83 | 0.08 |
|  | Level | − 0.194 | − 0.20 | 0.85 |
|  | Resonance | − 0.734 | − 0.60 | 0.55 |
| MDI/PDI | $F_0$ | 0.011 | 0.20 | 0.84 |
|  | Duration | 26.012 | 1.24 | 0.22 |
|  | Level | − 0.585 | − 0.30 | 0.76 |
|  | Resonance | − 1.176 | − 0.44 | 0.67 |

[a]$N = 35$.

*Table 8. Relationship between MDI, PDI, and MDI/PDI of the Bayley Test and 4 Cry Factors for Premature Infants' Fourth Week Cries[a]*

| Variable | Cry factors | Slope estimate | t | p |
|----------|-------------|----------------|------|------|
| MDI      | $F_0$       | 0.047          | 0.95 | 0.36 |
|          | Duration    | −10.546        | −1.11 | 0.28 |
|          | Level       | 0.350          | 0.37 | 0.71 |
|          | Resonance   | 0.368          | 0.30 | 0.77 |
| PDI      | $F_0$       | 0.080          | 1.18 | 0.26 |
|          | Duration    | − 2.033        | −0.19 | 0.85 |
|          | Level       | 3.595          | 2.98 | 0.01 |
|          | Resonance   | − 0.769        | −0.60 | 0.56 |
| MDI/PDI  | $F_0$       | 0.018          | 0.14 | 0.89 |
|          | Duration    | −21.462        | −0.94 | 0.36 |
|          | Level       | 3.373          | 1.65 | 0.12 |
|          | Resonance   | 0.933          | 0.32 | 0.75 |

[a]$N = 35$.

vary in their sound pressure level. There are no significant relationships between any of the first-week or fourth-week cry factors and the pooled MDI/PDI index of development of the Bayley Scales.

We are not reporting the results of the statistical tests in which the relationships between the Cry and the Bayley tests were explored in the sibling group. The number of infants in the sibling groups was too small to permit any meaningful statistical conclusions. Two trends may be of interest, however, and they underscore the need for additional cry developmental data for this group. First, there appears to be a strong negative relationship between the fourth-week Fundamental Frequency factor and the MDI scale for the sibling group. Second, we observed a strong positive relationship between the Resonance cry factor in the first week of life and the MDI scale. These findings could be due to chance, or they may reflect slight differences in the physiological maturation of the sibling infant in contrast to a non-SIDS sibling. One may speculate that these differences reflect a different neurophysiological process or dysfunction in the SIDS sibling infant. Further study of the possibility seems warranted.

## 9. THE CRY, RESPIRATORY INSTABILITY, AND DEVELOPMENT: IMPLICATIONS FOR INFANTS AT RISK

One of the results reported in this chapter is that there is greater respiratory instability in infants at risk for SIDS. The causative factors for this instability are not known exactly, but they could be peripheral abnormalities or dysfunctions (e.g., obstruction in the air way), or they could be central in origin. Furthermore, the respiratory instability observed has occurred when the infant was sleeping. We know little about the characteristics of the respiratory system or the degree of respiratory instability when the infant is awake. These factors should be considered when evaluating the relationship between respiratory instability, cry, and development.

One could hypothesize that the underlying cause of the respiratory instability during sleep, the different acoustic cry characteristics, and the delayed development of the SIDS sibling (and by analogy the SIDS victim) are due to some form of central nervous system dysfunction. This presumed dysfunction could be a localized lesion, affecting only parts of the respiratory system. It may, however, reflect a more diffuse deficit with a more generalized effect. Although not conclusive, the data reported here fail to support the notion of a generalized, diffuse central nervous system dysfunction. Perhaps the more localized CNS dysfunction hypothesis is, at the present time, the most tenable. Other hypotheses need also be considered if we are to fully understand these relationships among respiratory instability, cry, and development.

In spite of difficulties with the large number of variables and subjects, the relationships between cry and later development exist and suggest that knowledge of the infant cry characteristics, even in the first week of life, may assist in the prediction of the later development of the infant. Furthermore, with respect to those infants at risk for SIDS, the cry may provide significant and additional sources of information about the severity of the infant's physiological distress, thereby assisting the physician in any decision concerning intervention. Analysis of cry characteristics is also noninvasive, and recordings can be obtained with a minimum of equipment. In the future, the analysis of the cry may become more automated, allowing for a more routine clinical use (Golub, 1979).

We should stress one last important generalization—the deficits noted, although significant for groups of infants, do not appear to be a product of a few deviant cases. Rather, we are observing many cases with small differences, largely within a normal range. These small differences in combination with others may provide the means for identifying those infants at risk for prolonged sleep apnea, delayed development, or SIDS.

## 10. REFERENCES

Bayley, N. *Manual for the Bayley Scales of Infant Development*. New York: The Psychological Corp., 1969.

Black, L. *Sleep apnea and SIDS: Developmental correlates* (Final report of NICHD contract N01-HD-9-2808). Syracuse University, Syracuse, N.Y., 1981.

Black, L., Steinschneider, A., & Sheehe, P. Neonatal respiratory instability, home apnea monitors and infant development. *Child Development*, 1978, *50*, 561–564.

Brazelton, T. B. Neonatal Behavior Assessment Scale. *Clinics in Developmental Medicine 50.* Philadelphia: Lippincott, 1973.

Colton, R. H., & Steinschneider, A. Acoustic relationships of infant cries to the sudden infant death syndrome. In T. Murry & J. Murry (Eds.), *Infant communication: Cry and early speech.* Houston: College Hill Press, 1980.

Colton, R. H., & Steinschneider, A. The cry characteristics of an infant who died of the sudden infant death syndrome. *Journal of Hearing Disorders*, 1981, *46*, 359–363.

Fant, G. *Acoustic theory of speech production.* The Hague: Mouton, 1960.

Fisichelli, V. R., & Karelitz, S. The cry latencies of normal infants and those with brain damage. *Journal of Pediatrics*, 1963, *62*, 624–634.

Froggatt, P. Epidemiologic aspects of the Northern Ireland study. In A. Bergman, J. E. Beckwith, & C. G. Ray (Eds.), *Sudden Infant Death syndrome.* Seattle: University of Washington Press, 1970.

Golub, H. A physioacoustic model of the infant cry and its use for medical diagnosis and prognosis. In J. Wolf & D. Klatt (Eds.), *Speech communication papers.* New York: Acoustic Society of America, 1979.

Karelitz, S., & Fisichelli, V. Infant's vocalizations and their significance. *Clinical Pro Child Hospital*, 1969, *25*, 345–361.

Langlois, A., Baken, R. J., & Wilder, C. Pre-speech respiratory behavior during the first year of life. In T. Murry & J. Murry (Eds.), *Infant communication: Cry and early speech.* Houston: College Hill Press, 1980.

Lenneberg, E. H. *Biological foundation of language.* New York: Wiley, 1967.

Lester, B. M., & Zeskind, P. Brazelton scale and physical correlates of neonatal cry features. *Infant Behavior and Development*, 1978, *4*, 393–402.

Lieberman, P. *Speech physiology and acoustic phonetics: An introduction.* New York: Macmillan, 1977.

Lingoes, J. C., & Schonemann, P. H. Alternative measures of fit for the Schonemann–Carroll matrix fitting algorithm. *Psychometrika*, 1974, *39*, 423–427.

Michelsson, K., & Wasz-Höckert, O. The value of cry analysis in neonatology and early infancy. In T. Murry & J. Murry (Eds.), *Infant communication: Cry and early speech.* Houston: College Hill Press, 1980.

Murry, T., & Murry, J. (Eds.). *Infant communication: Cry and early speech.* Houston: College Hill Press, 1980.

Naeye, R. L., Messmer, III, J., Specht, T., & Merritt, T. A. Sudden Infant Death syndrome temperament before death. *Journal of Pediatrics*, 1976, *88*, 511–515.

Parmelee, A. H. Infant crying and neurological diagnosis. *Journal of Pediatrics* 1962, *61*, 801–802.

Prechtl, H., & Beintema, D. Neurological examinations of the full term newborn infant. *Little Cub Clinics in Developmental Medicine 12.* London: William Heinemann Medical Books, 1964.

Prechtl, H., Theorell, K., Gramsbergen, A., & Lind, J. Statistical analysis of cry patterns in normal and abnormal newborn infants. *Developmental Medicine and Child Neurology*, 1969, *11*, 142–152.

Scarr-Salapatek, S., & Williams, D. The effects of early stimulation on low birth weight infants. *Child Development*, 1973, *44*, 94–101.

Schonemann, P. H., & Carroll, R. M. Fitting one matrix to another under choice of central dilation and a rigid motion. *Psychometrika*, 1970, *35*, 245–255.

Stark, R. E., & Nathanson, S. Unusual features of cry in an infant dying suddenly and unexpectedly. In J. Bosma & J. Showacre (Eds.), *Development of upper respiratory anatomy and function: Implications for Sudden Infant Death syndrome*. Washington, DC: U.S. Department of Health, Education and Welfare, 1975.

Steinschneider, A. Prolonged sleep apnea and the Sudden Infant Death syndrome: Clinical and laboratory observations. *Pediatrics*, 1972, *50*, 646–654.

Steinschneider, A. Prolonged sleep apnea and the Sudden Infant Death syndrome: Clinical and laboratory observations. *Pediatrics*, 1972, *50*, 646–654.

Steinschneider, A. Prolonged sleep apnea and respiratory instability: A discrimination study. *Pediatrics*, 1977, *59*, 962–970.

Stevens, K., & House, A. An acoustical theory of vowel production and some of its implications. *Journal of Speech and Hearing Research*, 1961, *4*, 303–320.

Valdes-Dapena, M. *Sudden unexplained infant death: An evolution in understanding*. Rockville, MD: DPED Public Health Service, 1980.

Wasz-Höckert, O., Lind, J., Vuorenkoski, U., Partanen, T., & Valanne, E. The infant cry: A spectrographic and auditory analysis. *Clinics in Development Medicine 29*. London: Heineman, 1968.

Zeskind, P., & Lester, B. Acoustic features and auditory perceptions of the cries of newborns with prenatal and perinatal complications. *Child Development*, 1978, *49*, 580–589.

# 7

# The Communicative and Diagnostic Significance of Infant Sounds

## PETER F. OSTWALD AND THOMAS MURRY

## 1. INTRODUCTION

Our interest in the cry behavior of infancy stems from a general concern with the clinical significance of human sound. Audible sonic events appear to serve a unique function in social communication, facilitating the exchange of information not only in those precise, phonetic forms called speech but also in more ambiguous ways, via emotional expressions, music, and noises. Sounds are known to have alerting as well as sedating properties. They enter into many aspects of interpersonal relationships and seem to play an especially vital role in the regulation of intimacy. Thus, an infant with its fascinating acoustic repertoire and a mother with her special attachment to the tiny soundmaker offer rich opportunities for scientific research. In this chapter, we will invite the readers' attention to five dimensions of this subject area that are of particular interest to us: (1) the context of infant crying behavior; (2) its

PETER F. OSTWALD • Department of Psychiatry, Langley Porter Psychiatric Institute, School of Medicine, University of California at San Francisco, San Francisco, California 94143.    THOMAS MURRY • Audiology and Speech Pathology Service, Veterans Administration Medical Center, San Diego, California 92161.

patterning in disease and health; (3) factors that influence cry performance; (4) methodological issues; and (5) the communicative function of
crying.

## 2. THE CONTEXT OF INFANT CRY BEHAVIOR

A fundamental assumption underlying our work in this field is
that crying establishes a continuity between prenatal biological inter-
dependence of mother and child and their postnatal environment of
gradually increasing distance. Thus, the antecedents for cry behavior
seem to appear long before birth. Tryphena Humphrey's (1969) beautiful
cinematic studies of very young fetuses demonstrate clearly a variety of
spontaneous and induced movements that foreshadow later behavior.
For example, when touched near the mouth, a 7½-week fetus—merely
an inch long—turns away from the stimulus. A week later, it shows
more extensive body rotation and begins to open its mouth and to spread
its fingers when stimulated. By 11 weeks of age, the mouth snaps open
and shut in a reflex fashion, taking less than 1 second. Swallowing,
ventral flexion of the head, and coordinated movements between mouth,
face, and arms follow shortly, and by 14 weeks of age, inspiratory gasps
and rib cage movements can be elicited by tickling the fetus.

These observations suggest a very early integration of behavior,
due presumably to closing of the neural tube at the midcervical level
that allows nerve cells located there to begin functioning earlier than
those in the lower parts of the body. Bergström (1969) reports electrical
activity in the fetal nervous sytem as early as the 10th week. The pontine
brain stem, so essential in coordinating motor behavior later on, begins
to mature around this time. Mothers may begin to perceive fetal movements during the 15th to 16th weeks of pregnancy, and this perception
heralds, in our opinion, the onset of the desire to engage in communication with the child. Mothers (and, of course, fathers who discuss
such matters with their spouses) form mental images of the baby they
will have, expectations that are reinforced when the nurse or the doctor
listens to the fetal heart beat, a baby's first audible sound.

What, if anything, does a fetus hear before birth? Attempts have
been made to record intrauterine sounds, and Armitage, Baldwin, and
Vince (1980) have successfully placed a hydrophone into the amniotic
sacs of fetal lambs during gestation. They describe definite noises from
within the mother—swallowing, drinking, breathing, and muscle movements—as well as "periods of quiet." More remarkable is that sounds
external to the mother were also transmitted, attenuated by 16 to 37

decibels. Conversation at normal levels outside the animal often could be understood, and one is led to the assumption that similar events take place during a human pregnancy. Indeed, the human auditory system matures remarkably quickly. The middle ear and inner ear structures attain nearly full-adult size by the fifth month of gestation, and Tanner (1970) reports that fibers of the sound-receiving system of the brain begin to myelinate during the sixth fetal month. The late Philip Peltzman (Ostwald & Peltzman, 1974) succeeded in recording fetal electroencephalographic responses to acoustical stimuli prior to birth. It thus seems fair to assume that the neonate probably emerges into light and air with auditory experiences, which are registered perhaps subcortically in the form of early rhythm and tone memories. That might help to explain why infants as early as 3 days postpartum are able not only to discriminate their mothers' voice but also to indicate a definite preference for this familiar acoustical pattern (De Casper & Fifer, 1980).

The baby has, by this time, already become a fairly accomplished soundmaker. Excellent sound films are available to document the various "cries, struggles, and coughs" (Bosma, Truby, & Lind, 1966) emitted at birth. It has even been reported that if air leaks into the amniotic sac, babies may cry before birth (Thiery, Yo Le Sian, Vrijens, & Janssens, 1973). Environmental influence immediately starts shaping an infant's behavioral repertoire. For example, late clamping of the umbilical cord has an effect on vocal output (Yao, Lind, & Vuorenkoski, 1971). Ostwald's study of a male infant's first 24 hours (1963) showed that some of the most intense, hyperphonated screams occurred during circumcision, whereas other cries, whines, squeaks, and oral noises seemed related to the nursing care received as well as the baby's inner states of arousal and quiescence. Three internal mechanisms appear to be involved in neonatal vocalization, each reflecting physiological processes that are not as yet completely understood. Periodicity of the central nervous system (CNS) regulation of diurnal cycles from deepest sleep to maximal awakeness is one process; coordination of laryngeal actions with respiratory cycles is another. The third process seems to involve a neonate's nutritional state, now that after months of continuous umbilical feeding, he or she is dependent upon a discontinuous oral input. Hence, the appearance, at regular intervals, of spontaneous "hunger" cries.

Our first systematic exploration of infant cries focused on these spontaneous expressions of emotion. We visited the homes of 32 newborn babies and we studied 16 pairs of twins along many dimensions to assess the differential effects of heredity and environment. On the basis of clinical experience with older twins, we assumed that the cries of identical, monozygotic babies would be more similar than fraternal, dizygotic pairs. To maximize the effects of internal factors on the cry sounds, we avoided any form of external stimulation that might arouse the babies. To our surprise, there was no correlation between zygocity and crying (Ostwald, Freedman, & Kurtz, 1962). Some pairs that sounded almost identical were, in fact, twins whose blood tests showed unmistakable genetic dizygocity. Thus, we concluded that developmental processes that may be active long before a newborn has ever emitted a cry sound (for example, single placenta monozygocity) could substantially influence the quality and quantity of its crying after birth.

## 3. THE PATTERNING OF INFANT CRIES

Several other investigators have demonstrated that the patterning of infant vocalization is subject to prenatal influences. For convenience, these studies are separated into (1) genetic; (2) growth; and (3) toxic factors. Readers should be reminded that future research will probably show interactions between these factors. (Methodological problems currently make it extremely difficult to analyze such interactions.)

### 3.1. Genetic Anomalies

One of the first disturbances to be studied was Down's syndrome, a diffuse brain disorder resulting from chromosome reduplication. Fisichelli, Haber, Davis, and Karelitz (1966), in a study of 21 afflicted infants, observed that the amount of crying was significantly reduced and that individual cries were of shorter duration, more monotonous, and more difficult to evoke than with normals. In their spectrographic study, Wasz-Höckert, Lind, Vuorenkoski, Partanen, and Valanne (1968) established the following acoustic parameters: a typically flat melody form, low pitch, periodic high tension (especially when attacks of glottal "pressure" are superimposed on the phonation), and half voicing. It proved possible to train auditors in the correct identification of these cries after only 5 minutes of work with a test tape.

Cries of an infant afflicted with Trisomy 13–15 syndrome have been described by Ostwald, Peltzman, Greenberg, and Meyer (1970). We found an unusually hard or abrupt onset of phonation, unsteady or quavery pitch patterns, and a marked drop of pitch at the end of each cry. The spectrograms revealed excessively long durations of individual cries, containing as many as four distinguishable microsegments within which the typical tonal instabilities seemed to take place. A striking feature of the frequency patterns of these cries was the unusually low pitch level at the end of each phonation; one cry terminated at 100 Hz, whereas none remained above 250 Hz. Clicklike noises possibly resulting from glottal activity were noted near the end of several cries.

A study of the Smith-Lemli-Optiz syndrome (Wasz-Höckert, Simila, Rosenberg, Vuorenkoski, & Lind, 1969) reveals a flat melody contour in eight of the nine cries analyzed, some of which were of unusually long duration. However, the late age of these cases—one child was already 2 years old when tape-recorded—makes comparison with neonatal cry patterns difficult.

Cri-du-chat syndrome, so named because of the strikingly abnormal pattern of vocalization, has been described in several studies. Luchsinger, Dubois, Vasselli, Joss, Gloor, and Wiesman (1967) showed the typically high fundamental tone in spectrograms plus the pronounced upper formants (at 4000 Hz). Vuorenkoski, Lind, Partanen, Lejeune, Lafourcade, and Wasz-Höckert (1966) also called attention to the dichotomous and inspiration/expiration cry types found in such cases plus the absence of vocal fry and the presence of pitch levels at or above 600 Hz, which makes these babies sound so characteristically feline.

Michelsson, Tuppurainen, and Aula, in Helsinki (1980), have recently analyzed 135 pain cries from 14 children with various karyotype abnormalities. Those who had an anomaly of chromosome 4 or 5 showed significantly higher fundamental frequencies than the controls. The cri-du-chat group had a flat, monotonous melody, whereas those children with 13- or 18-trisomy manifested hoarse, low-pitched cries without shift. Michelsson and Wasz-Höckert (1980) summarized the pitch and melody contours of a variety of genetic and other disease factors.

## 3.2. Growth Factors

In her study of 310 neonates, Michelsson (1980) divided a subgroup of 105 low-birth-weight infants into those who were small for date and those who were delivered prematurely. This enabled her to show that the cries of small-for-date neonates resembled those of healthy, normal-birth-weight infants much more than those of prematures, which differed significantly in terms of the location of the fundamental frequency ($F_0$), the maximum pitch of shift, and the occurrence of biphonation and gliding. The signals were more high pitched the more immature the neonate; the increase in minimum pitch was significant in the smaller prematures; and the maximum pitch was significantly increased in all prematures irrespective of gestational age. Unfortunately, it was not possible to do follow-up studies to find out how long these changes persist. It is thus difficult to distinguish between temporary and more permanent effects of prematurity on the developing cry. That criticism pertains to much of the research on infant cry reported to date. Michelsson, however, has compared her data with cries obtained from asphyxiated newborn infants, a group that shows many of the abnormalities reported by others who have studied the cries of so-called brain-damaged babies (Wasz-Höckert *et al.*, 1968). She reports striking differences between the cries of infants whose oxygen depletion resulted from peripheral respiratory distress—increased duration of phonation, increase in the crying period, higher pitch, occurrence of biphonation—and of those with central respiratory failure.

Complicating conditions have also been studied—hydrocephalus and jaundice, for example (Sirvio & Michelsson, 1976). It is from these investigations, with careful sound-spectrographic analysis, that one gains a sense of confidence in the potential diagnostic value of cry analysis. Certain acoustical features seem almost pathognomonic—for example, furcation with jaundice, biphonation with cerebral lesions, and noise concentrations in cases of brain damage associated with herpes infection.

## 3.3. Toxic Influences

An ingenious demonstration of the diagnostic value of abnormalities of the cry is the study of variations in birth cries of newborn infants from heroin-addicted mothers. Blinick, Tavolga, and Antopol (1971) collected 31 such cases and proposed a schema of three types of patterns for comparing them with 338 nonaddicted babies. Distinct abnormalities of crying were noted in 53 cases, and there was a strong association between cry abnormality and heroin abuse. Even in the Type II category of "common variants" (long duration, low intensity, strong distortion, high pitch, low pitch, and strong inspiration), every individual from a drug-addicted mother seems to produce a high-pitched squealing cry (Blinick *et al.*, 1971).

Some of the previously mentioned prenatal influences merge, of course, with peri- and postnatal effects, for example, hyperbilirubinemia, which may compromise a child's development in the first week of life and produce those cry anomalies that have been described by the Scandinavian group of investigators (Wasz-Höckert, Koivisto, Vuorenkoski, Partanen, & Lind, 1971). In our study of the diagnostic potentials inherent in cry analysis, we searched for general characteristics that might give early warning of disease. Specifically, we wanted to know whether the two acoustical features that have so often been implicated, namely, duration and pitch of expiratory phonation, showed any relationship to clinical evaluation of the babies (Ostwald, Phibbs, & Fox,

1968). Diagnostic rating based on all clinical data available about each infant and the mother plus the postpartum history were felt to be preferable to specific disease categories because it often happened that pediatricians, in spite of considerable knowledge of the case, could not make a definite diagnosis, even postmortem.

We were able to categorize 13 babies this way (Group 1, five normals; Group 2, five questionably impaired; Group 3, three abnormals). The analysis of 356 cries showed that only among the questionably impaired infants (Group 2) were there any excessively long vocalizations of the type reported by Lind, Wasz-Höckert, Vuorenkoski, and Valanne (1965). Normals (Group 1) could not be differentiated from abnormals (Group 3) on the basis of duration, which averaged 1.29 seconds among the former and 1.23 seconds among the latter. The occurrence of longer durations (1.62 seconds) in Group 2 remains unexplained. This might have been a statistical artifact produced by the inclusion of one infant in the group whose cries were persistently prolonged (25 cries; range from 1.00 to 6.65 seconds; mean 2.02; SD 1.07). This infant had had a perilous course, with repeated intrauterine transfusions because of Rh incompatiblity, a C-section delivery, and lengthy hospitalization. Of interest also was the persistence of auditory unresponsiveness in this child, suggesting deafness. Jones (1965) has described greater variability of cry duration among deaf children. Or, it may be that these cry prolongations reflect some temporary change of homeostasis among impaired infants due, as Lester and Zeskind (1982) have suggested, to the loss of parasympathetic inhibition.

Expiratory cry pitch proved to have a more positive diagnostic value in our study. Cries of excessively high pitch occurred only among those infants who were questionably impaired or definitely abnormal (Groups 2 and 3) and not in the normal group. In Group 1 only two infants reached a higher level than 600 Hz in the course of a single cry, and none ever achieved this level either at onset or termination of a cry. Although the question of statistical artifacts may be raised again—unequal numbers of cries were included in the three groups that, among themselves, were not equally balanced—little doubt can remain that a persistently elevated cry pitch points to serious trouble. One of the children in Group 3 died at 3 months with severe cardiopulmonary anomalies, having completely failed to develop normally. His pitches went as high as 900 Hz at the beginning and 1100 Hz at the peak of crying. Of additional interest in this case was that we had difficulty obtaining *any* cries from this infant when he was only 2 days old and before other signs of pathology had as yet been disclosed. One Group 3 infant suddenly died at age 7 months, after emitting some of the most extraordinarily hyperphonic cries we have ever heard or recorded in our laboratory. Stark and Nathanson (1975) have reported similar "high and extremely high" pitches among SIDS infants. Colton and Steinschneider (1980) have reported high-frequency cries from both SIDS infants and their siblings.

However, before too much confidence is expressed in the validity of acoustical analysis as a clinical tool, let us look at some of the factors that influence cry performance in infancy.

## 4. FACTORS THAT INFLUENCE CRY PERFORMANCE

Infant cry is a product of the respiratory and phonatory systems whose output has been shown to have a high degree of variability with regard to pitch and intensity. Perhaps the respiratory system, which is undergoing rapid maturational changes, accounts for much of the variability. The breathing rate of an infant varies as a function of age, health, general activity, and the presence of vocalization. Initially, as Fisichelli *et al.* (1966) have pointed out, there is inspiratory voicing in the neonatal cry. This inspiratory sound often makes it difficult to identify an expiratory cycle. As the infant matures, these vocalized inspiratory periods become more like sobs, and virtually all cry becomes expiratory. Langlois, Baken and Wilder (1980) reported that at the age of 1 month, the quiet breathing rate is 87 breaths per minute (bpm) and 50 bpm while crying. This gradually decreases to 42 quiet bpm and 19 bpm for crying at the end of 1 year. The rate of 19 bpm is very close to the adult breathing rate of approximately 16 bpm. Thus, by 1 year of age, infants have acquired the quick inspiratory and long expiratory phases of respiration associated with adult speech and breathing. Shortly after birth, the infant adds to the abdominal movement of early cry by involving the thorax. After 6 months, rib cage movements and the activity of the costal cartilages allow for deeper breathing, leading to the reduced rates of ventilation.

Crying behavior varies according to the cry-evoking events or stimuli. The birth cry, which is a unique sequence of vocal behaviors made within minutes of birth, may be partially pain related as well as hunger and environmentally related. The infant is taken from a dark, warm, quiet environment with a nutritional source and is subjected to noise and noxious stimuli. This results in a cry that has a short repetitive cycle (due primarily to the infant's respiratory characteristics) and a relatively high average fundamental frequency, presumably due to the high laryngeal position (Lieberman, Harris, Wolff, & Russell, 1971; Truby, Bosma, & Lind, 1965). Thus, the birth cry is primarily a response to the infant's external stimulus. Further, it serves to assist in the cardiorespiratory organization in the new environment.

Following the birth cry, the infant cries for several possible reasons: pain, hunger, discomfort, or startle (shock). Early work by Sherman (1927) also considered anger and fear; however, these states are difficult to verify. There is now evidence to show that as early as 2 weeks of age, the cry-evoking situation contributes to a distinct acoustic profile. Murry, Gracco, and Gracco (1979) reported on one infant who produced cries prior to feeding (hunger) and prior to having her diaper changed (discomfort). At 2 weeks of age, the hunger cries were characterized by a higher fundamental frequency of phonation ($F_0$), greater $F_0$ range, longer mean cry durations, a larger proportion of phonation to silence, and a more complex melodic countour than the discomfort cry. The discomfort cries with their limited $F_0$ range and higher incidence of a flat melody were interpreted as reflecting the constraint or physiological tension associated with discomfort. Although these results suggest an early discriminative use of cry by an infant, it must be remembered that withholding food or allowing the infant to remain in a soiled diaper actually may be interpreted as two variations of a discomforting situation.

Most of the literature describes pain and hunger cries as the two cry types used in the study of infant cry behavior. A third—startle—has been used in several recent investigations. These three types have been operationally defined by us as well as by other investigators (Michelsson & Wasz-Höckert, 1980; Murry, 1980). Pain cry is considered as any cry from suddenly inflicting a painful stimulus to the infant. Muller, Hollien, and Murry (1974) stung the base of the foot with a rubber band. Others have recorded the cry coincident with taking a blood sample. Still others have used a pin prick on the heel of the foot to elicit the pain cry.

The hunger cry is usually defined as the cry produced by withholding food from the infant at the normal feeding time. In some instances, feeding is begun and then stopped, resulting in what is operationally defined as a hunger cry. The startle cry has been elicited in a number of ways, from a loud clap near the infant's head to suddenly dropping the child toward a table top.

Prior to the controlled investigations of the 1960s, no clear evidence was available to indicate the presence of physical differences or any communicative functions of the various cry types. In 1963, Wasz-Höckert, Valanne, Vuorenkoski, Michelsson, and So Vijarvi (1963) reported on the acoustic patterns of birth, pain, and hunger cries using sound spectrography. They described the rising/falling patterns in the birth cry but only qualitative differences between the pain and hunger cries. Sedláckova (1964) noted the birth cry to be a high frequency signal.

Murry, Amundson, and Hollien (1977) systematically examined the frequency characteristics of pain, hunger, and startle cries from four male and four female infants. For all three types of cries, the males produced a higher mean $F_0$ than the females. The cries were not only differentiated on the basis of sex but also according to cry type. Pain cries resulted in the highest $F_0$, followed by the hunger cry; the startle cries had the lowest mean $F_0$. However, the differences in $F_0$ were not statistically significant, and each infant had a large standard deviation for at least one cry type. The consistent finding of higher $F_0$ in males for all cry types verifies a trend reported by Sheppard and Lane (1968); namely that male infants have a higher $F_0$ than females and also speculation by Hollien (1980) that the male voice fundamental frequency is higher than the female voice during the first 6 years of life.

The majority of studies of cry duration and cry intensity are based on data derived from pain cry stimuli. Ringel and Kluppel (1964) studied 10 neonates 4 to 40 hours of age and found the expiratory cycle to be 1.47 seconds long and 82 dB sound pressure level (SPL) in intensity. This value compares favorably with the respiratory rates reported for 1-month-old infants by Langlois et al. (1980). The data by Caldwell and Leeper (1974) for 1–3-day-old neonates, however, indicated a duration on the order of .65 seconds; this was much shorter than would be expected from respiratory cycle data. Hollien (1980) has summarized the cry duration data from 12 studies of infants ranging from 4 hours to 12 months. The data obviously represent a wide range of ages, sampling techniques, and definitions of cry cycle. The difficulty in interpreting data of this sort reflects the need to standardize terminology, experimental protocols, and data analysis procedures.

More information regarding trends in age, sex, and cry types (especially pain and hunger) is available with each new generation of investigators. These results that are not yet integrated due to divergent populations, methodologies, and definitions have provided those investigators of abnormal cry with a corpus of data on the normal child from which differences now may be identified.

The acoustic patterns of cries have given rise to numerous investigations of auditors' perceptions of these events. The notion of cry as a meaningful mode of communication stems from early perceptual studies of infant vocalizations. In 1927, Sherman attempted to elicit distinctive emotional responses from neonates using four stimuli: restraint of the head, pricking with a needle, withholding feeding, and suddenly dropping toward a table top. She found that both trained subjects (nurses, medical students, and graduate psychology students) and untrained observers (college freshmen) were unable to match correctly the emotional responses with the cry-evoking stimuli. Although Sherman argued that the nature of the discomfort could not be distinguished on the basis of the cry, the techniques for testing the two observer groups did not allow for separation of the visual and auditory components of the infant's cry responses, nor were their judgments based solely on the auditory perception of the cry sounds. Wasz-Höckert, Partanen, Vuorenkoski, Valanne, and Michelsson (1964a) tested the notion that different types of infant vocalizations are perceptually distinguishable. Recordings of vocalizations "typical" to the situations of birth, pain, hunger, and pleasure were obtained from normal neonates. Eighty nurses, who were trained in the care of young children, listened to the randomized cry recordings and were able to identify the type of vocalization 67% of the time. (Many of the correct responses were to the pleasure sounds that really cannot be considered as a type of cry.) In a follow-up study, Wasz-Höckert *et al.* (1964b) used the same experimental method to examine the effect of training on the ability of the listener to identify the cry-evoking stimulus. They found that the trained listeners were able to identify the types of cry-evoking stimuli better than the untrained listeners.

Muller *et al.* (1974) reported on the perceptual responses of mothers to the cries of their children. In a very carefully controlled experimental protocol, they elicited three types of cry—pain, hunger, and startle—from four male and four female infants age 3 to 5 months. All the children were healthy, and the samples were obtained in a quiet environment. After all recordings were made, the first and third 15-second segments of each of the 24 recordings (eight infants by three stimulus conditions) were extracted, randomized, and presented to two groups of listeners. Group A consisted of the mothers of the eight infants recorded in the study. They were asked to indicate on their answer sheets whether the stimuli that originally evoked the cry were pain (P), hunger (H), or startle (S), and whether or not the sample was from their infant. Group B consisted of ten mothers of children whose ages were comparable with the infants recorded in the study but who had no previous contact with the eight subjects.

The results indicated that, whereas some of the hunger cry samples were correctly identified as hunger cries, a significant number of times by both groups of listeners, a number of other samples also were incorrectly identified as hunger cries a significant percentage of the time. Therefore, it must be concluded that the mothers incorrectly perceived an excessive number of samples as hunger cries and that those hunger samples that were correctly identified merely reflect this general bias. These results were similar for the samples of mothers judging only their own infant as well as for judging all infants.

These results support the contention that the acoustic characteristics of the cries of normal infants carry little perceptual information to the mother with respect to the cry-evoking situation (Murry, Hoit-Dalgaard, & Gracco, 1983). It might be hypothesized, therefore, that within the normal situation, the cry generally acts simply to alert the mother and that any of her suppositions concerning the situation that evoked the cry behavior must be based upon additional cues from the environment or the context of the situation.

In further studies (Murry, Hollien, & Muller, 1975), it was observed that mothers could recognize their own children simply on the basis of a 15-second cry, despite the fact that they could not recognize the cry type. Correct responses ranged from 86% to 98% correct, which was much higher than the chance level. Thus, there was more information common to all three cry types of each child than for any one cry type influencing a mother's decision.

When it came to judging the sex of the criers, mothers had difficulty with this task, except when judging their own children. After acoustically analyzing the cries, the investigators (Murry et al., 1977) concluded that the perceptual cues relating the fundamental frequency and vocal tract that are utilized in judging the sex of adult voices are not evident in the voices of infants. Moreover, the finding of higher $F_0$ values in males from infancy to age 6 would be expected to lead judges to erroneous conclusions about the sex because $F_0$ is so extensively used in perceptual judgment of speakers' sex (Sing & Murry, 1978).

## 5. TECHNICAL AND METHODOLOGICAL CONSIDERATIONS

Infant cry can be considered in terms of its signal and sign properties. As signal, the sound is a complex wave form, requiring sophisticated acoustical devices for analysis. To avoid the problem of signal/noise interactions, most investigators record crying at its source, that is, the infant's mouth. This approach skirts the perceptual issue, namely, what is the sound when it reaches the listener? Our initial efforts utilized fixed (octave, half-octave, and third-octave) band filters. Ignoring the element of time, we were able to describe certain features associated with the intrusive, alerting quality of these recorded sounds, specifically their intensity (83–85 dB) and the prominence of octave harmonics

(Ostwald, 1972). Sound spectrography has the advantage of preserving the temporal configuration. This method also gives a fairly reliable "picture" of certain events that cannot be described by listeners, that is, microsegments containing shifts, biphonations, and the like occurring subliminally probably but still adding to the total "impact" the cry makes on the listener. In this respect, spectrography represents a most important technical innovation. However, when large samples have to be analyzed, spectrography becomes an overly time-consuming procedure, and there is also some loss of accuracy in the temporal realm resulting from discontinuities between adjacent sonagrams. For this reason, we have been using continuous spectrography (a Rayscan apparatus designed at the Stanford Research Institute in Menlo Park, California) for coping with long stretches of sound produced by aquatic mammals (Poulter, 1968). In one study, when it was necessary to process many cries produced by craniopagus twins, we also relied on computer-averaged spectra to compare the two babies (Peltzman, Ostwald, Yaeger, & Manchester, 1970). Several cry studies using high-speed digital computation have appeared since then (Lester & Zeskind, 1982; Tenold, Crowell, Jones, Daniel, McPherson, & Popper, 1974), and it seems reasonable to assume that future research will begin to exploit automated methods more and more.

In terms of data collection, crucial decisions have to be made about the *sign properties* of infant sounds, especially under conditions of continuous bedside monitoring (Vuorenkoski, Lind, Wasz-Höckert, & Partaken, 1971). If spontaneous vocalizations are to be included in the analysis, it becomes difficult to know when to label a sound a *cry* as distinct from a *noncry*. And how is one to define the conditions causing a cry? Gastric intubation (to measure contractile events presumably related to hunger), skin electrodes (to measure EEG or EMG correlates), and other required instruments tend to be seen as invasive and restrictive methods; today they are often unacceptable in terms of the ethics of human experimentation. To inflict pain deliberately is another objectionable technique, especially when the subjects cannot give informed consent. Efforts have been made to minimize these objections by recording the cries produced by so-called routine procedures, for example, blood sampling or circumcision. But such stimuli tend to be excessive and can produce exaggerated vocal responses. Also, the presence of ancillary personnel—lab technicians, nurses, and the like—in the recording area adds unwanted noise and makes for a less than ideal experimental environment.

In our studies of cry with infants from birth to 5 months, three cry types appear to emerge with a definable construct: birth cry, pain cry, and hunger cry. Although the hunger cry may actually embody other characteristics such as distress, discomfort, and irritability, feeding tends to eliminate the cry behavior and may therefore be operationally defined as hunger cry. Future investigations of cry will require more specific definition of the cry types and more rigorous control of the events leading to the cry.

## 6. THE COMMUNICATIVE FUNCTION OF CRYING

If we consider the extraordinary helplessness of the human neonate who cannot obtain nourishment independently or cling to or follow a caretaker, it becomes possible to assume that survival mechanisms have evolved that assure against abandonment and promote contact with family members. Crying seems to be the primary mechanism of this sort, linked reflexively at its very onset to respiration and gradually modified to serve the purpose of speech. That is why we have likened this biosocial phenomenon to an "acoustic umbilical cord," (Ostwald, 1972) which is essential during the first postpartum months, after which the baby has usually gained sufficient neuromuscular coordination to emit "coos" and smiles, which are social signals that do not so blatantly call attention to his or her helplessness.

Crying as the elicitor of parental behavior has been thoughtfully discussed by Murray (1979). She examined the concept of crying as a "releaser" of caregiving behavior and as an "activator" of egoistic and altruistic motives. Evidence in support of the acoustic *releaser model* includes (1) contagious crying among newborns; and (2) the finding that deaf parents who can only see an infant's distress do not react as do hearing parents. Evidence favoring the *emotional activator model* includes (3) the observation that crying is a "graded" signal that increases in intensity with distress and is reduced by nurturance; (4) the compelling nature of the cry; and (5) the observation that responses to crying appear to range from hostility, through empathy, to affection for the tiny soundmaker.

There appears to be a period of physiological hypersensitivity on the mother's part, related probably to hormonal factors (Vuorenkoski, Wasz-Höckert, & Partanen, 1969), which assists in the achievement of homeostasis—that ideal state described by Middlemore (1941) as a "nursing couple." However, it should be mentioned that not only a baby's vocalizations but also its reflexively organized muscular activity, skin reddening, and facial contorting provide the sorts of graded signals that enable mothers (and other caretakers) to judge the level of distress and to act accordingly. Brody and Axelrod (no date) have made a film that demonstrates a number of distinctive response patterns at 6 weeks, when crying ordinarily reaches its peak. Some women pick up the infant almost immediately and eagerly search for the source of his or her discomfort. Having located the source of trouble, they quickly correct it and leave the infant alone. Others continue to fuss with a child even after the crying has stopped. There are also mothers who allow the baby to cry for a while before attempting to intervene. Finally, one can observe helpless and ineffective behavior, with mothers exhibiting various degrees of apathy, frustration, or anger toward the infant in distress.

The possibilities for maladaptive as well as adaptive patterns between growing babies and their social environment have recently been summarized by Greenspan and Lourie (1981). Four "stages" in the development from infant to toddler have been proposed:

I. Homeostasis (0–3 months)
II. Attachment (2–7 months)
III. Somatopsychological differentiation (3–10 months)
IV. Behavioral organization, initiative, and internalization (9–24 months)

It seems reasonable to assume that transformation of vocal sound patterning corresponds to these states. The early cries and screams of Stage I (homeostasis), whether resulting from respiratory distress, nutritional needs, or painful stimulation, are of such intensity, noisiness, and persistence that any listener within earshot, not only the baby's own mother, can be alerted. Tavolga (1970) calls these types of vocalizations "biosocial" signals. They elicit general protective nurturant responses from adults and remain available for the rest of the organism's life if needed under emergency conditions. With the onset of Stage II (attachment), vocalizations of much lower intensity, briefer duration, and less repetitiveness emerge in the infant–mother interaction, sounds that contrast dramatically with the distress vocalizations of the first month. These are the so-called "pleasure" sounds related to smiling (Ohala, 1980). One may hear them first as a soft "hum" while the baby is breast-feeding, a sound that seems not to be in phase with the baby's oral sucking which, when recorded by contact microphone (Applebaum, 1968), contains a characteristic smacking rhythm. The infant, while humming, is a responsive participant in the mother's behavior. More varied patterns of non-rhythmic vocalization called *cooing* appear to be effective social reinforcers (Ostwald, 1973). Together with visual and tactile cues, these pleasure sounds seem to govern playful interactions between mother and child that precede reciprocal speech.

Further elaboration of meaningful vocal behavior takes place during Stage III (somatopsychological differentiation) when, for the first time, the baby's acoustical repertoire can be said to contain elements referable to interpersonally shared events, that is, to have symbolic properties. The child's inner representation of the external world seems as yet to consist of fragmentary, indefinite, and syncretic percepts (Solley, 1966), and the association areas of his/her cortex are probably incapable of forming symbolic abstractions. Nonetheless, vocal utterances heard at this time (up to the 10th month) betoken increasingly precise responses to certain aspects of the mother—her voice, facial expressions, motor activities, and so forth (Schwartz, Rosenberg, & Brackbill, 1970). Therefore, by a process of linguistic generalization, perhaps it now becomes possible for people other than just the mother to understand what a child is trying to communicate.

The first "words" to be heard in infant–mother dyads are so closely related, both phonologically and functionally, to "babbling" that it becomes a matter of probabilistics to decide with each individual sound where the border between incomprehensibility and speech may lie.

To comment at greater length on these crucial maturational steps during Stage IV (behavioral organization, initiative, and internalization) would take us far beyond the emotional behavior of crying, which has been our primary concern in this chapter. Suffice it to say that it seems characteristic of most normal infants after the eighth or ninth month to continue engaging in noncry vocalization even after one stops interacting with them. Duplication and repetitions are heard, and two to five semi-discrete phonetic elements may appear within a single utterance. The baby plays with sounds as if talking to himself or herself using patterns that sound gradually more speechlike (Winitz, 1969).

Having by now been exposed for many months to human language, the year-old baby begins to echo back into the environment some of the sounds made by its inhabitants. As Crystal has pointed out, when an utterance "can be consistently assigned a specific semantic interpretation, it is no longer wholly affective in character, and has a stable phonetic form" (Crystal, 1969, p. 44), one can say with conviction that the baby "speaks."

Perhaps it is the persistence of the capacity for uttering nonspecific sounds, for vocalizing emotions, and for producing phonetically unstable entities that guarantees the immediacy and universality of social response to cry one has come to expect since infancy. Older children, teenagers, and even mature adults may revert at times to crying as their most basic and sometimes the only satisfactory way to communicate human emotions.

Singing, too, is related to crying. The purity of a singer's voice may depend on her or his ability to duplicate certain movements that infants spontaneously make when they cry. For example, by elevating the cheeks like a baby and drawing the jaw back to raise the soft palate, it becomes possible to emit vocalic sounds resembling the pure, highly communicative cries of an infant, a technique that is practiced and taught by some opera singers.

## 7. SUMMARY AND CONCLUSION

The results of cry research conducted within the past two decades have been reviewed. We are keenly interested in developing a better understanding of the acoustical properties of infant sounds and of the role these sounds play in communication between the infant and the social environment. Toward that goal, we have presented information about the gradual transformation of infant–mother communication from its prenatal origins into the first year of life.

Both the receptive and the productive apparatus for some communication appears to be present before birth, and the onset of vocalization is associated with dramatic changes is respiration and phonation at the time of delivery. One then observes a variety of different patterns of crying associated with states of health, illness, and emotion. How to define these states and the objective analysis of various acoustical events pose certain methodological problems that we have discussed. It seems that pitch, emotion, harmonic structure, and temporal changes in noise components of cry are important variables, and that in the context of good caretaking and reliable pediatric evaluation, the assessment of these and possible other parameters of cry may have diagnostic significance.

Another important problem for future investigation is to clarify the relationship between infantile sound-making and emotional expression in subsequent stages of personality development. One should not forget that the singing voice as much as the speaking voice probably has its origin in the baby's cry, so that research in this area may have something to offer not only to physicians, psychologists, and linguists but also to music teachers, drama coaches, singers, and public speakers.

## 8. REFERENCES

Applebaum, R. M. Infant vocalization breast-feeding, and the mother–child relationships. *La Leche League News*, 1968, *10*, 26–27.

Armitage, S. E., Baldwin, B. A., & Vince, M. A. The fetal sound environment of sheep. *Science*, 1980, *208*, 1173–1174.

Bergström, R. M. Electrical parameters of the brain during ontogeny. In R. J. Robinson (Ed.), *Brain and early behavior*. New York: Academic Press, 1969.

Blinick, G., Tavolga, W. N., & Antopol, W. Variations in birth cries of newborn infants from narcotic addicted and normal mothers. *American Journal of Obstetrics and Gynecology*, 1971, *110*, 948–958.

Bosma, J. F., Truby, H. M., & Lind, J. Cry motions of the newborn infant. *Acta Paediatrica Scandinavica* (Suppl.), 1966, *163*, 61–92.

Brody, S., & Axelrod, S. *Mother–infant interaction: Forms of feeding at six weeks.* New York: New York University Film Library.

Caldwell, H. S., & Leeper, A., Jr. Temporal patterns of neonatal vocalization: A normative investigation. *Perceptual and Motor Skills*, 1974, *38*, 911–916.

Colton, R. H., & Steinschneider, A. Acoustic relationships of infant cries to Sudden Infant Death Syndrome. In T. Murry & J. Murry (Eds.), *Infant communication: Cry and early speech.* Houston: College Hill Press, 1980.

Crystal, D. *Non-segmented phonology in first-language acquisition.* Paper read at the Second International Congress of Applied Linguistics, Cambridge, England, 1969.

De Casper, A. J., & Fifer, W. P. Of human bonding: Newborns prefer their mother's voices. *Science*, 1980, *208*, 1174–1176.

Fisichelli, V. R., Haber, A., Davis, J., & Karelitz, S. Audible characteristics of the cries of normal infants and those with Down's syndrome. *Perceptual and Motor Skills*, 1966, *23*, 744–746.

Greenspan, S., & Lourie, R. S. Developmental structuralist approach to the classification of adaptive and pathologic personality organizations: Infancy and early childhood. *American Journal of Psychiatry*, 1981, *138*, 725–735.

Hollien, H. Developmental aspects of neonatal vocalization. In T. Murry & J. Murry (Eds.), *Infant communication: Cry and early speech.* Houston: College Hill Press, 1980.

Humphrey, T. Postnatal repetition of human prenatal activity sequences with some suggestions of their neuroanatomical basis. In R. J. Robinson (Ed.), *Brain and early behavior.* London: Academic Press, 1969.

Jones, M. C. An investigation of certain acoustic parameters of the crying vocalization of young deaf children. *Dissertation Abstracts International*, 1965.

Langlois, A., Baken, R. J., & Wilder, C. Pre-speech respiratory behavior during the first year of life. In T. Murry & J. Murry (Eds.), *Infant communication: Cry and early speech.* Houston: College Hill Press, 1980.

Lester, B. M., & Zeskind, P. S. A biobehavioral perspective on crying in early infancy. In H. E. Fitzgerald, B. M. Lester, & M. W. Yogman (Eds.), *Theory and research in behavioral pediatrics.* New York: Plenum Press, 1982.

Lieberman, P., Harris, K. S., Wolff, P., & Russell, L. H. Newborn infant cry and nonhuman primate vocalization. *Journal of Speech and Hearing Research*, 1971, *14*, 718–727.

Lind, J., Wasz-Höckert, O., Vuorenkoski, V., & Valanne, E. The vocalization of a newborn, brain-damaged child. *Annale Paediatrica Fenn*, 1965, *11*, 32–37.

Luchsinger, V. R., Dubois, C., Vasselli, F., Joss, E., Gloor, R., & Wiesman, U. Spektralanalyses des Miauens bei Cri-du-Chat Syndrom. *Folia Phoniatrica*, 1967, *19*, 27–33.

Middlemore, M. P. *The nursing couple.* London: Hamish-Hamilton, 1941.

Michelsson, K. *Cry analyses of symptomless low birth weight nenoates and of asphyxiated newborn infants.* Academic dissertation, Department of Paediatrics, University of Oulu, Helsinki, Finland, 1980.

Michelsson, K., Tuppurainen, N., & Aula, P. Cry analysis of infants with karyotype abnormalities. *Neuropediatrics*, 1980, *11*, 365–376.

Michelsson, K., & Wasz-Höckert, O. The value of cry analysis in neonatology and early infancy. In T. Murry & J. Murry (Eds.), *Infant communication: Cry and early speech.* Houston: College Hill Press, 1980.

Muller, E., Hollien, H., & Murry, T. Perceptual response to infant crying: Identification of cry types. *Journal of Child Language*, 1974, *1*, 89–95.

Murray, A. D. Infant crying as an elicitor of parental behavior: An examination of two models. *Psychological Bulletin*, 1979, *86*, 191–215.

Murry, T. Acoustic and perceptual characteristics of infant cries. In T. Murry & J. Murry (Eds.), *Infant communication: Cry and early speech*. Houston: College Hill Press, 1980.

Murry, T., Amundson, P., & Hollien, H. Acoustical characteristics of infant cries: Fundamental frequency. *Journal of Child Language*, 1977, *3*, 321–328.

Murry, T., Hoit-Dalgaard, J., & Gracco, V. Infant vocalization: A longitudinal study of acoustic and temporal parameters. *Folia Phoniatrica*, 1983, *35*, 245–253.

Murry, T., Hollien, H., & Muller, E. Perceptual responses to infant crying: material recognition and sex judgments. *Journal of Child Language*, 1975, *2*, 199–204.

Murry, T., Gracco, V., & Gracco, C. *Infant vocalization during the first twelve weeks*. Paper presented at American Speech and Hearing Association, Atlanta, 1979.

Ohala, J. J. The acoustic origin of the smile. *Journal of the Acoustical Society of America*, 1980, *2*, 199–204.

Ostwald, P. F. *Soundmaking, the acoustic communication of emotion*. Springfield: Charles C Thomas, 1963.

Ostwald, P. F. The sounds of infancy. *Developmental Medicine Child Neurology*, 1972, *14*, 350–361.

Ostwald, P. F. *The semiotics of human sound*. The Hague: Mouton, 1973.

Ostwald, P. F., & Peltzman, P. The cry of the human infant. *Scientific American*, 1974, *230*, 84–90.

Ostwald, P. F., Freedman, D. G., & Kurtz, J. H. Vocalization of infant twins. *Folia Phoniatrica*, 1962, *14*, 37–50.

Ostwald, P. F., Phibbs, R., & Fox, S. Diagnostic use of infant cry. *Biology of the Neonate*, 1968, *13*, 68–82.

Ostwald, P. F., Peltzman, P., Greenberg, M., & Meyer, J. Cries of a trisomy 13-15 infant. *Developmental Medicine and Child Neurology*, 1970, *12*, 472–477.

Peltzman, P., Ostwald, P. F., Yaeger, C. L., & Manchester, D. Sensory-vocal studies of a twin pair with cephalic union. *Neuropaediatrie*, 1970, *2*, 79–97.

Poulter, T. C. Marine mammals. In T. A. Sebeok (Ed.), *Animal communication*, Bloomington: Indiana University Press, 1968.

Ringel, R. L., & Kluppel, D. O. Neonatal crying—A normative study. *Folia Phoniatrica*, 1964, *16*, 1–9.

Schwartz, A., Rosenberg, D., & Brackbill, Y. Analysis of the components of social reinforcement of infant vocalization. *Psychonomic Science*, 1970, *20*, 323–325.

Sedáčková, E. Analyse acoustique de la voix de nouveau-nés. *Folia Phoniatrica*, 1964, *16*, 48–58.

Sheppard, W. C., & Lane, H. L. Development of the prosodic features of input vocalizing. *Journal of Speech and Hearing Research*, 1968, *11*, 94–108.

Sherman, M. The differentiation of emotional responses from motion picture views and from actual observation; (II) The ability of observers to judge emotional characteristics of the crying infant and the voice of an adult. *Journal of Comparative Psychology*, 1927, *7*, 265–284.

Sing, S., & Murry T. Multidimensional classification of normal voice qualities. *Journal of the Acoustical Society of America*, 1978, *64*, 81–87.

Sirvio, P., & Michelsson, K. Sound-spectrographic cry analysis of normal and abnormal newborn infants. *Folia Phoniatrica*, 1976, *28*, 161–173.

Solley, C. M. Affective processes in perceptual development. In A. Kidd & J. Rivoire (Eds.), *Perceptual development in children*. New York: International Universities Press, 1966.

Stark, R. E., & Nathanson, S. N. Unusual features of cry in an an infant dying suddenly and unexpectedly. In J. F. Bosma & J. Showacrew (Eds.), *Development of upper respiratory anatomy and function*. Washington, DC: U.S. Government Printing Office, 1975.

Tanner, J. M. Physical growth. In P. H. Mussen (Ed.), *Carmichael's manual of child psychology*. New York: Wiley, 1970.

Tavolga, W. N. Levels of interaction in animal communication. In L. R. Aronson, E. Tobach, D. S. Lehrman, & J. S. Rosenblatt (Eds.), *Development and evolution of behavior— essays in memory of T. C. Schneirla*. San Francisco: Freeman, 1970.

Tenold, J. L., Crowell, D. H., Jones, R. H., Daniel, T. H., McPherson, D. F., & Popper, A N., Cepstral and stationary analyses of full-term and premature infants' cries. *Journal of Acoustical Society of America*, 1974, *56*, 975–980.

Thiery, M., Yo Le Sian, A., Vrijens, M., & Janssens, V. U. *Obstetrics and Gynecology of the British Commonwealth*, 1973, *80*, 183–185.

Truby, H. M., Bosma, J. F., & Lind, J. Newborn infant cry. *Acta Paediatrica Scandinavica* (Suppl. 163), 1965.

Vuorenkoski, V., Lind, J., Partanen, T. J., Lejeune, J., Lafourcade, J., & Wasz-Höckert, O. Spectrographic analysis of cries from children with maladie du cri du chat. *Annale Pediatrica Fenn*, 1966, *12*, 174–180.

Vuorenkoski, V., Wasz-Höckert, O., & Partanen, T. J. The effect of cry stimulus on the temperature of the lactating breast of primiparas. A thermographic study. *Experientia*, 1969, *25*, 1286–1287.

Vuorenkoski, V., Lind, J., Wasz-Höckert, O., & Partanen, T. J. Cry score. A method for evaluating the degree of abnormality in pain cry response of the newborn and young infant. *Speech Transmission Laboratory Quarterly Report* (Stockholm, Takniska Hogskalen), 1971, *1*, 68–75.

Wasz-Höckert, O., Valanne, E., Vuorenkoski, V., Michelsson, K., & So Vijarvi, A. Analysis of some types of vocalization in the newborn and in early infancy. *Annale Paediatrica Fenn*, 1963, *9*, 1.

Wasz-Höckert, O., Partanen, T. J., Vuorenkoski, V., Valanne, E., & Michaelsson, K. Effect of training on ability to identify preverbal vocalizations. *Developmental Medicine and Child Neurology*, 1964, *6*, 393–396. (a)

Wasz-Höckert, O., Paranen, T. J., Vuorenkoski, V., Valanne, E., & Michelsson, K. The identification of some specific meanings in infant vocalization. *Experientia*, 1964, *20*, 154. (b)

Wasz-Höckert, O., Lind, J., Vuorenkoski, V., Partanen, T. J., & Valanne, E. The infant cry, a spectrographic and auditory analysis. *Clinics in Developmental Medicine* No. 29. London: Heinemann, 1968.

Wasz-Höckert, O., Simila, S., Rosenberg, G., Vuorenkoski, V., & Lind, J. El síndrome de Smith-Lemli-Optiz en dos niñas, con especial atención a los patrones de sur gritos de dolor. *Revista Mexicana de Pediatría*, 1969, *38*, 63–68.

Wasz-Höckert, O., Koivisto, M., Vuorenkoski, V., Partanen, T. J., & Lind, J. Spectrographic analysis of pain cry in hyperbilirubinemia. *Biology of the Neonate*, 1971, *17*, 260–271.

Winitz, H. *Articulatory acquisition and behavior*. New York: Appleton-Century-Crofts, 1969.

Yao, A. C., Lind, J., & Vuorenkoski, V. Expiratory grunting in the late clamped normal neonate. *Pediatrics*, 1971, *48*, 865–870.

# 8

# A Developmental Perspective of Infant Crying

PHILIP SANFORD ZESKIND

## 1. INTRODUCTION

Infant crying has great significance for many aspects of infant development and has thus been studied within a variety of contexts. In one context, crying is a salient social behavior of the newborn and young infant that influences the infant's interactions with the caregiving environment. As such, researchers have examined the effects of crying on the responses of listeners (e.g., Frodi, Lamb, Leavitt, & Donovan, 1978) and the effects of those listeners' responses on future expressions of crying (e.g., Bell & Ainsworth, 1972; Rheingold, Gewirtz, & Ross, 1959). Also within this context, investigators have examined variations in the expression of crying as they relate to different levels of infant arousal (e.g., Wolff, 1969) and different perceptions of why the infant is crying (e.g, Sherman, 1927). As a social behavior, we can study the development of crying as we would the development of other early social behaviors.

In a traditionally separate context, infant crying has long been an integral part of standard newborn neurological examinations (Prechtl & Beintema, 1964). Early studies of newborn and young infants showed

PHILIP SANFORD ZESKIND • Department of Psychology, Virginia Polytechnic Institute and State University, Blacksburg, Virginia 24061.

that several measures of the threshold and production of crying (Fisi-chelli & Karelitz, 1963; Karelitz & Fisichelli, 1962) and the spectral char-acteristics of the cry sound (Vuorenkoski, Lind, Partanen, Lejeune, Lafourcade, & Wasz-Höckert, 1966) could be used to support the diag-nosis of a wide range of central nervous system (CNS) disorders. In particular, an usually high-pitched cry sound is a frequent and most notable attribute of the damaged infant (for reviews, see Lester & Zes-kind, 1979, 1982). There has been increasing evidence that the measures of infant crying used to distinguish infants with CNS disorders from healthy infants also differentiate relatively healthy infants in the normal newborn nursery who show signs of being at risk for nonoptimal devel-opment. For example, a response to a painful stimulus, a higher thresh-old for cry elicitation, a longer latency to the cry response, a shorter duration of crying, and the characteristically high-pitched cry sound have differentiated infants who showed obstetric (Zeskind & Lester, 1978) and/or anthropometric (Zeskind & Lester, 1981) index of increased risk for poor social and intellectual development. One recent formulation suggests that these cry features may reflect the organization of auto-nomic nervous system (ANS) functioning and thus can be useful in the assessment of the infant at risk (Lester & Zeskind, 1982).

Ultimately, the purpose of early assessment is to provide the basis for predicting the infant's developmental course so that an appropriate treatment can be implemented if required. Accurately predicting the developmental courses of healthy infants who show various pediatric signs of being at increased risk, however, is most difficult. Although there is an increased probability that an infant with a particular pediatric history will show a less than optimal pattern of development, many of these infants will show patterns of development that are indistinguish-able from those of "normal" infants. Individual differences in the con-stitutional integrity of infants, variations in the nature of the caregiving environments in which the infants develop, and the interaction of these two sources of variations are but a few of the factors that contribute to the continuum of possible developmental courses. For this reason, the concept of *risk* is a probabilistic one. Although this probabilistic course of events may appear to be problematic in the context of pediatric assess-ment, probabilistic principles of development have often been basic to the study of behavioral development. In these formulations, the course of development is not fixed by either the infant's biological character-istics, the characteristics of the environment in which the infant survives, or the static interaction of the two; instead, different developmental pathways have different probabilities of occurring based on the idiosyn-cratic and changing bidirectional interaction between the infant's biological and environmental attributes. Students of behavioral development have long confronted this issue with useful conceptual and methodological strategies (See Immelmann, Barlow, Petrinovich, & Main, 1981).

These mutual issues and concerns of traditionally distinct contexts provide the basis for a synthesis of the pediatric and behavioral views of infant crying. Within this synthetic context, the development of the infant at risk can be conceptualized as an example in which the probablistic course of the infant's developmental path, by definition, has been emphasized. The development of this infant's crying, in particular, may be an especially useful target of study because the cry at once may reflect individual differences in neonatal biological functioning and is a social behavior to which the principles of behavioral development can be applied. By applying the principles of normal behavioral development to the assessment of the infant at risk, not only can we illuminate the processes affecting the development of the infant and thus increase our ability to assess correctly and predict the infant's developmental course, but, also, through the study of the development of the cry features of the infant at risk, we are offered a view of a phenomenon in which the processes of normal infant development are accentuated and perhaps more clearly observed.

Unfortunately, we know very little about the development of crying. Although crying has been studied as an index of a number of developmental processes such as attachment (Schaffer & Emerson, 1964) and fear (Ricciuti, 1974) and has been the focal point of theoretical discussions regarding the effects of parental responsivity on future crying bouts (Ainsworth & Bell, 1977; Bell & Ainsworth, 1972; Gewirtz & Boyd, 1977a, 1977b), the development of crying has rarely been studied as an independent area. The purpose of this chapter is to conceptualize the study of crying as one part of the behavioral repertoire of the infant at risk within a model of "normal" behavioral development. I will attempt to put the paucity of existing developmental research on infant crying and the cry research of infants who show obstetric and/or anthropometric indices of risk into a developmental perspective that may guide future research questions. The focus of this chapter will be to ask *how* one can study the development of crying rather than *what* actual changes characterize the development of this behavior.

## 2. DEVELOPMENTAL PERSPECTIVE

Before we can study infant crying from a developmental perspective we must decide what a developmental perspective is. Conceptions of infant development range widely from within and between disciplines of scientific study with each discipline proffering its own nuance of meaning. These conceptual variations are not only associated with genuine differences in methods and theories but also are often the result of differences in the issues and levels of analysis selected for study (see Harris, 1957). Although the examination of a phenomenon undergoing change is central to most, if not all, perspectives, differences in the elements of change that are actually measured provide the basis for making relevant distinctions among the various views of development. For our purposes, we can distinguish between the investigation of development as a *product* of change and as a *process* of change.

As a *product*, development is measured by changes in behavior as they are manifested over time or different ages. In this perspective, the processes of development produce changes in the expression of crying, and what we actually measure are the changes in that product. For example, we can describe how the occurrence (e.g., Brazelton, 1962) or acoustic characteristics (e.g., Prescott, 1980) of crying change as the infant gets older. This approach offers a rich catalog of descriptions of changes in behavioral expression with regard to the changing age of the infant; however, for our purposes, studying age-related differences in behavioral expression may better be described as a *comparative* perspective than as a *developmental* one. That is, studying how the cries of an infant are different at various points along an ontogentic scale of evolution (development of the individual) may be comparable to studying how the behaviors of animals differ at various points along a phylogenetic scale of evolution (development of the species). We measure behavioral products at various ages, but we must infer the processes by which the changes occurred. Thus, in addition to the problems in design of developmental research based on the use of age as the independent variable (see Kessen, 1960; Wolhwill, 1973), this comparative approach offers little insight into the causes of behavioral development.

If we are interested in examining these causal elements of changes in infant crying, a process-oriented approach to development is more appropriate. In this approach, the targets of study are both the specific changes in behavior and the complex system of factors that led to those changes. As Rosenblatt and Lehrman (1963) have so eloquently demonstrated, we can illuminate the processes underlying the development of behavior at a particular point in time by analyzing the ways in which that behavior has arisen from preceding points in development and the ways that behavior influences or gives rise to succeeding points in development. This analysis emphasizes the functional significance of crying because behavior is viewed as an adaptive response to the preceding conditions in development (both ontogenetic and phylogenetic) and as a contributor to the infant's adaptations to the succeeding conditions in development.

The continuing adaptations of the infant to these conditions provides a set of experiences that guide his or her course of development. Experience, in this sense, is defined by the effects of changes in the infant's internal and external environments. As Carmichael (1963) suggested, even at the physiological level, changes resulting from environmentally released activity are not necessarily unlike those resulting from so-called inner processes of growth. I shall refer to experience as having both biological and external environment components that can serve to change the biological development of the infant even if the stimulation is self-produced by the infant's own structural growth and maturation. This conceptualization of experience has been applied to the development of several sensory perceptual and motor functions (e.g., Gottlieb, 1976) and to patterns of variable social behaviors (Sackett, Sameroff, Cairns, & Suomi, 1981). In this capacity, the *process* of development is neither the unfolding of the innate nor the direct result of environmental contingencies in which genetic activity provides only an initial push. Instead, development can be seem as proceeding out of a continuing interaction within the infant and his or her internal environment (including genetic activity) and between the infant and his or her outer environment (cf. Lehrman, 1953). This interaction is a dynamic bidirectional process in which changes in biological functioning result in behaviors that affect the environment such that its responses feed back to make further changes in biological functioning and behavior. New organizational levels of biological and behavioral functioning arise from these continuing interactions.

The probabilistic component of this bidirectional process is that the course of development is not fixed or teleologically predetermined; rather, there are many possible outcomes with differential probabilities based on the specific set of experiential conditions to which the infant must adapt. As new levels of biobehavioral functioning come into existence, early deficits may or may not be transmitted from one level of functioning to another, depending on whether or not the nonoptimal conditions that produced that deficit are still present or influential at that particular new level of functioning. Throughout this chapter, I will focus on this continuing process of adapation as the source of developmental changes in the crying of the infant at risk.

## 3. THE DEVELOPMENT OF CRYING

Crying is an organized behavioral response that, unlike other reflexes such as rooting and sucking, occurs at birth without any previous functioning of the total operating behavioral system. Crying has its discrete beginning at birth because this is usually the first time that the maturational capabilities of the infant interact with an environmental condition that allows the potential crying behavior to be realized. Although the fetus is maturationally capable of crying as early as 6 months after conception (see Carmichael, 1970), the presence of amniotic fluid and the absense of air in the prenatal environment, among other reasons, prevent the infant from being able to inhale, exhale, or produce a cry sound. Once these environmental conditions change, however, the maturational capabilities of the infant can be potentiated, even if the changes occur prenatally. For example, just as some avian species prenatally vocalize after their beaks penetrate the fetal sac at the large end of the egg (Vince, 1969), the human fetus has been heard to cry after the fetal sac has been ruptured prior to delivery (e.g., Graham, 1919).

The functional and adaptive significance of the newborn infant's crying can be seen at various levels of analysis. At a physiological level, the dramatic increase in ventilation associated with the newborn's crying may assist in ductal closure and thus help reorganize the infant's cardiorespiratory system from that of a fetus to that of a neonate (Vaughan, McKay, & Behrman, 1979). Newborn crying also improves pulmonary capacity and helps maintain the infant's homeostasis (Brazelton, 1962). At a social behavioral level, the survival value of infant crying has been long and frequently observed. As mentioned, theorists may differ in their views regarding the results of contingent responses to infant crying on the frequency of future crying bouts, but there is general agreement among these and other investigators from diverse theoretical positions (e.g., Ostwald, 1972; Rheingold, 1968) that the cry may often attract the attention of those who will provide care beneficial to the survival of the infant.

Variations in the pattern of crying have long intrigued those who are interested in the functional and adaptive significance of early emotional expressions (e.g., Darwin, 1855). The birth cry of the infant has been described as having a distinctive sound (Wasz-Höckert, Lind, Vuorenkoski, Partanen, & Valanne, 1968) that is probably related to the first use and strength of the mechanical and respiratory systems and the presence of various fluids in the vocal tract. Distinctive patterns of infant crying during the newborn period, however, reflect more than the status of the vocal tract and respiratory systems. The spectrographic studies relating rhythmical (Wolff, 1967) and spectral features (Wasz-Höckert et al., 1968) of infant crying to various eliciting conditions such as hunger and pain indicate that different patterns of infant crying may reflect the arousal of the infant (Lester & Zeskind, 1982). For example, in response to a presumably painful stimulus, initial portions of the cry show longer expirations of sound and between-sound pauses (Wolff, 1967) and more sudden shifts to a higher pitch (Wasz-Höckert *et al.*, 1968) than cries in response to presumably less arousing conditions. Some evidence suggests that as infant arousal to the painful stimulus subsides, the rhythmical (Wolff, 1967) and harmonic (Blinick, Tavolga, & Antopol, 1971) characteristics of the pain cry become more similar to the characteristics of cries in response to less arousing conditions. There are, for example, shorter expirations of sound and fewer shifts in pitch.

It is in cry features such as these that we again see the contributions of both environmental and biological influences on the manifestation of crying. The presumed arousal manifested in different cry sounds reflects the interaction of the nature of the eliciting stimulus condition (from either internal or external environmental sources) and the manner in which the biological system of the infant organizes a response to that stimulus condition. As mentioned previously, sudden shifts in pitch are more often associated with cry responses to the sharp stick of a needle or the pinch of the skin than with cry responses to the more gradual effects of rising hunger. However, that same painful stimulus may produce different cry sounds, depending on the biological response systems of the infant. For example, Truby and Lind (1965) found that infant cries, in response to presumably the same skin pinch, may show substantial differences in sound quality. These authors classified pain cries as either (1) phonated—characterized by a smooth and regular harmonic structure (at 400 to 500 Hz); (2) dysphonated—characterized by turbulence and noise at a higher pitch (less harmonic form); or (3) hyperhonated—characterized by an abrupt, upward shift in pitch (up to 2000 Hz). Thus, although shifts to a high-pitched cry sound appear to be associated with the characteristics of a painful stimulus, the high-pitched effects appear to be manifested only in some infants.

This particular pattern of infant responsivity appears to be a phenomenon more frequently evident among newborn infants who are at increased risk. Provided with a standard painful stimulus, infants who have experienced prenatal and perinatal events that affect biological functioning show high-pitched cries more frequently than infants who have not experienced these events. Just as in studies of "normal" infants, this high cry pitch appears to result from sudden pitch shifts. Whereas some studies of infants with anthropometric signs of risk, for example, have examined the heightened fundamental frequency ($F_0$) averaged over the first cry expiration (e.g., Lester, 1979; Zeskind & Lester, 1981), other studies of these infants at risk (Michelsson, 1971; Zeskind, 1983a) show that the heightened pitch may be the average of shifts between hyperphonated and phonated cry segments.

Because infants with an increased risk status may go unnoticed in the normal newborn nursery, we do not know if the infants in the preceding studies of "normal" infants who showed hyperphonation were actually infants who would actually have been considered to be at increased risk under closer scrutiny. For example, in one study (Zeskind & Lester, 1978), low- and high-risk infants who showed these differential cry features were found within a sample of full-birth-weight, full-term, appropriate weight-for-gestational-age infants who had Apgar scores of 7 or better at both 1 and 5 minutes and who showed no abnormal clinical signs on routine neurological and physical examinations. Rather than separating infants into groups of "at risk" and "normal" newborns, however, we can suggest that among the "normal" newborn population there are some infants whose previous developmental conditions provided the experiences that have led to a particular high-pitched cry sound. For some of these infants, we have isolated some of the prenatal events that are associated with this cry feature and, as in the previously mentioned study, these prenatal experiences are associated with an increased risk status. From our developmental perspective, then, we would like to know what this expression of crying reflects about the biobehavioral organization of newborn infants, what the conditions were that led to that expression of crying, and how that particular expression of crying will contribute to the development of future expressions of crying.

## 4. CRYING AND PRESENT BEHAVIORAL ORGANIZATION

Whereas various peripheral vocal mechanisms produce variations in pitch (Lieberman, 1967) and, in particular, hyperphonation (see Chapter 3), the high pitch and other cry features associated with the infant at risk may ultimately be determined by nervous system control of these mechanisms (Lester & Zeskind, 1979). Parmelee (1962) suggested that the amount of stimulation required to produce a sustained cry, the duration of crying, and the tonal quality of the cry sound might reflect the capacity of the infant's nervous system to be activated and then to inhibit that activation. Increasing evidence supports a model that suggests that, among relatively healthy infants, these cry features may reflect the activation and inhibition processes of the autonomic nervous system (ANS) (Lester & Zeskind, 1982). The sympathetic nervous system component of the ANS provides generalized physiological responses of excitation and arousal. In the normal process of maintaining homeostasis, the parasympathetic nervous system component provides oppositional inhibitory influences on the level of arousal. These processes are integrated in the hypothalamus.

Lester and Zeskind (1982) hypothesized that the threshold and duration of crying and the tonal variations in cry pitch were related, respectively, to the sympathetic and parasympathetic activities of the ANS. Threshold and duration of crying are thought to be related to sympathetic activation because of the ANS component's excitatory effect on infant arousal. Modulation of the cry sound may be under parasympathetic control via the effect of the ANS component on vagal input to the larynx. Normally, the inhibitory action of increase vagal tone prevents the contraction of the laryngeal muscles that maintains a well-modulated sound. Golub (1979; see also Chapter 3) suggests that the sudden shift in pitch that characterizes hyperphonation may be due to shifting of the vocal registers that results from the noncontinuous manner in which neonates control tension in their laryngeal muscles. According to the ANS model of infant crying (Lester & Zeskind, 1982), these laryngeal contractions producing the hyperphonated cry sound occur during reduced parasympathetic activity and reduced vagal tone.

Accordingly, a high pitch cry should be more evident in pain cries, especially the initial portions of the cry when arousal is highest (and parasympathetic activity is at its lowest), but it should be accentuated in infants at risk. This issue was examined directly in a study in which the cries of a full-term, full-birth-weight infants who were at increased risk based on either a low or high ponderal index (PI) were compared to the cries of infants with similar characteristics but who were at low risk based on an average ponderal index (Zeskind, 1983a). The ponderal index is a ratio of the infant's birth weight and birth length used in the assessment of fetal malnutrition (Miller & Hassanein, 1971, 1973) and has been previously associated with differential cry features in underweight-for-length or low-PI (Lester, 1979; Lester & Zeskind, 1978) and overweight-for-length or high-PI newborns (Zeskind, 1983a; Zeskind & Lester, 1981).) A qualitative categorization of the amount of high-pitched hyperphonation was performed on the (1) initial segment of a pain cry; (2) the final segment of that cry; and (3) a random segment of crying resulting from the presumably less intense arousal of handling the infant during administration of a newborn behavioral examination. The results of this study showed that when upward shifts in pitch occurred in low-risk infant cries, they were briefly evident in the pain cry (congruent with the findings of Wasz-Höckert et al., 1968). For the high-risk infants, hyperphonation was found in all three segments, but a continuously long occurrence of this high-pitched sound was found only in pain cries, and mostly in the initial segment. Thus, the occurrence of a high cry pitch is more frequently associated with the intense arousal of painful stimulation, but the response system of the infants with atypical anthropometric signs appears to accentuate the effects of stimulation.

Other research, mostly in studies of newborn and young infants who show anthropometric indices of fetal and/or postnatal malnutrition, provides preliminary support for this model of infant crying. Lester (1976) found that the fundamental frequency of the cries of malnourished 1-year-old infants was related to cardiac deceleration such that infants who cried at a higher fundamental frequency showed lower cardiac deceleratory responses to a pure-tone stimulus. A high cry pitch and cardiac decelerations may be the result of the same decrease in vagal tone. Studies using the Neonatal Behavioral Assessment Scale (NBAS) (Brazelton, 1973) have also shown a relationship between infant pain cry features and relevant dimensions of biobehavioral organization among infants who showed differential patterns of fetal growth. In a multiple regression analysis of 40 2-day-old infants (Lester & Zeskind, 1978), poor performances on the NBAS plus a short gestation and a low ponderal index were associated with infant cries of a short duration, a high fundamental frequency, a high maximum frequency, and fewer harmonics in the cry sound. A between-group analysis (Lester, 1979) of the low ponderal index (low PI) and average ponderal index (average PI) infants from the sample of the study previously mentioned showed that underweight-for-length infants showed poorer scores on all four *a priori* dimensions of the NBAS and were differentiated by most of the cry features. The poorer NBAS scores were correlated to differences in the cry features but most notably to a higher fundamental frequency.

Building on these studies relating NBAS biobehavioral dimensions to neonatal cry features, the relationships among cry features and the NBAS cluster were examined in the low-, average- and high-PI infant sample described previously (Zeskind, 1983a). The threshold and duration of crying (production features) and the dominant frequencies (spectral features) of the initial, final, and NBAS cry segments also previously discussed were factor analyzed with the seven biobehavioral dimensions of the NBAS described by Lester, Als, and Brazelton (1982). The factor analysis showed that (1) the threshold and duration of crying loaded on a single factor separate from that of a second factor loaded by the spectral components of crying; (2) the NBAS clusters of Motoric and Orienting capabilities were related to both cry factors, with a stronger loading of the Motoric scores on the factor described by the spectral features; (3) the

NBAS clusters of Autonomic Stability and Range of State (indicating general automonic arousal) were related to the threshold and duration of crying; and (4) Muscle Tone and Motor Maturity were related specifically to the pitch components of the cry sound. This study showed that the NBAS measures of general autonomic arousal were related to the production components of crying. Further, those infants whose laryngeal muscles may more frequently act noncontinuously, resulting in a shift of vocal registers and a hyperhonated cry sound (Golub, 1979), were also infants who demonstrated poorer scores on measures of motor maturity, motor activity, and muscle tonus.

To examine further the relation between the production features of crying and general autonomic stability of the infant, the resting heart rates of 28 healthy, full-term, full birthweight 2-day-old infants were studied (Zeskind & Field, 1982). Fourteen infants who required one rubber band snap to elicit a sustained pain cry (typical of low-risk infants) were compared to 14 similar infants who required multiple snaps (typical of high-risk infants). The two groups did not differ in mean rate over a 30-minute period of quiet resting, but the multiple stimulus infants showed a greater heart rate peak, a lower heart rate depth,and a greater statistical variance of heart rate. These infants also showed a shorter cry duration and a more frequent occurrence of hyperphonation in the cry sound. This study is interesting because it provides an empirical demonstration of the changes in ANS activity associated with the differential cry features characteristic of the infant at risk as will be described later.

Changes in heart rate reflect a summation of influences on the infant's autonomic nervous system from both internal and external sources of stimulation. In order to maintain homeostasis, the inhibitory influences of parasympathetic reactions may be directly related to the magnitude of the preceding excitatory responses of the sympathetic system as these two systems work reciprocally (Gelhorn, 1957). The lower HR depths of the multiple stimulus infants may represent a point in time when the infant is temporarily showing greater parasympathetic inhibition to conditions of arousal during a resting state. As the infant's system attempts to maintain homeostasis, the excitatory influences of sympathetic activation may be commensurate with the previous degree of inhibition, thus resulting in a higher HR peak. Although this balancing act is part of the normal homeostatic process, infants requiring multiple snaps to elicit crying may show greater fluctuations in this "seesaw" activity of the opposing system. Thus, we can speculate that one aspect of the functional organization that the cry features of the infant at risk may reflect is a greater autonomic instability to the changing stimulation of internal and external conditions of arousal. Our next question in our developmental perspective is, what were the previous conditions in development that gave rise to this form of biobehavioral organization?

## 5. EFFECTS OF PREVIOUS DEVELOPMENT

Because we have been studying the biobehavioral organization of newborn infants, the previous conditions in development that give rise to crying are points in the prenatal and perinatal periods. Unfortunately, our knowledge of specific prenatal experience is severely limited in the study of human infants by ethical constraints. However, even behaviors such as normal neonatal vocalizations develop as a function of specific prenatal conditions. For example, ducklings and other precocial birds vocalize several days before hatching and thus provide for themselves prenatal auditory stimulation in addition to mother-produced sounds. Environmental effects such as short-term reductions in incubation temperature result in a reduction in the amount of embryonic vocalizations (Oppenheim & Levin, 1975) and, therefore, the amount of auditory self-stimulation. Scoville (1982) has demonstrated in neonatal ducklings that a reduction in embryonic auditory stimulation can disrupt the rhythmical organization of the duckling's distress calls. Classic experiments by Gottlieb (1975a, 1975b, 1975c) have also demonstrated that preventing ducklings from vocalizing during the embryonic period reduces their posthatching ability to recognize maternal species-identification vocalizations. Experiments such as these emphasize the importance of specific prenatal experiences that influence "innate" maturational and social processes, even if the experiences are self-produced.

In the developing human fetus, some ANS activity may provide functional stimulation in and of itself. For example, the premature breathing movements of the fetal chest, or "Ahlfeld movements," help prepare the respiratory mechanisms for later breathing, while they also function prenatally to facilitate fetal circulation (Carmichael, 1970). Other ANS activity shows direct influences from the mother's internal environment. For example, Sterman and Hoppenbrouwers (1971) recorded fetal activity over a 4-month period (5 to 9 months gestation) by placing sensors on the mother's abdomen while she was sleeping. Computer analysis of apparently irregular rhythmic fluctuations extracted two basic cycles in rhythmic activity: a stronger cycle recurred every 40 minutes, whereas a weaker one appeared at 96 minutes. The 96-minute cycle of fetal activity may represent the influences of maternal ANS activity on the developing fetus' ANS activity. This cycle, which almost exactly approximates the REM sleep cycle in adults, was no longer evident in the fetal system immediately following birth.

During this prenatal period we can see the effects of both structural and functional development on the development of the potential sound of the cry. Depending on when during gestation the infant is born, the cry will reflect the then-present status of structural growth and functional organization. In a cross-sectional study of the birth cries of prematurely born infants, the fundamental frequency of the cry remained unchanged from 7 to 9 months gestation, whereas the pitch of the cry at the higher frequencies of the first and second formants tended to decrease with increasing gestational age (Gardosik, Ross, & Singh, 1980). Gardosik *et al.* suggested that the higher pitched formant frequencies of the more premature infant might be the result of a less matured structural system in which the larynx had a higher physical position and thus a shorter vocal tract. Shifts in the pitch of the cry sound are also frequent in preterm infants (Michelsson, 1971) and may be the most salient feature discriminating cries of preterm and term infants (Tenold, Crowell, Jones, Daniel, McPherson, & Popper, 1974). To the extent that shifts in cry pitch reflect the stability of autonomic functioning, in preterm infants the frequent pitch shifts may indicate a less mature organization of the autonomic nervous system (Lester & Zeskind, 1982).

During the development of these maturational and functional activities, the infant at risk may have experienced any number of factors that could detrimentally affect the ANS functioning associated with the distinguishing cry features. In many cases, the infant is besieged by multiple biological, social, economic, cultural, and familial hazards that may act separately or in combination to produce the nonoptimal obstetric conditions (Birch & Gussow, 1970) and/or differential patterns of fetal growth (Ounsted & Ounsted, 1973; Waisman & Kerr, 1970) associated with increased risk. For example, infants with these indices of risk often develop in a maternal environment characterized by such influences as inadequate nutrition, poor health and prenatal care, and increased maternal stress; the detrimental effect of one factor is exacerbated by the presence of others.

The complexity of these interacting influences can be underscored when we examine the role of fetal malnutrition associated with the risk indices of nonoptimal obstetric conditions and differential patterns of fetal growth. First, as suggested before, malnutrition often does not occur in the absence of other nonoptimal conditions. For example, even within the same level of low socioeconomic status, mothers who have infants with a low ponderal index also have more previous miscarriages and other health-related obstetric problems than do mothers who have infants with an average ponderal index (Zeskind & Ramey, 1981). Second, the effects of fetal malnutrition can operate at both direct and indirect levels on the development of the nervous system. Inadequate amounts of protein in the maternal diet may not only fail to provide the nutrients essential to optimal neural development, but also this protein deficiency interacts with the production of glucocorticoids (Greengard, 1978) and the neurotransmitter serotonin (Lytle, Messing, Fisher, & Phebus, 1975). Maternal stress can also lead to increased glucocorticoidal levels that have been shown in infrahuman species to alter embryonic neural development by changing the timing of genetic activity (Jonakait, Bohn, & Black, 1980). Similarly, placental dysfunction may reduce both the nutrients essential to neural development and the blood and oxygen transfer required for optimal fetal growth (Alexander, 1978), Third, malnutrition may bidirectionally interact with the existing developmental status of the individual to affect future impacts of malnutrition. For example, malnutrition increases the likelihood and severity of infection and, in turn, an increase in the severity of infection exacerbates the likelihood and severity of malnutrition (Scrimshaw, Taylor, & Gordon, 1968).

This array of neurochemical, maturational, and functional influences on the developing nervous system may provide the experiences that produce the distinguishing cry features of the infant at risk by affecting the manner in which the organization of the ANS responds to stressful conditions. For example, malnutrition interferes with the normal development of the pituitary–adrenocorticoid axis (Greengard, 1978) that is part of a hypothalamic feedback loop system monitoring the arousal level of the infant (Ganong, 1965). Under stressful conditions, such as when the infant is subjected to the painful stimulus of a rubber band snap to the foot, there is an increased production of ACTH and, consequently, an increase in the production of glucocorticoids. Higher levels of glucocorticoids inhibit ACTH secretion thereby increasing the threshold of the infant with regard to further stimulation and functionally inhibiting a further rise in arousal. This feedback system directly relates to the excitatory and inhibitory influences of the sympathetic and parasympathetic nervous systems (also mediated by the hypothalamus) thus influencing the general biobehavioral activity of the infant.

We can speculate that the sympathetic and parasympathetic influences on infant crying (Lester & Zeskind, 1982) and the instability in neonatal heart rate associated with an increased threshold for crying (Zeskind & Field, 1982) may be associated with a disruption in the organization of such feedback activities. These speculations certainly need to be examined further. The point to be emphasized, however, is that, although the cry sound of the infant at risk has been described as an innate adaptive form of distal communication (Lester & Zeskind, 1978), to suggest that specific cry patterns occur at birth *because* they are innate arbitrarily establishes the infant's birth as the time at which experiences begin to affect the development of crying importantly. From our developmental perspective, we need to elucidate these adaptive experiences even if they occur prenatally. The probabilistic conceptions of prenatal development contributed by Gottlieb (1976) may provide useful guidelines for future questions.

## 6. EFFECTS ON SUCCEEDING POINTS IN DEVELOPMENT

Thus far we have been concerned with what the characteristics of crying reflect about the biobehavioral organization of the newborn infant and what the conditions were at preceding points in development that may have led to those characteristics. As the last part of our developmental analysis, we must ask, how does the expression of crying change, and what are the experiences that give rise to those changes? As we shall indicate, in the days and months following birth, the characteristics of crying continue to reflect the changing biobehavioral organization of the infant.

The acoustic features of crying show evidence of rapid reorganization soon after birth. In the first few days, the number of pitch shifts drops dramatically from the cry sound (Wasz-Höckert et al., 1968), a phenomenon that may reflect recovery from the stressful conditions of the birth process. During the first few months, the fundamental frequency increases slightly (Fairbanks, 1942; Prescott, 1975; Sheppard & Lane, 1968) and shows more variability in melody (Prescott, 1975), suggesting that there is increasing lung strength and flexibility in the vocal mechanisms. Over time, a more efficient air uptake system changes the rhythmic pattern of the cry sound. Whereas the duration of air inspiration during crying remains constant in the first 8 months, the duration of expiratory segments increases during this period (Prescott, 1980). That is, the infant is capable of longer outbursts of air even though the time in which air is taken in is the same. This may result from a behavioral reorganization of the components of the inspiratory/expiratory cry cycle. For example, during this age period, inspiratory voicing (sound production during inhalation) decreases (Fisichelli, Karelitz, Fisichelli, & Cooper, 1974), thus permitting the air to flow into the lungs without being blocked by constriction of the larnyx. In experiments studying the distress calls of precocial ducklings, a similar process of reorganization has been suggested to be the result of an increasing coordination of laryngeal, glottal, and respiratory mechanisms (Scoville, 1982).

The patterns of crying activity also reveals changes in the infant's developing biobehavioral organization. Individual differences in patterns of crying activity are generally stable in the first few days of life (Korner, Hutchinson, Koperski, Kraemer, & Schneider, 1981) with the characteristics of the pain cry showing greater stability than the characteristics of cries in response to less arousing conditions (Prechtl, Theorell, & Gramsbergen, 1969). The amount of crying increases gradually until it peaks at about 6 weeks of age (Brazelton, 1962; Rebelsky & Black, 1972) at which time the fluctuations in infant state begin to be less liable. Both the frequency of changes to a crying state and the frequency of transitions between sleep and wakefulness decline over the next months (e.g., Shirley, 1933; Snow, Jacklin, & Maccoby, 1980). Emde and Gaensbauer (1981) have suggested that there are two major shifts in biobehavioral organization that would be reflected in these changing patterns of infant crying activity. One shift occurs at approximately 2 months of age and is reflected in a change from endogenous to exogenous control of crying. That is, crying may be more reflexive in the first few months of life and more under control of contingent responsivity following the shift. For example, Bell and Ainsworth (1972) observed that whereas an infant initially seemed to cry in order to promote proximity with his or her mother, in the later months of that first year the infant cried when the mother was already nearby. This change from reflexive crying occurs at a time when a number of other reflexes drop out, possibly reflecting the development of forebrain inhibitory areas (Peiper, 1963), and are concomitant with increases in exogenous smiling, quiet sleep, social-perceptual skills, and the ability to demonstrate habituation and classical and operant conditioning (see Emde & Gaensbauer, 1981). At 7 months, a second shift occurs in which changes in affective attachment, cognition, and state and heart rate organization develop.

At one level, the act of crying, in itself, may feedback to provide experiences important to changes in the infant's biobehavioral organization. Thelen (1981) theorizes that the manifestation of rhythmical behavior may serve as a mode of self-stimulation that, in the absence of other stimulation, improves behavioral organization. For example, according to Konner's (1972) descriptions of hunter-gatherer societies, when much of human evolution occurred, the infant received more vestibular stimulation and also cried less, both as a result of being carried by the mother more often than infants in today's Western cultures who are frequently left in a crib. In addition to the possible feedback effects of rhythmic stimulation, auditory feedback from crying may also provide important experiences. For example, reduced auditory stimulation has been found to affect the rhythmic organization of the distress calls of other species (Scoville, 1982). Although the processes by which auditory feedback may affect the development of crying is unexplored, we have evidence that indicates that newborn infants cry in response to hearing the sound of crying (Sagi & Hoffman, 1976) and that the lack of auditory feedback in deaf infants may affect other early vocalizations such as prelinguistic phonemic babbling (Lach, Ling, Ling, & Ship, 1970) as early as 6 months of age (Lenneberg, 1967).

At the second level, the act of crying contributes to the changing nature of the external caregiving environment whose responses will feedback to provide experiences important to changes in the biobehavioral organization of the infant. For example, any parent can attest to changes in their own sleep/wake cycles that result from the demands of their newborn infant's cry when the infant is hungry. Feeding, in return, changes the infant's autonomic arousal and, thus, pattern of crying. In studies of mother–pup interactions, a number of experiments (Hofer & Weiner, 1975) have shown that the mother rat regulates the heart rates and levels of arousal of her pups by the amount of milk she supplies them. In humans, similar interoceptive stimulation of the stomach affects autonomic system activity and reduces infant arousal. By 12 weeks of age, the infant's rhythmic organization of crying begins to conform to the feed/sleep patterns of the caregiving environment (Rebelsky & Black, 1972). Concordance between the infant's and caregiving environment's rhythms, however, is not preordained. The concept of a "difficult" infant, for example, focuses on the lack of a good fit between the infant's rhythms and behavioral style and the caregiving environment's goals and expectations (e.g., Thomas & Chess, 1977).

Similarly, the sound of the infant crying is an important behavior to which parents will respond, but the nature of the response is also not preordained. Although some suggest that the cry can be seen as a releaser of supportive parental behavior (e.g., Bowlby, 1969), in her thoughtful review, Murray (1979) concludes that altruistic parental responses to infant crying must be viewed within the context in which they occur. From the perspective of this chapter, we can suggest that parental attention results as a function of both the nature of the cry sound and the specific context in which it occurs. For example, the initial characteristics of the pain cry may send a parent running to attend to the infant (Wolff, 1967), but parental responsivity to crying will also depend on conditions such as how long it has been since the infant was fed (Bernal, 1972) or the nature of previous interactions with the infant (e.g., Frodi & Lamb, 1980). It is this kind of relationship between the characteristics of the cry and the characteristics of the caregiving environment that underscore the probabilistic process of infant development, especially as demonstrated in the infant at risk.

First, not all infants who have been classified as "at risk" by some pediatric standard have high-pitched cry sounds. Although there are significant differences in the cry features between groups of low- and high-risk infants, there are also significantly larger within-group differences in cry features for high-risk infant groups than there are for low-risk infant groups (Zeskind, 1981, 1983a; Zeskind & Lester, 1981). This could be due to (1) the false-positive identification of individual infants as having experienced some nonoptimal prenatal or perinatal condition based on the infant's deviation from some statistical norm such as being below the 10th percentile of fetal growth or having high numbers of birth complications; or (2) the individual infant's response to some real nonoptimal prenatal or perinatal condition such that not all infants are detrimentally affected by the factors that produced poor fetal growth or high numbers of birth complications. At this early stage of researching the cry of the infant at risk, we may speculate that, within a group of infants labeled as *at risk*, the cry may reflect which infants may truly have had an adverse biological response to their previous conditions of development. For example, as indicated in a previous section, there are a number of studies that have shown that these differential features of the cry sound are reliably related to other measurements of biobehavioral functioning (Lester, 1979; Lester & Zeskind, 1978; Zeskind, 1981, 1983a). Thus, the probablistic course of development may first be a function of the fact that some infants within a risk group have experienced some biological handicap, whereas others have not. Those who did may emit a particularly distinctive cry sound and concomitant behaviors.

The second factor in this probabilistic process is the nature of the environment in which the different biobehavioral systems develop. Although researchers have long attempted to find if adult listeners can identify cries that have been elicited by different stimuli, recent research has suggested that adult perceptions of infant crying are based on the nature of the cry sound rather than on the nature of the eliciting stimulus (Zeskind, Sale, Maio, Huntington, & Weiseman, in press). For example, in a study of mothers listening to a series of pain cries, we found a linear relationship between the fundamental frequency of the cries and the degree to which those cry sounds were grating and aversive (Zeskind & Marshall, 1984). In this context, the distinctive cry of the infant at risk is a most salient signal that will provide part of the basis of interactions with the care-giving environment. Ostwald (1972) once described the high-pitched cry characteristic of the infant at risk as a "biological siren" that calls attention to the special condition of the infant. Other reports have referred to the "biological synchrony" between the activity of the infant's nervous system that produces a high-pitched cry sound and the activity of the listener's nervous system that is especially responsive to high-pitched sounds (Zeskind, 1980; Zeskind et al., 1984). For example, whereas the fetal malnutrition that may result in a high-pitched neonatal cry sound affects such autonomic activity as the pituitary-adrenocorticoid feedback axis (Greengard, 1978), high-pitched sounds, in turn, have a synchronous stimulatory effect on the pituitary-adrenocorticoid axis in the adult listener (Arguelles, Ibeas, Ottone, & Chekherdemain, 1962).

Thus, even though two infants may be crying for the same reason, infants may receive differential treatment depending on the nature of the cry sound. In all cases, the cry of the infant at risk is a particularly potent signal and seems to bring to the surface potential differences in the nature of different caregiving environments. For example, in a recent cross-cultural study of maternal perceptions of the pain cries of low- and high-risk infants, the cries of the high-risk infants elicited perceptions and responses that paralleled the characteristics of parent–child interactions previously found to be dominant in each culture, whereas the low-risk infant cries did not, in this laboratory situation (Zeskind, 1983b). In another experiment (Zeskind & Lester, 1978), the pain cries of low-risk infants elicited ratings that represented a single perceptual dimension of how "distressing" the cry sounded. On the other hand, the pain cry of the high-risk infants not only elicited a similar perceptual dimension in which the cries were rated as even more "distressing" but also produced an additional perceptual dimension that the infant sounded "sick." This special message may be unique to the hyperphonated cry characteristic of the infant at risk. For example, although there may be acoustic differences between the cries of temperamentally "easy" and "difficult" infants that affect the parent's perceptions of their infants (Lounsbury & Bates, 1982), the cries of "difficult" infants do not reveal this distinct perceptual dimension under similar methodological and statistical procedures (Boukydis & Burgess, 1982). This dual set of perceptual dimensions may provide the basis for differential patterns of parental responsivity. In a laboratory setting, the cry of the infant at risk elicits caregiving choices that are rated as (1) more "immediate" in their action in terminating the cry sound that is particularly distressing and aversive; and (2) more "tender and caring" for an infant who sounds sick (Zeskind, 1980).

Thus, the cry of the infant at risk may bring out different environmental responses, each with their own differential probabilities of occurring. In one environment, the extremely distressing and aversive quality of the cry sound may be focused upon. In this nonsupportive caregiving environment, the behavioral repertoire of the especially lethargic or irritable infant with a high-pitched distressing cry sound may violate the limits of caregiver control (Bell, 1971) and suppress the optimal patterns of caregiver necessary to facilitate the recovery of the infant. These nonoptimal caregiving patterns could exacerbate the condition of the infant's biobehavioral organization, thus establishing a cycle of irritating infant behavior operating in an environment that will continue to provide nonoptimal experiences. In extreme conditions, this cycle could lead to failures in the parent–infant interaction process, with the result that the child is abused or totally neglected. In many anecdotal references regarding child abuse, for example, excessive patterns of high-pitched aversive cry sounds are often reported (Gil, 1970; Parke & Collmer, 1975; Ramey, Heiger, & Klisz, 1972).

In a supportive environment, however, where the structure of the caregiving environment can integrate the behavioral repertoire and rhythmic patterns of the infant at risk, the sick and urgent message of the cry sound may elicit responses that may feedback and facilitate recovery and optimal development. For example, the actual responses chosen by parents in laboratory experiments ("pick up" and "cuddle" the infant) may best provide the upright position (Korner & Thoman, 1972) and rocking motion (Byrne & Horowitz, 1981) that provide vestibular stimulation and efficiently bring the infants into an alert state. As these conditions provide the experiences necessary for optimal development, the recovery of the infant will be reflected in a reorganization of the infant's biobehavioral system. Some evidence suggests that as the infant shows recovery, the distinctive high-pitched cry components may disappear (Michelsson, Sirvio, & Wasz-Höckert, 1977), thus optimizing future transactions.

Support for this model is found in a study (Zeskind & Ramey, 1978) of the cognitive and social development of full-birth-weight and full-term low-PI and average-PI infants from low socioeconomic status homes who were randomly assigned to a supportive day-care environment or left in a home environment that had been shown to be nonsupportive or social and intellectual development. Not only did the low-PI infants in the nonsupportive caregiving environment show recovery, as did the low-PI infants in the supportive caregiving environment by 18 months, but they also began to obtain less maternal interaction relative to average-PI infants in the same environment and relative to the low-PI infants in the supportive environment. This indicated that the behavioral characteristics of the low-PI infants resulted in a withdrawal of maternal interaction when the infant did not show recovery. A follow-up study (Zeskind & Ramey, 1981) of these infants at 3 years of age indicated that the low-PI infants in the nonsupportive environment, unlike the other infant groups, still showed the withdrawn and unresponsive behavioral attributes characteristic of the low-PI newborn. In this study, the condition of the infant was either ameliorated or exacerbated, depending on the quality of the caregiving environment, an environment that the infant helped to create. Because the environment that results in nonoptimal prenatal conditions associated with an increased risk status is also the environment that results in similar nonoptimal postnatal conditions, there are unequal probabilities outside of this intervention program that the infant born at risk will experience supportive or nonsupportive postnatal caregiving environments, and thus, there is an increased probability of nonoptimal development.

## 7. CONCLUSION

Crying in the newborn and young infant has traditionally been viewed as either a social behavior that influences the quality of care the infant receives or as a reflexive response that may have diagnostic value. A synthesis of these two views may provide the basis for a developmental assessment tool in the care of the infant at risk. Unfortunately, a paucity of developmental research has resulted in little being known about the development of infant crying *per se*. This chapter has attempted to provide a developmental perspective within which future questions can be asked.

A developmental perspective of the cry of the infant at risk was presented that was based on the same bidirectional and probabilistic processes as those involved in normal infant behavioral development. To say that a behavior such as the cry of the low-risk infant is "normal" imparts a statistical evaluation of its occurrence—that there are behaviors that have a higher probability of occuring in a given set of conditions than other behaviors. They are behaviors that have a higher probability of occurring because both the specific biological and environmental conditions in which they developed have a higher probability of occurring. However, to the extent that there are variations in this "normal" condition, there will be variations in the development of behavior. Within the range of normality there are particular patterns of infant behavior such as the cry of the infant at risk that may have lesser probabilities of occurring at birth in the general population but that have arrived via present functioning of the newborn's autonomic nervous system as it has arisen from previous development exercises, but its also contributes to the experiences that direct the future course of infant development. This bidirectional and probabilistic process of development may contribute to either the fulfillment of the outcome prophesized by the risk status or to the eventual recovery of the infant.

## 8. REFERENCES

Ainsworth, M. S., & Bell, S. M. Infant crying and maternal responsiveness: A rejoinder to Gewirtz and Boyd. *Child Development*, 1977, *48*, 1208–1216.

Alexander, G. Factors regulating the growth of the placenta: With comments on the relationship between placental weight and fetal weight. In F. Naftolin (Ed.), *Abnormal fetal growth: Biological bases and consequences*. Berlin: Life Sciences Research Reports, 1978.

Arguelles, A. E., Ibeas, D., Ottone, J. P., & Chekherdemain, M. Pituitaryadrenal stimulation by sound of different frequencies. *Journal of Clinical Endocrinology and Metabolism*, 1962, *22*, 846–852.

Bell, R. Q. Stimulus control of parent or caretaker behavior by offspring. *Developmental Psychology*, 1971, *4*(1), 63–72.

Bell, S. M., & Ainsworth, M. D. S. Infant crying and maternal responsiveness. *Child Development*, 1972, *43*, 1171–1190.

Bernal, J. Crying during the first ten days of life and maternal responses. *Developmental Medicine and Child Neurology*, 1972, *14*, 362–372.

Birch, H. G., & Gussow, J. D. *Disadvantaged children: Health, nutrition and school failure*. New York: Grune & Stratton, 1970.

Blinick, G., Tavolga, W. N., & Antopol, W. Variations in birth cries of newborn infants from narcotic addicted and normal mothers. *American Journal of Obstetrics and Gynecology*, 1971, *110*, 948–958.

Boukydis, C. F. Z., & Burgess, R. L. Adult physiological response to infant cries: Effects of temperament of infant, parental status and gender. *Child Development*, 1982, *53*, 1291–1298.

Bowlby, J. *Attachment and loss* (Vol. 1). New York: Basic Books, 1969.

Brazelton, T. B. Crying in infancy. *Pediatrics*, 1962, *29*, 579–588.

Brazelton, T. B. Neonatal behavioral assessment scale. *Clinics in Developmental Medicine 50*. London: Heineman; Philadelphia, Lippincott, 1973.

Byrne, J. M., & Horowitz, F. D. Rocking as a soothing intervention: The influence of direction and type of movement. *Infant Behavior and Development*, 1981, *4*, 207–218.

Carmichael, L. A re-evaluation of the concepts of maturation and learning as applied to the early development of behavior. *Psychological Review*, 1936, *43*, 450–470.

Carmichael, L. The onset and early development of behavior. In P. H. Mussen (Ed.), *Carmichael's manual of child psychology*. New York: Wiley, 1970.

Darwin, C. *The expression of emotion in man and animals*. New York: Philosophical Library, 1855.

Emde, R. N., & Gaensbauer, T. Some emerging models of emotion in human infancy. In K. Immelman, G. Barlow, L. Petrinovich, & M. Main (Eds.), *Behavioral development*. Cambridge: Cambridge University Press, 1981.

Fairbanks, G. An acoustical study of the pitch of infant hunger wails. *Child Development*, 1942, *13*(3), 227–232.

Fisichelli, V., & Karelitz, S. The cry latencies of normal infants and those with brain damage. *Journal of Pediatrics*, 1963, *62*, 724–734.

Fisichelli, V., Karelitz, S., Fisichelli, R., & Cooper, J. The course of induced crying activity in the first year of life. *Pediatric Research*, 1974, *8*, 921–928.

Frodi, A. M., & Lamb, M. F. Child abusers' responses to infant smiles and cries. *Child Development*, 1980, *51*, 238–241.

Frodi, A., Lamb, M., Leavitt, L., & Donovan, W. Fathers' and mothers' responses to infant smiles and cries. *Infant Behavior and Development*, 1978, *1*(2), 187–198.

Ganong, W. F. *Review of medical physiology*. Los Altos, Calif.: Lange Medical Publications, 1965.

Gardosik, T., Ross, P., & Singh, S. Acoustic characteristics of the first cries of infants. In T. Murry & J. Murry (Eds.), *Infant communication: Cry and early speech*. Houston: College-Hill Press, 1980.

Gelhorn, E. *Autonomic imbalance and the hypothalus*. Minneapolis: University of Minnesota Press, 1957.

Gewirtz, J. L., & Boyd, E. F. Does maternal responding imply reduced infant crying? A critique of the 1972 Bell and Ainsworth report. *Child Development*, 1977, *48*, 1200–1207. (a)

Gewirtz, J. L., & Boyd, E. F. In reply to the rejoinder to our critique of the 1972 Bell and Ainsworth report. *Child Development*, 1977, *48*, 1217–1218. (b)

Gil, D. *Violence against children*. Cambridge, MA: Harvard University Press, 1970.

Golub, H. L. A physioacoustic model of the infant cry and its use for medical diagnosis and prognosis. In J. J. Wolf & D. H. Klatt, (Eds.), *Speech communication papers presented at the 97th meeting of the Acoustical Society of America*, 1979.

Gottlieb, G. Development of species identification in ducklings: I. Nature of perceptual deficit caused by embryonic auditory deprivation. *Journal of Comparative and Physiological Psychology*, 1975, *89*, 387–399. (a)

Gottlieb, G. Development of species identification in ducklings: II. Experiential prevention of perceptual deficit caused by embryonic deprivation. *Journal of Comparative and Physiological Psychology*, 1975, *89*, 675–684. (b)

Gottlieb, G. Development of species identification in ducklings: III. Maturational rectification of perceptual deficit caused by auditory deprivation. *Journal of Comparative and Physiological Psychology*, 1975, *89*, 899–912. (c)

Gottlieb, G. Conceptions of prenatal development: Behavioral embryology. *Psychological Review*, 1976, *83*(3), 215–234.

Graham, M. Intrauterine crying. *British Medical Journal*, 1919, *1*, 675.

Greengard, O. Relationship of enzymes to normal and abnormal fetal growth. In F. Natolin (Ed.), *Abnormal fetal growth: Biological bases and consequences*. Berlin: Life Sciences Research Reports, 1978.

Harris, D. B. (Ed.). *The concept of development*. Minneapolis: University of Minnesota Press, 1957.

Hofer, M. A., & Weiner, H. Physiological mechanisms for cardiac control by nutritional intake after early maternal separation in the young rat. *Psychosomatic Medicine*, 1975, *37*, 8–24.

Immelmann, K., Barlow, G. W., Petrinovich, L., & Main, M. (Eds.). *Behavioral development*. Cambridge: Cambridge University Press, 1981.

Jonakait, G. M., Bohn, M. C., & Black, I. B. Maternal glucocorticoid hormones influence neurotransmitter phenotype expression in embryos. *Science*, 1980, *210*, 551–553.

Karelitz, S., & Fisichelli, V. The cry thresholds of normal infants and those with brain damage. *Journal of Pediatrics*, 1962, *61*, 679–685.

Kessen, W. Research design in the study of developmental problems. In P. H. Mussen (Ed.), *Handbook of research methods in child development*. New York: Wiley, 1960.

Konner, M. Aspects of the developmental ethology of a foraging people. In N. J. Blurton Jones (Ed.), *Ethological studies of child behavior*. Cambridge: Cambridge University Press, 1972.

Korner, A. F., & Thoman, E. B. The relative efficacy of contact and vestibular-proprioceptive stimulation in soothing neonates. *Child Development*, 1972, *43*, 443–453.

Korner, A. F., Hutchinson, C., Koperski, J., Kraemer, H., & Schneider, P. Stability of individual differences of neonatal motor and crying patterns. *Child Development*, 1981, *52*, 83–90.

Lach, R., Ling, D., Ling, A., & Ship, N. Early speech development in deaf infants. *American Annals of the Deaf*, 1970, *15*, 522–526.

Lehrman, D. S. A critique of Konrad Lorenz's theory of instinctive behavior. *Quarterly Review of Biology*, 1953, *28*, 337–363.

Lenneberg, E. H. *Biological foundations of language*. New York: Wiley, 1967.

Lester, B. M. Spectrum analysis of the cry sounds of well-nourished and malnourished infants. *Child Development*, 1976, *47*, 236–241.

Lester, B. M. A synergistic process approach to the study of prenatal malnutrition. *International Journal of Behavioral Development*, 1979, *2*, 377–393.

Lester, B. M., & Zeskind, P. S. Brazelton scale and physical size correlates of neonatal cry features. *Infant Behavior and Development*, 1978, *1*(4), 393–402.

Lester, B. M., & Zeskind, P. S. The organization and assessment of crying in the infant at risk. In T. M. Field, A. M. Sostek, S. Goldberg, & H. H. Schuman (Eds.), *Infants born at risk*. New York: Spectrum, 1979.

Lester, B. M., & Zeskind, P. S. A biobehavioral perspective on crying in early infancy. In H. E. Fitzgerald, B. M. Lester, & M. W. Yogman (Eds.), *Theory and research in behavioral pediatrics* (Vol. 1). New York: Plenum Press, 1982.

Lester, B. M., Als, H., & Brazelton, T. B. Regional obstetric anesthesia and newborn behavior: A reanalysis toward synergistic effects. *Child Development*, 1982, *53*, 687–692.

Lounsbury, M. L., & Bates, J. E. The cries of infants of differing levels of perceived temperamental difficultness: Acoustic properties and effects on listeners. *Child Development*, 1982, *53*, 677–686.

Lytle, L. D., Messing, R. B., Fisher, L., & Phebus, L. Effects of long-term corn consumption on brain serotonin and the response to electric shock. *Science*, 1975, *190*, 692–694.

Michelsson, K. Cry analysis of symptomless low birthweight neonates and of asphyxiated newborn infants. *Acta Paediatrica Scandinavica* (Supp. 216), 1971, 1–45.

Michelsson, K., Sirvio, P., & Wasz-Höckert, O. Pain cry in full term asphyxiated newborn infants correlated with later findings. *Acta Paediatrica Scandinavica*, 1977, 1–45.

Miller, H. C., & Hassanein, K. Diagnosis of impaired fetal growth in newborn infants. *Pediatrics*, 1971, *48*, 511–522.

Miller, H. C., & Hassanein, K. Fetal malnutrition in white newborn infants: Maternal factors. *Pediatrics*, 1973, *52*, 504–512.

Murray, A. Infant crying as an elicitor of parental behavior: An examination of two models. *Psychological Bulletin*, 1979, *86*(1), 191–215.

Oppenheim, R. W., & Levin, H. L. Short-term changes in incubation temperature: Behavioral and physiological effects in the chick embryo from 6 to 20 days. *Developmental Psychobiology*, 1975, *8*, 103–115.

Ostwald, P. The sounds of infancy. *Developmental Medicine and Child Neurology*, 1972, *14*, 350–361.

Ounsted, M., & Ounsted, C. On fetal growth rate. *Clinics in Developmental Medicine NO. 46.* Phildadelphia: Lippincott, Spastics International Medical Publications, 1973.

Parke, R. D., & Collmer, C. W. Child abuse: An interdisciplinary analysis. In E. M. Hetherington (Ed.), *Review of child development 5.* Chicago: University of Chicago Press, 1975.

Parmelee, A. Infant crying and neurological diagnosis. *Journal of Pediatrics*, 1962, *61*, 801–802.

Peiper, A. Cerebral function in infancy and childhood. In J. Wortis (Ed.), *The international behavioral science series*. New York: Consultants Bureau, 1963.

Prechtl, H. F. R., & Beintema, D. The neurological examination of the full term infant. *Clinics in Developmental Medicine, 12.* London: Heinemann; Philadelphia: Lippincott, 1964.

Prechtl, H. F. R., Theorell, K., Gramsbergen, A., & Lind, J. A. Statistical analysis of cry patterns in normal and abnormal newborn infants. *Developmental Medicine and Child Neurology*, 1969, *11*, 142–152.

Prescott, R. Infant cry sound: Developmental features. *Journal of the Acoustic Society of America*, 1975, *57*, 1186–1991.

Prescott, R. Cry and maturation. In T. Murry & J. Murry (Eds.), *Infant communication: Cry and early speech*. Houston: College Hill Press, 1980.

Ramey, C. T., Heiger, L., & Klisz, D. Synchronous reinforcement of vocal responses in failure-to-thrive infants. *Child Development*, 1972, *43*, 1449–1455.

Rebelsky, F., & Black, R. Crying in infancy. *The Journal of Genetic Psychology*, 1972, *121*, 49–57.

Rheingold, H. L. Infancy. *International encyclopedia of the social sciences* (Vol. 7). New York: Crowell-Collier and Macmillan, 1968.

Rheingold, H. L., Gewirtz, J. L., & Ross, H. Social conditioning of vocalizations in the infant. *Journal of Comparative and Physiological Psychology*, 1959, *52*, 68–73.

Ricciuti, H. N. Fear and the development of social attachments in the first year of life. In M. Lewis & L. A. Rosenblum (Eds.), *The origins of fear*. New York: Wiley, 1974.

Rosenblatt, J. S., & Lehrman, D. S. Maternal behavior of the laboratory rat. In H. L Rheingold (Ed.), *Maternal behavior in mammals*. New York: Wiley, 1963.

Sackett, G. P., Sameroff, A., Cairns, R. B., & Suomi, S. J. Continuity in behavioral development: Theoretical and empirical issues. In K. Immelman, G. Barlow, L. Petrinovich, & M. Main (Eds.), *Behavioral development*. Cambridge: Cambridge University Press, 1981.

Sagi, A., & Hoffman, M. L. Empathetic distress in the newborn. *Developmental Psychology*, 1976, *12*(2), 175–176.

Schaffer, H. R., & Emerson, P. E. The development of social attachments in infancy. *Monographs of the Society for Research in Child Development*, 1964, *29* (serial no. 94).

Scoville, R. *The embryonic development of neonatal vocalizations in Peking ducklings* (Anas platyrhynchos). Unpublished doctoral dissertation, University of North Carolina, Chapel Hill, 1982.

Scrimshaw, N. S., Taylor, C., & Gordon, J. E. Interactions of nutrition and infection. *WHO Monograph Series*, 1968, No. 57.

Sheppard, W. C., & Lane, H. L. Development of the prosodic features of infant vocalizing. *Journal of Speech and Hearing Research*, 1968, *11*, 94–108.

Sherman, M. The differentiation of emotional responses in infants. *Journal of Comparative Psychology*, 1927, 7, 265–284.

Shirley, M. *The first two years: A study of twenty-five babies, Vol. 3: Personality manifestations.* Minneapolis: University of Minnesota Press, 1933.

Snow, M. E., Jacklin, C. N., & Maccoby, E. E. Crying episodes and sleep–wakefulness transitions in the first 26 months of life. *Infant Behavior and Development*, 1980, 3, 387–394.

Sterman, M. B., & Hoppenbrouwers, T. The development of sleep–waking and rest–activity patterns from fetus to adult in man. In M. B. Sterman, D. J. McGinty, & A. M. Adinolfi (Eds.), *Brain development and behavior*. New York: Academic Press, 1971.

Tenold, J. L., Crowell, D., Jones, R., Daniel, T., McPherson, F., & Popper, A. Cepstral and stationarity analyses of full-term and premature infants' cries. *Journal of the Acoustical Society of America*, 1974, 3, 975–980.

Thelen, E. Rhythmical behavior in infancy: An ethological perspective. *Developmental Psychology*, 1981, 17, 237–257.

Thomas, A., & Chess, S. *Temperament and development*. New York: Brunner/Mazel, 1977.

Truby, H. M., & Lind, J. Cry sounds of the newborn infant. In J. Lind (Ed.), Newborn infant cry. *Acta Paediatrica Scandinavica*, 1965, (Suppl. 163).

Vaughan, V., McKay, R., & Behrman, R. E. *Nelson textbook of pediatrics* (11th ed.). Philadelphia: Saunders, 1979.

Vince, M. A. Embryonic communication, respiration, and the synchronization of hatching. In R. A. Hinde (Ed.), *Bird vocalizations*. London: Cambridge University Press, 1969.

Vuorenkoski, V., Lind, J., Partanen, T., Lejeune, J., Lafourcade, J., & Wasz-Höckert, O. Spectrographic analysis of cries from children with maladie du cri du chat. *Annales Paediatrias Fenniae*, 1966, 12, 174–180.

Waisman, H. A., & Kerr, G. R. *Fetal growth and development*. New York: McGraw-Hill, 1970.

Wasz-Höckert, O., Lind, J., Vuorenkoski, V., Partanen, T., & Valanne, E. The infant cry. *Clinics in Development Medicine 29*. London: Heinemann; Philadelphia: Lippincott, 1968.

Wohlwill, J. F. *The study of behavioral development*. New York: Academic Press, 1973.

Wolff, P. The role of biological rhythms in early psychological development. *Bulletin of the Meninger Clinic*, 1967, 31, 197–218.

Zeskind, P. S. Adult responses to cries of low-risk and high-risk infants. *Infant Behavior and Development*, 1980, 3, 167–177.

Zeskind, P. S. Behavioral dimensions and cry sounds of infants of differential fetal growth. *Infant Behavior and Development*, 1981, 4, 321–330.

Zeskind, P. S. Production and spectral analysis of neonatal crying and its relation to other biobehavioral systems in the infant at-risk. In T. Field & A. Sostek (Eds.), *Infants born at-risk: Physiological and perceptual processes*. New York: Grune & Stratton, 1983. (a)

Zeskind, P. S. Cross-cultural differences in maternal perceptions of cries of low- and high-risk infants. *Child Development*, 1983, 54, 1119–1128. (b)

Zeskind, P. S., & Field, T. M. Neonatal cry threshold and heart rate variability. In L. P. Lipsitt & T. M. Field (Eds.), *Infant behavior and development: Perinatal risk and newborn behavior*. Norwood, NJ: Ablex, 1982.

Zeskind, P. S., & Lester, B. M. Acoustic features and auditory perceptions of the cries of newborns with prenatal and perinatal complications. *Child Development*, 1978, 49(3), 580–589.

Zeskind, P. S., & Lester, B. M. Cry features of newborns with differential patterns of fetal growth. *Child Development*, 1981, *51*, 207–212.

Zeskind, P. S., & Marshall, T. *The relation of cry pitch and duration to mothers' perceptions of infant cries*. Paper presented to the Southeastern Conference on Human Development, Athens, Ga., 1984.

Zeskind, P. S., & Ramey, C. T. Fetal malnutrition: An experimental study of its consequences on infant development in two caregiving environments. *Child Development*, 1978, *49*(4), 1155–1162.

Zeskind, P. S., & Ramey, C. T. Preventing intellectual and interactional sequelae of fetal malnutrition: A longitudinal, transactional and synergistic approach to development. *Child Development*, 1981, *52*, 213–218.

Zeskind, P. S., Sale, J., Maio, M. L., Huntington, L., & Weiseman, J. Adult perceptions of pain and hunger cries: A synchrony of arousal. *Child Development*, in press.

# 9

# Perception of Infant Crying as an Interpersonal Event

## C. F. ZACHARIAH BOUKYDIS

## 1. INTRODUCTION

Recent studies have examined the infant cry as one form of preverbal, interpersonal communication. Emphasis has been on the cry as an adaptive distress signal evolved to elicit nurturing and protective responses from adults in the surrounding environment. Murray (1979) indicated that there are two basic types of information in any cry signal, the "categorical" and the "affective," or motivational, message. The distinction between *categorical* and *affective* information derives from the distinction between lexical and prosodic features of speech. Prosodic features, timing, amplitude, and fundamental frequency, convey the affective message in the cry (Lester, 1982). Categorical information refers directly to known predisposing conditions associated with crying, and generally the cause of crying is presumed to be physical rather than psychological. In order to examine the categorical information in cries, a typology of cries was developed by obtaining cry samples from infants in known conditions (3 hours from last feed = hunger cry; first cry after being born = birth cry) and then studying the ability of adults to identify the type of cry (Wasz-Höckert, Lind, Vuorenkoski, Partanen, & Valanne,

C. F. ZACHARIAH BOUKYDIS • Department of Medicine, Harvard Medical School, and Department of Pediatrics, The Children's Hospital, Boston, Massachusetts 02115.

1968). The focus of this research has been on adults' ability to identify correctly the type of cry from a range of several alternatives rather than on assumptions about affective quality or self-report about how the cry was experienced by the listener.

The attempt to understand adult perception of the affective meaning embodied in infants' cries has led to an examination of the features of the cry, such as variability in pitch (Lester & Zeskind, 1982) and signal intensity (Pratt, 1981). These features are presumed to affect the motivation or disposition of the listener to respond (Murray, 1979), for example, either nurturantly or at least to terminate crying. Concurrently, there has been an effort in some studies to view the cry not as a unidirectional signal evolved to elicit invariant patterns of response but as a transactional event where the predictability of response is affected by infant state, patterns of cry features, a complex understanding of adult interpretive processes, contextual factors such as time since last feed (Bernal, 1972), cultural influence, and the history of the relationship between parent and infant, which may concurrently affect adult perception and response. This chapter will begin by reviewing recent studies on adult perception of the cry as an interpersonal signal. This review will provide a critique of the questions asked about what factors influence peoples' perception of babies' crying. Then, some recent research by the author will be presented to highlight some important features of influence on perception of crying. Following a discussion of this research, a new integrative model will be outlined that draws on the insight and limitations of previous work.

## 2. REVIEW OF RECENT CRY PERCEPTION RESEARCH

This section considers the findings of the body of research in Table 1, which are related to adult perception of crying, and it illustrates the paradigms employed to study perception of the cries. The studies in Table 1 fit the category of analog studies and have been useful in highlighting and examining some important parameters. The term *analog studies* means that representative samples of crying are recorded on audiotape, and responses to the tape are assumed to approximate responses to cries in an *in vivo* situation. The developmental aspects of infant cry and parental understanding have largely been held in abeyance in order to examine more refined aspects of the process of perception and physiological response. It is the intent of this review section to illustrate important findings that can be incorporated to improve developmental research in the future. As in all attempts to deal with perception *per se*, not just of the sound of babies' cries as a psychophysical signal but of the cry as an important interpersonal event, these studies offer some better and largely unexplored questions in understanding how adult perception of crying translates into action, into caretaking behavior, and into the complex ontogenesis of the relationship between parents and their babies.

## 2.1. Perception of Cries from Different Populations of Infants

Adult perception of cries is studied by having subjects listen to cries and rate each cry using rating scales tapping their impressions of the cry. Using this paradigm, differences in self-report measures of adults listening to cries have been found in (1) moderate-risk preterm versus low-risk preterm and healthy full-term neonates (Friedman, Zahn-Waxler, & Radke-Yarrow, 1982): (2) high complications versus low complications full-term infants' pain cries (Zeskind, 1980; Zeskind, & Lester, 1978); (3) Down's syndrome versus normal full-term infants (Freudenberg, Driscoll, & Stern, 1978); (4) premature versus full-term infants (Frodi, Lamb, Leavitt, & Donovan, 1978; Frodi, Lamb, Leavitt, Donovan, Neff, & Sherry, 1978); (5) difficult versus average or easy-temperament-rated infants (Lounsbury, 1978; Lounsbury & Bates, 1982); and (6) parents' own versus other babies (Wiesenfeld, Zander Malatesta, & DeLoach, 1981).

## 2.2. Sound Features That Affect Perception

There may be many different factors (including prior knowledge of infant status) that influence adult perception of the cries of babies from different populations. In order to examine the relative importance of the cry as an acoustic signal influencing adult perception, those studies will be discussed that give information about the acoustic parameters of the cries employed.

As we can see in Table 1, the studies done by Zeskind and Lester (1978), Zeskind (1980), Lounsbury (1978), and Wiesenfeld *et al.* (1981) all provide analysis of some of the sound characteristics of cries used in their research. Several authors have implicated the fundamental frequency or dominant pitch of cries as one salient feature related to differences in adult perception and response. The higher pitched pain cry of the high-complications infants in the Zeskind and Lester (1978) study

Table 1. Recent Studies on Adult Perception of Infant Cries

| Study | Characteristics of infants | Characteristics of adults | Task | Analysis of cry features |
|---|---|---|---|---|
| Friedman et al., 1981 | Health full-term neonates ($N = 4$) Low-risk preterms ($N = 4$) Moderate risk preterms ($N = 4$) Risk status (low, mod) based on cost of hospitalization | 2 studies Mothers ($N = 30$) Mothers ($N = 31$) Self-rated sensitivity to irritating noise (low, high) | Rate cries | No sound feature analysis cries recorded during Littman/Parmelee neurological Required greater than 30 sec continuous crying record male/female infant |
| Zeskind & Lester, 1978 | Clinically healthy full-term neonates Measure pre/ perinatal complications Low complications ($N = 24$) High complications ($N = 24$) | Men ($N = 30$) Women ($N = 30$) ½ parents ½ students | Rate cries | Pain cry elicited by rubber band snap at heel Used spectrum analyzer to plot Fourier transformation of the first cry expiration (see results) Random assignment into two groups of male/ female and black/white babies' cries |
| Zeskind, 1980 | Same as Zeskind & Lester, 1980 | Men ($N = 30$) Women ($N = 30$) ½ parents (mixed parity) ½ students | Rate cries | Used cry tapes from Zeskind & Lester, 1978 |
| Freudenberg et al., 1978 | Use Karelitz cry tapes 6 Down's syndrome 6 normal full term | Men ($N = 21$) Women ($N = 21$) ½ little experience with infants ½ moderate to extensive experience | Rate cries | Cries of Down's syndrome infants were flat, lower pitched Karelitz' analyses of the cries were not used directly in data analyses in this study |

| Measures | Findings |
| --- | --- |
| 5 scales (urgent/not urgent, pleasing/grating, healthy/ sick, soothing/arousing, mature/immature) | Modern risk cries more urgent, etc. than low-risk or full term<br>Full-term and low-risk males infants rated higher (i.e., more aversive) than females, moderate risk males and females given similar ratings three cry types perceived along two dimensions (1 = grating/arousing; 2 = immature/sick)<br>No differences in mothers' responses as a function of self-rated sensitivity to noise |
| 8 scales (urgent, grating, sick, arousing, piercing, discomforting, aversive, distressing) | High-complications infants require more stimulation to elicit the cry, had a longer latency to cry onset, a shorter first cry expiration, a higher cry pitch (high comp. = 813 Hz; low comp. = 468 Hz), and cried less in total time than low-complications infants<br>High-complications cries more urgent, etc. than low-comp. etc.<br>Low-complications cries described along one dimension (discomfort)<br>High complications cries described along two dimensions (discomfort and sickness)<br>Parents rated cries overall as less aversive than nonparents |
| (1) Caregiving responses (feed, cuddle, pick up, clean, give pacifier, wait and see)<br>(2) How tender & caring your response is<br>(3) How immediately effective the response is at terminating the cry | The cries from the high-risk infants elicited from parents but not from nonparents, responses that were intended as more "tender and caring" and more "immediately effective at terminating the crying" than the cries from low-risk infants'<br>Responses by parents but not by nonparents, were more consistent to high-risk infant cries than to low-risk cries<br>Parents gave a high percentage of contact-comfort kinds of responses to the high-risk cries, whereas none gave undirected responses |
| 2 scales<br>How strong is feeling that infant needs immediate attention?<br>How pleasant/unpleasant does cry sound to you? | Normal infants were rated as in greater need of attention, and their cries were more unpleasant than Down's syndrome infants (need for attention and unpleasantness were positively correlated)<br>Neither gender of rater nor raters' experience with infants effected the ratings |

(continued)

*Table 1.* (continued)

| Study | Characteristics of infants | Characteristics of adults | Task | |
|---|---|---|---|---|
| Wiesenfeld et al., 1981 | 5-month-olds | Mothers (N = 16) Fathers (N = 16) | Rate cries identify own infant | 15 sec cries 6 segments (2 own, 2 other, 2 tone) for own & other 1 anger cry (physical restraint, removal of pacifier), and 1 pain cry (rubber band snap at heel) X pacifier removal = 418 Hz X restraint = 455 Hz X pain = 539 Hz |
| Frodi, Lamb, Leavitt, Donovan, Neff, & Sherry, 1978 | 1 premature taped at time of discharge 1 normal full-term neonate | Couples (N = 32) having own 5-month-old infant Mixed parity (24 have 1; 7 have 2; 1 has 4) | Watch video (quiescent/ crying/. quiescent baby) Rate reaction | No sound feature analysis ½ see tape of normal ½ see tape of premature Sound track dubbed so ½ hear cry of premature; ½ hear cry of full-term |
| Lounsbury, 1978 | 4–6-month-old normal full-term Difficult (N = 4) Average (N = 4) Easy (N = 4) Rated on Infant Characteristics Questionnaire Tape crying before feeds | Primiparous mothers (N = 45) having own infants 4–6 mths. | Rate cries | Yes Difficult infants' cries Longer pauses between cries Longer total pause time during cry Tend to cry at higher fundamental frequencies |

| Measures | Findings |
| --- | --- |
| Heart rate<br>Skin conductance<br>(1) Identify own versus other infant<br>(2) Pleasantness (1–10)<br>(3) Self-tension (1–10)<br>(4) Novelty (1–10)<br>(5) Type of cry (pain, anger or other) | Heart rate—own infant—mother had cardiac deceleration, then acceleration—father had cardiac deceleration only<br>Heart rate—other infant—both parents had cardiac deceleration<br>Skin conductance—highest (both parents) for own infant pain cry<br>Own infant's pain cry most unpleasant, especially for mothers<br>Mothers report highest tension; higher than fathers for own infant's pain cry<br>Mothers correctly identify own 97%; unfamiliar infant 75%<br>Fathers correctly identify own 84%; unfamiliar infant 44%<br>Mothers correct ident. (anger, pain, other) 55% significantly above chance; and identify own infant (pain, etc.) 65% versus other infant 44% (significantly more accurate for own infant)<br>Fathers not sig. above chance for identifying type of cry; and no difference in identifying type of cry for own versus other |
| Heart rate<br>Skin conductance<br>(1) Mood adjective checklist (how much each mood applies; happy, annoyed, irritated, disturbed, indifferent, attentive, alert, distressed, frightened, sympathetic)<br>(2) Guess baby's gender<br>(3) How pleasant baby is; how much you like to interact; how distressed is baby while crying<br>(4) Rank strategy for soothing | Higher arousal while viewing crying infant; SC increase in response to either infant cry was more pronounced when the premature, rather than the normal baby's face was seen<br>All mood adjective checklist ratings higher for crying versus quiescent infant<br>Parents more irritated, less indifferent, etc. while hearing premature baby's cry; found the normal baby more pleasant and said they'd rather interact with it<br>Highest arousal when face and cry of premie occurred together<br>Premie cry elicited more rapid acceleration of heart rate<br>Significant correlations between arousal and mood adjective items<br>No gender differences in psychophysiological measures<br>Women reported more extremes in mood adjective checklist ratings than men |
| (1) Hypothetical behavioral intervention (tickle, feed, change diaper, etc.)<br>(2) Emotional reaction (sad, angry, irritated, spoiled, etc.)<br>(3) Perceived cause of crying (hunger, wet diaper, fatigue, too hot/cold) | More reported anger, irritation to cries of difficult infants<br>Difficult infants perceived as more spoiled<br>Difficult infants crying because of psychological/emotional reasons (fright, frustration, wants attention) versus easy infants who cried for routine physical discomfort (cold/hot, hunger, fatigue) |

is strongly related to the perceived aversiveness of these cries. This was true of parental perception and skin conductance response to the high-pitched pain cries of parents' own babies in the Wiesenfeld *et al.* (1981) study. Perception of the aversiveness of the cries in Lounsbury's (1978; Lounsbury & Bates, 1982) research varied according to temperament rating of the baby, with the cries of difficult temperament infants perceived as most aversive. These cries had the highest average fundamental frequency at peak. In addition, the difficult cries used in Lounsbury's research were shown to have longer pauses between cry bursts and longer pauses overall during the cry vocalization. This indicates that it may also be the arhythmic, low predictability in temporal patterning that is influencing parents' cycles of physiological response and perceived aversiveness of the cries as well as rapid shifts in fundamental frequency. Thus, it may not only be average fundamental frequency per se but rapid and less predictable shifts in vocal registers that are connected with differential adult perception and physiological response. These cry features may be more characteristic of babies that are immature or disorganized in the complex coordination of systems that modulate their cries. These babies appear to have cries that have a different pattern from the basic or rhythmic pattern of crying that Wolff (1969) has described.

In the original work of Truby and Lind (1965), three patterns of crying were described: phonation, hyperphonation, and dysphonation. "Phonation" ranges in pitch from 200 to 600 Hz and is characterized by a relatively symmetric spectral and intensity pattern. "Dysphonation" is caused by overloading along the vocal tract causing noise that obscures the harmonics of the phonated cry. "Hyperphonation" indicates a sudden shift in pitch between 1000 and 2000 Hz to produce a high-pitched, whistle-like cry. Adult perception of the aversiveness of any particular cry sample may well be affected by the relative proportion of each of the three patterns and by the predictability of shift from one cry pattern to the next.

Pratt (1981) has developed the "cry index," which is represented as a function of the density (amount of time spent crying per unit of time) and the amplitude (loudness distribution of high- and low-amplitude peaks) of crying in order to establish patterns or "forms" of crying in normal infants. Three main forms appeared in Pratt's research. The first form is characterized by a continuous rising slope in the cry index and appears when there is some kind of physical discomfort such as hunger. The second form has a rapid rise to maximum values in the slope of the cry index, where maximum values are maintained, and indicates a sudden change in state. The third form has a rapid rise to medium values of the cry index and may arise in situations where the infant is frustrated or annoyed. Again, adult perception of the aversiveness of crying would be affected by the rapidity of buildup and the distribution of high- and low-amplitude peaks characterized in the information given by the cry index.

There are other influences that must be accounted for. The pain cries of high-complications infants were perceived not only on a dimension that incorporated the aversiveness of the cry but on a second dimension that seemed to convey the sickness or urgency of the infant cry. As will be discussed later in this section on adult differences in perception, Zeskind (1980) used these same cry tapes with parents and nonparents. The high-complications cries received more tender (immediately effective at terminating) contact comfort responses from parents. A partial explanation for the importance of this second dimension comes from work of Ferber and Wolff (1981) on "cry attempts" in the development of crying in preterm infants. This work suggests that very immature preterm babies have trouble coordinating a full-blown cry. Both the spontaneous and elicited cries seem to incorporate a series of preliminary inspiration/expiration respiratory cycles with little voiced elements before arising to a short-duration, high-pitched, sometimes rhythmical cry. This pattern of "cry attempts" is represented in the cries of very young premature infants. Although decreasing in length, the "cry attempt" feature is still present in the second or third month of the baby's life. Here, Zeskind and Lester's (1978) second dimension of sickness/urgency in adult perceptions of the cries is relevant, and it may be that the saliency of this constellation for parents overrides the perceived aversiveness of cries in very young premature or at-risk infants. It is likely that a threshold exists above which a cry has long enough expirations, organized pitch and intensity, and so forth, where the first dimension of aversiveness becomes predominant. Developmental work on crying in preterm infants and parental perception should take the presence and distribution of the "cry attempt" pattern into account when studying influences of specific cry features on perception.

Lounsbury and Bates (1982) have also demonstrated that the difficult cry samples used were perceived along a different dimension related to the perceived underlying psychological/emotional complexity of why the infant was perceived to be crying. This dimension was foreshadowed by Wolff (1969) in his description of the "basic" versus "mad," or angry cry. Again, this pattern may have higher proportions of hyperphonation, as described by Truby and Lind (1965). In the Lounsbury study, cries of all infants were recorded just before a feed. Hunger was the presumed cause of crying. Lounsbury found that the cries of average or easy temperament infants were thought by parents to be caused by routine physical discomfort (hunger, wet diapers, hot/cold), whereas the cries of difficult temperament infants were more frequently thought to be caused for more psychological/emotional reasons (fright, frustration, wants attention). These findings represent one example where the emotional information in the cry and the acoustical features that convey this information become predominant over the categorical information.

Other dimensions related to the cause of crying that are relevent are the perceived intentionality or the perceived "legitimacy" of the cry communication. Crying to communicate physical needs has a high tendency to be seen as legitimate by parents, and the issue of intentional manipulation, especially in young babies, is less at stake. When we move into the realm of the communication of so-called psychological needs, the issue becomes less clear. Communication of various forms of distress are seen as legitimate, and the issues of intentionality and volitional control are less critical. With perceptions related to "wanting attention" or possibly "frustration," the perceived legitimacy of crying is more variable, and the perceived intentionality of crying as a willful manipulation can become more of an issue.

There are differences in when babies are able to attain volitional control of their crying, which is paralleled by a shift from what Emde, Gaensbauer, and Harmon (1976) have described as endogenous to exogenous organization. Again, there are differences in parental assumptions about when intentional control of crying can be expected. There may be differences in the perceived intentionality of infants' crying from different populations of infants. Systematic research on the factors influencing perceived intentionality would enrich an overall understanding of parental perception of the cry as an interpersonal signal.

Other features of cries that have not been systematically assessed in their influence on cry perception include (1) quality of noise (i.e., "raspiness" influences judgments about sickness and health); (2) loudness (i.e., "robustness" of crying may influence judgments about health and about demandingness of the crying); (3) richness of harmonic structure (the flat, low-pitched cries of Down's syndrome babies [Freudenberg *et al.*, 1978] were perceived as less in need of attention and more pleasant than the cries of normal infants); and (4) melody, including pattern of inspiration/expiration, periodicity of pauses, and so on.

## 2.3. Adult Population Differences

Two studies indicate that parental status is related to the perception of cries. In the Zeskind and Lester (1978) study, parents rated both high- and low-risk infant cries as less aversive than nonparents did. In a second study using the same cries, Zeskind (1980) reported that parents rated their expected response to high-risk infant cries as more tender and caring and included more contact-comfort responses than nonparents. Parents, having had more exposure to crying in general than nonparents, and being able to make more distinctions between different cries, perceived the high-risk infant cries in terms of their own internal reactions as less aversive. Thus, they saw these cries as more deserving of special attention.

Several studies examined differences in the self-report and physiological responses of men and women. Frodi, Lamb, Leavitt, and Donovan (1978) and Frodi, Lamb, Leavitt, Donovan, Neff, and Sherry (1978), using heart rate and skin conductance measures, did not find differences in men's and women's overall patterns of physiological response. Wiesenfeld *et al.* (1981) did show differences in mothers' versus fathers' cardiac acceleration/deceleration patterns to the pain cries of their own baby, with mothers having a unique cardiac deceleration followed by acceleration upon hearing their own child's pain cry.

On self-report measures, Frodi, Lamb, Leavitt, and Donovan (1978) and Frodi, Lamb, Leavitt, Donovan, Neff, and Sherry (1978) found that women reported more extremes, both positive and negative, in mood adjective checklist response to cries than men did. Zeskind and Lester (1978) reported that women had higher "arousal" scale ratings. Wiesenfeld *et al.* (1981) found that own infant's pain cry was rated as most unpleasant, especially for mothers, and that mothers reported highest levels of self-tension overall and higher levels than fathers for own infant's pain cry. Also, mothers had higher percentages of correct identification of own infant's cries and correct identification of type of cry (anger, pain, other) overall. This finding was especially true for identification of the type of cry for own infants' cries. In these studies, it is not possible to tease out the effects of prior exposure to infant crying and particularly in the Wiesenfeld *et al.* (1981) study, to own infant crying. Mothers in this study may have had more exposure to their own babies' crying, were more able to identify their own infant's cries, and therefore gave evidence of unique patterns of physiological response as a function of learning particular unique features of their own baby's cries.

Work by Zeskind (1982) on cross-cultural perceptions of cries of infants at risk employed the same cry stimuli used in previous work on parental perception (Zeskind, 1980; Zeskind & Lester, 1978). Cuban-American, Anglo-American, and Black-American mothers recorded their perception of cries of low-risk and high-risk infants. There were no differences between the three groups in perception of low-risk infants' cries. The Black-American mothers reported lower ratings on distress, arousing, urgent, and sick scales than did Cuban-American and

Anglo-American mothers. Generally, Anglo-American mothers had highest ratings on these scales with Cuban-American mothers rating at an intermediate level. Anglo-Cuban-American mothers chose "cuddle" as a possible response to high-risk cries more frequently than did Black-American mothers. Black-American mothers chose to "wait and see" more frequently. All mothers selected "pick up the baby" as a high-frequency response to the high-risk infants' cries.

This study gives some evidence for differing cultural expectations that influence perception of crying and appropriate caretaking response. However, the high-risk infants' cries appeared to be more demanding, urgent, sick, and so forth, and therefore they attracted a more consistent response. We can speculate that although there is wider variation for culturally influenced response to "moderate" ranges of infant crying, the cries of high-risk babies are perceived more universally as extreme and requiring more immediate attention.

## 2.4. Some Methodological Issues

A review of the studies on Table 1 reveal several methodological issues of concern.

### 2.4.1. Cry Samples

Given that we know little about the "normal" development of crying in the various populations represented in Table 1, we must be cautious in our interpretation of the data. It is hard to know how representative the cry samples used were of the population from which they were taken (Lester & Zeskind, 1982). Most of the studies use only a few cry samples from one or two contrast populations. The samples may be so radically divergent in sound characteristics that differences in scaled perception are to be expected strictly as a function of contrast. In some instances, results were affected by anticipation of differences due to prior knowledge of infant status, such as prematurity. This is especially important where adult perception is related to a "type" of cry; yet the acoustic features of the cry are not known (Lester, 1983). For example, some studies used a "premie" cry, but it is not known if there is a distinctive premie cry.

### 2.4.2. Population Parameters

In all of this research, as in other work where gender has been examined as a variable, there is a need for more exhaustive understanding of the effects of prior experience with infants, current attitudes to parenting, and particular relational history with a parent's own baby, when parental perception and response to crying is the focus, in order to sort out experimental versus constitutional influences on perception.

One potentially important omission in this body of work is that studies have not controlled for feeding status. Mothers' physiological response to crying and perception of crying can be expected to be quite different as a function of whether women are breast-feeding or not at the time a study was conducted because hormonal level may effect arousal levels on physiological measures. Further, common sense features such as time since last feed have a strong effect on perception of the compelling or demanding aversive quality of cries.

Past work by Vuorenkoski, Wasz-Höckert, Koivisto, and Lind (1969) used thermography to measure correlates of the effect of crying on the let-down reflex of lactating primiparous mothers. There was a predictable increase in the temperature of the breasts within 7 minutes of the onset of crying. The interaction between hormonal effects due to lactation and measures such as heart rate and skin conductance is not well understood, but it should be of prime concern in studies of physiological responsiveness. Physiological responsiveness to auditory stimulation has been shown to be related to hormonal levels during the menstrual cycle (Little & Zahn, 1974). Therefore, mothers' physiological arousal and auditory sensitivity may be affected by hormonal levels during lactation. The tendency to interpret higher arousal as a function of the perceived aversiveness of cries will have to be modified according to differences in arousal patterns, as these are influenced by lactational status and hormonal activity.

### 2.4.3. Relation between Cry Parameters and Physiology

None of the published work has been provided a moment-to-moment analysis of the relationship between change in cry parameters such as fundamental frequency and change in parental physiological measures. Wiesenfeld *et al.* (1981) (Table 1) reported different patterns of parental heart rate acceleration in relation to pain and discomfort cries of own and other babies, but patterns of change in physiological paramaters were not analyzed as contiguous with change in cry parameters. In this review, it has been hypothesized that not only high pitch per se but rapid and unpredictable shifts in pitch are associated with higher perceived aversiveness. Following on this, in order to see if there is a predictable relationship between perceived aversiveness and physiological parameters, studies are required that measure the temporal patterning of sound features, such as pitch, as related to differences in patterns of parental physiological response.

## 2.4.4. Relation of Cry Perception to Parent–Infant Interaction

There is a tendency in the studies reviewed in Table 2 for authors to talk about perception as if they were talking about interaction. Many scales ask adult respondents to indicate how they *would* expect to act upon hearing a given cry. Because the action of parents does not always concur with their statements of what they would do, it is time to integrate the information gained from these studies into observational and longitudinal designs.

First, this means taking into account quantitative and qualitative differences in the sound pattern of babies' cries while observing parent–infant interaction. Recording cries and analyzing cry features can give an independent, more detailed measure of what parents were responding to during an observed interaction.

Second, analysis of the temporal patterning of cry features may tap the integrity and maturity of the autonomic nervous system, and this may influence rhythmic patterns of parent–infant interaction. Recent work by Lester (1983) presents useful strategies for calculating spectral analyses on the fundamental frequency ($F_0$) of the spontaneous cries of

*Table 2. Factor Loadings on ICQ*

| Fathers ($N = 24$) | | | | | |
|---|---|---|---|---|---|
| **Factor 1 (25%)** | | **Factor 2 (16%)** | | **Factor 3 (12%)** | |
| Mood Energy | | Adaptability | | Fussy/Difficult | |
| Mood | (.84) | New person | (.72) | Calm | (.68)* |
| Smile | (.92) | New place | (.86) | Amount fuss | (.88)* |
| Excite | (.82) | Adaptability | (.40) | Number fusses | (.35)* |
| Games | (.90) | Hold | (.80) | Loud protest | (.40)* |
| Eat | (.53) | Change | (.76) | Difficultness | (.74)* |
| | | | | Upset | (.51) |
| | | | | Sleepy | (.65) |
| Mothers ($N = 24$) | | | | | |
| **Factor 1 (30%)** | | **Factor 2 (14%)** | | **Factor 3 (12%)** | |
| Mood Energy | | Fussy/Difficult | | Adaptability | |
| Mood | (.88) | Amount fuss | (.69)* | New person | (.64) |
| Smile | (.74) | Number fusses | (.69)* | New place | (.78) |
| Excite | (.83) | Difficultness | (.82)* | Adaptability | (.59) |
| Games | (.89) | Change mood | (.54)* | Change | (.87) |
| Dress | (.72) | Upset | (.61) | | |
| | | Sleepy | (.78) | | |

*Same item as original "fussy/difficult" dimension on ICQ.

full-term and preterm infants collected during neonatal assessments. This information is used to predict, for instance, the correlation between rhythmic affective state change for infants interacting with their mothers at 3 months of age.

Third, it means developing ways for relating data that account for observed patterns of interaction, parent and infant physiological correlates of observed patterns, *and* concurrent parental report of the felt meaning of the events that take place (see Section 4).

If the focus of a research study is on the perception of the sound quality of the cry, then we have reliable strategies for testing and comparing individual differences in perception and response. However, some psychoacousticians have claimed in the past that a psychophysical model is limited when applied to sounds that convey emotional meaning (Kryter, 1971). When research questions are directed toward measuring the cry as an affective signal or adults' own psychological reactions to crying, we need new models for understanding the process of interpersonal perception. (Section 4 presents a theoretical model for examining the interpersonal aspect of cry perception.)

## 3. CURRENT RESEARCH ON ADULT PERCEPTION OF INFANT CRYING

The research in this section was developed using the cry stimuli collected by Lounsbury (1978) and Lounsbury and Bates (1982) whose findings were reported previously. The present research (Boukydis & Burgess, 1982) was developed to examine the motivational or affective message perceived in babies' cries. Following on the speculation about fundamental frequency, combined with rhythmic predictability of temporal parameters as reflecting central nervous system stress (Lester & Zeskind, 1982), it was expected that cries with higher fundamental frequencies and less periodic patterning of pauses would be associated with higher physiological arousal and more extreme self-report ratings in adult listeners. Thus, these cries may not only reflect internal stress in the autonomic regulating functioning of the CNS, but they may be more "costly" in terms of the more extreme physiological responses associated with auditory perception in the listener. The research was designed to examine the responses of three parental-status groups (nonparents, primiparous parents, and multiparous parents) and to compare responses of women and men. The stimulus tapes included the cries of difficult-, average-, and easy-temperament rated infants. Therefore, it was possible to compare adult response to the cries of infants of differing temperament.

Three groups, each of 24 adults, were studied: (1) primiparous parents having their own child 3 to 5 months of age at the time of the study; (2) multiparous parents also having a child 3 to 5 months of age; and (3) a control group of nonparents matched with the two parent groups on age and social class variables. The babies were normal, full term, from uncomplicated vaginal deliveries, and none had any serious postnatal illness. All participants listened to a tape recording of 12 randomly ordered, 25-second samples of babies' crying. The audiotapes were analyzed and were used by Lounsbury and Bates (1982) in research on sound spectrographic patterns of babies' cries from babies who were rated on three temperament levels (difficult, average, easy) on the Infant Characteristics Questionnaire (Bates, Bennett-Freeland, & Lounsbury, 1979). The tape included four segments each of difficult, average, and easy cries. Lounsbury showed that there were differing pitch and temporal patterns that distinguished the cries of babies rated on the three temperament levels and that these cry patterns were related to differences in parental perception. Difficult cries tended to have higher fundamental frequencies at peak and longer, irregular pauses during cry bouts. The difficult cries were perceived as more aversive and were thought to be caused by more psychologically complex reasons such as frustration rather than routine physical discomfort.

In the present study, the skin potential response (SPR), a generally accepted measure of autonomic arousal, was recorded while the three groups of adults listened to the cries. After each cry, the subjects recorded their perceptions using a paper and pencil on response sheets that included the following sections: (1) cry characteristics (Zeskind & Lester, 1978) (nine, 7-point Likert-type scales—urgent/not-urgent, pleasing/grating, sick/healthy, soothing/arousing, piercing/not piercing, comforting/discomforting, aversive/nonaversive, distressing/not distressing, and manipulative/not manipulative); (2) reaction to cry (four 7-point Likert-type scales: anger/irritation, sadness, spoiled, care for); and (3) perceived cause of crying (eight choices: wet or dirty diapers, fatigue, wants attention, teething, hunger, too hot or too cold, pain, illness, fright, frustration).

## 3.1. Perception of Crying: Results

### 3.1.1. Skin Potential Response

On the SPR data, there was an important relationship between parental status and type of cry (difficult, average, easy). Both nonparents and multiparous parents showed statistically significant higher levels of arousal to difficult infant cries and lower arousal to easy infant cries. Primiparous parents showed higher arousal to the average infant cries, with difficult infant cries next, and easy infant cries lowest. Multiparous and nonparents showed the expected order of arousal (difficult = high; easy = low) to the distress-related cues in the cries. Lounsbury and Bates's (1982) work indicated that the average infant cries were most representative of the hunger cry pattern shown in other research. Picking up cues for feeding may be of predominant importance for primiparous parents (Bernal, 1972), and this may have accounted for the higher arousal to average infant cries.

There were no differences between men and women in overall SPR. In the work of Frodi, Lamb, Leavitt, and Donovan (1978) and Frodi, Lamb, Leavitt, Donovan, Neff, and Sherry (1978), there were no gender differences in physiological arousal. Within parental-status groups, men and women showed similar patterns of SPR arousal and seemed to be responding to the same stress-related cues across the three types of cries.

Overall, primiparous parents showed the highest level of arousal to cry stimuli, with multiparous parents having the lowest levels of arousal. Primiparous parents, being parents for the first time, were more anxious to learn about infant crying and to discriminate between cry sounds. This may account for their higher levels of arousal when listening to the cry tape. Multiparous parents, with much exposure to infant crying, showed lowest levels of arousal, but they responded with their highest levels of arousal to the difficult cry samples. They were attending to the distress-related cues in the cry samples. Nonparents, not having had generally as much exposure to infant crying, showed more arousal than multiparous parents. However, the nonparents may have had lower investment in attending to infant crying compared with the primiparous parents, and therefore they had lower levels of SPR arousal. Nonparents, too, responded primarily to the distress-related cues in the cry samples.

### 3.1.2. Self-Report in Relation to Cry Samples

There were several important findings on the "reaction to cry" items. On the "irritation/anger" item, men reported significantly more anger than women, and difficult infant cries received higher irritation/anger responses than easy infant cries. Similarly, men rated the cries as more "spoiled," and difficult cries received higher "spoiled" ratings. Difficult infant cries elicited lower "care for" responses than average or easy infant cries, meaning that they felt they would be less likely to care for these infants. Nonparent women were lower on "care for" responses than primiparous or multiparous women, whereas there were no differences in "care for" responses between the three groups of men. Primiparous and multiparous women had higher "care for" ratings than men, whereas there were no differences between nonparent men and women in these ratings. Difficult infant cries were rated as more grating, arousing, piercing, and aversive than average or easy infant cries, and they were rated as more discomforting than easy infant cries. Average infant cries were rated as more healthy than difficult or easy infant cries. Generally, difficult infant cries produced more extreme responses on the reaction to cry ratings. This confirmed the work of Lounsbury (1978) in which primaparous mothers gave similar extreme ratings to the difficult infant cries.

As indicated, the difficult infant cries tended to receive more extreme responses. The cry characteristics scales were developed to study perception of the cries of high- versus low-complications infants (Zeskind & Lester, 1978). Findings reported elsewhere (Boukydis & Burgess, 1982) have indicated that the average fundamental frequency of the difficult infant cries (498.19 Hz) fell between the average fundamental frequency of the high- (813.9 Hz) and low- (468.3 Hz) complications infants, whereas mean ratings on the cry characteristics scales for the difficult infant cries also fell consistently between the scale ratings for high- and low-complications infants in the Zeskind and Lester (1978) research. This supports the CNS stress model (Lester & Zeskind, 1982), reflecting higher fundamental frequency at peak in the cries of difficult temperament-rated infants. When stress is viewed in an interpersonal context, the difficult cries tended to cause higher SPR arousal and more extreme self-report ratings by the adults in this study. Further, on the "probable-cause" measures, difficult cries were seen to be caused for more psychologically complex reasons (frustration, wanting attention) and easy cries for more routine discomfort (hunger). This confirms Lounsbury and Bates's (1982) previous finding and suggests an important component to the cry samples of difficult temperament-rated infants. Of course, this study does not help to resolve the important question of whether the difficult temperament infant cries were related to constitutional factors or whether these particular babies learned to cry that way in order to attract attention from a less responsive caretaking environment, for instance. The question can only be answered by prospective longitudinal studies on crying, parental responsiveness, and concurrent perception of infant behavior and temperament.

There were no differences between men and women in average levels of SPR arousal. The work of Frodi, Lamb, Leavitt, and Donovan (1978) and Frodi, Lamb, Leavitt, Donovan, Neff, and Sherry (1978) also does not indicate differences between men and women on heart rate or skin conductance measures. There were some differences between men and women in psychological responses to their own infant's crying (especially pain cries) in the Weisenfeld *et al.* (1981) research. From the Wiesenfeld *et al.* study, it was not possible to tell whether these differences were a reflection of interactional history with one's own child (mothers were better at identifying own infant's cries) or differences in predisposing factors connected with auditory sensitivity.

In this study, both men and women reacted consistently with similar average SPR levels to the difficult-, average-, and easy-type cries. As indicated, there were differences between women and men on self-report measures. Berman's (1980) review of the extensive literature on gender differences in caretaker responses to children suggests that self-report measures may be more stable indices of differences than physiological measures taken alone. Frodi, Lamb, Leavitt, and Donovan (1978) and Frodi, Lamb, Leavitt, Donovan, Neff, and Sherry (1978) found that women reported more extreme feelings, both negative (irritated, disturbed) and positive (happy, alert). Frodi *et al.* suggested that this may be an indication of cultural permission for women to be more outwardly expressive of their feelings. The differences in self-report in the present research indicated that women consistently reported less extreme "negative" (irritation/anger, spoiled, care for) reactions. At the level of analysis in this study, this finding does not imply that men are potentially less "sensitive" to infant signals or are more likely to respond negatively in caretaking situations. However, the findings suggest that there may be more internally experienced disruption upon hearing the cries, which is symbolized by men's more consistently negative responses, and this sense of internal disruption forms the ground for further responses. The question becomes, how do people understand and begin to deal with this disruption that comes about upon hearing babies' cries?

## 3.2. Infant Temperament and the Transition to Parenthood: Results

In a second phase of this research, the parents ($N = 48$) (primiparas and multiparas) were asked to complete questionnaire material on themselves and their own infant. The material consisted of: (1) the Infant Characteristics Questionnaire (Bates *et al.*, 1979); (2) a modification of the transition to parenthood questionnaire (Wente & Crockenberg, 1976); and (3) parent participation in child care measures. Mothers and fathers separately completed the Infant Characteristics Questionnaire (ICQ) on

their own baby. This questionnaire has 24 7-point scale items that emphasize parental perception of their baby's daily behavioral and temperamental patterns by asking about recent caretaking events. The transition
to parenthood questionnaire consists of 14 items, each represented by
a statement (on a 7-point scale) about the emotional and practical realities
of becoming parents.

### 3.2.1. Parental Perception of Infant Temperament

Parental ratings of infant temperament on the Infant Questionnaire
were examined. There were six items that composed the "fussy/difficult"
dimension of the ICQ (Bates, *et al.*, 1979). There was a very high agreement between fathers and mothers on their rating of their babies on the
fussy/difficult dimension, including significant positive correlation on
five out of the six items (calm, number of fusses per day, amount of
fussing, loudness or vigor of protest, change of mood, and overall difficulty). Patterns of infant crying, reported in the fussy dimension, are
a major contribution to parents' ratings of their own baby's temperament
in the ICQ, and there is considerable independent agreement from both
parents on how babies appear on this dimension. Primiparous parents
rated their babies overall as *less* difficult than multiparous parents. Within
parity groups, however, fathers did not differ from mothers in average
ratings of their babies' temperament.

Factor analyses of the ICQ responses for fathers and mothers
revealed that fathers perceived their babies' temperament differently
than mothers, as shown in Table 2. Factor analyses revealed three main
dimensions for fathers (Table 2). The first factor (Mood/Energy) had
strong loadings on items that account for the baby's excitability and
overall mood; the second factor (Adaptability) had strong loadings on
items that relate to the baby's adaptation to new situations and to new
people; and the third factor (Fussy/Difficult) included five of the six
original items composing the fussy/difficult dimension of the ICQ.

In comparison, we see different emphasis for mothers. These were
three important dimensions in mothers' characterization of the temperament of the baby. The first factor (Mood/Energy) was almost identical
to fathers' first factor, with strong loadings on four of five identical items.
However, the second factor for mothers (Fussy/Difficult) includes four
of six original items composing the fussy/difficult dimension of the ICQ
and differs totally from fathers' second factor. The third factor (Adaptability) for mothers again differs from fathers' third factor and is similar
to the fathers' second factor in comparison.

### 3.2.2. The Transition to Parenthood

Following the strategy of Wente and Crockenberg (1976), who developed the original version of the transition to parenthood questionnaire, we composed a total adjustment difficulty score (TAD) from items that originally correlated significantly with the composite adjustment difficulty score. On the total adjustment difficulty scores, primiparous fathers reported significantly less adjustment difficulty than multiparous fathers and also significantly less adjustment difficulties than primiparous mothers, who had the highest adjustment difficulty scores of anyone. In these families, where primiparous mothers left work to have their first child, they experienced less continuity after their baby was born, in comparison with their spouses, who continued working. There were no significant differences between primiparous mothers and multiparous mothers or between multiparous mothers and multiparous fathers. Table 3 indicates the intercorrelations between individual adjustment difficulty items and total adjustment difficulty scores for everyone, and for fathers and mothers taken separately. From Table 3 we can see that, for fathers overall, and not for mothers, concerns about having to change long-range plans and worries about the additional expense of caring for a new child were significantly correlated with total adjustment difficulty. A separate analysis showed that this was especially true for multiparous parents. Concerns about having enough knowledge about parenting,

Table 3. Intercorrelations of Individual Adjustment Difficulty Items with Total Adjustment Difficulty (TAD)

| Item | Overall | Fathers (N = 24) | Mothers (N = 24) |
|---|---|---|---|
| Baby's crying | .52*** | .61*** | .42* |
| Missing sleep | .49*** | .47* | .50** |
| Not enough time for job | .21 | .20 | .28 |
| Not enough time for family | .05 | .30 | .04 |
| Less time with spouse | .48*** | .61*** | .39* |
| Being tied down to home | .19 | .28 | .05 |
| Change long-range plans | .39* | .50** | .05 |
| Additional expenses | .49*** | .60** | .26 |
| Need more knowledge about parenting | .20 | .06 | .47* |
| Less income, spouse not working | .17 | .20 | .24 |
| Changing diapers | .30* | .20 | .51** |
| Feeding the baby | .51*** | .46* | .58** |
| Visits from friends and relatives | .34* | .18 | .46* |
| More cooking and housework | .44** | .49** | .38* |

$*p < .05. **p < .01. ***p < .001.$

how to handle visits from relatives and friends, and having to handle child-care tasks such as changing diapers were significantly correlated for mothers but not for fathers with total adjustment difficulty. Although there were significant correlations between "having less time with spouse" and total adjustment difficulty for mothers and fathers, the strength of the relationship was stronger for fathers. This was also true for the correlation between the item *baby's crying* and total adjustment difficulty, with fathers showing a stronger correlation. Parity was also a factor on these items, with primiparous parents showing significantly more concern than multiparous parents about knowledge about parenting, less income from spouse not working, and being tied down to home more often.

A separate question asked fathers and mothers to self-rate on a 7-point scale the amount of experience they had with babies as compared with people who were similar to them. As expected, primiparous parents rated themselves as having less experience than did multiparous parents. Within parity groups, fathers and mothers did not differ in their self-rating of experience with infants.

There were several interesting relationships between major variables in this part of the study. For fathers, self-rating of experience was significantly correlated with the father's perception of his own infant's fussy/difficultness, such that the higher fathers rated their general experience with infants, the more they tended to see their babies as having difficult temperament. By comparison, with mothers, there was a significant relation between self-rating of experience with infants and total adjustment difficulty, such that the lower mothers rated their experience with infants, the more total adjustment difficulty was reported. The relationship did not hold for fathers. Mothers' perceptions of how well they were doing in the transition to parenthood appeared to be more closely tied than with fathers to mothers' perceptions of the temperamental difficultness of their baby. Finally, for all multiparous parents, total adjustment difficulty was related to how difficult one's infant was perceived, such that higher adjustment difficulty scores were positively correlated with greater perceived infant temperamental difficultness. Although multiparous parents have considerable experience with babies, having a second or third baby with difficult temperament was more closely associated with perceptions of difficulty in the transition to multi-parenthood.

These data suggest how infant crying patterns and infant temperament affect parents' perceptions of the smoothness of the transition to parenthood. Having an infant who was perceived as being temperamentally difficult was highly related to stress in becoming a parent, especially for mothers, and generally, for all multiparous parents. Mothers, who in these families had more exposure to their babies during the day, appeared to be more concerned about difficult temperament affecting their overall adjustment to parenthood. Recent work by Crockenberg (1981) showed that early maternal social support was significantly related to the security of the mother–infant attachment at 12 months. Further, support was most needed and had strongest effects with irritable infants and their mothers.

Multiparous parents, having had at least one previous child, could be expected to be more realistic in their appraisal of the temperament of their most recent child. The data presented before on cry perception showed that multiparous parents had lower general levels of arousal compared with primiparous parents to infant cries *per se*, but they still reacted with highest levels of arousal to the distress-related cues in the difficult cry samples. With older children to care for, the impact of a difficult temperament baby on the family was perceived to be associated strongly with overall difficulty in becoming parents for the second or third time. How a baby is viewed and the relative impact of that baby's daily pattern have been shown in this research to vary according to parity of the baby's parents. This suggests that parental perception of infant temperament and crying patterns is mediated by parity and previous infant care experience.

## 4. TOWARD A MODEL OF INTERPERSONAL PERCEPTION OF INFANT CRY

The focus on the cry as affective communication and as an interpersonal event has involved methodological difficulties as in most empirical studies of interpersonal perception (von Eckartsberg, 1978) because research questions have been directed toward several intertwining aspects: adult report of the measurable characteristics of the cry, underlying assumptions about the infant's psychological or physiological state, and, finally, report of own feelings, perceptions, and reactions in relation to the cry. Even when a research question is directed at one of these aspects, such as perception of characteristics of the cry, the other aspects come into play and influence measures on self-report scales. Asking how aversive a particular baby's cry sounds, for example, may call forth both a comparison from one's own standards of how aversive were the cry sounds compared to other cries one has heard *and* a report on one's internal reaction to the cry, including how much the cry made one want to avert. Further specifications of self-report scales may help in some instances (i.e., how much does this cry make you want to avert?), but it is because of the nature of the particular phenomenon of hearing a baby's cry that the "intertwining" of the different aspects of interpersonal space (self-reaction, perception-of-other reaction, perception of relationship between self and other) becomes important. The intent of the model portrayed in Figure 1 is that phenomenologically, upon hearing a baby's cry, there is an *a priori*, bodily experienced event. Even though there may be mechanisms that structure the incoming data of the cry signal, it is this preconceptual experiencing of the cry that forms the basis for further self-conceptualizing (Gendlin, 1962). Self-report on structured scales happens after the conceptualizing of this event. Physiological measures are necessarily correlated with this bodily experienced event but can only indirectly tap the salience, strength, and meaning of the event for the individual.

The cry is most typically characterized to be a gradation of a preverbal distress signal. With reference to perception of another salient distress-related phenomenon—pain, Bakan (1968) has argued that understanding of pain in another starts with each person's isolated internal reference to his or her own experience. Attempts to "measure" pain or to study pain as simply *one more* psychophysical sensation have been difficult, precisely because measurement must fall back on some form of introspective report by those experiencing pain. Our understanding of the pain in another begins with some form of analogizing from our own experience of pain or distress. So, it is because of this that the perception of the cry as an interpersonal signal will always have an element of *indefiniteness*. The distress of another effects people at a level that Bakan (1968) says is "prior to the mind/body split" and that, in this model, is called a bodily experienced event.

The question becomes how to study the individual's process of conceptualizing this *a priori* bodily experienced event, which has an

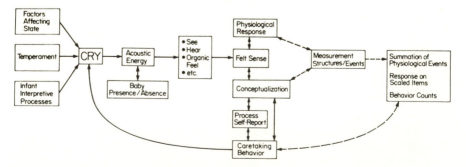

*Figure 1.* Interpersonal perception of infant cry.

element of indefiniteness. The simplest statement of this indefiniteness for the cry perceiver is, "Was my reaction caused by the cry signal alone or by some combination of the cry and my own internal 'potentiated' reaction?" The occasion of participating in a research project on cry perception has often been the setting where people explore this very question. They ask, how are these cries different and why do I react differently on hearing cries in different settings?

The model points toward two, non-mutually exclusive strategies: (1) asking people to report spontaneously on their reaction to particular cries after listening and before structuring their responses on scaled items; and (2) observing how people respond to crying during observations of parent–infant interaction (where physiological measures, cry analysis, and concurrent self-report may all be measured simultaneously).

The model does not imply that every response to a cry will be idiosyncratic or unique. It implies that there may be characteristic ways in which individuals conceptualize or interact with the bodily experienced event. In a broader context, this has already led to the search for personality and response history factors (learned helplessness [Chapter 11], egoistic versus altruistic motives for response [see Chapter 12] that affect perception of crying and predict physiological and caretaking response. As indicated in the previous section, there are some factors that have been delineated that account for the strength and salience of the bodily experienced event of hearing the cry and that predict more extremes in interpretation.

Lester and Zeskind (1982) have conceptualized the cry of a high-risk infant as indexing some amount of stress or internal imbalance (disorganization) in the physiological functioning of the organism. Simply put, I am saying that perception of the cry as an interpersonal signal also involves an amount of internal arousal or possibly stress in the "listener."

With Selye's explanation of stress (1956), there is a generalized stress reaction, which is initially adaptive, in the sense that the organism is prepared to fight or flee, but (1) the stress reaction can affect (sometimes damage) tissues and organ systems not connected with those systems necessary for functional preparedness; and (2) there can be a breakdown of hierarchical central nervous system organization of stress that provide the impetus for developing differentiated responses and specialized functioning in growth. Conflict can occur, however, when there are higher levels of stress, when there is a lack of hierarchically or centralized organized response, and when multiple systems are activated. Within moderate limits, crying is thought to be positively adaptive, leading to internal homeostasis or attracting regulatory input from the caretaking environment. At the extremes, there is a much finer *balance* between the movement toward organized response or toward disorganization and breakdown in functioning. Perception of the cry of the high-risk or difficult temperament infant in the research reviewed in this chapter reflects this finer balance. The cry is often characterized as "adaptive" in the sense that it is more demanding of immediate attention. Again, perception of the cry could be call neutrally, "more extreme," "more arousing," and so on. Yet the cry has a higher likelihood of tipping the balance toward disruption or distress in the listener. This does not mean that there is a simple contiguity between the potential stress experienced by the baby and that experienced by the adult. The difficult temperament cry caused high levels of arousal in multiparous parents, but these average levels were, in absolute terms, at medium levels, compared to the arousal levels of primiparous parents or non-parents. We can assume that, all other things considered, there is less likelihood of a disorganized, highly stressed caretaking response on the part of experienced parents and those parents without undue amounts of stress in other areas of their lives.

Being in the presence of a crying baby has some amount of cost, and without "successful" resolution, it can lead to disorganized response (egoistic motives for response [Hoffman, 1976]; learned helplessness, [Seligman, 1975]). Furthermore, the primacy of the bodily experienced event brings up the possibility that the adult's stress, without mediation, affects the baby at this level, and a "stressful cycle" can continue. Current theorizing must extend to include an understanding about what different babies in turn perceive or comprehend about parental response, and how this may differentially affect their crying. In terms of the developmental history of the parent–infant relationship, the baby may be responding to a situation where his or her signals are being misread and may have developed a particular crying pattern to attract adequate caretaking attention. This calls for careful longitudinal observation of parent–infant interaction that includes strategies for examining how parents interpret and respond to babies' cries and how effective different babies are at signaling their needs.

## 5. CONCLUSION

Research on the cry as in interpersonal communication has itself been motivated in clinical settings by an attempt to account for the burden of irritable, virtually unconsolable crying bouts on parental caretaking energy and the implication of crying as a possible precipitant to failures in parent–child interaction that, at the extreme, may culminate in child abuse. One major concern of parents in early postnatal visits with health-care professionals is the inability to cope with crying and the feelings of inadequacy that this reflects or engenders. In concert with other developmental research on infant temperament and risk populations, it is hoped that we can identify babies who are more difficult to console, more unpredictable in daily patterns, and are more susceptible to bouts of unexplained fussiness, or colic, and *concurrently* improve the understanding of effective ways of helping parents to deal with these babies.

The work reviewed in this chapter has been useful in isolating some cry features and some adult characteristics that influence perception of the cry as an affective, interpersonal signal. As indicated, much of the work reviewed has eliminated or controlled contextual cues in the effort to isolate other phenomena affecting cry perception. With the questions generated by the studies reviewed, it is once again important to study crying in the context of the developing parent–infant relationship and the importance of crying patterns in parents' conceptions of their babies' overall temperament or personality. For, without doubt, it ultimately takes two to make a perceiving event occur. Crying occurs in the context of a mutually regulated, dynamic relationship between infant and parent. Theoretical questions must be able to address simultaneously the different levels of transaction involved.

## 6. REFERENCES

Bakan, D. *Disease, pain and sacrifice.* Chicago: University of Chicago Press, 1968.

Bates, J., Bennett-Freeland, C. A., & Lounsbury, M. L. Measurement of infant difficultness. *Child Development*, 1979, *50*, 704–713.

Berman, P. Are women more responsive than men to the young? A review of developmental and situational variables. *Psychological Bulletin*, 1980, *88*(3), 668–695.

Bernal, J. Crying during the first 10 days of life and maternal responses. *Developmental Medicine and Child Neurology*, 1972, *14*, 362–372.

Boukydis, C. F. Z. Adult perception of infant appearance: A review. *Child Psychiatry and Human Development*, 1981, *11*(4), 241–254.

Boukydis, C. F. Z., & Burgess, R. Adult physiological response to infant cries: Effects of temperament of infant, parental status, and gender. *Child Development*, 1982, *53*, 1291–1298.

Crockenberg, S. Infant irritability, mother responsiveness, and social influences on the security of infant–mother attachment. *Child Development*, 1981, *52*, 857–865.

Emde, R. N., Gaensbauer, T. J., & Harmon, R. J. Emotional expression in infancy: A behavioral study. *Psychological Issues* (Monograph 37), 1976.

Ferber, R., & Wolff, P. *Development of cry in preterm infants.* Children's Hospital Medical Center, Boston. Personal communication, 1981.

Freudenberg, R. Driscoll, J., & Stern, G. Reactions of adult humans to cries of normal and abnormal infants. *Infant Behavior and Development*, 1978, *1*, 224–227.

Friedman, S. L., Zahn-Waxler, C., & Radke-Yarrow, M. Perceptions of cries of full-term and preterm infants. *Infant Behavior and Development*, 1982, *5*, 161–173.

Frodi, A. M., Lamb, M., Leavitt, L., & Donovan, W. Fathers' and mothers' responses to infant smiles and cries. *Infant Behavior and Development*, 1978, *1*, 187–198.

Frodi, A. M., Lamb, M., Leavitt, L., Donovan, W., Neff, C., & Sherry, D. Fathers' and mothers' responses to the appearance and cries of premature and normal infants. *Developmental Psychology*, 1978, *14*, 490–498.

Gendlin, E. *Experiencing and the creation of meaning*. Glencoe, IL: Free Press, 1962.

Hoffman, M. Developmental synthesis of affect and cognition and its implications for altruistic motivation. *Developmental Psychology*, 1975, *11*, 607–622.

Kryter, K. *The effects of noise on man*. New York: Academic Press, 1971.

Lester, B. M. Infant crying and the development of communication. In N. Fox, & R. Davidson (Eds.), *Affective development: A psychobiological perspective*. Hillsdale, NJ: Erlbaum, 1982.

Lester, B. M. A biosocial model of infant crying. In L. Lipsitt (Ed.), *Advances in infant behavior and development* (Vol. 3). New York: Ablex, 1983.

Lester, B. M., & Zeskind, P.S. A biobehavioral perspective on crying in early infancy. In H. E. Fitzgerald, B. M. Lester, & M. W. Yogman (Eds.), *Theory and research in behavioral pedicatrics*. New York: Plenum Press, 1982.

Little, B. C., & Zahn, T. P. Changes in mood and autonomic functioning during the menstrual cycle. *Psychophysiology*, 1974, *11*, 579–590.

Lounsbury, M. L. *Acoustic properties of maternal reactions to infant cries as a function of infant temperament*. Unpublished doctoral dissertation, Indiana University, Lafayette, Indiana, 1978.

Lounsbury, M. L., & Bates, J. E. The cries of infants of differing levels of perceived temperamental difficultness: Acoustic properties and effects on listeners. *Child Development*, 1982, *53*, 677–686.

Murray, A. Infant crying as an elicitor of parental behavior: An examination of two models. *Psychological Bulletin*, 1979, *86*, 191–215.

Pratt, C. Crying in normal infants. In W. I. Fraser & R. Grieve (Eds.), *Communicating with normal and retarded children*. Bristol, U.K.: J. Wright & Sons, 1981.

Seligman, M. E. *Helplessness: On depression, development and death*. San Francisco: Freeman, 1975.

Selye, H. *The stress of life*. New York: McGraw-Hill, 1956.

Truby, H., & Lind, J. Cry sounds of the newborn infant. *Acta Paediactrica Scandinavica*, 1965, 8–54 (Supp. 163).

von Eckartsberg, R. Person perception revisited. In R. Valle & M. King (Eds.), *Existential-phenomenological alternatives for psychology*. New York: Oxford University Press, 1978.

Vuorenkoski, V., Wasz-Höckert, O., Koivisto, E., & Lind, J. The effect of cry stimulus on the temperature of the lactating breast of primipara: A thermographic study. *Experientia*, 1969, *25*, 1286–1287.

Wasz-Höckert, O., Lind, J., Vuorenkoski, V., Partanen, T., & Valanne, E. The Infant Cry: A Spectrographic and Auditory Analysis. *Clinics in Developmental Medicine 29*. London: Heinemann Medical, 1968.

Wente, A. S., & Crockenberg, S. B. Transition to fatherhood: Lamaze preparation, adjustment difficulty and the husband–wife relationship. *Family Coordinator*, 1976, *24*, 351–357.

Wiesenfeld, A., Zander Malatesta, C., & DeLoach, L. Differential parental responses to familiar and unfamiliar infant distress signals. *Infant Behavior and Development*, 1981, 4(3), 281.

Wolff, P. The natural history of crying and other vocalizations in early infancy. In B. M. Foss (Ed.), *Determinants of infant behavior* (Vol. 4). London: Methuen, 1969.

Zeskind, P. S. Adult responses to cries of low and high risk infants. *Infant Behavior and Development*, 1980, 3, 167.

Zeskind, P. S. *Cross-cultural perceptions of cries of infants at risk.* Paper presented at the International Conference on Infant Studies, Austin, Texas, 1982.

Zeskind, P. S., & Lester, B. M. Acoustic features and auditory perceptions of the cries of newborns with prenatal and perinatal complications. *Child Development*, 1978, 49, 580–589.

# 10

# Aversiveness Is in the Mind
# of the Beholder
## Perception of Infant Crying by Adults

## ANN D. MURRAY

*And still Caroline cried, and Martha's nerves vibrated in extraordinary response, as if the child were connected to her flesh by innumerable invisible fibers.*

—Doris Lessing, *A Proper Marriage*

## 1. INTRODUCTION

The research reported in this chapter grew out of a long-standing interest in the compelling nature of infant cries and their seemingly paradoxical capacity to elicit either nurturant or hostile responses from caregivers. On the one hand, the biological significance of the cry for survival seems obvious (Bowlby, 1969), but crying also may be maladaptive because it is so frequently cited as a major trigger for child abuse (Frodi & Lamb, 1980; Lester & Zeskind, 1982). Furthermore, if crying has adaptive significance, it seems odd that parental sensitivity and responsiveness to crying are reported to vary so widely between cultures (Mead & Newton,

ANN D. MURRAY • High Risk Infant Development Laboratory, Boys Town National Institute for Communication Disorders in Children, Omaha, Nebraska 68131.

1967). In primitive and traditional societies, the cry is treated as an emergency signal and responded to immediately, but in Western cultures, responses are delayed, and infants may cry for several hours each day.

A description of the various mechanisms that could account for the cry's compelling nature will be summarized (see Murray, 1979, for more detail), which will be followed by presentation of data bearing on the adequacy of these models to account for the cry's paradoxical impact.

## 2. CONCEPTUAL MODELS OF THE CRY'S IMPACT

### 2.1. The Cry as an Innate Releaser of Parental Behavior

In this theoretical framework, the cry is viewed as a distress signal that originally evolved, along with other attachment behaviors, to promote proximity between infants and their caregivers for protection from predators (Ainsworth, 1969; Bowlby, 1969). To ensure species survival, reciprocal mechanisms would have evolved in adults to promote immediate and appropriate responses to the cry signal. In this context, it has been hypothesized that the cry may act as a releaser—a sign stimulus that acts figuratively as a key to unlock a stereotyped motor response from the receiver. The recognition of the signal and production of the motor responses are said to be under the control of an hypothesized neural filtering system that is referred to as an innate releasing mechanism (Eibl-Eibesfeldt, 1975). A cardinal feature of the releaser model is that the cry is viewed as a unique stimulus that is matched, like other biologically significant sounds, with specialized detection capabilities or processing modes in the receiver (Worden & Galambos, 1972). The emphasis is on stimulus recognition that leads to an involuntary, reflexive response by the receiver.

The existing evidence that most strongly supports the view of the cry as an innate releaser includes the finding of contagious crying in newborns (Sagi & Hoffman, 1976), the suggestion that deaf parents do not exhibit an urgency about responding to crying (Lenneberg, Rebelsky, & Nichols, 1965), and the near universality of interventions that involve close physical contact (Bell & Ainsworth, 1972; Bernal, 1972). On the other hand, the cry signal, unlike most releasers, does not appear to be a simple and discrete stimulus with a single meaning, but rather its meaning and responses to it depend upon intensity cues and contextual factors (Murray, 1979).

Because the releaser formulation originated with observations of invertebrates and lower vertebrates such as insects and frogs, the concept in its strictest sense may not be useful when applied to higher mammals and primates (Wilson, 1975). As one ascends the phylogenetic scale, there is a tendency away from discrete sign stimuli toward signals that do not communicate fixed messages but are graded in intensity, reflecting the motivational state of the sender (Wilson, 1975). Similarly, the messages conveyed by graded signals have their effect by influencing the motivational state of the listener (Bastian, 1965). Correct interpretation of graded signals depends on both acoustic cues of intensity and nonacoustic cues such as the context in which the signal is employed (Wilson, 1975). Therefore, a conceptualization that allows for motivational and cognitive factors may further our understanding of adult responses to infant cries. A model of the cry as a graded signal may nevertheless be compatible with the broadened "social releaser" concept used by the English ethologists (cf. Hinde, 1974) who tend to view innate releasing mechanisms as motivational entities.

## 2.2. The Cry as an Aversive Stimulus

In arguments advanced against the releaser model, researchers in the learning theory tradition (Moss & Robson, 1968) have suggested that parents respond to the cries of their infants for the same reason that they respond to any noxious sound—that is, to reduce aversive stimulation. In contrast to the releaser formulation, the aversive stimulus model accords no special properties or powers to the cry sound but combines principles of negative reinforcement and psychophysics in relating the quality of the auditory experience to the physical characteristics of the sound. Whereas the releaser model emphasizes the uniqueness of a particular stimulus and its receptor mechanism, the psychophysical approach stresses the general properties of the auditory processing system. The aversive stimulus model is summed up by this quote from Ostwald (1983).

> One can appreciate why the parent must interfere with the baby's cry: This sound is too annoying to be tolerated beyond a short period of time, particularly at close range. Thus, the cry cries to be turned off. The listener who cannot escape usually reduces the noise by soothing whatever baby needs occasion it. (p. 46)

The psychophysical approach to the explanation of the perceptual and motivational mechanisms underlying responses to the cry may have some validity, but the greatest weakness of this approach is that it accounts best for escape from or avoidance of the crying child and less well for approaches to remove the source of the distress. The motivation is egoistic or self-serving in that the parent is described as motivated to reduce his or her own distress rather than the baby's. By contrast, Hoffman's

(1975) empathy model, which will be presented next, tries to integrate both egoistic and altruistic motives into a single perspective.

## 2.3. The Cry as an Elicitor of Empathy and Altruism

Hoffman (1975) has proposed that observers of another's distress experience emphatic distress or an involuntary and forceful experiencing of the other's painful emotional state. The intensity of the observer's affect increases with the number of pain cues emitted by the victim. The primitive empathic reaction may exist early in infancy if not at birth, and it subsequently develops with a cognitive sense of the other into a reciprocal concern for the victim, which Hoffman labels *sympathetic distress*. At first, young children observing another in distress are unable to differentiate their own distress from that of the victim. With the development of the concept of the self as distinct from others, the child's concern for his or her own discomfort is transformed into a concern for the other's distress. However, the child lacks understanding of the cause or remedy of the other's distress and attempts to help are egocentric. By middle childhood, children are capable of true sympathetic distress— they know that the source of their affect is something happening to the other person, and they have a sense of what the other person is feeling. At the highest level, the older child and adult can respond not only to situation-specific cues of distress but also to a general representation of the welfare of the victim regardless of the victim's momentary state.

According to Hoffman (1977a), sympathetic distress—that is, empathy with a cognitive awareness of the other's painful emotional state—is a more reliable predictor of helping behavior than the primitive empathic reaction alone. Without the cognitive component, observers of another's distress may be more concerned with their own discomfort than with that of the victim. Hoffman (1975) contends that the altruistic basis for helping behavior differs qualitatively from an egoistic one in that the motivation to respond is aroused by another's distress rather than one's own; the major goal is to help the other rather than one's self; and gratification is contingent on reducing another's distress rather than one's own.

Hoffman (1977a) has also hypothesized that there may be an optimal range of distress cues. Distress cues from another must be sufficient to activate distress in the observer but must not be so disturbing as to elicit avoidance or aggression toward the victim. Excessive and prolonged crying, or particularly aversive-sounding crying, may exceed limits of tolerability and overly tax parents' abilities to withstand continuing high levels of emotional arousal.

## 2.4. Ontogenetic Considerations

Because care of the young is crucial for genome survival in mammalian species, it would seem that there may be other mechanisms that foster responsiveness toward infants in particular. Mammalian parental behavior may be under control of two separate but interacting mechanisms. One major influence is exposure to the young and its enhancement of the attractiveness of the young for adult male and female species members (Harper, 1971). For example, in rats, enforced exposure to the young over the course of several days elicits appropriate caregiving behavior such as nest building and retrieving in virgin females and in males (Rosenblatt, 1970). However, a more rapid initiation of caregiving behavior occurs in females that have been primed by the hormonal changes associated with pregnancy and parturtition (Moltz, 1974). Caregiving is not dependent on physiological changes for its appearance, but the hormonal changes associated with parturition in the female reduce the duration of exposure to the young that is required to effect a change from attacking or avoidance to caregiving behavior.

In the human literature, an analogy has been drawn to research on mother–infant bonding (Klaus & Kennell, 1976) that suggests that there may be a period immediately following birth when the mother's sensitivity to care-eliciting cues from her baby may be enhanced. Prenatal hormonal events (Money & Erhardt, 1972) and hormonal changes at puberty may also bias human females toward the eventual adoption of the caregiving role. The net effect of the interaction of organismic and experiential factors may account for greater participation by females in infant care among mammals. However, sex differences among humans would be expected to vary within and between cultures, depending on the opportunities for males to be exposed to the eliciting effect of stimuli from the young. It may then be fruitful to view responsiveness to crying infants in the context of ontogenetic processes (experiential and constitutional) that may sensitize adults to infantile cues and enhance the attractiveness of the young for them.

## 3. STUDIES OF THE CRY'S IMPACT

A series of four studies was designed with the general aim to investigate and describe the emotional significance and arousal powers of infant cries for the listener. Two types of questions were addressed. One was the question of whether the cry could be demonstrated to have a greater impact than other sounds with similar annoying features but with little biological utility. Such a demonstration would provide some support for the notion that the cry is a biologically significant sound in that there is a selective response. Evidence for a selective response would be consistent with either a releaser model of the cry's impact or a model of the cry as a graded signal activating emotions in the listener, as both models stress the involuntary aspect of the listener's response. Such a finding would, however, suggest that a conceptualization of the cry's compelling nature must go beyond a simple psychophysical formulation or aversive stimulus model.

A second type of question dealt with individual differences in the impact of cries for experienced and inexperienced caregivers and for male and female listeners. The literature on the ontogeny of parental behavior suggests that the contributions of sex and experience to responsiveness may be similar and parallel rather than qualitatively different. The pathways to altering thresholds to infantile stimulation appear to be twofold—changes in sensitivity consequent to hormonal stimulation in the female and changes in sensitivity brought about by prolonged exposure to the young in both sexes. Thus, it was expected that any sex and experience differences found in responsiveness to cries would be qualitatively similar and mirror each other.

In the next section, the paradigms, measures, and subject populations for the four studies will be briefly described. Subsequently, rather than report the findings study by study, results across all studies that pertain to salient theoretical issues are presented together.

## 3.1. Paradigms, Measures, and Subject Populations

Significant features of each of the four studies (comparison groups, numbers of subjects, stimuli, and response measures) are listed in Table 1. Two different paradigms were used. In Studies 1 and 4, four newborn cries, which were selected to provide a range of intensity cues, were used as stimuli. The cries included a birth cry, a pain cry, a hunger cry, and a cry for attention. Cry segments that were not accompanied by extraneous sounds and that could be described as rhythmical active crying (Wolff, 1969), rather than fussing, were selected. The birth cry was recorded several minutes after birth from a male infant. The pain cry was recorded from a 20-hour-old female neonate when her heel was pricked as part of normal hospital procedure to draw a blood sample. The hunger cry, recorded approximately 30 minutes before a midday feeding, was from a 32-hour-old male infant. The fourth cry was obtained from a 45-hour-old female after a midday feeding. This cry was labeled an *attention cry* by an obstetrical nurse who had determined that the

Table 1. Subjects, Stimuli, and Response Measures

| Study | Comparison groups | 4N | Stimuli | Psychol. measures | Physiol. measures |
|---|---|---|---|---|---|
| 1. | No experience (nonparents)<br>Some experience<br>(nonparents)<br>Parents<br>Females<br>Males | 139 | 4 newborn cries | Pleasant/unpleasant, weak/<br>strong, active/passive,<br>annoying/not annoying,<br>sympathetic/unsympathetic | — |
| 2. | Obstetrical nurses<br>General Nurses | 16 | 4 newborn cries<br>4 animal sounds<br>2 mechanical sounds | Evaluation, potency, and<br>activity ratings (see text) | Pulse rate, pulse<br>amplitude,<br>blood volume |
| 3. | Nulliparous<br>Primiparous<br>Multiparous<br>Females<br>Males | 64 | 4 newborn cries<br>6 animal sounds<br>2 mechanical sounds | Evaluation, potency, and<br>activity ratings (see text) | Pulse rate, pulse<br>amplitude,<br>blood volume |
| 4. | Oral contraceptive users<br>Nonusers | 48 | 4 newborn cries | Active/passive, annoying/not<br>annoying, sympathetic/not<br>sympathetic | — |

newborn's obvious physical needs had been met. The attention cry seemed to be occasioned by minor discomfort and was qualitatively different from the other cries that were noisy, raucous, and strident.

In Studies 2 and 3, another paradigm was used in which listeners' reactions to the four cries were compared to their responses to animal and mechanical sounds that were matched, on the basis of spectrographic analyses, with the infant cries for annoying physical features. The animal sounds included a Siamese cat cry, the crowing of a raven, the fear squawks of a chicken, and orangutan "kiss squeaks." The mechanical sounds were constructed by Simner (1971) to simulate the properties of a newborn cry. These included a synthesized infant cry and a series of white noise bursts. The animal and mechanical sounds were similar to the infant cries in a number of temporal and physical features that contribute to the annoyance value of sounds (cf. Kryter, 1971), including impulsiveness, average burst length, average interval between bursts, peak fundamental frequency ($F_0$), and the presence of turbulence or noise obscuring the harmonics of the signals. The characteristics of the newborn cries and the other sounds are described in Table 2.

Subjects' reactions to the cries and the other sounds were measured on both a physiological and a psychological level. In Studies 2 and 3,

Table 2. Characteristics of the Sounds Used as Stimuli

| Sounds | Average burst length (sec) | Average interval (sec) | Peak $F_0$ (Hz) | Presence of noise |
|---|---|---|---|---|
| Infant cries | | | | |
| Birth | .5 | .5 | 550 | yes |
| Pain | .9 | .3 | 375 | yes |
| Hunger | .8 | .3 | 450 | yes |
| Attention | .6 | .2 | 425 | no |
| Mean | .7 | .4 | 450 | (3 yes/ 1 no) |
| Animal Sounds | | | | |
| Siamese cat | 1.0 | .8 | 400 | no |
| Raven | .7 | .5 | 350 | no |
| Chicken | .5 | .4 | 600 | yes |
| Orangutan | .5 | .6 | 300 | yes |
| Mean | .7 | .6 | 413 | (2 yes/ 2 no) |
| Mechanical Sounds | | | | |
| Synthesized cry | .7 | .1 | 475 | no |
| White noise | .9 | .5 | — | yes |
| Mean | .8 | .3 | 475 | (1 yes/ 1 no) |

measures of vasoconstriction in the finger (decreases in finger pulse amplitude and blood volume) were used as indicators of general sympathetic nervous system arousal (Brown, 1972). Pulse rate was also monitored for acceleratory changes indicative of active coping or stress reactions and for deceleratory changes that correlate with orienting or attentional responses (Obrist, 1976). Psychological measures were used to impute the nature of the arousal (e.g., distress or anger) beyond the active/passive coping distinction.

The emotional significance of the sounds for listeners was measured using 5-point semantic differential scales (Osgood, Suci, & Tannenbaum, 1957). In Studies 2 and 3, the ratings selected for each dimension were kind/cruel, pretty/ugly, and good/bad for evaluation; weak/strong, heavy/light, and hard/soft for potency; and slow/fast, active/passive, and sharp/dull for activity. Scores on the three ratings were averaged to provide a summary rating for the three dimensions. In Studies 1 and 4, the semantic differential scales listed in Table 1 were used in addition to ratings of the annoyance value of the cries and the amount of sympathy evoked by them.

Listeners were tested in groups in Studies 1 and 4. Ten-second samples of hunger, birth, attention, and pain cries were played with an interval of approximately 30 seconds between cries during which the listeners filled out the rating scales for each cry. For Studies 2 and 3, eight random orders of the infant, animal, and mechanical sounds were constructed, with 10-second segments of each sound followed by an interval of 15 to 20 seconds of silence. Each listener was assigned one order of presentation. During the first presentation, the listener's physiological responses were monitored, using a finger plethysmograph. During a second presentation, listeners completed the rating scales immediately after hearing one sound.

The comparison groups were selected to explore various parameters of experience and biological influences on responsiveness to infant cries. For example, the effects of no experience and casual baby-sitting experience were compared with parenthood in Study 1. In this study, subjects with no experience had never or only rarely cared for an infant of less than 12 months of age. Subjects with some experience had cared for an infant on at least 10 occcasions. Study 2 examined the effects of professional experience with infants by comparing the responses of female obstetrical and general nurses. Study 3 looked at the effects of having no children compared with having one or more than one child. In Studies 1 and 3, sex differences were examined, and in Study 4, the issue of hormonal sensitization of females was addressed by comparing responses of nonusers and users of oral contraceptives, simulating the condition of pregnancy. Except for the nurses in Study 2, all subjects were college students.

Analyses of variance were used to analyze the data. Subsequently, mean comparisons were carried out. In Study 1, the main comparison of interest across the repeated factor was that between the mild attention cry and the combined mean across the more urgent pain, hunger, and birth cries. (More detailed analyses by cry type were not considered appropriate as the cry segments selected may not have been representative of their cry types.) To make these planned comparisons, $t$ tests were used. In Studies 2 and 3, $t$ tests were also used within the repeated factor to compare the mean across all infant cries with the combined mean for animal and mechanical sounds. The Scheffe test was used to make comparisons within the experience factors in Studies 1 and 3. Significant $F$ values are reported in the text. Findings with the potency ratings were not replicable from study to study and are therefore not reported.

## 3.2. Physiological Arousal to Cries

Both studies that included physiological measures provided evidence that infant cries were more arousing than other sounds that were nevertheless similar in annoying features. In Study 2, the nurses reacted to the cries with greater decreases in pulse amplitude, $F(2,28) = 3.593$, $p < .041$, and blood volume, $F(2,28) = 7.798$, $p < .002$, than to the animal and mechanical sounds indicating sympathetic arousal. There were no differences in pulse rate across the types of sounds in this study. In Study 3, the vasoconstriction measures showed a similar pattern with greater decrease in pulse amplitude, $F(2,110) = 12,121$, $p < .001$, and blood volume, $F(2,110) = 6.515$, $p < .005$, to the infant cries than to other sounds. In this study, there was also a pattern of greater pulse rate acceleration, $F(2,110) = 5.333$, $p < .01$, to the infant cries. The results of these analyses suggest that infant cries are more arousing than other types of sounds, and furthermore, that the nature of this arousal is an active coping or stress response rather than a more passive orienting to a stimulus. The studies provided no evidence of either sensitization or habituation to the sound of crying as a function of experience with infants (Studies 2 and 3) or gender of the listener (Study 3).

## 3.3. Annoyance Value of Cries

In Studies 2 and 3, infant cries were compared with other sounds in terms of their aversiveness to listeners. Because the sounds were matched for annoying features, the prediction on the basis of the aversive stimulus model would be that the cries and the other sounds would be similar in annoyance value. The data from both studies indicated that the question of the comparative aversiveness of the sounds had to be addressed within the context of the experience that the listener had had with young infants. For example, general nurses who had relatively little exposure to infants did not differentiate between the cries and the other sounds in aversiveness (mean = 2.5 for cries; mean = 2.5 for other sounds); obstetrical nurses, on the other hand, found the cries to be significantly less aversive than the other sounds (mean = 3.3. for cries; mean = 2.4 for other sounds, $F(2,110) = 4.194$, $p < .027$, for the sound × nurse group interaction) and significantly less aversive than did the general nurses. Only the nurses who were relatively unfamiliar with infants perceived the cries and the other sounds to be similar in annoyance value, just as the aversive stimulus model would predict. Obstetrical nurses, on the other hand, found the cry sounds to be neutral if not somewhat pleasant to listen to. Similarly, in the third study using the same paradigm, those with no caregiving experience and parents of an only child rated the cries and other sounds as equally unpleasant, but the multiparous parents rated the cries as more pleasant than other sounds, $F(4,110) = 4.228$, $p < .005$, for the sound × parity interaction. In the first study, there was also evidence that the cries increased in pleasantness, $F(2,133) = 3.496$, $p < .05$, and decreased in annoyance, $F(2,133) = 7.856$, $p < .01$ with caregiving experience, such that those with no baby-sitting experience found the cries to be less pleasant and more annoying than either baby-sitters or parents.

## 3.4. Sympathetic Responses to Cries

As the cries became less annoying and more pleasant with experience, self-ratings of sympathy significantly increased, $F(2,133) = 9.037$, $p < .005$, in Study 1. This apparent inverse relationship between annoyance and sympathy ratings raises the question of whether the increases in sympathy with experience simply reflect a reduction in the aversiveness of cry sounds for experienced caregivers. Perhaps baby-sitters and parents are more sympathetic, not because they are more altruistic but because the cry sound is less disturbing for them. If this is so, then the aversive stimulus model could still apply. Although this explanation is plausible, it may not provide the whole story for several reasons. First, although annoyance and sympathy ratings were significantly correlated, the correlation was moderate, and the ratings only shared 12% of variance in common ($r = -.35$, $p < .01$). The dimensions of sympathy and annoyance may not be redundant, even though experience with infants may mediate changes in both components of the listener's reaction.

Another way to address this question is to look at how sympathetic responses vary with the urgency or intensity of the cries. If the aversive stimulus model is accurate, subjects should be more concerned about their own distress than the infant's, and the more urgent cries should evoke the least sympathy. Conversely, an altruistic model would predict that sympathy should increase with the number of pain cues (Hoffman, 1975). Looking at the relationship between cry intensity and sympathy, there was a significant interaction between experience and cry type, $F(6,399) = 2.615$, $p < .025$, that is illustrated in Figure 1. Persons with no experience did behave as the aversive stimulus model would predict—the urgent, pain, birth, and hunger cries evoked less sympathy than the unobtrusive attention cry. On the other hand, the responses of experienced caregivers indicate a breakdown of this inverse relationship between sympathy and the urgency of the cry. The amount of sympathy reported for the birth and hunger cries increased with

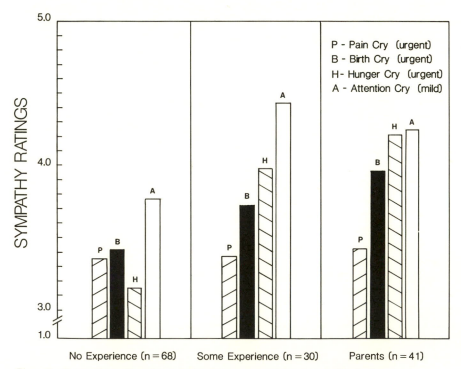

*Figure 1.* Sympathy ratings by experience groups and cry type in Study 1.

experience until, for the parent group, these urgent cries evoked as much sympathy as the mild attention cry. However, the pain cry continued to evoke little sympathy even from parents.

## 3.5. Experiential and Biological Influences on Responsiveness

A review of the literature on sensitization of adult mammals to cues from their young suggested the hypothesis that sex and experience influences on responsiveness to cries would be parallel. Thus, whenever an experience effect was observed, a gender effect in the same direction was predicted. Studies 1 and 3, with both male and female subjects, provided an opportunity to test this hypothesis.

Although both studies provide consistent evidence that the aversiveness of cries (as measured by evaluation, pleasantness, and annoyance ratings) decreases with caregiving experience, there were no comparable sex differences indicating that females find cries to be less aversive than males. In addition, a consistent sex effect with no comparable experiential influences was found on ratings of activity. In Study 1, females perceived the cries to be more active than did males, $F(1,133) = 11.186$, $p < .001$ (mean for females = 3.96, mean for males = 3.59). In Study 3, there was an interaction between gender and sound type, $F(2,110) = 4.905$, $p < .01$, such that females rated the infant cries (mean = 3.92) as more active than the other sounds (mean = 3.53), but males did not differentiate between the sound types in terms of activity. These findings, which may indicate a greater psychological arousal value of the cries for women than for men, were not reflected in measures of physiological arousal that showed neither gender nor experience effects.

The hypothesis that sex and experience differences would mirror each other was confirmed only for self-reports of sympathy. In Study 1, experience with infants was associated with increases in sympathetic responses, but females (mean = 3.83) were consistently more sympathetic than males (mean = 3.26) in all experience categories, $F(1,133) = 15.072$, $p < .001$. Greater overall levels of sympathy by females could reflect a greater sensitivity to infant crying due to more exposure to the young by females than males within experience categories. For example, the women classified as baby-sitters may have had more actual experience than the male baby-sitters in the sample. However, if this were the case, then one would have expected to find sex differences in pleasantness and annoyance ratings that were clearly sensitive to experience effects. Thus, it does not appear that mere exposure to infants can account for the gender differences in sympathetic reactions.

Failure to find strictly parallel gender and experience effects suggests that there may be qualitative differences between the sexes in their reactions to infant cries. One hypothesis is that socialization pressures could account for a qualitatively different affective response by women. An alternative hypothesis is that there may be hormonal factors that not only sensitize women to care-eliciting cues from infants but that result in a qualitatively different reception of these cues. This latter hypothesis was investigated in the fourth study of the series.

Although rodent studies indicate that the most dramatic increases in caregiving behavior by females occur at parturition, there is also evidence of an increase in the display of maternal behavior throughout the pregnancy period (Noirot, 1972). This increase is generally attributed to the hormonal changes taking place in the female rodent during pregnancy. Because previously pregnant females require no hormonal priming to elicit adequate nest-building and retrieving behaviors (Moltz, 1971), there is some reason to believe that once the mechanism is triggered, it continues to operate, regardless of current levels of circulating hormones. If such hormonal sensitization takes place in the human case, it was reasoned that it could occur as a result of taking oral contraceptives that prevent conception by simulating the condition of pregnancy. Subjects were recruited who had taken oral contraceptives for at least one 9-month period, and their responses were compared with the responses of women who had never used the pill. The period of time that the women in the pill group had taken the oral contraceptives ranged from 9 to 84 months, with a mean of 30 months. About half of the women had discontinued use of the pill at the time of the study. Analyses of the sympathy and activity ratings of pill users and nonusers yielded no significant differences, and therefore they provide no evidence that stimulation by hormones associated with a simulated pregnancy alters women's responsiveness to infant cries. An alternative test of hormonal involvement would be to assay current levels of circulating hormones, but such an investigation was beyond the scope of this research.

## 4. EVALUATION OF THE CONCEPTUAL MODELS

### 4.1. The Releaser Model Reconsidered

The strongest evidence in favor of the releaser model is the finding of greater physiological arousal to infant cries than to other sounds with similar annoying features. The nature of this arousal can be described as an active coping or stress reaction. Other investigators have monitored physiological arousal to infant cries and have reported similar reactions. Frodi and her colleagues (Frodi & Lamb, 1978; Frodi, Lamb, Leavitt, & Donovan, 1978; Frodi, Lamb, Leavitt, Donovan, Neff, & Sherry, 1978) reported a pattern of autonomic arousal involving increases in heart rate, skin conductance, and diastolic blood pressure to a videotaped segment of a baby crying. Frodi interpreted these and other results to suggest that infant cries are aversive and aggression provoking and that infants may elicit abuse if their cries are either particularly aversive or interminable or if their cries are perceived as particularly aversive by their parents. Using audiotaped cries of infants, Boukydis (1980) found that the cries of temperamentally "difficult" infants elicited greater autonomic arousal in terms of skin potential compared with the cries of average or easy infants. Wiesenfeld and Klorman (1978) reported heart rate acceleration to videotaped cries but only when mothers were viewing the cries of their own compared with unfamiliar infants.

In the present studies, the findings that listeners were selectively aroused by the infant cries compared with other annoying sounds is compatible with either the releaser model of the cry's impact or the empathy model. Both models stress the uniqueness of the cry stimulus and the involuntary aspect of the receiver's reaction. However, even if the cry functions as a releaser at the elementary level of physiological arousal, the empathy model seems to be a more inclusive, though perhaps not incompatible, formulation because it goes beyond the primitive empathic response to include cognitive factors that may influence importantly the nature of the adult's overt responses to crying.

## 4.2. A Reexamination of the Aversive Stimulus or Egoistic Model

The aversive stimulus model suggests that the motivation to respond to crying is to escape aversive stimulation. The cry is, therefore, not conceived as a unique or special stimulus but one of a general class of sounds that possess annoying physical features. On several counts, the findings reported in this chapter suggest that the aversive stimulus model is incomplete.

First, this model does not account for the finding of greater autonomic arousal to the cries than to other sounds with similar annoying features. It would seem, then, that an adequate explanation of the cry's compelling nature must go beyond a formulation based on the typical responses of the sense organs to the physical features of sounds. The selective response to infant cries may reflect higher central nervous system organization over and above the general capacities of auditory reception and processing mechanisms.

Second, although inexperienced caregivers react to cries on a psychological level as they do to other annoying sounds, experience with infants seems to reduce markedly the aversiveness of cries for listeners. The fact that the mean ratings of obstetrical nurses fell on the positive side of the evaluation rating scale suggests that extended experience may eliminate the aversiveness of most cries altogether. Zeskind and Lester (1978) similarly reported that parents rate cries as less aversive sounding than nonparents. These findings are consistent with psychoacousticians' claims that a psychophysical model is inappropriate when applied to sounds that convey emotional meaning (Kryter, 1971). The physical characteristics of a sound may set some broad fundamental limits on its tolerability, but knowledge of the source of the sound may greatly alter tolerability within these limits. The annoyance values of sounds may depend not so much on their physical features but on the highly annoyed person's tendency to attribute intentions to the responsible party and thereby distort the sound's perception (Miller, 1974). The studies by Frodi and her colleagues (Frodi, Lamb, Leavitt, & Donovan, 1978; Frodi, Lamb, Leavitt, Donovan, Neff, & Sherry, 1978) show that the mere labeling of a cry as that of a *difficult* baby or a *premature* baby is sufficient to raise arousal levels and perceived aversiveness.

Third, the findings suggest that the aversive stimulus model may be correct in its egoistic characterization of adults with no caregiving experience, but the responses of experienced caregivers reflect a more altruistic concern for the baby's distress. For inexperienced caregivers, the more urgent and aversive the cries, the less sympathy they evoke. A similar inverse relationship between annoyance and sympathy was reported by Frodi and Lamb (1980) for child abusers. However, the data reported in this chapter suggest that for experienced caregivers, there may be a shift away from egoism toward a more altruistic tendency to be equally sympathetic toward discomforting urgent cries and mild unobtrusive cries. Nevertheless, a pain cry evoked little sympathy even from parents suggesting that egoism may come into play for experienced caregivers when cries are extremely raucous. The low level of sympathy for the pain cry may relate to Hoffman's (1977a) hypothesis that there may be an optimal range of distress cues beyond which observers are too concerned about their own distress to be concerned about the victim. The pain cry segment used in this study was a particularly unpleasant cry recorded when a needle was inserted in the infant's heel to draw a blood sample. Cries of such intensity may exceed limits of tolerability and would probably not be heard often by adults in the normal course of caregiving.

## 4.3. The Adequacy of the Empathy Model

The data reported seem to be most compatible with the empathy model. The finding that subjects responded to the cries with a stress reaction is consistent with Hoffman's (1975) claim that distress cues from another trigger empathic distress or an involuntary and forceful vicarious emotional experience and that this primitive response is not simply a reaction to an aversive stimulus (Sagi & Hoffman, 1976). The pervasiveness of this stress reaction despite differing amounts of exposure to the cry stimulus and despite differences in the emotional meaning of the cries for listeners suggests that adults may indeed be preadapted such that they are aroused and motivated to action by crying.

Also consistent with the empathy model is the finding that, although subjects were equally aroused by the cries, their reactions on a psychological level could tend toward either egoism or altruism. In the framework of Hoffman's empathy model (1975), one's cognitive sense of the other determines whether this primitive empathic distress response is accompanied by an egoistic concern to alleviate one's own distressed state or whether the empathic arousal is transformed into a more altruistic concern to alleviate the other's distress. The shift toward altruism with experience probably reflects not only changes in the hedonic value of the cry sound but also changes in the listener's cognitive understanding of the needs and capabilities of young infants.

Hoffman (1977a) has also suggested that egoistic elements may predominate when distress cues are extremely aversive. The cries of some infants may be particularly unpleasant, thereby making these infants more vulnerable to abuse by their parents. For example, Zeskind and Lester (1978) found that the pain cries of infants with many nonoptimal obstetric conditions are high pitched and that listeners find them to be more aversive, grating, distressing, sick, urgent, piercing, discomforting, and arousing than the cries of infants with low numbers of nonoptimal conditions. Frodi, Lamb, Leavitt, Donovan, Neff, and Sherry (1978) also reported that the high-pitched cry of a premature baby is considered more aversive and elicits greater autonomic arousal than the cry of a full-term infant. Similarly, Boukydis (1980) found that the cries of temperamentally difficult infants are high pitched and elicit greater autonomic arousal, more "anger/irritation," less "care-for," and more "spoiled" responses than the cries of easier babies. In addition to aversive-sounding cries, the parents' limits of tolerability may be exceeded by the interminable crying of an infant with poor state organization and self-quieting abilities.

## 4.4. The Ontogeny of Human Parental Behavior

Studies of caregiving behavior in a wide range of mammals suggest that exposure to the young enhances their attractiveness for adults (Harper, 1971). The findings of experience effects on aversiveness and sympathy in the studies reported show that exposure to human infants does indeed produce changes in the perception and meaning of cries in a manner that might be expected to facilitate altruistic responses by adult caregivers. The reduced aversiveness of cries may reflect changes on a purely affective level, that is, changes in the hedonic relevance of the sound of crying for the listener. Changes in sympathy, on the other hand, may reflect a higher level cognitive shift in the extent to which the listener views the use of crying as justifiable or beyond the infant's personal control.

The occurrence of similar affective changes mediated by experience both in lower level mammals and in humans implies that the sensitization process does not involve complex cognitive factors. Furthermore, these exposure effects may not depend on conventional reward or reinforcement principles because even traumatic experiences with infants do not seem to impede the sensitization process. One process that could be evoked to explain these findings is that attachments are formed by mammals with any indiviual with which the animal has been maintained in a proximate relationship. It is the number of interactions rather than their quality that determines attachment strength (Cairns, 1966). A more positive appraisal of cry sounds with caregiving experience may be accounted for by a similar associative conditioning process.

The increase in sympathy ratings with caregiving experience may instead reflect changes in one's cognitive understanding of the painful emotional state of the distressed person. Some hypotheses about the nature of these cognitive changes can be formulated on the basis of studies of the attribution process (Shaver, 1975). There are at least three levels on which parents and caregivers can distort the infant's objective capabilities and characteristics in ways that could either facilitate or impede the interaction process. First, the crediting of infants with intentions begins as early as in the delivery room (MacFarlane, 1977), although true intentionality does not emerge until about the age of 8 months (Piaget, 1952). Crying, for example, may not be fully goal oriented until the second half of the first year, according to Bell and Ainsworth (1972). However, parents do ascribe intentionality to early infant behaviors, and this may, in fact, be a necessary distortion for the establishment of anything but a routine, impersonal relationship (Bennett, 1971). A second level of distortion is the attribution of personality traits to infants from the moment of birth. The trait labels that are applied to infants in the first 2 weeks of life have great importance for the kinds of care that infants receive (Bennett, 1971) and could result in self-fulfilling prophecies (Shaver, 1975). At a third level, attributions of intentionality and personal dispositions usually lead to judgments of responsibility and evaluations of the individual in terms of praiseworthiness or blameworthiness (Shaver, 1975).

Whether an individual describes his or her emotional arousal at the sound of distressful crying as predominantly that of annoyance to that of sympathy may depend importantly on the individual's cognitive understanding of the infant at the three levels of intentionality, attribution of traits, and responsibility. Because crying is not a neutral behavior but has hedonic relevance, assignments of blame may be extreme unless the behavior is also seen as justifiable (Shaver, 1975). It may be that those unfamiliar with young infants are more likely to view the use of negative behavior like crying as intentional, manipulative, or otherwise reprehensible, or they may see crying as reflecting stable dispositions, such as "naughtiness" or "crankiness." With greater familiarity with infants, adults may come to view crying as a justifiable means for communicating infants' needs.

Last in the discussion of ontogenetic factors is the question of sex differences in activity and sympathy ratings. Zeskind and Lester (1978) reported a similar finding with females reporting that cries are more arousing than males. Boukydis (1980) found that men compared with women give more "anger/irritation," less "care-for," and more "spoiled" responses. The gender differences in the psychological arousal value of cries reported in this chapter and by Boukydis (1980) were not accompanied by similar differences on measures of physiological arousal. Berman (1980) also concluded from her recent view of the literature that self-report measures give more consistent support for gender differences in responsiveness to the young than physiological or behavioral measures. The gender differences reported in this chapter do not appear to be a function of differential amounts of experience in infant care, nor is there support for one hypothesis concerning hormonal determinants, although other hormonal hypotheses need to be investigated. Alternatively, the effects of gender on reactions to infant cries may stem from (1) the anticipation of motherhood and preparation of young girls for this role by socializing agents (Berman, 1980); or (2) a less negative evaluation by these agents toward the feeling and expression of emotional states by young girls than by boys (Hoffman, 1977b).

## 5. NEW DIRECTIONS FOR CRY RESEARCH

A major question for future research is the relationship between actual and perceived features of infant cries and the caregiver's behavioral response. Do parents whose infants have particularly high-pitched cries (e.g., premature infants or those with medical complications or with difficult temperaments) respond less promptly or less appropriately than parents whose infant's cries possess fewer aversive cry features? The length of the cry segments used as stimuli in the studies to date has been limited to a few seconds or, at most, to a few minutes, and yet it is estimated that young babies cry on the average of 1.5 to 2 hours per day (Brazelton, 1962). Studies are needed to determine how judgments of aversiveness and behavioral responses are affected by length of exposure to the sound. Conversely, are pleasant-sounding cries more likely to be ignored altogether or rather to lead to positive interactions with caregivers (Friedman, Zahn-Waxler, & Radke-Yarrow, 1980)?

Perhaps, as Hoffman (1977a) has implied, the aversiveness of the distress cues is a less reliable predictor of helping behavior than the cognitive factors that transform empathic distress into sympathetic distress. Parke (1977) also has argued that the caregiver's cognitive and affective mediational sets may be more important in directing the interaction process than the objective behaviors or characteristics of the infant. Studies are needed to determine how attributions of intentionality, responsibility, and personality traits relate to the perceived aversiveness of cries, the amount of sympathy evoked by them, and caregiving behavior. The caregiver's perceived control over the termination of crying may also be important: Bouts of crying from a relatively unconsolable infant may be seen as more aversive and may be ignored, compared with the cries of an infant who is easily consoled (cf. Bennett, 1971). Another level at which cognitive and affective processes could affect behavioral responsiveness relates to the caregiver's ascription of causes to particular cries (e.g., hunger, pain, attention, naughtiness). Although it has been argued that cries vary primarily in intensity and are not uniquely different according to evoking situation (Murray, 1979), caregivers do use intensity and contextual cues to make qualitative distinctions between cries on the basis of their presumed causes. How do these causal assignments affect the emotional and affective impact of cries and the caregiver's subsequent behavior?

The findings reported in this chapter that the meaning of cries changes through exposure to infants suggests that future research should focus not only on the identification of these mediational processes but on their development. By charting normal developmental changes in the perception and evaluation of specific infant behaviors, some light will be shed on the conditions that foster the development of positive and negative mediational sets that can either facilitate or impede the interaction process. The identification of these conditions will have important practical implications for preventive intervention with parents and for therapeutic intervention when the interaction process has become destructive in nature.

## 6. REFERENCES

Ainsworth, M. Object relations, dependency, and attachment: A theoretical review of the mother–infant relationship. *Child Development*, 1969, *40*, 969–1025.

Bastian, J. Primate signalling systems and human language. In I. Devore (Ed.), *Primate behavior: Field studies of monkeys and apes.* New York: Holt, Rinehart, & Winston, 1965.

Bell, S., & Ainsworth, M. Infant crying and maternal responsiveness. *Child Development*, 1972, *43*, 1171–1190.

Bennett, S. Infant–caretaker interactions. *American Academy of Child Psychiatry Journal*, 1971, *10*, 321–335.

Berman, P. Are women more responsive than men to the young? A review of developmental and situational variables. *Psychological Bulletin*, 1980, *88*, 668–695.

Bernal, J. Crying during the first 10 days of life and maternal responses. *Developmental Medicine and Child Neurology*, 1972, *14*, 362–372.

Boukydis, C. F. Z. An analog study of adult physiological and self-report responding to infant cries. *Cry Research Newsletter*, 1980, *2*(2), 2–5.

Bowlby, J. *Attachment and loss: Vol. 1 Attachment.* New York: Basic Books, 1969.

Brazelton, T. B. Crying in infancy. *Pediatrics*, 1962, *29*, 579–588.

Brown, C. Instruments in psychophysiology. In N. Greenfield & R. Steinbeck (Eds.), *Handbook of psychophysiology.* New York: Holt, Rinehart, & Winston, 1972.

Cairns, R. Attachment behavior of mammals. *Psychological Review*, 1966, *73*, 409–426.

Eibl-Eibesfelt, I. *Ethology: The biology of behavior* (2nd ed.). New York: Holt, Rinehart & Winston, 1975.

Friedman, S., Zahn-Waxler, C., & Radke-Yarrow, M. *Perception of cries of full-term and preterm infants.* Paper presented at the American Psychological Association Meetings, Montreal, Canada, September. 1980.

Frodi, A., & Lamb, M. Sex differences in responsiveness to infants: A developmental study of psychophysiological and behavioral responses. *Child Development*, 1978, *49*, 1182–1188.

Frodi, A., & Lamb, M. Child abuser's responses to infant smiles. *Child Development*, 1980, *51*, 238–241.

Frodi, A., Lamb, M., Leavitt, L., & Donovan, W. Fathers' and mothers' responses to infant smiles and cries. *Infant Behavior and Development* 1978, *1*, 187–198.

Frodi, A., Lamb, M., Leavitt, L., Donovan, W., Neff, C., & Sherry, D. Fathers' and mothers' responses to the faces and cries of normal and premature infants. *Developmental Psychology*, 1978, *14*, 490–498.

Harper, L. The young as a source of stimuli controlling caretaker behavior. *Developmental Psychology*, 1971, *4*, 73–88.

Hinde, R. *Biological bases of human social behavior.* New York: McGraw-Hill, 1974.

Hoffman, M. Developmental synthesis of affect and cognition and its implication for altruistic motivation. *Developmental Psychology,* 1975, *11,* 607–622.

Hoffman, M. *A three component model of empathy.* Paper presented at a meeting of the Society for Research in Child Development, New Orleans, 1977. (a)

Hoffman, M. Sex differences in empathy and related behaviors. *Psychological Bulletin,* 1977, *84,* 712–722. (b)

Klaus, M., & Kennell, J. *Maternal–infant bonding.* St. Louis: C. V. Mosby, 1976.

Kryter, K. *The effects of noise on man.* New York: Academic Press, 1971.

Lenneberg, E., Rebelsky, F., & Nichols, I. The vocalization of infants born to deaf and hearing parents. *Human Development,* 1965, *8,* 23–37.

Lessing, D. *A proper marriage.* St. Albans, England: Panther Books, 1976.

Lester, B. M., & Zeskind, P. A biobehavioral perspective on crying in early infancy. In H. E. Fitzgerald, B. M. Lester, and M. W. Yogman (Eds.), *Theory and research in behavioral pediatrics.* New York: Plenum, 1982.

Macfarlane, A. *The psychology of childbirth.* London: Fontana/Open Books, 1977.

Mead, M., & Newton, N. Cultural patterning of perinatal behavior. In S. Richardson & A. Guttmacher (Eds.), *Childbearing: Its social and psychological aspects.* Baltimore: Williams & Wilkins, 1967.

Miller, J. The effects of noise on people. *Journal of the Acoustical Society of America,* 1974, *56,* 729–764.

Moltz, H. The ontogeny of maternal behavior in some selected mammalian species. In H. Moltz (Ed.), *The ontogeny of vertebrate behavior.* New York: Academic Press, 1971.

Moltz, H. Some mechanisms governing the induction, maintenance, and synchrony of maternal behavior in the laboratory rat. In. W. Montagna & W. Sadler (Eds.), *Reproductive behavior.* New York: Academic Press, 1974.

Money, J., & Erhardt, A. *Man and woman, boy and girl.* Baltimore: Johns Hopkins University Press, 1972.

Moss, J., & Robson, K. *The role of protest behavior in the development of mother–infant attachment.* Paper presented at the annual meeting of the American Psychological Association, San Francisco, August–September, 1968.

Murray, A. Infant crying as an elicitor of parental behavior: An examination of two models. *Psychological Bulletin,* 1979, *86,* 191–215.

Noirot, E. The onset of maternal behavior in rats, hamsters, and mice: A selective review. In D. Lehrman, R. Hinde, & E. Shaw (Eds.), *Advances in the study of behavior* (Vol. 4). New York: Academic Press, 1972.

Obrist, P. The cardiovascular-behavioral interaction—As it appears today. *Psychophysiology,* 1976, *13,* 95–107.

Osgood, S., Suci, G., & Tannenbaum, P. *The measurement of meaning.* Urbana: University of Illinois Press, 1957.

Ostwald, P. *Soundmaking: The acoustic communication of emotion.* Springfield, Ill.: Charles C Thomas, 1963.

Parke, R. Parent–infant interaction: Progress, paradigms, and problems. In G. Sackett (Ed.), *Observing behavior: Vol. 1. Theory and application in mental retardation.* Baltimore: University Park Press, 1977.

Piaget, J. *The origins of intelligence in children.* New York: International Universities Press, 1952.

Rosenblatt, J. Views on the onset and maintenance of maternal behavior in the rat. In L. Aronson, E. Tobach, D. Lehrman, & J. Rosenblatt (Eds.), *Development and evolution of behavior.* San Francisco: Freeman, 1970.

Sagi, A., & Hoffman, M. Empathic distress in the newborn. *Developmental Psychology*, 1976, *13*, 175–176.

Shaver, K. *An introduction to the attribution process.* Cambridge, Mass.: Winthrop Publishers, 1975.

Simner, M. Newborn's response to the cry of another infant. *Developmental Psychology*, 1971, *5*, 136–150.

Wiesenfeld, A., & Klorman, R. The mother's psychophysiological reactions to contrasting affective expressions by her own and an unfamiliar infant. *Developmental Psychology*, 1978, *14*, 294–304.

Wilson, E. O. *Sociobiology: The new synthesis.* Cambrige, Mass.: Belknap Press, 1975.

Wolff, P. The natural history of crying and other vocalizations in early infancy. In B. M. Foss (Ed.), *Determinants of infant behavior* (Vol. 4). London: Methuen, 1969.

Wordon, F., & Galambos, R. Auditory processing of biologically significant sounds. *Neurosciences Research Program Bulletin*, 1972, *10*, 1–117.

Zeskind, P. S., & Lester, B. M. Acoustic features and auditory perception of the cries of newborns with prenatal and perinatal complications. *Child Development*, 1978, *49*, 580–582.

# 11

# Physiology and Behavior
## Parents' Response to the Infant Cry

WILBERTA L. DONOVAN and LEWIS A. LEAVITT

## 1. INTRODUCTION

This chapter reviews studies of parental response to the infant cry. In this review, the cry is considered as a social signal that mediates developing parent–infant interaction. The studies examine links between the cry as a signal, processing of the cry by caregivers, and consequences of their behavioral response to the cry.

## 2. THE CRY AS AN ELICITOR OF CAREGIVER RESPONSE

One prominent conceptualization of the mechanisms by which the cry has its powerful impact is attachment theory that was formulated by Bowlby (1969) and Ainsworth (1969). Within a context of evolutionary biology, the cry is considered an attachment behavior that promotes proximity to the caregiver, thus increasing the probability of survival for

WILBERTA L. DONOVAN and LEWIS A. LEAVITT • Infant Development Laboratory, Waisman Center on Mental Retardation and Human Development and Department of Pediatrics, University of Wisconsin, Madison, Wisconsin 53706. The research reported in this chapter was supported in part by the Department of Health, Education, and Welfare Grants HD-03352 and HD-082400 and by Grant 100665 from the Graduate School of the University of Wisconsin–Madison.

the young. In this framework, the cry is viewed as a releaser of caregiving behavior. Central to this theorizing has been the increasing attention devoted to the theme that maternal sensitivity to a variety of signals from the human infant, including the cry, is important for the infant's development as well as for its survival. Sensitivity entails interpreting the infant's signals accurately and responding appropriately and promptly (Ainsworth, 1969). The thesis underlying the emphasis on maternal sensitivity is that responsiveness during social interaction is related to the quality of attachment behavior exhibited toward the mother. To quote Ainsworth, Blehar, Waters, and Wall (1978, p. 152), "Sensitive responsiveness to infant signals and communication seems to be the key variable accounting for environmental influences on the development of a secure versus an insecure attachment relationship."

Whereas Bowlby had emphasized protection as being sufficient for the evolution of attachment behavior in many species, the function of attachment behavior was broadened by Ainsworth to include the concept of the attachment figure as a secure base for exploration. She views human adaptation and survival as equally dependent upon exploration and protection. The securely attached infant elicits protection from its mother but also uses her as a secure base from which to explore. A consequence of the infant's exploration is mastery of the environment and competency in cognitive skills and social interactions.

## 3. INFANT DEVELOPMENT AS A FUNCTION OF MATERNAL RESPONSE

Many studies have demonstrated that maternal response contingent upon infant behavior has a significant effect on developing a secure attachment. Bell and Ainsworth (1972) have shown that rapid maternal behavioral response to early crying is associated not only with a decline in crying but also with the development of noncrying modes of communication. Additional work by S. M. Bell (1970) supports this emphasis on maternal sensitivity. Her data demonstrated a relation between a secure attachment and advanced scores on the Piagetian task of object permanence. Furthermore, person permanence, which developmentally anticipates object permanence, was seen in securely attached infants, but insecurely attached infants failed to demonstrate a similar acceleration in person permanence. Correlations between quality of attachment and intelligence have been found by Ainsworth and Bell (1974) as well as by Beckwith, Cohen, Kopp, Parmelee, and Marcy (1976). In a longitudinal study in our laboratory, we also found differences between infants paired with more versus less sensitive mothers (Donovan & Leavitt, 1978). Our data, to be described in detail in this chapter, extend those reported earlier and underscore the importance for infant development of a mother's response being contingent upon her infant's behavior.

Not only have more advanced cognitive skills of infants paired with the more sensitive mothers been reported, but also these infants more readily comply to maternal commands during their first year of life than do infants of less sensitive mothers (Stayton, Hogan, & Ainsworth, 1971). Matas, Arend, and Sroufe (1978) have reported that quality of attachment is related to compliance with maternal requests, help seeking, and problem-solving behavior at age 2. Infants securely attached at 12 or 18 months exhibited enthusiasm and positive effect in approaching problems at age 2. In contrast, insecurely attached infants were more easily frustrated and less able to use the caregiver for help, were more negativistic, and gave up more quickly. Thus, the patterns established early have consequences for behavior in the following year.

## 4. STIMULUS PROCESSING AND PHYSIOLOGICAL RESPONSE TO INFANT SIGNALS

The studies attesting to the importance of a mother's responses being contingent on her infant's behavior (cf. Ainsworth & Bell, 1974) and the converging theme that infants direct and modulate the nature of social interactions (R. Q. Bell, 1971) stimulated a series of studies in our laboratory (Donovan & Leavitt, 1978; Donovan, Leavitt, & Balling, 1978; Leavitt & Donovan, 1979). In our studies, we assessed the caregiver's processing of infant signals by measuring her physiological response to these signals. Both skin conductance and heart rate response are frequently used as indices of stimulus processing or the orienting response (Hare, Wood, Britain, & Shadman, 1971; Lacey & Lacey, 1970). The orienting system serves to maximize the effects of stimulation, and cardiac deceleration is observed during periods when attention is directed to the external environment. Several investigators have provided evidence that cardiac deceleration following stimulus onset is a reliable index of this orienting response (Graham & Clifton, 1966; Kagan & Lewis, 1965) and can be used as a physiological reflection of attentional processing (Lacey, 1967). In contrast, cardiac acceleration is a component of the defensive response and is observed in situations where external stimulation is intense, painful, and/or is to be minimized. This arousal system serves to buffer or minimize the effects of stimulation when the external environment is "rejected" or attention is turned inward such as during mental arithmetic (Lacey, 1967).

The direction of heart rate change and habituation rate to simple stimuli is in large part a function of stimulus parameters, whereas cardiac response to complex stimuli is additionally affected by other factors labeled as *experiential* or *cognitive*. In effect, stimuli may be attention provoking and elicit cardiac deceleration even though labeled as *unpleasant* (Hare, Wood, Britain, & Shadman, 1971; Libby, Lacey, & Lacey, 1973).

To measure the physiological concomitants of processing infant signals, we developed an analog strategy for studying the mother–infant dyad. This enabled us to control various stimulus parameters, such as onset, intensity, and duration of the signals. In our analog situation, caregivers (usually the mothers) of young infants are shown videotapes of an infant exhibiting varying facial expressions of interest. Single or multiple physiological responses are monitored while the caregivers view the selected images. Analysis of repeated presentations of the stimulus figure yields information concerning changes in autonomic arousal and permits determination of whether differences exist between the facial expressions in their ability to command continued attention from the caregiver.

Our initial study (Donovan *et al.*, 1978) examined autonomic responses to videotaped images of a smiling or crying infant. Heart rate and skin conductance responses were recorded continuously throughout viewing. One of two "standard" infants was selected for viewing so as to ensure that stimulus parameters would be held constant across mothers. The stimuli were 10-second silent images on a videotape monitor of a 3-month-old infant, *en face*, exhibiting either a smiling or a crying facial expression. The stimulus tape, constructed from a naturalistic tape, showed a full-face view of the head and shoulders of the baby reclining in an infant seat against an undifferentiated background. A sequence of six identical episodes of one expression was followed by six episodes of the other expression. A blank screen followed each stimulus presentation.

As expected, the infant facial expressions with a strong affective component were potent elicitors of physiologic response in mothers with young infants. As can be seen in Figure 1, the infant smile, as manipulated in our study, initially elicited a biphasic heart rate response with an initial acceleratory component followed by cardiac deceleration. Although acceleration is considered to be the cardiac component of the defensive response (Graham & Clifton, 1966), an interpretation of the acceleratory response as being equivalent to the defense response in this instance seemed inappropriate because defensiveness is not the only

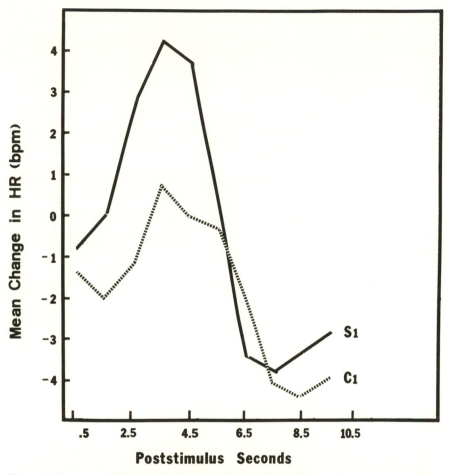

*Figure 1.* Mean second-by-second changes in heart rate on Trial 1 in response to a smiling infant ($S_1$) and a crying infant ($C_1$).

elicitor of acceleration. It has been shown that in addition to mental activities eliciting cardiac acceleration, smiling in response to a stimulus elicits acceleration (Emde, Campos, Gaensbauer, & Reich, 1975). As is often noted, a smiling infant, indeed, elicits a similar facial expression from many mothers.

The cry signal elicited deceleration—the cardiac component of the orienting response. We interpreted this deceleratory response to the cry stimulus within the context of the evolutionary-ethological approach as discussed earlier (Ainsworth, 1969; Bowlby, 1969; Sroufe & Waters, 1977). Our finding that cardiac deceleration accompanies the viewing of a crying infant is predicted by the ethological view that the function of mammalian and avian cries is to activate maternal attention. Cries of the young are usually emitted when the infant has lost proximity with its mother, and for many species in their natural environment, survival depends upon eliciting immediate attention followed by maternal behaviors aimed at terminating the cry and preventing its recurrence.

These initial data from the Donovan *et al.* study (1978) indicated that the paradigm developed to tap maternal attentive processes might indeed be useful as a means to understand better a mother's behavioral response during interaction. Hence, the study served as an impetus for many of the following studies, each of which attempted to delineate further those variables affecting physiologic and behavioral response to infant signals, especially the cry. For convenience, we have labled those variables affecting response as being either *receiver variables* or *infant/ stimulus variables*. Included under the former are variables such as the mother's perception of her own infant's temperament affecting response to a standard stimulus figure or experiential factors affecting response. Examples of infant/stimulus variables affecting response include those variables specifically manipulated in the stimulus array, such as the stimulus figure being a familiar or an unfamiliar infant or varying acoustic features of the cry stimulus.

## 4.1. Receiver Variables

The influence of experiential factors on physiologic response can be demonstrated either by specific experimental manipulations or by comparing groups of mothers with contrasting experiences. As an example of the former, the Donovan *et al.* (1978) data indicated that the cry and the smile differentially affected both skin conductance and cardiac responses to subsequent signals. The smile that initially elicited a biphasic cardiac response and an increase in skin conductance failed to elicit either physiologic response when it was viewed following the cry stimulus. In contrast, the viewing of the cry signal following the smile elicited the skin conductance response and cardiac deceleration. It was of particular interest to us that cardiac deceleration to the cry signal viewed second was more persistent than response to the cry viewed first. From these data, we speculated that infants may increase the probability of eliciting maternal attention in crying situations by having previously presented the mother with more positive signals from the infant's behavioral repertoire such as clinging, sucking, and, for human infant, smiling. This differential effect of the preceding signal upon response to future signals implicates the role of prior experience in predicting maternal response.

By comparing mothers with contrasting perceptions of their own infant's temperament, another important receiver variable was found to affect physiologic response to the cry signal. Many investigators have become increasingly interested in the effect of early differences in infant temperament on developing mother–infant reciprocity (cf. Bates, 1980; Carey, 1970; Thomas, Chess, Birch, Hertzig, & Korn, 1963). Difficult infants have been described as displaying not only irregularity in biological functioning, but they also have low thresholds for arousal and, when aroused, react intensely (Carey, 1970). Such babies are described as being irritable and fussy. A decrease in the mother's behavioral response to negative behaviors of difficult infants has been reported. Mothers of 3-month-old difficult infants vocalized less and were less responsive to their infant's cries than mothers of less difficult infants (Campbell, 1979), and mothers of 4-month-old difficult infants tended to respond negatively to infants' negative emotions (Kelly, 1976).

Each mother in the Donovan *et al.* (1978) study had answered the Carey Infant Temperament Questionnaire (Carey, 1970). Based on their responses, mothers were dichotomized as having either an "easy" or a "difficult" baby. A striking difference between the mothers who described their infants as "easy" versus those who described their infants as "difficult" emerged when their heart rate responses were compared. The mothers of easy infants responded physiologically to changes in infant signals. They exhibited cardiac deceleration to the stimulus change from a smile to a cry, and they exhibited a biphasic response as the stimulus changed from a cry to a smile. Mothers of difficult infants failed to respond physiologically to these changes. This finding that the smile following the cry failed to elicit attention, indexed by cardiac response, of mothers of difficult infants has important implications if our analog of the mother–infant dyad taps processes operative in nonlaboratory settings. A consequence of being confronted with an infant perceived as difficult may be that response to positive signals is reduced. The finding that mothers of difficult infants have a low vocalization rate (Campbell, 1979) supports our contention that reduced sensitivity generalizes to signals other than negative ones, such as fussiness and crying. Sameroff (1977) reports that mothers of 12-month-old difficult infants avoid social interaction with their infants more than other mothers.

In these several studies reporting on the effects of a difficult temperament, the various questionnaires (e.g., Carey's Infant Temperament Questionnaire) taps the mother's perception of her infant's behavior. Theorists generally agree that reports of early temperamental differences have a functional significance for parent–child interaction despite the disagreement over whether the differences reflect actual attributes of the child (Thomas, Chess, & Korn, 1982) or "parental perceptions" (Bates, 1983).

Whereas our study did not address the question of direction of causality between maternal physiologic response and infant temperament, a consequence of the mother being less responsive may be that both mother and infant fail to benefit from the mutual interchange of positive behaviors such as smiling during episodes of mother–infant interaction. Furthermore, the finding of reduced sensitivity generates several questions of interest. For example, the degree to which being less responsive might be adaptive for the mothers who are continually confronted with negative behaviors is still to be determined.

In the Leavitt and Donovan study (1979), mothers' physiologic concomitants of processing an infant's direct gaze and its averted gaze were assessed. Although the response to the cry was not investigated, the finding that physiologic response was a function of perceived infant temperament makes a brief mention of this study relevant to this chapter. As before, mothers of young infants were shown repeated presentations of videotaped images of an infant face but with *eye contact* possible on only half the trials. As in the Donovan *et al.* study (1978), Leavitt and Donovan (1979) found mothers who described their infants as being easy to be physiologically sensitive to changes in infant signals. These mothers responded with cardiac deceleration to the change from the infant's averted gaze to its direct gaze. Mothers of difficult infants did not respond physiologically to this change in infant gaze behavior. Together with the earlier data, these suggest that as a consequence of stressful caregiving experiences, mothers who perceive their infants as more difficult may fail to engage in the interchange of positive signals (e.g., smiling or eye contact).

The replication of the finding that mothers of "easy" and "difficult" babies differ in their physiologic response to visual presentations of infant stimuli appeared important enough to merit further investigation to determine the extent to which parental expectations may influence subsequent interaction or response. Frodi, Lamb, Leavitt, and Donovan (1978) attempted to establish cognitive sets (expectations) experimentally by describing the identical stimulus infant as "difficult," "normal," or "premature." Donovan *et al.* (1978) had reasoned that the failure of mothers of difficult infants to respond was a consequence of caretaking experiences that had been so stressful that the women failed to attend to changes in their infant's behavior. Frodi, Lamb, Leavitt, and Donovan (1978) reported that skin conductance response to the "premature" infant cry signal was significantly greater than to the "normal" infant. Furthermore, crying and smiling infants labeled as *premature* and *difficult* elicited fewer verbal responses of sympathy than the *normal* infant. These findings are important because they demonstrate that the cognitive sets implied by the Donovan *et al.* (1978) data can be established by brief experimental manipulations involving labels alone.

As more attention is being drawn to the father's role in his child's development, it was naturally of interest to determine how similar (or different) mothers' and fathers' physiological responses were to the infant cry. Frodi, Lamb, Leavitt, and Donovan (1978) found that physiologic response did not discriminate between mothers and fathers; however, mothers gave more extreme descriptions of their moods and feelings than did the fathers. Boukydis and Burgess (1982), however, have recently reported that men report more "irritation/anger" to cries, although they, too, report that men and women do not differ in their physiologic response (i.e., skin potential response) to the cries. Recently, Wiesenfeld, Malatesta, and DeLoach (1981) reported that a pain cry is rated as especially unpleasant by parents, especially mothers. Also, mothers were more accurate than fathers in recognizing their own infants' cries from unfamiliar infants' cries and in differentiating the anger and pain cries. However, both mothers and fathers responded physiologically to unfamiliar infants' cries with heart rate decelerations. To their own infants' cries, fathers again responded with deceleration, whereas mothers responded with a brief cardiac deceleration followed by a secondary acceleration. Frodi and Lamb's data (1978) agree with this general finding of no sex differences in physiologic response. They reported that boys and girls aged 8 and 14 years did not differ in physiologic responses to infant smiles and cries. Behaviorally, however, the girls interacted more than did the boys.

Parity effects in response to the cry have been reported by Boukydis and Burgess (1982). Primiparous parents showed highest levels of arousal (i.e., skin potential response) in response to the cry signal, with nonparents showing the next highest level, and multiparous parents exhibiting the lowest levels of response.

## 4.2. Infant/Stimulus Variables

In addition to the several receiver variables just reviewed, there are many stimulus variables that affect response to the cry. Wiesenfeld and Klorman (1978) sought to determine the similarities and differences in maternal physiologic response as a function of a mother's viewing her *own* or an *unfamiliar* infant. The infant stimuli were again 10-second silent black-and-white videotaped segments of the infant's either crying or smiling. In addition, affectively neutral landscape scenes were included as control stimuli. Subjective reports of tension and perceived unpleasantness of these scenes were also obtained. Their results showed that mothers responded to their *own* babies' smiles with cardiac acceleration. As argued earlier, an interpretation of the acceleratory response reflecting defensiveness again seems inappropriate because a smiling infant frequently elicits a smile from his or her mother. In contrast, response to the *unfamiliar* smiling infant was one of slight deceleration on the first trial. The accelerating component of the biphasic response reported in the Donovan *et al.* (1978) study was not replicated by Wiesenfeld and Klorman. The inclusion of the mother's own infant in the Wiesenfeld and Klorman results were similar to those from the Donovan *et al.* (1978) study, showing that the image portraying the *unfamiliar* crying infant elicited a sharp deceleratory cardiac response. A small acceleratory response was observed on Trial 1 to the cry of one's *own* infant. Although not emphasized in their report, by Trial 3, maternal cardiac response to one's own infant cry was also deceleratory. Recall also that we noted earlier that mothers and fathers responded with cardiac deceleration to the unfamiliar infant's cry and that fathers exhibited a similar deceleratory response to their own infant's cry. Mothers, though, responded with a biphasic response of deceleration followed by acceleration to their own infant's cry (Wiesenfeld, Malatesta, & DeLoach, 1981). The several findings of deceleration in response to the cry support our argument that physiologic mechanisms may operate to help ensure maternal attention to this basic infant signal. Although subjects' verbal reports indicate the infant cry to be unpleasant, the finding that cardiac deceleration accompanies the viewing of the cry signal agrees with other findings that report that stimuli labeled as *unpleasant* may be attention provoking and hence elicit heart rate deceleration (Hare *et al.*, 1971; Libby *et al.*, 1973).

Wiesenfeld and Klorman (1978) found that images of the mother's own infant evoked large electrodermal response. Skin conductance response was greatest to the image of one's own infant's crying, followed by the image of one's own infant's smiling. Not surprisingly, their data show that ratings of tension during the episode portraying the subject's own child's crying exceeded those ratings given to all other images. The image depicting one's own child smiling was rated most pleasant.

Data from two additional studies indicate that stimuli generated by atypical babies, such as prematures, elicit a response pattern that differs from the response elicited by full-term infants (Frodi, Lamb, & Willie, 1981; Frodi, Lamb, Leavitt, Donovan, Neff, & Sherry, 1978). In particular, the premature's auditory signal, rather than her/his facial features, elicited greater increases in diastolic blood pressure, skin conductance, and heart rate, although the most marked differences in response occurred when both the cry and the face were those of the premature infant. This finding is of special interest because Lenneberg, Rebelsky, and Nichols (1965) report that deaf parents are not compelled to attend to their crying infants although they can see their distressed state. In effect, a cognitive awareness of distress without the urgency conveyed by the sound itself may be ineffective in eliciting a response. More recently, Frodi, Lamb, and Wille (1981) report that mothers with premature babies respond with especially pronounced arousal to a premature infant's cry. Furthermore, those mothers who described their own premature baby as "easy" exhibited less physiologic arousal and were more willing to interact with the stimulus babies than were the mothers who viewed their own baby as "difficult." It is possible that maternal expectations developed through labeling (cf. Frodi, Lamb, Leavitt, & Donovan, 1978) contributed to this effect.

Acoustic features of the infant cry vary as a function of infant temperament and also affect the physiologic response of both parents and nonparents (Boukydis & Burgess, 1982). Specifically, cries from difficult infants had the highest pitch and the most irregular patterns of pauses. Overall, the cries of these difficult infants elicited highest levels of skin potential responses, with average cries next, and easy cries least for nonparents and multiparous parents. Primiparous parents reacted to the average cries with significantly higher levels of arousal than they did to the other two cry tapes. The "difficult" cries were also rated as significantly more grating, piercing, and aversive than the "average" and "easy" cries. Lounsbury and Bates (1982) have reported a similar finding of difficult cries being rated as more irritating and spoiled sounding than easy infant cries.

The series of studies just reviewed demonstrate that physiologic response to the infant cry signal is determined not only by acoustic features of the cry stimulus but also by one or more important cognitive/experiential variables of the perceiver. Because the impetus to study physiological responding stemmed from the knowledge that the child's development was affected by the mother's behavioral response, we, therefore, sought to determine whether differences in physiologic response predicted behavioral response and thus had implications for the child's development (Donovan & Leavitt, 1978). In this study, we demonstrated links between measures of maternal physiologic response, the mother's behavioral response, and her infant's cognitive development. We confirmed that there are patterns of social transactions between infant and caregiver that are correlated with the infant's advanced development and, more importantly, we demonstrate that physiologic indices of maternal attentive processes predict the mother's behavioral response. Mothers whose physiologic responses to infant signals had been recorded at an earlier date (Donovan *et al.*, 1978; Leavitt & Donovan, 1979) participated in a follow-up study requiring that the mother–infant dyad visit the laboratory on two separate occasions. The first session involved observing each dyad during a feeding session when the infant was approximately 9 months of age; the second session involved testing the infants on the object permanence task within 1 week of their 15-month birthday. Our results revealed that the infant scoring high on the object permanence task had a mother whose responses during the feeding session were contingent upon her infant's behavior. It is significant that only these behaviorally sensitive mothers during the feeding session at 9 months had earlier shown cardiac orienting (attention) to changes in infant signals. These data are shown graphically in Figure 2. In constrast,

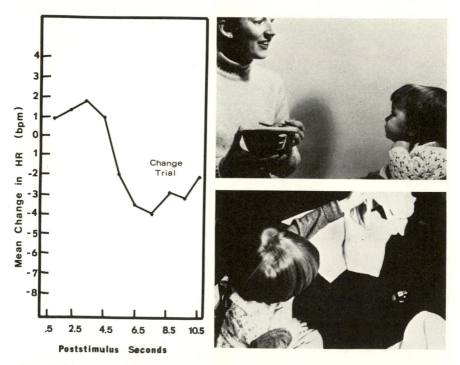

*Figure 2.* Mean second-by-second changes in heart rate to a change in the infant's signal (left) of behaviorally sensitive mothers (upper right) and their infants who score high on the object permanence task (lower right).

the low-scoring infants had mothers who were, at 3½ months, physiologically, and at 9 months, behaviorally, less sensitive to changes in infant behaviors. This study is significant because it brings together data collected in a naturalistic environment (the feeding session) with those collected under the confines of an experimental setting (the earlier session recording physiologic responses).

In summary, data from several studies underscore the importance of maternal response contingent upon infant behavior for the infant's development. We have shown how the study of the mother's attentional processing of signals prior to her behavioral response may help us to better understand underlying processes affecting developing reciprocity and to determine which variables are responsible for differential patterns of interaction that leave some infants at risk for deviant social and cognitive development.

## 5. LEARNED HELPLESSNESS—A MODEL OF MATERIAL RESPONSE

Given the importance of maternal response—physiologic and behavioral—for the infant's development, we have recently proposed that the learned helplessness theory (Seligman, 1975, 1978) be used as a model to account for observed differences in responsiveness to infant signals and especially to the distress signal of crying (Donovan, 1981). In general terms, the theory of learned helplessness claims that individuals exposed to uncontrollable events learn that responding is futile. Decreased motivation to act is accompanied by feelings of failure and the inability to cope with future events. Applying this theory to a developmental issue, we have attempted to evaluate a central aspect of maternal behavior—a mother's effectiveness in responding to her infant's signals as it relates to the mother's future responsivity. We suggest that maternal competence is dependent upon the mother's learning that her efforts during interaction with her child are effective. Processing her infant's signals provides both information to the mother concerning the needs of her child and an opportunity to learn about her effectiveness in handling the child. With specific reference to crying behavior, we argue that if a mother has previously been unsuccessful in controlling her infant's crying, a state of helplessness will ensue. This resulting state of helplessness will interfere with current and future attempts in controlling crying behavior. In other words, decreased attentiveness to her infant may be an enduring consequence of earlier experiences in which a mother has learned that her response to the infant distress signal of crying is not effective.

Typically, with the learned helplessness procedure, performance on some instrumental task is assessed as a function of various pretreatments that involve exposure to an aversive stimulus but differ in the control over the termination of the stimulus. In order to isolate the effects of controllability *per se* from the effects of the physical stimulus, a "triadic" design is employed. The first of three groups is presented, as its pretreatment, a task that can be controlled by some response. A second group of yoked subjects receives the same physical outcomes as their counterparts in the first group, but there is no response these yoked subjects can make that modifies the outcome of the task. A third group receives no pretreatment and hence serves as a control. Later, all groups are tested on a second and different task. Performance on this second task has been found to be a function of control exercised during the pretreatment (Seligman, 1975).

To test the usefulness of the helplessness model in accounting for differences in maternal response, we exposed mothers of young infants to varying degrees of control over the termination of infant crying (Donovan, 1981). The apparatus used during the pretreatment that was designed to induce varying levels of control consisted of a spring-loaded button in the center of a base. Each mother was tested on an instrumental shuttle box task following exposure to one of three instrumental pretreatments: (1) escape—four button presses terminated the infant cry; (2) no escape—button press was unrelated to cry termination; and (3) control—mothers passively listened to the cry. The instrumental shuttle box task followed the pretreatment. All mothers had the opportunity to solve the shuttle box task. The escape response that controlled cry termination consisted of sliding a knob alternately from either side of the box (see Figure 3).

Physiologic responses were also monitored because we were particularly interested in integrating our earlier application of physiological measures in the study of social interaction and our present proposed model of maternal response. We sought to determine whether characteristic physiologic response patterns differentiated mothers who had learned to terminate infant crying (response-outcome dependence) from those who had been unsuccessful in their attempts at termination (response-outcome independence, or learned helplessness). We focused on possible physiologic changes accompanying belief in control that would be manifested during anticipatory periods—periods during which a mother prepares her response to infant crying. Our decision to focus on the physiologic correlates during the anticipatory period was derived from data collected within reaction-time paradigms. Although control

## TASK I

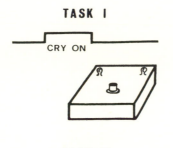

## TASK II

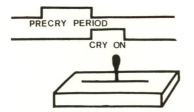

*Figure 3.* The learned helplessness pretreatment and test apparatuses. The pretreatment apparatus for Task I consisted of a spring-loaded button in the center of a base. The test apparatus for Task II consisted of a shuttle box with a sliding knob.

is not specifically manipulated in these studies, physiologic responses are used to index an individual's sustained attention to external stimuli and readiness to respond. The findings show an anticipatory cardiac deceleration during the preparatory interval (i.e., the foreperiod), and the faster the response, the greater the cardiac deceleration (Lacey & Lacey, 1970). We predicted that mothers who had learned that they were successful in controlling crying behavior would show cardiac deceleration during the anticipatory period when they prepare their response to the impending cry. In contrast, we predicted that those mothers who had learned they were not effective in terminating the cry would not exhibit this characteristic deceleratory response in anticipation of the cry.

In general, the results confirmed our predictions. The behavioral data parallel those findings reported by Seligman and others working within the learned helplessness paradigm (Seligman, 1975, 1978). It has been found that subjects pretreated with an inescapable aversive stimulus show a performance decrement on a subsequent task requiring instrument responding. Mothers in the present study who were pretreated with inescapable infant crying (they attempted, but failed to stop the cry) showed debilitated performance on the second task. Mean number of trials to escape criterion (shown in Figure 4), mean number of failures to escape, and mean response latency to the cry were all greater for the nonescape group as compared to escape and control mothers,

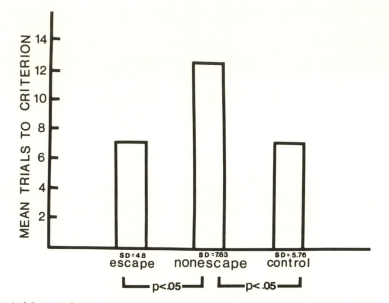

*Figure 4.* Mean trials to escape criterion for the three pretreatment groups.

with the exception that nonescape and control mothers did not differ significantly on response latency scores. Recent work from our laboratory (Donovan & Leavitt, 1982) has replicated this finding but with the cry presented at a 65 dB intensity level as compared to the 80 dB level in the Donovan (1981) study. Again, mothers pretreated with inescapable, as compared with escapable, cries showed debilitated performance. With no experience at failure, through our pretreatment manipulation, control mothers performed quite adequately when the opportunity arose. These data are consistent with other studies using the helplessness paradigm.

The cardiac data provide suggestive evidence that the important behavioral differences between the escape and nonescape mothers may, in part, be attributable to differential processing of cues signaling the onset of the cry. Only mothers with prior experience controlling the cry (escape group) showed cardiac deceleration indicative of attention during these anticipatory periods. Others failed to show a similar deceleratory response. Behaviorally, mothers with prior experience controlling the cry showed a slight but consistently shorter latency in response to cry termination. A history of successfully terminating the cry perhaps primes a mother to attend to cues signaling the onset of crying behavior. Attentional differences are then reflected behaviorally in more rapid termination of the cry.

Given this finding of debilitated performance of mothers who were unsuccessful, we were eager to assess the effect of an intervention designed to reduce the debilitating effects of prior experience with failure. For an intervention strategy, we drew upon current learned helplessness theory. Current theory predicts that an attribution for failure that is specific to a particular situation will be less likely to produce a state of helplessness than an attribution for failure that entails failing in many situations—a global attribution (Abramson, Seligman, & Teasdale, 1978). To test the effect of altering the mothers' attribution for failure, we studied an additional group of mothers (intervention group) (Donovan & Leavitt, 1982). We pretreated this group identically to the nonescape group (button press was unrelated to cry termination). Following this pretreatment designed to induce helplessness, we told the intervention group that performance on the second task was unrelated to performance on the first task. As predicted, we found that following this specific attribution the nonescape-intervention group performed significantly better than the nonescape group on both mean trials to criterion and mean response latency. These data have important implications in that, without an intervention, decreased attentiveness and debilitated performance of mothers who have been unsuccessful in interactions with their infants may result in long-term consequences for the infants' development.

The finding of debilitated performance of mothers pretreated with inescapable crying and the equally significant finding that an appropriate intervention works to break up the helplessness effect appear important enough to merit further testing of this model of mother–infant interaction. The usefulness of this model as an aid to understanding underlying processes affecting mother–infant interaction will depend upon future testing of its generalizability to spontaneous day-to-day interaction. Certainly, important questions arise from the finding of reduced attentiveness and responsiveness of mothers pretreated with inescapable crying. It will be important to determine whether the performance decrement of these mothers generalize, resulting in decreased responsiveness to infant behaviors other than the cry. A central theme of learned helplessness theory is that experience with uncontrollable events generalizes to situations beyond the immediate one (Seligman, 1975). From the Donovan (1981) experiment in which the signaling cue was paired only with the cry, it is not known whether the observed decreased attentiveness followed by a performance decrement generalizes to other signals, including positive ones emitted by the infant. Recall that earlier data (Donovan et al., 1978) suggested that an image of the crying infant decreased maternal physiologic response to the smile signal. One would predict that the patterns of interaction established by the dyad would be a function of the degree to which suppressed responsiveness to the cry generalizes to signals other than the cry.

Our model is also useful for extending the interpretation of our data indicating that only mothers of easy infants exhibited cardiac response to a change in signals (e.g., to the cry signal viewed second). The data demonstrating that dampened sensitivity to infant signals may be learned given the proper environmental contingencies suggests that the physiological differences observed earlier between mothers who perceive their infants as "difficult" versus "easy" were, in part, the result of learning. As mentioned earlier, when cognitive sets (created by attributions) were experimentally manipulated by describing an identical stimulus infant as "difficult," "normal," or "premature," we found that expectations affected physiologic responses (Frodi, Lamb, Leavitt, & Donovan, 1978). These data, together with reports of variations in the patterning of mother–infant interaction as a function of infant temperament (Bates, 1980; Campbell, 1979; Crockenberg, 1981; Gordon, 1983; Kelly, 1976) and reports of parental perceptions of difficult infant cries as being more grating, arousing, and piercing (Boukydis & Burgess, 1982) and more irritating and spoiled sounding (Lounsbury & Bates, 1982) than easy infant cries, suggested that varying attributions of infant temperamental style would effect susceptibility to learned helplessness.

In a replication of the helplessness study (Donovan & Leavitt, 1984), we labeled an identical stimulus cry as produced by an "easy" or a "difficult" infant. Similar to having repeated experience with failure, simply labeling the cry as being produced by a "difficult" infant had a debilitating effect on mothers' performance on our learning task. The manipulation of the cry attribution indicates that reduced responsiveness of the mother may stem from the perception of the infant as being "difficult." The implications of these data are clear. Even though earlier behavioral differences disappear, the previously established sets may continue to exert their influence on the caregiver's response. Furthermore, these data suggest a possible mechanism whereby interaction with an infant perceived as "difficult" affects developing reciprocity. To the degree that a mother feels a loss of control over her "difficult" infant this state of helplessness will be evidence in reduced responsiveness.

## 6. SUMMARY

In this chapter, we have summarized a series of recent studies that share in common the use of physiologic measures to index the attentional processing of infant signals. Response to the cry has been emphasized because the cry is an especially important mediator of caregiver–infant interaction. The data indicate that parental response is determined by both stimulus features of the cry as well as by characteristics of the perceiver, such as cognitive and experiential variables. Especially important variables are the mother's perceptions of her infant's behavior as well as experience with the consequences of her behavioral response to the cry. Learned helplessness theory was proposed as a model to increase our understanding of the observed differences in response, with special emphasis on response to infant crying. In support of this model, we report data that demonstrate that mothers confronted with infant crying they could not terminate showed decreased attention and debilitated performance during episodes of listening to infant cries. We propose that mothers who learn through experience that their response to infant signals is ineffective develop patterns of interaction that fail to optimize their infant's development. Learned helplessness theory allows us to generate testable hypotheses concerning infant–mother interaction and their implications. The demonstration that our experimental intervention can remedy the learned helplessness effect has implications for the development of preventive and therapeutic measures outside of the laboratory.

## 7. REFERENCES

Abramson, L. Y., Seligman, M. E. P., & Teasdale, J. D. Learned helplessness in humans: Critique and reformulation. *Journal of Abnormal Psychology*, 1978, *87*, 49–74.

Ainsworth, M. D. S. Object relations, dependency and attachment: A theoretical view of the mother–infant relationship. *Child Development*, 1969, *40*, 969–1025.

Ainsworth, M. D. S., & Bell, S. M. Mother–infant interaction and the development of competence. In K. S. Connolly & J. S. Bruner (Eds.), *The growth of competence.* New York: Academic Press, 1974.

Ainsworth, M. D., Blehar, M. C., Waters, W., & Wall, S. *Patterns of attachment.* Hillsdale, N.J.: Erlbaum, 1978.

Bates, J. E. Issues in the assessment of difficult temperament: A reply to Thomas, Chess and Korn. *Merrill-Palmer Quarterly*, 1983, *29*(1), 89–97.

Bates, J. G. The concept of difficult temperament. *Merrill-Palmer Quarterly*, 1980, *26*, 300–319.

Beckwith, L., Cohen, S., Kopp, C., Parmelee, A., & Marcy, T. Caregiver–infant interaction and early cognitive development in preterm infants. *Child Development*, 1976, *47*, 576–587.

Bell, R. Q. Stimulus control of parent or caretaker behavior by offspring. *Developmental Psychology*, 1971, *4*, 63–72.

Bell, S. M. The development of the concept of object as related to mother–infant interaction. *Child Development*, 1970, *41*, 291–311.

Bell, S. M. and Ainsworth, M. D. S. Infant crying and maternal responsiveness. *Child Development*, 1972, *43*, 1171–1190.

Boukydis, C. F. Z., & Burgess, R. Adult physiological response to infant cries: Effects of temperament of infant, parental status, and gender. *Child Development*, 1982, *53*, 704–713.

Bowlby, J. *Attachment and loss: Vol. 1. Attachment.* New York: Basic Books, 1969.

Campbell, S. B. G. Mother–infant interaction as a function of maternal ratings of temperament. *Child Psychiatry and Human Development*, 1979, *10*, 67–76.

Carey, S. B. A simplified method of measuring infant temperament. *Journal of Pediatrics*, 1970, *77*, 188–194.

Crockenberg, S. B. Infant irritability, mother responsiveness, and social support influences on the security of infant–mother attachment. *Child Development*, 1981, *52*, 857–865.

Donovan, W. Maternal learned helplessness and physiologic response to infant crying. *Journal of Personality and Social Psychology*, 1981, *40*, 919–926.

Donovan, W., & Leavitt, L. Early cognitive development and its relation to maternal physiologic and behavioral response. *Child Development*, 1978, *49*, 1251–1254.

Donovan, W. L. & Leavitt, L. A. *Maternal learned helplessness and response to infant crying.* Paper presented at the International Conference on Infant Studies, Austin, Texas, March 1982.

Donovan, W. L. & Leavitt, L. A. *Effects of experimentally manipulated attributions of infant cries on maternal learned helplessness.* Paper presented at the International Conference on Infant Studies, New York, April 1984.

Donovan, W. L., Leavitt, L. A., & Balling, J. D. Maternal physiologic response to infant signals. *Psychophysiology*, 1978, *15*, 68–74.

Emde, R. N., Campos, J. J., Gaensbauer, T. J., & Reich, J. *Smiling to strangers and mothers at 5 and 9 months: Analyses of movement and heart rate.* Paper presented at Society of Research in Child Development, Denver, 1975.

Frodi, A., Lamb, M. Sex differences in responsiveness to infants: A developmental study of psychophysical and behavioral responses. *Child Development*, 1978, *49*(4), 1182–1188.

Frodi, A. M., Lamb, M. E., Leavitt, L., & Donovan, W. Fathers' and mothers' responses to infant smiles and cries. *Infant Behavior and Development*, 1978, *1*, 187–198.

Frodi, A. M., Lamb, M., Leavitt, L., Donovan, W., Neff, C., & Sherry, D. Fathers' and mothers' responses to the appearance and cries of premature and normal infants. *Developmental Psychology*, 1978, *14*, 490–498.

Frodi, A. M., Lamb, M., Leavitt, L., Donovan, W., Neff, C., & Sherry, D. Fathers' and mothers' responses to the appearance and cries of premature and normal infants. *Developmental Psychology*, 1978, *14*, 490–498.

Frodi, A. M., Lamb, M. E., & Wille, D. Mothers' responses to the cries of normal and premature infants as a function of the birth status of their own child. *Journal of Research in Personality*, 1981, *15*, 122–133.

Gordon, B. N. Maternal perception of child temperament and observed mother–child interaction. *Child Psychiatry and Human Development*, 1983, *13*(3), 153–167.

Graham, F., & Clifton, R. Heart-rate changes as a component of the orienting response. *Psychological Bulletin*, 1966, *65*, 305–320.

Hare, R., Wood, K., Britain, S., & Shaman, J. Autonomic responses to affective visual stimulation. *Psychophysiology*, 1971, *7*, 408–417.

Kagan, J., & Lewis, M. Studies of attention in the human infant. *Merrill-Palmer Quarterly*, 1965, *11*, 95–128.

Kelly, P. The relation of infant's temperament and mother's psychopathology to interactions in early infancy. In K. F. Riegel & J. A. Meacham (Eds.), *The developing individual in a changing world* (Vol. 3). Chicago: Aldine, 1976.

Lacey, J. Somatic response patterning and stress: Some revision of activation theory. In
    M. Appley & R. Trumbell (Eds.), *Psychological stress: Issues in research.* New York:
    Appleton-Century-Crofts, 1967.
Lacey, J. I., & Lacey, B. C. Some autonomic-central nervous system relationships. In
    P. Black (Ed.), *Physiological correlations of emotion.* New York: Academic Press, 1970.
Leavitt, L. A., & Donovan, W. L. Perceived infant temperament, locus of control, and
    maternal physiological response to infant gaze. *Journal of Research in Personality,*
    1979, *13,* 267–278.
Lennenberg, E., Rebelsky, F., & Nichols, I. The vocalization of infants born to deaf and
    hearing parents. *Human Development,* 1965, *8,* 23–32.
Libby, W. J., Lacey, B. C., & Lacey, J. I. Pupillary and cardiac activity during visual
    attention. *Psychophysiology,* 1973, *10,* 270–294.
Lounsbury, M. L., & Bates, J. E. The cries of infants of differing levels of perceived
    temperamental difficultness: Acoustic properties and effects on listeners. *Child
    Development,* 1982, *53,* 677–686.
Matas, L., Arend, R., & Sroufe, L. Continuity of adaptation in the second year: The
    relationship of quality of attachment and later competence. *Child Development,* 1978,
    *49,* 547–556.
Sameroff, A. J. Concepts of humanity in primary prevention. In G. Albee & J. M. Jaffe
    (Eds.), *Primary prevention of psychopathology* (Vol. 1). Hanover, N.H.: University Press
    of New England, 1977.
Seligman, M. E. P. *Helplessness: On depression, development, and death.* San Francisco: Free-
    man, 1975.
Seligman, M. E. P. Comment and integration. *Journal of Abnormal Psychology,* 1978, *87,*
    165–179.
Sroufe, L. A., & Waters, E. Attachment as an organizational construct. *Child Development,*
    1977, *48,* 1184–1199.
Stayton, D. J., Hogan, R. T., & Ainsworth, M. D. S. Infant obedience and maternal
    behavior: The origins of socialization reconsidered. *Child Development,* 1971, *42,*
    1057–1069.
Thomas, A., Chess, S., Birch, H. G., Hertzig, J. E., & Korn, S. *Behavioral individuality in
    early childhood.* London: University of London Press, 1963.
Thomas, A., Chess, S., & Korn, S. J. The reality of difficult temperament. *Merrill-Palmer
    Quarterly,* 1982, *28*(1), 1–20.
Wiesenfeld, A. R., & Klorman, R. The mother's psychophysiological reactions to con-
    trasting expressions by her own and an unfamiliar infant. *Developmental Psychology,*
    1978, *14,* 294–304.
Wiesenfeld, A. R., Malatesta, C. Z., & DeLoach, L. L. Differential parental response to
    familiar and unfamiliar infant distress signals. *Infant Behavior and Development,* 1981,
    *4,* 281–295.

# 12

# When Empathy Fails
## Aversive Infant Crying and Child Abuse

ANN FRODI

## 1. INTRODUCTION

In recent years, there has been a growing research interest in the various qualities of the infant cry. In some investigations, the acoustic features of the cry have been analyzed (e.g., Vuorenkoski, Lind, Wasz-Höckert, & Partanen, 1971; Zeskind & Lester, 1978), whereas in others, the effects of the cries on the listener have been examined (e.g., Frodi, Lamb, Leavitt, & Donovan, 1978; Frodi & Lamb, 1980b; Lounsbury, 1978). This chapter will focus on the latter. Within this perspective, the infant cry is seen as a proximity-eliciting and proximity-maintaining signal, which is functional virtually from the time of birth.

In a comprehensive review, Murray (1979) examined the infant cry as an elicitor of parental behavior. She suggested that the infant cry is a graded signal that conveys important information to the caregiver about the infant's distress, the intensity of that distress, and perhaps even its likely causes. Following Hoffman's (1975) formulation of altruistic motivation, it was argued that infant crying provides distress cues that trigger a sympathetic distress response in the listener. The listener's initial tendency is to act out of empathy and to relieve the cause of the

ANN FRODI • Department of Psychology, University of Rochester, Rochester, New York 14627. The work reported in this paper was financed in part by a grant from Riksbankens Jubileumsfond, Sweden.

infant's distress. However, infants differ in soothability and temperament. Caretakers vary in child-rearing philosophies regarding the handling of infant crying as well as in parenting skills. Alone, or in combination, these facts may produce a situation in which the parent is exposed to crying beyond the level of what is tolerable. In his discussion of emotions elicited in the listener by infant cries, Tomkins (1963) referred to the "critical toxicity" problem. There may be an optimal range of distress cues. These distress cues must be sufficient to activate distress in the caregiver but should not exceed the level beyond which they trigger either avoidant or aggressive behavior. What defines the level of tolerance is not clear, however. It may be related to the duration of the cry or it may be its pitch, amplitude, or temporal patterning. These features of the cry may furthermore interact with interindividual differences in parental sensitivity. One possibility is that the cry triggers physiological changes that may become intolerable beyond a certain limit. Several studies have demonstrated cry-elicited autonomic changes that were perceived as aversive (e.g., Frodi, Lamb, Leavitt, & Donovan, 1978; see Chapter 10).

As Murray has stated

> Continued exposure to the sounds [of the cry] with the attendant involuntary experiencing of a high level of emotional arousal in the parent tips the parent's motivation from altruistic to egoistic, that is, the motivation is no longer to alleviate the infant's distress but to alleviate the parent's distress at having to listen to the sound of crying for prolonged periods of time. (1979, p. 206)

Thus, distress cues from an infant typically elicit empathic responses but may at times exceed the limits of tolerability, thereby activating nonempathic behaviors such as avoidant or even aggressive behavior from the caretaker.

A number of investigators have emphasized the aversive feature of cries. Ostwald (1963) writes,

> One can appreciate why the parent must interfere with the baby's cry: This sound is too annoying to be tolerated beyond a short period of time, particularly at close range. Thus, the cry cries to be turned off. (p. 46)

Some cries may also be perceived as more aversive than others. Zeskind and Lester (1978) found that college students rated infant cries as piercing, grating, aversive, distressing, discomforting, and arousing, especially the cries of infants whose mothers had experienced pre- or perinatal complications. Similarly, Lounsbury (1978) showed that mothers rated infant cries as irritating, especially the cries of temperamentally difficult babies.

Prematurely born babies (Frodi, Lamb, & Wille, 1981) and abnormal babies (Vuorenkoski, Lind, Wasz-Höckert, & Partanen, 1971) typically emit cries that are either higher or lower in pitch than normal cries; they have greater variability and different temporal patterns marked by either shorter or longer cry durations and cry intervals. One study suggests (Milowe & Lourie, 1964) that some abnormal cries are so unpleasant that even experienced caretakers, such as nurses, tend to avoid these infants and try to place the infants' cribs where the cries cannot be heard.

There is a substantial amount of anecdotal evidence suggesting that infant crying may serve as a final spark triggering an abusive outburst by a caretaker, especially if he or she is already angered or frustrated (Frodi, Humke, & Demro, 1979; Kadushin, 1975; Murray, 1979). Frodi *et al.* (1979) reported from interviews with abusive mothers that a majority of subjects mentioned "incessant crying," the "grating sound of the cry," and "whining for prolonged periods of time" as factors precipitating the abusive event. Weston (1968) found in one study of infants battered by their parents that excessive crying was given as the reason for battering by 80% of the parents of infants less than a year old. Child abuse is, however, a multiply determined phenomenon, and it is important not to overemphasize any one contributing factor at the expense of other equally important determinants.

## 2. THE CONTRIBUTION OF INFANT CHARACTERISTICS TO CHILD ABUSE

Before attempting to link infant crying to child abuse, I will first review the development of a theoretical framework into which infant crying can be fruitfully incorporated.

In a review of theorizing and research on child abuse, Parke and Collmer identified three major explanatory models: the psychiatric, the sociological, and the social-situational (or transactional) models (Parke, 1977; Parke & Collmer, 1975). In the psychiatric perspective, the pathology of the parent/perpetrator is emphasized, whereas in the sociological model, abuse is viewed as the manifestation of an individual's inability to cope with intolerably stressful and unsupportive social circumstances. These two perspectives failed, however, to account for the fact that certain children are more likely to become targets of abuse than are others (Parke, 1977). For example, prematurely born or "difficult" infants have been found to be particularly at risk for abuse.

The transactional model attempts to integrate these facts with the major components of the psychiatric and sociological approaches. In this model, abuse is seen as the joint product of characteristics of the child, parental dispositions, and patterns of parent–child interaction as well as stressful environmental events. A recent explanation of this framework (Belsky, 1980) suggests the inclusion of an additional component, namely the cultural context in which the abuse occurs. Thus, viewed in this light, some atypical infants may contribute to their own abuse (e.g., Martin, Beezley, Conway, & Kempe, 1974). Or put differently, some features of particular infants may constitute one component of the abuse complex.

A number of investigators have pointed to prematurity and low birth weight as factors closely linked to abuse (e.g., Friedrich & Boriskin, 1976). Klein and Stern (1971), for example, found that 23.5% of their Canadian sample of 51 abused children who were followed over a 9-year period were low-birth-weight infants (less than 2400 g at birth). Simons, Downs, Hurster, and Archer (1966) found that 20% of the abused babies in their New York sample, for whom the investigators could obtain access to birth records, weighed less than 2500 g at birth. According to these investigators, this percentage was approximately twice the abuse rate of the city as a whole at the time. Furthermore, Fontana (1973) reported that one-half of the 25 abused children he examined had been premature. Elmer and Gregg (1967) found one-third of their sample to have been low birth weight. Frodi et al. (1979) reported that 4 out of 14 of their sample were premature.

Numerous factors could be listed as potential explanations for the link between prematurity/low birth weight and abuse. The physical characteristics of premature infants violate parental expectations because these infants are small, unattractive, developmentally retarded (relative to others born at term), and typically require special care. Because they do not look like full-term infants, they may have more difficulty eliciting the "cute" response from parents (Lorenz, 1970). In addition, parents may be ill prepared when the infants arrive several weeks sooner than expected. Parent–infant separation and isolation of the infants may disrupt the process of parent–infant bonding (Klauss & Kennell, 1976). I will argue, however, that the typically high-pitched and nonrhythmic cry of the premature infant (e.g., Murray, 1979; Zeskind & Lester, 1978) may be of particular importance in the elicitation of an abusive event. Infant crying may alter the listener's initially altruistic motivation in favor of an egoistic disposition, and crying that is particularly aversive may trigger abusive behavior. In the following paragraphs, I will attempt to outline a model that links crying to child abuse.

## 3. THE ROLE OF INFANT CRYING IN CHILD ABUSE

A fundamental assumption of the model linking cry to abuse is that certain child characteristics are perceived as aversive, either because of their objectively aversive features or because of the perceivers' idiosyncrasies. According to Berkowitz's (1974) model of impulsive aggression, aversive stimuli may function as aggression-eliciting stimuli: The probability of aggressive behavior is enhanced when an aroused individual is exposed to an aversive stimulus. As discussed previously, infant cries are generally perceived as aversive, and when an infant cries a great deal (whether for constitutional, temperamental, or medical reasons or because the parent is lacking in parenting skills), the child may itself become an aversive stimulus through a process of conditioning. The child's behavior may thereafter be perceived as aversive (and thus aggression eliciting) even after the initially aversive features have been outgrown.

Thus, infant crying viewed as an aversive stimulus may serve as an aggression-eliciting cue, either directly or by way of classical conditioning, whereby the child itself is perceived as aversive. Atypical infants commonly cry a great deal or exhibit unusual aversive cry patterns. These facts may help explain the overrepresentation of atypical children among the abused.

## 4. PARENTAL PHYSIOLOGICAL RESPONSES TO INFANT CRYING

Although an experimental examination of abuse of children *per se* is not possible, the effects of infant cries on the emotional and behavioral dispositions of the caretaker can be assessed. In a series of experimental investigations, my colleagues and I have attempted to assess the effects of various infant characteristics and signals on the physiological and emotional responses of young parents. In all the studies, parents were shown a 6-minute videotape of an infant. In the first and last 2-minute segments of the tape, the infant was seen quiet and alert, whereas in the middle 2-minute segment, the infant was either crying or smiling. The cry was elicited by snapping the baby's heels with two fingers. When the cry was heard on the videotape, the sound was adjusted to reach peaks of 70 dB. Heart rate and skin conductance responses of the subjects were recorded continuously throughout the videotaping that was always preceded by a 5 to 10 minute rest period. The analyses of the physiological data was based on averages from the first and last 30 seconds of each 2-minute videotape segment, during which blood pressure measurements were also taken. In all cases, the data recorded in the last 30 seconds of the first (quiet/alert) segment served as a baseline to ensure adaptation to tape exposure. All physiological data were expressed as change scores, that is, deflections from the baseline.

The choice of the three physiological indices was guided by previous research in psychophysiology: Heart rate was chosen because it is a measure capable of discriminating between attentive (orienting) and defensive reactions (Lacey, 1967); blood pressure for its ability to tap aversion or feelings of anger (e.g., Schachter, 1957); and skin conductance because it is a more general index of autonomic activation.

In the first study, 96 parents *viewed* and *heard* a videotape of a 5-month-old infant who was either smiling or crying (Frodi, Lamb, Leavitt, & Donovan, 1978). Some parents were told that the infant was "normal"; others were told that it was "difficult"; and the remainder were told that it had been born prematurely. In reality, all parents viewed the same infant. After the session, the parents filled out a checklist of 10 bipolar mood adjectives, referring to each of the three videotape segments.

As can be seen in Table 1, the results showed that the parents' responses differed, depending on whether the baby smiled or cried. The cry elicited a pattern of autonomic arousal involving increases in skin conductance and diastolic blood pressure. The parents viewing the crying baby also reported negative emotions. They rated themselves as significantly more annoyed, irritated, distressed, disturbed, and indifferent as well as significantly less happy and attentive than those who saw the smiling baby.

Smiling, on the other hand, elicited negligible physiological changes. Separate analyses indicated that the "premature" infant triggered greater

Table 1. The Effects of Infant Smiling and Crying on Diastolic Blood Pressure (DBP) and Skin Conductance (SC)[a]

| Physiological measures (change scores) | Infant signal | | F (1,84) | p |
| --- | --- | --- | --- | --- |
| | Cry | Smile | | |
| DBP (mm Hg) | | | | |
| At onset of signal | 1.96 | −.04 | 7.64 | .007 |
| At end of signal | 2.73 | −.00 | 14.36 | .0003 |
| SC (log micromhos) | | | | |
| At onset of signal | 0.270 | 0.095 | 11.75 | .001 |
| At end of signal | 0.076 | −0.024 | 4.30 | .04 |

[a]From "Infant Behavior" by A. M. Frodi, M. E. Lamb, M. Leavitt, and W. Donovan, 1978, *Infant Behavior and Development, 1*, pp. 187–198. Copyright 1978 by the American Psychological Association. Adapted by permission.

autonomic arousal on the measure of skin conductance when it was crying than did any other infant. In addition, the "premature" and "difficult" infants elicited less sympathy when crying than did the "normal" infant. These results suggest that the parents experienced more sympathy vis-à-vis a needy infant when the costs of caregiving were low (i.e., when the infant was smiling contently) than when the caregiving demands were high (i.e., when the baby was crying). Clearly, the crying infant was perceived as aversive and triggered a specific physiological response pattern. This pattern has been shown to be related to a readiness to aggress. Several investigators have demonstrated a relationship between feelings of anger and increases in diastolic blood pressure (e.g., Schachter, 1957) or anger and increases in both diastolic blood pressure and skin conductance (Frodi, 1978; Weerts & Robert, 1975). The parents' aversive reactions were more pronounced when the stimulus baby was labeled as "premature," and both "atypical" infants reduced the parents' sympathetic reactions. Apparently, this experimental manipulation created a cognitive set that affected the parents' autonomic arousal as well as their subjective feelings.

## 5. PARENTAL RESPONSES TO PREMATURE INFANTS' CRYING

In the next study (Frodi, Lamb, Leavitt, Donovan, Neff, & Sherry, 1978), 64 parents were shown videotapes of either premature or term infants. The cry of a premature or of a full-term infant was dubbed onto the tapes in such a way as to ensure an independent assessment of the effects of the infants' cries and facial features. On two of the tapes, the face of the premature infant was seen with either an accompanying premature or term infant's cry. On the other two video sequences, the face of the term infant was seen with either a full-term infant's or a premature baby's cry. As in the first study, analyses showed that the cries elicited marked autonomic arousal on indices of diastolic blood pressure, skin conductance, and heart rate. The parents also reported experiencing aversion, annoyance, and disturbance. More importantly, the cry of the premature infant elicited significantly greater autonomic arousal and more negative emotions than did the cry of the term infant. In addition, the parents indicated that the premature infant was less pleasant and that they were less willing to interact with it than with the term infant (see Table 2). There were consistent significant main effects for type of cry on all physiological indices and significant or near-significant face × cry interaction effects, suggesting that the sound of

Table 2. The Effects of Infant Characteristics on Physiological Measures and Self-Report[a]

| Physiological measures (change scores) | Infant cry | | F df = 1,56 | p |
|---|---|---|---|---|
| | Normal | Premature | | |
| Diastolic blood pressure (mm Hg) | | | | |
| At cry onset | .82 | 3.13 | 4.35 | .04 |
| At cry onset | −1.88 | 2.07 | 3.90 | .05 |
| Skin conductance amplitude (log micromhos) at cry onset | .06 | .29 | 15.06 | .003 |
| Heart rate at cry onset | −1.47 | 1.0 | 5.64 | .02 |
| Mood adjective checklist (scale 1–5) | | | | |
| Irritated | 1.92 | 2.24 | 5.96 | .02 |
| Annoyed | 1.60 | 2.35 | 6.37 | .01 |
| Disturbed | 2.30 | 2.50 | 2.86 | .09 |
| Indifferent | 2.00 | 1.53 | 6.01 | .02 |
| Self-report (scale 1–5) | | | | |
| How pleasant did you find the baby? | 3.6 | 2.9 | 6.97 | .01 |
| To what extent would you like to interact with the baby? | 3.53 | 2.88 | 6.48 | .01 |

[a]From "Fathers' and Mothers' Responses to Infant Smiles and Cries" by A. M. Frodi, M. E. Lamb, L. Leavitt, W. Donovan, C. Neff, and D. Sherry, 1978, *Development Psychology*, 14, pp. 490–498. Copyright 1978 by the American Psychological Association. Adapted by permission.

the cry had a more powerful physiological impact than did the facial features. On the measures of heart rate and skin conductance, the most marked autonomic increases occurred in response to the premature face and premature cry in combination.

A complex interaction between sex of parent, infant face, and infant cry was evident for the mood adjective *sympathetic*. Fathers felt more sympathy overall than did mothers, but they were most sympathetic to the term baby with its own cry and least sympathetic to the infants with the incongruous characteristics (i.e., premature face with term infant's cry or term infant's face with premature cry). Mothers, on the other hand, were most sympathetic toward the premature infant with a normal cry and significantly less sympathetic to all other babies, in particular to the premature baby with the premature cry. When this study was in progress, the investigators were not able to analyze the cries for any sound parameters. Spectrographic analyses were, however, performed a year later using a Kay Sonagraph Analyzer. The fundamental frequency was found to be approximately 710 Hz for the premature infant and around 330 Hz for the baby born at term.

At the time of filming, the infants on videotape were all scheduled to be released from the hospital to their parents with 36 hours. The term infants were then 3 days old, and the prematures were approximately 3 weeks old. Thus, the aversive features of the premature's appearance and cry are evident not simply at birth but at the critical time when the baby is placed in the care of his or her parents.

In another study also using physiological indices, Boukydis (1980) further examined adults' physiological responses to the cries of different classes of infants. This researcher played audiorecordings of 12 infant cries to 24 parent couples and 12 nonparent couples. Four of the stimulus infants (whose cries had been recorded) had previously been rated as "difficult," four as "easy," and four as "average" on the Infant Characteristics Questionnaire (Bates, Bennet-Freeland, & Lounsbury, 1979). While the adults listened to the recordings, their skin potential level was monitored. The results showed that the cries of the difficult infant elicited the highest level of skin potential, the easy infant the lowest, with the average baby falling at an intermediate level. Viewing these studies together, it appears as though atypical babies, or infants either labeled or perceived as atypical, triggered a response pattern consistent with a readiness to aggress. Thus, the aversiveness of objective characteristics of an infant may be supplemented by expectations regarding atypical infants.

## 6. RESPONSES OF MOTHERS WITH PRETERM INFANTS

In the third study of our series (Frodi, Lamb, & Wille, 1981), the effect of the birth status of the subjects' own children was systematically assessed. Sixteen mothers of premature babies and sixteen mothers of term babies viewed and heard videotapes of premature and full-term infants. According to spectrographic analyses performed on the cries, the fundamental frequency of the premature cry centered around 600 Hz and that of the term infant around 330 Hz. As in the earlier studies, the onset of crying by both infants elicited physiological arousal as evident on blood pressure, skin conductance, and heart rate increases in the adults. However, the mothers of premature babies as compared to mothers of term babies responded with a more pronounced arousal to the infants' cries. The most parsimonious explanation of these results appears to be that the mothers who interacted daily with their premature babies had become sensitized to their aversive features and therefore exhibited an exaggerated response to the stimulus babies. Mothers of prematures reported feeling more sympathetic to the stimulus baby than did mothers of full terms but only when the baby on the videotape was a term baby, that is, different from their own.

The infant's crying in all three studies elicited a physiological response pattern similar to that shown in investigations where subjects were asked to imagine the most anger-provoking scene possible (Weerts & Roberts, 1975), where they were repeatedly insulted (Schachter, 1975), treated in a hostile or condescending fashion (Frodi, 1978), or given electric shock (Geen, Stonner, & Shope, 1975).

Our studies confirmed our prediction that infant cries are aversive and arousing and that the cries of premature infants are especially aversive. Our data also suggested that mothers who have had extended experience with atypical infants exhibit an exaggerated response pattern to aversive infant stimuli.

## 7. CHILD ABUSERS' RESPONSES TO CHILD-RELATED STIMULI

We turn next to an examination of another population whose child-rearing experiences deviate from the norm, namely abusive parents. Two recent studies provide converging evidence that the psychophysiological responses to infant cries of abusive and nonabusive parents are significantly different. Frodi and Lamb (1980a,b) compared the heart rate, blood pressure, and skin conductance responses of 14 abusive and 14 nonabusive mothers who were shown the videotapes of the smiling and the crying babies used in the Frodi et al. (1978a) study. The same procedure was used as in the previous studies by these investigators. As can be seen in Table 3, the results indicated that the abusive mothers were significantly more annoyed by, and less sympathetic toward, the crying infant than were the nonabusive mothers. They also found the crying baby less pleasant than the control mothers did. Furthermore, the cry elicited greater increases in heart rate and skin conductance but smaller increase in blood pressure. Compared to the nonabusers, the abusers reported consistently more negative reactions to the smiling baby as well. Although the smiling baby had a negligible physiological effect and a positive emotional effect on the control mothers, it elicited increased blood pressure and conductance from the abusers. Significant interaction effects between mother classification and infant signal indicated that the abusers responded to both the cry and the smile with annoyance and heart rate increases. The nonabusive mothers reacted to the cry in a way similar to that of the abusive mothers but with a

*Table 3. Responses of Abusers and Nonabusers to the Cry and Smile Signals[a]*

| | Abusers | Nonabusers | $F(1,24)$ | $p$ |
|---|---|---|---|---|
| Cry stimulus | | | | |
| Mood adjectives | | | | |
| Annoyed | 2.50 | 1.50 | 4.26 | .05 |
| Sympathetic | 3.57 | 4.43 | 3.96 | .06 |
| How pleasant | 3.36 | 4.21 | 3.09 | .09 |
| Physiological measures (change scores) | | | | |
| DBP at cry onset[b] | 2.43 | 4.43 | 5.71 | .03 |
| DBP at cry onset | 1.14 | 3.57 | 3.37 | .03 |
| SC (peak) at cry onset[b] | 1.42 | 1.13 | 4.97 | .04 |
| SC (peak) at end of cry | 1.38 | 1.14 | 6.11 | .02 |
| HR at cry onset[b] | 2.29 | .21 | 3.96 | .05 |
| HR at end of cry | 2.00 | −.07 | 4.65 | .04 |
| | | | | |
| Smile stimulus | | | | |
| Mood adjectives | | | | |
| Attentive | 2.86 | 4.07 | 4.11 | .05 |
| Happy | 3.35 | 4.38 | 4.20 | .05 |
| Indifferent | 1.80 | 1.00 | 4.22 | .05 |
| How pleasant | 3.20 | 4.30 | 4.18 | .05 |
| Willingness to interact? | 3.42 | 4.43 | 4.29 | .04 |
| Physiological measures (change scores) | | | | |
| DPB at smile onset | 1.14 | −1.85 | 3.10 | .09 |
| DBP at end of smile | 1.00 | −3.14 | 5.83 | .02 |
| SC (peak) at smile onset | .82 | .26 | 3.13 | .08 |

[a]From "Child Abusers' Responses to Infant Smiles and Cries" by A. M. Frodi and M. E. Lamb, 1980, *Child Development*, 51, pp. 238–241. Copyright 1980 by the Society for Research in Child Development, Inc. Adapted by permission.
[b]DBP = diastolic blood pressure; SC = skin conductance; HR = heart rate.

reduction of autonomic activation when viewing the smiling baby. Furthermore, Figures 1 and 2 show the mothers' second-by-second heart rate changes in response to the infant signals. Although the nonabusive mothers showed a significantly differential response to the cry and the smile, the corresponding heart rate responses of the abusers were indistinguishable. The abusive mothers apparently responded as if both social signals were equally aversive to them. The observed acceleratory heart rate responses or the heart rate that remained above baseline for the duration of the 10 seconds following the onset of the cry are similar to what Lacey (1967) labeled the DR or *defense response*. According to this investigator, this pattern of responses reflects an attempt on the part of the organism to tune out, or defend against, external stimulation. Thus, is appears as though the abusive mothers were attempting to block out the infant signals—both the cry and the smile.

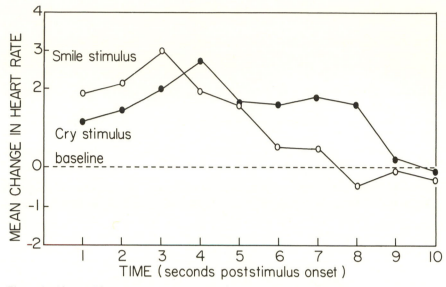

Figure 1. Abusers' heart rate responses to infant crying and smiling.

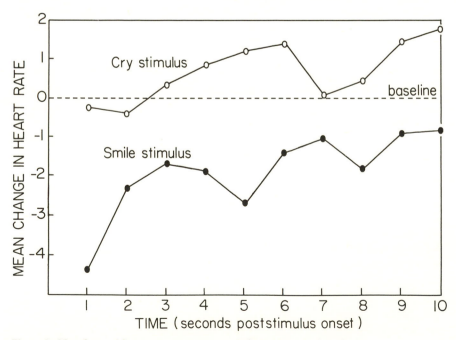

Figure 2. Nonabusers' heart rate responses to infant crying and smiling.

Doerr, Disbrow, and Caulfield (1977) have provided comparable findings. These investigators showed an hour long videotape to 33 identified abusive parents, 34 parents found to be neglectful, and 55 control parents. The videotape consisted of a series of 10-minute episodes depicting parent–child interaction of either an unpleasant/aversive or pleasant/positive nature. A number of physiological measurements were recorded continuously. Their results indicated that the abusers exhibited higher, and the neglectors lower, heart rate levels than did the controls. This was evident throughout the video session. In addition, in their heart rate and skin conductance responses, both the abusive and the neglectful parents failed to differentiate between pleasant and unpleasant scenes, whereas the control parents did so significantly on both physiological measures. In their conclusions, Frodi and Lamb (1980a) and Doerr and his co-workers (1977) similarly argued that abusive mothers responded defensively and insensitively to child-produced stimuli, both pleasant and unpleasant.

Unfortunately, we lack the necessary data to provide an etiological explanation of the anomalous responses of the abusers. I would like to suggest, however, that the abusers' overall higher levels of physiological arousal and their lack of sensitivity to child-related stimuli may have developed as a consequence of unsuccessful transactions with their own children. Either their own children had been unusually difficult to deal with, or the adults were unskilled at parenting. Whichever the case, or a combination of both, their interactions with their own children may have become aversive. Their response patterns observed in the laboratory could thus be a manifestation of a generalized aversion to child-related stimuli.

## 8. SUMMARY AND CONCLUSION

It is clear that certain infant signals such as the cry, and the atypical cry in particular, are aversive to adults. And the more aversive the infant stimulus, the less sympathy it tends to elicit. Because aversive stimuli may facilitate the expression of aggressive behavior (Berkowitz, 1974), the findings reported previously may help explain the link between infant crying and child abuse. The dominant adult response to infant crying is to act empathically to relieve the cause of the infant's distress. Under certain circumstances, however, continued exposure to the aversive sound or exposure to particularly aversive cries, with the attendant involuntary high level of emotional arousal, may suppress the empathic response tendency in favor of an egoistically motivated predisposition.

Whether the egoistic tendency will be translated into actual abuse or not will depend on other exacerbating factors in the situation. The etiology of child abuse is highly complex and multifaceted and is affected by factors within the family as well as within the larger social context. The greater the social stress and isolation, for instance, or the greater the degree to which cultural values condoning violence exist, the greater is the likelihood that caretakers will respond with abusive behavior to aversive crying.

## 9. REFERENCES

Bates, J. E., Bennett-Freeland, C. A., & Lounsbury, M. L. Measurement of infant difficultness. *Child Development*, 1979, *50*, 704–803.

Belsky, J. Child maltreatment: An ecological integration. *American Psychologist*, 1980, *5*, 320–335.

Berkowitz, L. Some determinants of impulsive aggression: Role of mediated associations with reinforcements for aggression. *Psychological Review*, 1974, *81*, 165–176.

Boukydis, C. F. Z. An analog study of adult physiological and self-report responding to infant cries. *Cry Research Newsletter*, 1980, *2*, 1–5.

Doerr, H. O., Disbrow, M. A., & Caulfield, C. *Psychophysiological response patterns in child abusers*. Paper presented to the Society for Psychophysiological Research, Philadelphia, October 1977.

Elmer, E., & Gregg, G. S. Developmental characteristics of abused children. *Pediatrics*, 1967, *40*, 596–602.

Fontana, V. J. The diagnosis of the maltreatment syndrome in children. *Pediatrics*, 1973, *51*, 780–782.

Friedrich, W. N., & Boriskin, J. A. The role of the child in abuse: A review of the literature. *American Journal of Orthopsychiatry*, 1976, *46*, 580–590.

Frodi, A. M. Experiential and physiological responses associated with anger and aggression in women and men. *Journal of Research in Personality*, 1978, *12*, 335–349.

Frodi, A. M., & Lamb, M. E. Child abusers' responses to infant smiles and cries. *Child Development*, 1980, *51*, 238–241.

Frodi, A. M., & Lamb, M. E. Infants at risk for child abuse. *Infant Mental Health Journal*, 1980, *1*, 240–247.

Frodi, A. M., Lamb, M. E., Leavitt, L., & Donovan, W. Fathers' and mothers' responses to infant smiles and cries. *Infant Behavior and Development*, 1978, *1*, 187–198.

Frodi, A. M., Lamb, M. E., Leavitt, L., Donovan, W., Neff, C., & Sherry, D. Fathers' and mothers' responses to the appearance and cries of premature and normal infants. *Developmental Psychology*, 1978, *14*, 490–498.

Frodi, A. M., Humke, C., & Demro, J. *A pilot interview study of abusive mothers*. Unpublished manuscript, University of Michigan, Ann Arbor, Michigan, 1979.

Frodi, A. M., Lamb, M. E., & Wille, D. Mothers' responses to the cries of normal and premature infants as a function of the birth status of their child. *Journal of Research in Personality*, 1981, *15*, 122–133.

Geen, R. G., Stonner, D., & Shope, G. L. The facilitation of aggression by aggression: Evidence against the cartharsis hypothesis. *Journal of Personality and Social Psychology*, 1975, *31*, 221–226.

Hoffman, M. Developmental synthesis of affect and cognition and its implications for altruistic motivation. *Developmental Psychology*, 1975, *11*, 607–622.

Kadushin, A. University of Wisconsin, personal communication, 1975.

Klaus, N. H., & Kennell, J. H. *Maternal-infant bonding.* St. Louis: C. V. Mosby, 1976.

Klein, M., & Stern, L. Low birth weight and the battered child syndrome. *American Journal of Diseases of Childhood*, 1971, *122*, 15–18.

Lacey, J. Somatic response patterning and stress: Some revisions of activation theory. In M. Appley & R. Trumbell (Eds.), *Psychological stress: Issues in research.* New York: Appleton-Century-Crofts, 1967.

Lorenz, K. Companions as factors in the bird's world. In K. Lorenz (Ed.), *Studies in animal and human behavior.* Cambridge: Harvard University Press, 1970.

Lounsbury, M. L. *Acoustic properties of and maternal reactions to infant cries as a function of infant temperament.* Unpublished doctoral dissertation, Indiana University, Lafayette, Indiana, 1978.

Martin, H. P., Beezley, P., Conway, E. F., & Kempe, C. H. The development of abused children. *Advances in Pediatrics*, 1974, *21*, 25–73.

Milowe, I., & Lourie, R. The child's role in the battered child syndrome. *Society for Pediatric Research*, 1964, *65*, 1079–1081.

Murray, A. Infant crying as an elicitor of parental behavior: An examination of two models. *Psychological Bulletin*, 1979, *86*, 191–215.

Ostwald, P. *Soundmaking: The acoustic communication of emotion.* Springfield, Ill.: Charles C Thomas, 1963.

Parke, R. D. Socialization into child abuse. A social interactional perspective. In J. L. Tapp & F. J. Levine (Eds.), *Justice and the individual in society: Psychological and legal issues.* New York: Holt, Rinehart & Winston, 1977.

Parke, R., & Collmer, C. Child abuse: An interdisciplinary review. In M. E. Hetherington (Ed.), *Review of child development research* (Vol. 5). Chicago: University of Chicago Press, 1975.

Schachter, J. Pain, fear, and anger in hypertensives and normotensives. *Psychosomatic Medicine*, 1957, *19*, 71–79.

Simons, B., Downs, E. G., Hurster, M. M., & Archer, M. Child abuse: Epidemiological study of medically reported cases. *New York State Journal of Medicine*, 1966, *66*, 2738–2385.

Tomkins, S. *Affect, imagery and consciousness: Vol. 2. Negative affects.* London: Tavistock, 1963.

Vuorenkoski, V., Lind, J., Wasz-Höckert, O., & Partenen, T. *Cry score: A method for evaluating the degree of abnormality in the pain cry response for the newborn young infant.* Quarterly Progress and Status Report. Stockholm, Sweden: Speech Transmission Laboratory, Royal Institute of Technology, April 1971.

Weerts, T. C., & Roberts, R. *The physiological effects of imagining anger-provoking and fear-provoking scenes.* Paper presented to the Society of Psychophysiological Research, Toronto, October 1975.

Weston, J. The pathology of child abuse. In R. Helfer & C. Kempe (Eds.), *The battered child.* Chicago: University of Chicago Press, 1968.

Zeskind, P. S., & Lester, B. Acoustic features and auditory perceptions of the cries of newborns with prenatal and perinatal complications. *Child Development*, 1978, *49*, 580–589.

# 13

# A Comparative Model of Infant Cry

## JENNIFER S. BUCHWALD and CARL SHIPLEY

## 1. INTRODUCTION

Language is generally considered to be unique to the human species and, of its various forms, *vocal* language, or speech, clearly represents one of the most complex behaviors of any species. The linguistic aspect of speech involves a hierarchy of discrete elements that develop meaning as basic phonemic units are combined into syllables and words, and these, in turn, are organized by rules of syntax into meaningful phrases and sentences. The resulting expression is understandable either when produced by the human voice or by a speech synthesizer such as a computer. However, the marked difference in quality and ease of comprehension between natural and synthetic speech is, in large part, a function of a second nonlexical element—the "paralinguistic" or prosodic component of speech. The qualities of pitch, intensity, and duration combine to provide an overall intonation that makes the human voice recognizable and familiar, projects emotional states—happiness, anger, fear—and conveys general intent as, for example, the terminal rising inflection of a yes/no question versus the falling inflection of a declaration.

Speech can thus be separated into two components. On the one hand, it contains *lexical elements*, which can be arranged to generate an

JENNIFER S. BUCHWALD and CARL SHIPLEY • Department of Physiology, Brain Research Institute and Mental Retardation Research Center, School of Medicine, University of California at Los Angeles, Los Angeles, California 90024.

enormous array of messages, convey abstract ideas and remote occurrences, remain "open" so that new concepts can be named and added,
and require precise, often complex, articulations (Hockett, 1960; Marler,
1961). On the other hand, speech contains *paralinguistic elements*, such
as pitch, intensity, and duration that provide identification of a particular
individual and of an emotional state through acoustic dimensions that
are graded, have a variable content of information, and contain a relatively restricted scope of communication functions. It is this paralinguistic aspect of human language that appears first in the vocal behavior
of the human infant and that is also the major component in the vocalization of most mammals. Thus, in the paralinguistic or prosodic mode,
overall intonation conveys information about age, sex, individual iden-
tity, and emotional state in both human and animals, and it provides a
communicatory potential that is independent of lexical elements.

## 1.1. Relevance of Animal Models to Human Language

It is particularly relevant to discuss animal models in conjunction
with studies of the human infant cry insofar as paralinguistic vocalizations are common to both nonhuman mammals and human infants as
their primary form of vocal communication. The significance of animal
models for students of human language will, of course, appear differently to those individuals who believe that vocal behavior can be represented on a continuum, with speech only quantitatively different from
animal vocalizations, than to those who believe that qualitative differences separate the vocalizations of the human from all other species. In
either case, however, understanding mechanisms of vocal behavior in
species other than humans should be of interest, particularly because
these mechanisms are easier to investigate and manipulate experimentally in animal preparations and the effects of development and environmental conditions as well as the role of specific brain systems can be
more precisely determined.

The hypothesis that human speech is programmed by a specific
genetic code, the outcome of evolutionary pressures unique to our species, has been argued on theoretical grounds by both linguists and biol-
ogists. The occurrence of universals in child language development and
in adult grammars in natural languages of the world has provided a
substantial linguistic basis for describing human speech as innate. Moreover, the claim that any human language is constituted by an infinitely
open set of sentences has provided the basis for believing that human
language has certain unique properties (Chomsky, 1965). Similarly, Lenneberg (1975) has stated that there is "a special biological propensity in

man for the acquisition and use of natural language" (p. 19) and that human language is qualitatively different from the vocal behavior of animals. In its extreme form, this point of view maintains that there is a behavioral and neurological dichotomy between humans and non-humans in terms of the communicative function and neural basis of vocalization (Myers, 1976). If such qualitative contrasts exist, a major question would be how evolution proceeded from an innate, reflexive, noncortical communication system to a modifiable, voluntary, neocortical one.

Two fundamental characteristics of human language that have been suggested as support for a qualitative discontinuity between human and animal vocal behavior are vocal learning and volitional vocal responses (Lenneberg, 1967; Nottebohm, 1975; Steklis & Raleigh, 1979a).

*Vocal learning* indicates the ability to develop and regulate a vocal output that matches a remembered or ongoing auditory signal. Clearly, one aspect of such learning is dependence of the vocal behavior on auditory feedback. As the subject hears his or her own vocalization, central control mechanisms are activated to shape the signal in such a way that it reflects a particular auditory model. A second aspect of vocal learning is the subject's ability to perceive and remember the auditory signal to be copied. Not only must the subject be able to hear her own vocal output, but she must be able to store, as an accessible model, the auditory signal against which the vocal output will be compared and modulated until a match occurs. Thus, modifiability and imitation are qualities of vocal production that exemplify vocal learning.

In the human infant, imitation and vocal modifications are said to occur within the first 6 to 9 months of life (Lenneberg, 1975; Lenneberg, Rebelsky, & Nichols, 1965). Auditory feedback has, however, recently been indicated as already operative by 6 weeks of age. In a study of the vocalizations of normal and hearing-impaired infants during the first 30 weeks of life, systematic changes in the patterns of vocal behavior between the hearing and hearing-impaired infants began to appear as early as 6 weeks of age (Maskarinec *et al.*, 1981). These data suggest that at least one aspect of vocal learning may begin earlier in human development than had been previously reported (Lenneberg, 1967; Lenneberg *et al.*, 1965; Marilya, 1972; Winitz, 1969).

A second unique characteristic of human language has been considered to be *volitional control of vocal behavior*. Many kinds of vocal activity are involuntary and reflexive. The cry produced by sudden pain is involuntary, is triggered by the external environment, and the automatic vocal expression coincident with a rage response is internally generated by intense emotion. In contrast, speech is generally initiated voluntarily in a highly variable form and without any consistently correlated trigger stimuli in the external or internal environment.

In contrast to the view that human language is qualitatively unique in displaying characteristics of vocal learning and voluntary control, there is the alternate concept that places human language at the far end of a continuum. Although speech clearly represents the most evolved form, in terms of central nervous system mechanisms for reception, storage, and production, as well as articulator control, it is only *quantitatively*, not qualitatively, different from other animal modes of vocal communication. This point of view has continued to gain strength through the work of neurolinguists, physiologists, anatomists, and behavioral scientists (Brown, 1979; Dingwall, 1979; Jacobson, 1975; Lamendella, 1977; Steklis & Raleigh, 1979b; Zangwell, 1975). Steklis and Raleigh (1979a) conclude that neither the current behavioral nor the neurological data support the concept of an evolutionary dichotomy. Although tremendous differences exist between human and, for example, nonhuman primate vocal communication systems, these authors suggest that the contrasts are more reasonably regarded as the end products of quantitative rather than qualitative differentiation.

Some of the animal data that support the argument that neither vocal learning nor voluntary control are unique to human language will be summarized briefly. Of the two animal groups, birds and nonhuman primates, which have been most widely used in studies of vocal behavior, birds have been studied extensively in both developmental and experimental situations, but they represent an anatomy and physiology that are phylogenetically quite disparate from that of the mammal. Most of the information from nonhuman primates rests upon behavioral and ethological observations. Neither vocal development nor effects of experimental manipulations on vocal behavior have been studied extensively.

The bird has been the most widely exploited animal as a model for human language development in terms of experimental procedures and theoretical implications. From such studies, which have been exhaustively reviewed (Konishi, 1970; Nottebohm, 1975, 1979), it has been shown that there are marked species differences in vocal behaviors. Learning through auditory feedback and/or imitation is unnecessary for the development of a normal vocal repertoire in the case of the chicken, turkey, or ringdove. In contrast, the junco must hear, but it requires auditory feedback only from its own vocal output to establish a normal song. In this case, the bird does not need to imitate the song it strives to perfect, but, rather, utilizes an innate, genetically programmed species-specific song template to regulate its vocal output. A different level of vocal learning is apparent in the white-crowned and song sparrows.

These birds must not only hear themselves but also hear the song of their species during a restricted "sensitive" period of development in order for normal vocal behavior to occur. If the birds do not hear a model of their conspecific call, their adult song is markedly aberrant and only fractionally similar to the normal repertoire. If the adult with normal song is subsequently deafened so auditory monitoring is no longer possible, some deterioration in call structure occurs. Thus, within the bird family, there is a range of vocal behavior that at one extreme shows no aspect of learning and at the other extreme requires both auditory feedback and the reception, storage, and imitation of an auditory template.

A second major group of animal vocalization studies has centered on the nonhuman primate. Species differences are apparent, although relatively few developmental or neurophysiological studies have been carried out in this population, in part for practical reasons, and in part because of the popularity of the bird as a model for studies of vocal behavior.

The squirrel monkey is perhaps the most extensively studied nonhuman primate in terms of vocalization. The adult has a series of calls that are emitted under different behavioral situations and that are composed of a variety of syllablelike components. In this species, vocal learning apparently plays a minor role in the establishment of an adult repertoire. Although the number of studies is small and the vocalizations have not been subjected to rigorous quantification, neither auditory feedback nor conspecific vocal models appear to be essential for the development of normal adult calls. One animal deafened in infancy was subsequently reported to emit a range of normal calls at several months of age (Winter, Handley, Ploog, & Schott, 1973). Similarly, normal-hearing animals raised by muted mothers showed adult vocal production that was normal (Newman, 1979). Thus, the adult repertoire is generally considered to exemplify a genetically coded vocal output that is relatively insusceptible to modification or variation as a function of learning or experience (Ploog, 1974).

In contrast, studies of the macaque suggest that considerable modification of vocal output can be manifested by the animal during development as well as in adulthood. Pigtailed macaques deafened at birth exhibited vocal abnormalities as did three *Maccaca nemistrina* following total labyrinthectomy in the neonatal period (Sutton, 1979). Rhesus monkeys and Japanese macaques raised with normal hearing but in isolation from normally vocalizing adults showed abnormal adult repertoires insofar as some calls were lacking or poorly formed (Kawabe, 1973; Newman & Symmes, 1974). Such data suggest that vocal learning occurs in these species and is dependent upon both auditory feedback and imitation.

Conditioning procedures have indicated that the rhesus monkey is voluntarily able to produce a specific vocal response or to modify the rate, type, duration, and amplitude of its vocal output for food rewards (Sutton, 1979). In this case, vocal learning is apparent as well as volitional control of vocal behavior.

Outside of a formal laboratory setting, similar kinds of control over vocal behavior have been reported as, for example, the locale-specific dialects of three different Japanese macaque troops (Green, 1975). The call variants displayed by the different groups were considered to reflect vocal learning, with the altered call originally emitted in the new context by one troop member and thereafter imitated by others in that locale. Call variability has been documented for confined as well as for free-ranging macaque and rhesus monkeys (Steklis & Raleigh, 1979a). Several calls (e.g., coos, chirps, whistles) emitted under identical conditions exhibited both individual and intergroup differences. Although these data do not in themselves indicate vocal learning or volitional control, they suggest that individuals of these species can control a range of gradations in vocal output along the prosodic dimensions of intensity, duration, and frequency.

In summary, the paralinguistic or prosodic component of speech depends upon parameters of intonation—pitch, duration, intensity—that are common to the human infant cry and to animal vocalization. Whether human language is viewed as evolutionarily unique or at the extreme end of an evolutionary continuum, it seems clear that the two major characteristics of human vocal behavior, vocal learning and voluntary control, are shared to some extent by a number of animal species. In the human infant, vocal learning and volitional control of vocalization develop within the first 6 to 9 months (and possibly commence as early as 6 weeks). In mammalian animal models, there has been no systematic longitudinal study of vocal development, vocal learning, or volitional vocal control. To address some of these issues, we have focused upon the cat as an experimental subject for investigations of vocalization and, in particular, have utilized the vocal behavior of the kitten as a comparative model of the human infant cry.

## 1.2. Rationale for the Cat Vocalization Model

Cats represent a good potential model for the study of vocalization for several reasons. They are vocal animals and provide an opportunity for study of many different types of vocalizations. This is true not only for the domestic cat but also for other members of the family Felidae. Shaller (1972), in his study of the Serengetti lion, observes that "lions are vocal animals which seem to emit a bewildering variety of snarls, moans, growls, grunts, and roars" (p. 138). Peters (1978) has documented the large numbers of vocalizations by several species of cat including snow leopard, clouded leopard, tiger, and puma.

Another virtue of the domestic cat as a model of vocal behavior is the fact that the nervous system of this species has been extensively studied. A combination of factors, including size, tameness, and relatively high intelligence, has made the cat one of the most frequently used animals in research on the physiology of the mammalian nervous system; indeed, it is quite possible that more is known about the brain of the cat than about that of any other mammalian species, including the human. Because of the extensive knowledge that has been acquired about the cat's nervous system, vocal behavior in this species can be investigated in terms of its neurophysiological substrates. Recording and stimulating within the brain concurrent with vocal behavior is possible, as is the placement of precise lesions to interrupt the integrity of brain systems of suspected importance.

Still another advantage of the cat is the relative ease with which it can be studied developmentally in a controlled laboratory environment. Sexual maturity occurs within 6 months, and by this age adult vocal behavior has been established. Although the call repertoire of adults born and bred in the laboratory may be less extensive than that of feral cats, there are, nonetheless, a number of distinctly different call types that the laboratory cat emits under different behavioral circumstances.

## 2. PROBLEMS OF QUANTIFICATION

One of the most serious difficulties in the study of both animal and infant vocalizations is the problem of measurement. Several approaches have been used in an attempt to characterize these complex acoustic data. A common early approach to animal and infant vocal behavior was to describe sounds in terms of alphabetic notation or phonetic transcription. A fairly extreme example of this practice is contained in a description by Mellon (1940, p. 103) of the vocal repertoire of the domestic cat:

> Clark named them [the sounds made by cats] as b, d, f, l, m, p, r, t, v, w, and y. Dupont de Nemours, eighteenth century naturalist, Chateaubriand, and others agreed upon f, g, h, m, n, and v. Carl Van Vechten stresses p, r, s, t, and says he never heard a cat say v. Pollack doubted that cats ever use h or v. In the various cat sounds given by Beachcroft one may find c, h, k, m, p, q, r, s, t, v, w, and x. . . . Studies made by the author show that the cat uses ch, f, h, k, l, m, n, p, r, s, t, w, and the semivowel y.

This method of analysis is unsatisfactory for several reasons. The sounds made by most mammals have few, if any, common equivalents in the phonology of normal human speech. Thus, the attempt to describe them in terms of phonemes is inevitably prone to error. Indeed, because of differences between the anatomy of the vocal tracts of adult humans and other mammals, it is doubtful whether phonetic transcription would be accurate even in the case of sounds that bear some resemblance to words (Lieberman, 1968). In addition, phonetic transcription is a difficult task for trained linguists describing normal speech (Ladefoged, 1975), and even then it gives only an impressionistic rendition of the sound. Students of communication in animals have rarely had the background to use phonetic description of speechlike sounds with any precision, and the audience to which this work is addressed also generally lacks the skill to interpret such descriptions. Finally, although human speech is composed of discrete phonetic categories, the vocalizations of animals are not decomposable into constituent parts. Rather, these vocalizations are graded and highly variable. When such widely different sounds are placed into small classes, much information can be lost.

A common method of describing sounds, somewhat related to phonetic transcription, is the use of onomatopoeic labels such as *mew* or *hiss*. This technique is still widely used by students of animal communication. Like phonetic transcription, the use of onomatopoeic labels encourages the grouping of sounds that differ greatly into a single category. For example, black bear cubs make a contented noise when nursing from the mother. In different studies, this sound has been called a *purr*, a *hum*, and a *churkle* (Pruitt & Burghardt, 1977). In the cat, onomatopoeic labels have occasionally led investigators to term almost any vocalization a *meow*. For example, Bazett, Oxon, Eng, Penfield, & Oxon (1922) reported that some decerebrate cats had normal vocalizations because animals were observed to "mew," "growl," or "purr" after surgery.

By far the most common method of describing both infant and animal vocalizations is the sound spectrograph. This instrument converts a recorded sound wave into a graph of frequency versus time. The loudness of a given frequency is coded by the darkness of the graph. This method of analyzing vocalization data is greatly superior to the use of phonetic symbols or onomatopoeic labels because it is more objective and preserves much more information. However, the spectrograph has weaknesses of its own. One of the most important is the coding of loudness or intensity information by a "darkness" scale; any but the grossest differences in intensity are hard to evaluate. This limitation can be partially overcome by making an amplitude section, but the technique is extremely tedious, especially if intensity information is desired for all portions of the vocalization. As a result, intensity relationships within the call are frequently ignored in studies of vocal behavior.

A further serious limitation of the sound spectrograph is that it produces results that are not directly quantitative. In order to quantify frequency or temporal information, values must be measured from the ordinate and abscissa. This process is frequently done with a millimeter rule and is both laborious and somewhat subjective. Because of the lengthy analysis time associated with quantifying spectrographic data, most investigators present information from a small number of calls.

A most promising development in attempts to describe adequately the paralinguistic behavior of animals and infants is the use of digital computer techniques. Computer analysis of vocalization has the advantage of being fast, objective, and inherently quantitative. The field of computer analysis of speech has been an extremely active one in the last decade. Algorithms for the analysis of many features of speech are now well documented and should be easily adaptable for the study of infant or animal communication (see, for example, Carterette, Shipley, & Buchwald, 1979). A glimpse of the potential power of this method can be seen in a study by Sheppard and Lane (1968) on the development of pitch in infant cries. By using automatic analog to digital conversion of recorded cries and computer analysis of fundamental frequency, Sheppard and Lane were able to present a developmental function on which each point represented an average of 34,200 samples of vocal activities.

We have developed a computer analysis system that does an exact, automatic analysis of the cries of cats. In this system, calls are digitized at a sampling rate of 20,000 Hz and stored on a disk. The analysis program uses fast Fourier transform and linear prediction techniques to obtain call parameters such as the fundamental frequency for successive 256-point sections of the digitized call. Figures 1 and 2 illustrate some of the results from this analysis. Figure 1 presents a linear prediction analysis of the cry of a young kitten. For each function, amplitude is plotted on the ordinate and frequency on the abcissa. Time is plotted into the plane of the page; each frequency function in the graph results from an analysis of 12.8 milliseconds of the call. This kind of quasi–three-dimensional graph is extremely useful for visualizing frequency relationships within the call. In this respect, it is similar to a spectrogram. However, it has advantages relative to spectrographic analysis because the linear prediction technique is inherently quantitative so that frequencies and amplitudes can be specified exactly.

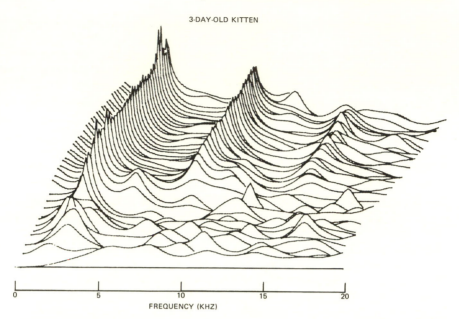

*Figure 1.* Three-dimensional plot of kitten isolation call with amplitude on the vertical axis and time on the oblique axis.

Figure 2 presents three functions from a computer program we have developed to summarize call characteristics. In these graphs, time is represented on the abcissa; each point on the three functions is derived from 12.8 milliseconds of the call. The pitch function shows the fundamental frequency of the vocalization. The energy ratio is a value representing the energy in the harmonic with maximum energy divided by the energy in the fundamental. The third function depicts the root mean

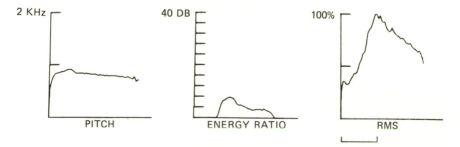

*Figure 2.* Three functions expressing acoustic parameters of the cry of a 50-day-old kitten. The functions were obtained by computer analysis of the digitized cry. The time calibration in the lower right is 200 msec.

square value of the amplitude for each analysis window of the call. With these analysis techniques, it is possible to approach the study of highly variable calls quantitatively, as will be discussed more fully later.


## 3. CHARACTERISTICS OF CAT VOCALIZATION

In discussing cat vocalizations, one must first introduce the issue of variability. As noted previously, bird songs (e.g., male white-crowned sparrows; Marler & Tamura, 1962) are highly stylized, and little variation is seen in the structure of particular calls. This lack of variability has facilitated the study of vocal behavior in birds because individual call types can easily be identified and factors that influence vocalization can be systematically studied. Even small changes in vocal behavior stand out against the normal background of stability. However, in the case of many mammalian vocalizations, the situation is much different. As Lillehei and Snowdon (1978, p. 270) have observed, regarding the calls of nonhuman primates: "If communication researchers were to agree on a single thing, it would be that a high degree of variability exists."

Because of this variability, many mammals, including cats, seem to have an almost unlimited number of vocalizations, so that the initial research problem of defining the vocal repertoire is difficult. A common approach has been to group calls on the basis of acoustic similarity. For example, Shaller (1972) has divided lion vocalizations into three general classes—meowing, roaring, and growling/snarling—within which nine "more or less" distinct expressions are noted. As Shaller admits, this scheme is somewhat arbitrary; there are often intermediate forms between general classes of vocalizations so that a major problem, as it is sometimes expressed, is where to split and where to lump. A further difficulty in the use of acoustic features by human observers for grouping animal sounds is that category boundaries obtained in this fashion may not correspond to boundaries the animals themselves perceive.

A second common approach to classifying animal vocalizations has been to group calls that occur in similar behavioral situations. Classifying responses by the typical interactions or environmental circumstances that evoke them offers some important advantages; the call-generating situation can be specified objectively, and the definition of a response category is, therefore, operational (Brown, Buchwald, Johnson, & Mikolich, 1978). This approach has been used in our classification of cat vocalizations.

## 3.1. Cat Vocal Repertoire

Figure 3 illustrates, in part, the vocal repertoire of the domestic adult cat and kitten. Classification is based primarily on the behavioral context in which the cries were emitted. However, measurements from sonographic records of call duration, initial and peak values of fundamental frequency, and changes in these parameters with development indicated that the vocalizations emitted in different behavioral situations also exhibited differences in these quantifiable dimensions (Brown *et al.*, 1978). Qualitative differences were exhibited in the overall structural pattern of certain call types emitted during different behaviors.

The call sonographically illustrated at the top of Figure 3 is the "isolation call," which is emitted by young kittens in a variety of circumstances, including isolation from the mother or littermates, hunger, cold, or mild restraint. This call is present at birth, becomes less frequently emitted with age, and disappears or merges into an adult cry around the time of weaning. The next call, the hunger cry of an adult cat, first appears during weaning and closely resembles the kitten isolation cry. The cry in response to painful stimuli has never been recorded in the neonate and does not normally appear until 4 to 6 weeks of age. The next two cries first appear at 4 to 5 weeks of age and are emitted in aggressive or defensive threat situations. Finally, the maternal vocalization in response to a kitten isolation call requires sexual maturity, pregnancy, and parturition. The regular developmental sequence of these various call types in the normal repertoire permits a variety of observations within the first year. Changes in repertoire, in response thresholds, response intensities, or in other parameters can indicate abnormal vocal behavior as a function of experimental manipulation of the animal.

## 3.2. The Kitten Isolation Cry

The isolation calls of individual kittens vary considerably, as is illustrated in Figure 4. Although these cries were all emitted by a single kitten when it was removed from its mother, it can be seen that a wide range of modulations of the general cry pattern occurred both within and across recording sessions.

In order to define the significant acoustic parameters within each of these highly variable cries, a behavioral assay was developed that utilized the adult cat's maternal retrieval response (Buchwald, 1981; Harrison, Buchwald, Norman, & Hinman, 1979). During the first 2 weeks postpartum, lactating females were found to retrieve kittens emitting the isolation call at virtually a 100% level whether or not the kittens were

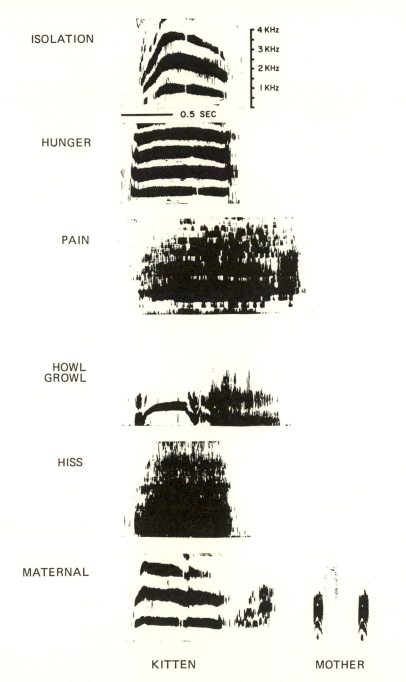

ISOLATION

HUNGER

PAIN

HOWL
GROWL

HISS

MATERNAL

KITTEN                    MOTHER

*Figure 3*. Classes of calls in cat vocal repertoire. From the top, these sonographs are typical of the kitten isolation cry, adult cat hunger cry, adult pain cry, cries emitted in territorial disputes or in threatening situations, and maternal response to kitten cry.

DAY 6                    DAY 13                    DAY 18

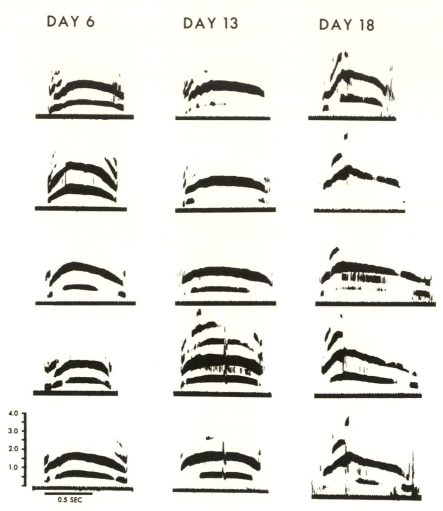

*Figure 4.* Isolation cries recorded from a single kitten over successive days.

seen. (In the experimental situation, a curtain separated the female from the kittens.) A tape-recorded series of naturally varying kitten cries and a tape-loop recording of a single kitten cry were subsequently found to trigger the same maternal retrieval response, although somewhat less reliably than the actual crying kitten. The naturally varying cries were more effective than the single repeated cry. Presentations of synthesized stimuli that contained only isolated components of the total call structure, for example, the fundamental frequency, the first formant, the initial segment or the terminal segment, were clearly less salient than initial segment or the terminal segment, were clearly less salient than either the varying or invariant total call, and little or no retrieval was elicited by these "component" stimuli.

From these experiments a number of conclusions are suggested. Maternal retrieval triggered by the kitten isolation cry, in the absence of visual, olfactory, or thermal cues, indicated that the acoustic signal *per se* had behavioral significance. Although variability appears to be an important feature, even without the parameter of novelty, an invariant cry resulted in relatively high response levels, whereas isolated acoustic components of the cry did not. Thus, the combined acoustic features of a normal isolation cry provide the kitten with a vocal behavior of significance. Vocal communication with the mother is enhanced by cry variability along prosodic dimensions of pitch, duration, and intensity and is diminished by decomposition of total call structure into isolated acoustic parameters.

## 4. VOCAL LEARNING IN THE KITTEN

Modulation of vocal behavior by mechanisms of auditory feedback exemplifies one level of vocal learning, whereas imitation and replication of externally generated auditory signals exemplify a second, more demanding level. We have approached the issue of vocal learning thus far by investigating the role of auditory feedback in the regulation of the kitten isolation cry. If vocal learning plays any role in the development of kitten cries, then the calls of deaf animals should differ from those of hearing littermate controls.

In our initial studies, kittens were deafened at 4 weeks of age by bilateral destruction of the cochlea (Buchwald & Brown, 1977). Sonographic studies of the isolation calls subsequently emitted by the deaf kittens indicated some disruption of call structure, although measurements of fundamental frequency did not reveal significant differences between the deafened kittens and their normal littermates. These data suggested that total call structure was more dependent upon auditory feedback than was fundamental frequency.

A more quantitative study currently ongoing in our laboratory has indicated that auditory feedback plays a role in the regulation of intensity, overall structure, and fundamental frequency stability in the kitten isolation cry (Shipley, Buchwald, Carterette, & Strecker, 1981). Comparison of the calls of a kitten deafened at 2 weeks of age by bilateral cochlear destruction with calls of a normal littermate control is presented in Figure 5. In each case, three different pitch functions are plotted in the same graph to indicate a range of variability. We have found that, on average, the cries of deaf kittens of 50 days of age are shorter than those of hearing littermates, and that there is less variability between the calls of the deaf animals than between those of the controls. In addition, although the pitch functions of deaf and hearing animals have similar overall frequencies, the calls of the deaf animals have more point-to-point variability, suggesting a lack of fine control of fundamental frequency.

We have also found that the cries of deaf kittens are, on average, much louder than those of hearing littermates. To investigate the causes of this difference, we designed miniature headphones for kittens (Figure 6). We played varying levels of white noise to the kittens and measured the loudness of their calls. As the level of noise was increased from 0 to 80 dB (SPL), the calls of normal animals increased approximately 10 dB (Shipley *et al.*, 1981). These manipulations had no effect on the cries of deafened animals. An effect similar to that observed in hearing kittens, known as the Lombard reflex, is also seen in humans. The Lombard reflex functions to adjust the level of vocal output so that it can be heard in varying levels of background noise. Lack of auditory feedback prevents this reflex from functioning in deaf kittens. Thus, the difference in the loudness of the cries of deaf and hearing animals appears to reflect, at least in part, active modulation of cry intensity by the hearing animals.

In terms of vocal modulation through mechanisms of auditory feedback, vocal learning can therefore be demonstrated in the developing kitten. To what extent kitten or cat vocal behavior shows the more complex imitative level of vocal learning has not been established.

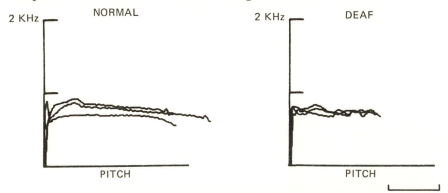

*Figure 5.* Pitch functions from deaf and hearing kittens at 50 days of age. For both animals, values from three different calls are plotted to indicate a range of variability. The time calibration in the lower right is 200 msec.

*Figure 6.* Thirty-day-old kitten fitted with headphones through which miniature speakers can deliver varying levels of white noise.

## 5. VOLUNTARY CONTROL OF VOCALIZATIONS IN THE CAT

In addition to vocal learning, a second basic characteristic of human vocal behavior is volitional control. However, as discussed in an earlier section, conditioning studies in some species of monkeys have demonstrated not only a capacity for vocal learning but also for volitional control of vocal behavior.

At an anecdotal level, we have frequently observed the conditioned vocalizations of household kittens and cats emitted for specific purposes, for example, to obtain food, to obtain egress from the house, and as a greeting. Cats and dogs have been trained to produce conditioned vocalizations in the laboratory with both classical and instrumental conditioning procedures (Salzinger & Waller, 1962; Soltysik, Nicholas, & Wilson, 1984). We are presently investigating the extent to which the adult cat can exercise volitional control and modulate its vocal behavior under formal experimental constraints within a laboratory setting.

## 6. SUBSTRATES OF CAT VOCAL BEHAVIOR

The foregoing data indicate that a repertoire of vocalizations can be produced by the cat that have behavioral correlates and identifying acoustic features. Furthermore, kitten and cat vocalizations appear to reflect some aspects of vocal learning and volitional control. These important characteristics of language are also manifested in a paralinguistic mode by the human infant. Substrates of vocal behavior in the cat, therefore, may also be relevant as a potential structural-functional model for the vocal production of the 6-week- to 6-month-old human infant.

### 6.1. Vocal Tract Properties

Lieberman and his associates have emphasized that the evolutionary development of the human pharyngeal cavity has provided humans with a unique ability to produce the wide variety of resonance patterns characteristic of most languages. Lieberman (1968) points out that humans can easily vary the area of the pharyngeal cavity, creating complex resonances because their tongues are positioned relatively far back in the vocal tract compared to other animals. In contrast, patterns of resonances in most ape vocalizations can be explained by considering the vocal tract as a simple tube, which is slightly flared at the mouth. Lieberman, Crelin, and Klatt (1972) used computer modeling to determine the theoretical number of sounds that such a vocal tract could produce and concluded that primates have extremely limited capacity for the production of speechlike sounds. The argument proposed by Lieberman for primates also applies to cats.

In the pharyngeal cavity of the cat, the tongue is positioned forward in the mouth, and the entire area of the tract can resonate sound as a simple tube. In the case of young kittens, these resonances are sometimes surprisingly near theoretical values for a tube closed at one end. Kitten cries have a fundamental frequency that usually varies between about 800 and 1500 Hz. Carterette et al. (1979) have argued that the natural resonance of the kitten's vocal tract is such that it closely matches the first overtone of this fundamental. Figure 1 presents a hidden-line plot of the frequencies of the isolation call of a 6-day-old kitten. The energy peaks are arranged throughout most of the call in a nearly perfect 1:3:5 ratio, exactly the theoretical resonances of a cylindrical tube closed at one end. This kind of resonance pattern may allow the kitten to produce maximum sound intensity in some of its calls.

However, not all cries of even the youngest kittens display this simple structure. Even if the vocal tract is considered only as a cylindrical tube, which is closed at one end, movement of the jaw and/or lips can be an important method of modulating the sound of the call. The resonances of a tube are partially a function of its length and, in the case of the mammalian vocal tract, the length of the pharyngeal tube is markedly affected by mouth opening and lip position. Holding the jaws in different positions also changes the flair of the opening of the vocal tract, and this directly influences the tract resonances. Thus, kittens have several articulatory gestures with which to modulate the acoustic features of their calls. These gestures may also be used by human infants.

At birth, the oropharyngeal anatomy of the human is similar to that of subhuman primates (Bosma, 1975), and separation of the epiglottis and palate does not occur until about 4 to 6 months of age (Sasaki, Levine, Laitman, & Crelin, 1977). The approximation of the epiglottis and palate has advantages for sucking and breathing but restricts the range of sounds available to the infant. Based largely on considerations of anatomy (although some spectrographic data were analyzed), Lieberman, Harris, Wolff, and Russell (1971) have argued that the vocal tract of infants can be assumed to resonate sounds as if it were a simple tube as discussed previously in the case of the kitten and cat.

Thus, the basic acoustic properties of the pharyngeal tract may be similar in kittens and human infants. Although obvious differences in scale exist, it seems reasonable to expect that articulatory gestures that are effective for kittens might also be effective for human infants. Figure 7 illustrates the similarity of structure found in the cries of human infants and kittens. The vocalization shown is a normal hunger cry from a 3-week-old human infant. In order to emphasize similarities between the structure of the call and that seen in the cries of kittens (e.g., Figure 4) the spectrograph was made by playing the cry at twice its normal speed. Similarities between such cries and those of kittens are striking both on the spectrograph and to the ear.

## 6.2. Neurophysiological Mechanisms

There has been considerable interest in the physiology of vocal behavior in animals; two research approaches have commonly been used. In one, different areas of the brain are electrically excited, and the vocal

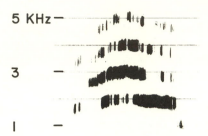

*Figure 7.* A hunger cry from a 3-week-old human infant. The cry was spectrographed at twice normal speed to emphasize similarities with the kitten isolation cry (see Figure 4).

reactions of the animal are noted. In a second approach, some area of the brain is lesioned, and the resulting effects on vocalization are observed. These methods have been used for study of the neural substrates controlling vocalization in a large number of mammals, including gibbons (e.g., Apfelbach, 1972); rhesus monkeys (e.g., Magoun, Atlas, Ingersoll, & Ranson, 1937); squirrel monkeys (e.g., Jurgens & Ploog, 1970); dogs (e.g., Skultety, 1962); rats (e.g., Waldbillig, 1975); and cats (e.g., Skultety, 1965).

In a review of this literature, Jurgens (1979) concludes that results from several species indicate that the vocalization areas of mammals, including the cat, can be organized into three hierarchical levels. The most caudal level consists of the cranial nerve nuclei involved in phonation, the respiratory motoneurons, and the interneurons connecting these areas with each other. These include the trigeminal, facial, rostral ambiguus, and hypoglossal nuclei for opening the mouth and for articulatory movements of the lips, soft palate and tongue, the caudal nucleus ambiguus for control of the vocal folds, the nucleus solitarius and anterior horn cells for control of respiration, and the lateral pontine and medullary reticular formation for integration of these areas.

A second major vocalization area is the caudal periaqueductal gray and laterally adjacent tegmentum between the inferior colliculus and brachium conjunctivum. Stimulation of this area produces vocalization in all mammals that have been studied but does not appear to alter affect. Lesion of this area in cats produces either total mutism or a severe reduction in vocal behavior (Skultety, 1958, 1965). The periaqueductal region receives direct inputs from almost all rostral vocalization-eliciting brain areas, most of which simultaneously represent motivation-eliciting areas. The periaqueductal gray has, in turn, a direct projection to the nucleus ambiguus that controls laryngeal musculature. Jurgens (1976) has argued that this region couples motivation with adequate vocal expression so as to trigger a specific vocal pattern. The fine motor integration and expression of this pattern then takes place within the pons and medulla. Jurgens also points out that the vocal functions of this brain region may have great phylogenetic age because stimulation of similar regions in birds, reptiles, and amphibians also elicits vocalization.

A third hierarchical level is composed of certain subcortical structures including the amygdala, septum, and hypothalamus. Stimulation in these areas reliably evokes vocalizations that are, in part, the result of changes in affective state. For example, in cats, stimulation of the hypothalamus can produce hissing and/or growling. Generally, these vocalizations are accompanied by other signs of anger such as flattened ears and piloerection (Hess & Brugger, 1943). The stimulated animal will also attack a stuffed cat (Hunsberger & Bucher, 1967). In man, stimulation of similar areas has been reported to produce rage or fright (King, 1961). Stimulation of the septum produces purring in the cat (Meyer & Hess, 1957) and reports of a feeling of well-being in humans (King, 1961).

Loci in the three levels discussed previously are not the only neural substrates involved in vocal behavior. However, they represent an organizational system that has been found in all mammals studied and that is almost certainly of primary importance in the production of most calls in most mammals. As such, this organizational system is also an ideal candidate for the neural control of human infant vocalizations.

## 7. SIMILARITIES BETWEEN INFANT AND KITTEN VOCAL BEHAVIOR

The vocal behavior of human and nonhuman infants is similar in many respects. For example, in both cases, pitch, intensity, and duration carry the meaning of the vocal signal in a nonlexical, paralinguistic mode. Moreover, infant mammals of a large number of species, including creatures as diverse as humans, cats, bats, elephant seals, and reindeer, communicate with their mothers by means of a distress cry used in situations in which the infant is isolated, hungry, or cold. The widespread presence of this behavioral feature in mammals suggests that human infant vocalization might be profitably approached with a comparative model such as the kitten isolation cry.

As in the case of animal, for example, cat, vocalizations, most investigators of human infant sounds have used the technique of grouping cries in terms of the behavioral situation in which they are given. Thus, probably the most frequently studied infant vocalization is the pain cry. This vocalization has been elicited by snapping a rubber band on the heel (e.g., Fisichelli & Karelitz, 1963; Fisichelli, Haber, Davis, & Karelitz, 1966) or by pinching the infant (e.g., Truby, 1965). Another frequently studied vocalization is the hunger cry, which is usually recorded at the infant's normal feeding time (e.g., Valanne, Vourenkoski, Partenen, Lind, & Wasz-Höckert, 1967). In addition, pleasure and anger cries are sometimes described (Wasz-Höckert, Lind, Vourenkoski, Partenen, & Valanne, 1968).

The kind of variability typically seen in nonhuman mammal vocal behavior, as in the kitten cries illustrated in Figure 3, is also found in the study of infants. Fairbanks (1942) recorded "hunger wails" from his son at monthly intervals over the first 9 months of life. The range of fundamental frequencies from different calls recorded in a given session sometimes exceeded 2000 Hz. For example, at 3 months, the range was from 89 to 2120 Hz; at 7 months from 150 to 2348 Hz. Fairbanks points out that although the normal singing range of an adult is about three octaves, that of his infant son was somewhat in excess of five octaves and the infant commonly used his entire range in the course of a 4-minute recording session.

Thus, the problem of variability in the vocal signal is similar in the study of both infants and animals, and similar methods have been used to approach the problem in both areas. Despite this similarity, researchers in one area almost never mention results in the other. Perhaps because of this separation, theoretical interpretations of variability in vocalization are much different in the two fields. Students of animal vocalization have consistently theorized that some aspects of variability have communicative significance, for example, the enhanced retrieval response of the female cat to the variable versus invariant kitten isolation cry. Students of infant crying have generally ignored the possible significance of varibility. It would be of considerable interest to know if the cry types used by human infants differed in amount of variability and if the amount of variability within different cry types changed developmentally. Such issues are difficult to study in human infants, but they can be addressed relatively easily in an animal model such as the cat.

## 8. CONCLUSIONS

Almost no attempt has been made to relate results from vocalization studies in animals to human infant vocal behavior. Research in both areas frequently deals with the same theoretical and methodological problems and could easily be complementary. Yet, with a few exceptions, such interaction has been surprisingly absent.

The word *infant* comes from Latin roots meaning "without speech." However, although the human infant is without speech, it is certainly not without an effective means of communication. And, as we have seen in the preceding discussion, this means of communication may have much in common with vocal behavior seen in a number of other mammals. If more attention were paid to such common features, our understanding of the paralanguage that precedes speech in the human infant might be greatly enhanced.

This chapter is a progress report that has presented arguments for the use of animal models of vocal behavior. Whether or not human language is considered as part of a continuum of vocal behavior that extends into the animal kingdom, a number of its behavioral characteristics are shared with nonhuman species. The qualities of pitch, duration, intensity, and overall intonation are parameters common to the prosody of adult speech, the infant cry, and animal vocalizations. Likewise, the behavioral characteristics of vocal learning and volitional control are common to speech, the infant cry, and to certain animal vocalizations.

Animal studies of vocal behavior have previously emphasized the songbird and the nonhuman primate. In the former species, much is known regarding the role of vocal learning in the development of adult song, but relatively little is known regarding volitional control of vocalization. The phylogenetic disparity between birds and mammals, moreover, makes comparisons with the mammal difficult at functional or structural levels. The vocal behavior of a number of species of nonhuman primates has been studied in some detail at ethological and physiological levels. However, in part because of practical considerations, the development of a call repertoire and the role of vocal learning during development and of volitional control in the infant have rarely been systematically investigated or quantified.

Studies of vocal behavior in the cat provide a mammalian model in which both developmental experimental manipulations can be assessed with relative ease, in terms of time to maturity (i.e., 6 to 9 months), availability of subjects, and knowledge of central nervous system anatomy and physiology. A vocal repertoire for cats raised in the laboratory environment can be defined by utilizing developmental, behavioral, and acoustic parameters.

The cries of cats resemble those of human infants in that both reflect a graded system of vocalization. Problems of phonetic description and accurate measurement are analogous. Infant cries are extremely variable as are the cries of cats (as well as those of many other mammals). In the kitten, this variability has positive significance relative to maternal responsiveness. Thus, techniques and approaches used to quantify and assess cat or kitten cries for their significant acoustic parameters might be profitably applied to studies of the infant cry.

At least one aspect of vocal learning—the modulation of vocal output controlled by auditory feedback—appears to occur in the cat model. Deafened kittens were found to emit cries that were louder and less variable than were those of their normal littermates. Moreover, normal kittens demonstrated the Lombard reflex; that is, they cried louder in the presence of background white noise, an additional indication of the role of auditory feedback in cry regulation. Such self-monitoring has also been implicated in the modulation of human vocal patterns, as is exemplified by vocal learning of the human infant as early as 6 weeks of age. Volitional control of vocal behavior in the cat is suggested by both formal conditioning procedures and informal observation. Studies are currently in progress to determine the extent of this control in the cat, a control that becomes increasingly prepotent in the human infant.

Finally, common to all nonhuman mammals, including the cat, in which invasive stimulation and lesion procedures have been carried out, there appears to be a hierarchy of subcortical integrative systems controlling vocal behavior. These systems are intriguing candidates for the control of vocalization in the human infant and of at least some aspects of prosody in adult speech.

A common thread through vocal communication in the mammalian species, including the cry of the human infant, is the utilization of pitch, intensity, and duration in a graded paralinguistic mode. Such vocalization provides a significant amount of information transfer. It may also serve as a phylogenetic and ontogenetic substrate for the emergence of the more complex lexical form of vocal communication. Mammalian models such as the cat and kitten provide a means of exploring the development and neurophysiological regulation of this form of vocal behavior and may ultimately assist us in understanding the mysteries of human speech, which emerges from in the infant cry.

## 9. REFERENCES

Apfelbach, R. Electrically elicited vocalizations in the gibbon *Hylobates lar* (Hylobatidae) and their behavioral significance. *Zeitschrift für Tierpsychologie*, 1972, *30*, 420–430.

Bazett, H. C., Oxon, M. D., Eng, F. R. C. S., Penfield, W. G., & Oxon, B. S. A study of the Sherrington decerebrate animal in the chronic as well as the acute condition. *Brain*, 1922, *45*, 185–265.

Bosma, J. F. Anatomic and physiologic development of speech apparatus. In D. B. Tower (Ed.), *The nervous system: Vol. 3. Human communication and its disorders*. New York: Raven Press, 1975.

Brown, J. W. Language representation in the brain. In H. D. Steklis & M. J. Raleigh (Eds.), *Neurobiology of social communication in primates*. New York: Academic Press, 1979.

Brown, K. A., Buchwald, J. S., Johnson, J. R., & Mikolich, D. J. Vocalization in the cat and kitten. *Developmental Psychobiology*, 1978, *11*, 559–570.

Buchwald, J. S. Development of vocal communication in an experimental model. In S. L. Friedman & M. Sigman (Eds.), *Preterm birth and psychological development*. New York: Academic Press, 1981.

Buchwald, J., & Brown, K. A. The role of acoustic inflow in the development of adaptive behavior. *Annals of the New York Academy of Sciences*, 1977, *290*, 270–284.

Carterette, E. C., Shipley, C., & Buchwald, J. S. Linear prediction theory of vocalization in cat and kitten. In B. Lundbloom & S. Ohman (Eds.), *Frontiers of speech communication research*. London: Academic Press, 1979.

Chomsky, N. *Aspects of the theory of syntax*. Cambridge, Mass.: M.I.T. Press, 1965.

Dingwall, W. O. The evolution of human communication systems. In H. Whitaker & H. A. Whitaker (Eds.), *Studies in neurolinguistics* (Vol 4). New York: Academic Press, 1979.

Fairbanks, G. An acoustical study of the pitch of infant hunger wails. *Child Development*, 1942, *13*, 227–232.

Fisichelli, V., & Karelitz, S. The cry latencies of normal infants and those with brain damage. *Journal of Pediatrics*, 1963, *62*, 724–734.

Fisichelli, V., Haber, A., Davis, J., & Karelitz, S. Audible characteristics of the cries of normal infants and those with Down's syndrome. *Perceptual and Motor Skills*, 1966, *23*, 744–746.

Green, S. Dialects in Japanese monkeys: Vocal learning and cultural transmission of locale-specific vocal behavior. *Zeitschrift für Tierpsychologie*, 1975, *38*, 304–314.

Harrison, J. B., Buchwald, J. S., Norman, R. J., & Hinman, C. Acoustic analysis of maternal retrieval to kitten stress call. *Society of Neuroscience Abstracts*, 1979, *5*, 22.

Hess, W. R., & Brugger, M. Das subkortikale Zentrum der affectiven Abwehrreaktion. *Helvetica Physiologica et Pharmacologica Acta*, 1943, *1*, 33–52.

Hockett, C. F. Logical considerations in the study of animal communication. In W. E. Lanyon & W. N. Tavolga (Eds.), *Animal sounds and communication*. Washington, DC: American Institute of Biological Science, 1960.

Hunsberger, R. W., & Bucher, V. M. Affective behavior produced by electrical stimulation in the forebrain and brain stem of the cat. *Progress in Brain Research*, 1967, 27, 103–127.

Jacobson, J. Brain development in relation to language. In E. H. Lenneberg & E. Lenneberg (Eds.), *Foundations of language development. An interdisciplinary approach* (Vol. 1). New York: Academic Press, 1975.

Jurgens, V. Neural control of vocalization in nonhuman primates. In H. D. Steklis & M. J. Raleigh (Eds.), *Neurobiology of social communication in primates*. New York: Academic Press, 1979.

Jurgens, V., & Ploog, D. Cerebral representation of vocalization in the squirrel monkey. *Experimental Brain Research*, 1970, *10*, 532–554.

Kawabe, S. Development of vocalization and behavior of Japanese macaques. In C. R. Carpenter (Ed.), *Behavioral regulators of primate behavior*. Lewisburg, Pa.: Bucknell University Press, 1973.

King, H. E. Responses to subcortical electrical brain stimulation in humans. In D. E. Sheer (Ed.), *Electrical stimulation of the brain*. Austin: University of Texas Press, 1961.

Konishi, M. Comparative neurophysiological studies of hearing and vocalizations in songbirds. *Journal of Physiology*, 1970, *66*, 257–272.

Ladefoged, P. *A course in phonetics*. New York: Harcourt Brace Jovanovich, 1975.

Lamendella, J. T. The limbic system in human communication. In H. Whitaker & H. A. Whitaker (Eds.), *Studies in neurolinguistics* (Vol. 3). New York: Academic Press, 1977.

Lenneberg, E. H. Speech as a motor skill with special reference to nonaphasic disorders. *Monographs of the Society for Research in Child Development*, 1964, *29*, 115–127.

Lenneberg, E. H. *Biological foundations of language*. New York: Wiley, 1967.

Lenneberg, E. H. The concept of language differentiation. In E. H. Lenneberg & E. Lenneberg (Eds.), *Foundations of language development. A multidisciplinary approach* (Vol. 1). New York: Academic Press, 1975.

Lenneberg, E. H., Rebelsky, F. G., & Nichols, I. A. The vocalizations of infants born to deaf and to hearing parents. *Human Development*, 1965, *8*, 23–37.

Lieberman, P. Primate vocalizations and human linguistic ability. *Journal of the Acoustic Society of America*, 1968, *44*, 1574–1584.

Lieberman, P., Harris, K. S., Wolff, P., & Russell, L. H. Newborn infant cry and nonhuman primate vocalizations. *Journal of Speech and Hearing Research*, 1971, *14*, 718–727.

Lieberman, P., Crelin, E. S., & Klatt, D. H. Phonetic ability and related anatomy of the newborn and adult human Neanderthal Man, and the chimpanzee. *American Anthropologist*, 1972, *74*, 287–307.

Lillehei, R., & Snowdon, C. T. Individual and situational differences in the vocalizations of young stumptail macaques (*Maccaca arctoides*). *Behavior*, 1978, *65*, 270–281.

Magoun, H. W., Atlas, D., Ingersoll, E. H., & Ranson, S. W. Associated facial, vocal and respiratory components of emotional expression; an experimental study. *Journal of Neurology and Psychiatry*, 1937, *7*, 241–255.

Maskarinec, A. S., Cairns, G. F., Jr., Butterfield, E. C., & Weamer, D. K. Longitudinal observations of individual infants' vocalizations. *Journal of Speech and Hearing Disorders*, 1981, *46*, 267–273.

Marilya, M. P. Spontaneous vocalization and babbling in hearing impaired infants. In G. Fant (Ed.), *International symposium on speech, communication, ability and profound deafness*. Washington, DC: Alexander Graham Bell Association for the Deaf, 1972.

Marler, P. The logical analysis of animal communication. *Journal of Theoretical Biology*, 1961, *1*, 295–317.

Marler, P., & Tamura, M. Song dialects in white-crowned sparrows. *Condor*, 1962, *64*, 368–377.

Mellon, I. M., *The science and mystery of the cat*. New York: Scribner's, 1940.

Meyer, A. E., & Hess, W. R. Diencephal ausgelostes sexual Verhalten und Schmeicheln bei der Katze. *Helv. Physiol. Pharmacol. Acta*, 1957, *15*, 401–407.

Myers, R. E. Comparative neurology of vocalization and speech: Proof of a dichotomy. *Annals of the New York Academy of Science*, 1976, *280*, 745–757.

Newman, J. D. Central nervous system processing of sounds in primates. In H. D. Steklis & M. J. Raleigh (Eds.), *Neurobiology of social communication in primates*. New York: Academic Press, 1979.

Newman, J., & Symmes, D. Vocal pathology in socially deprived monkeys. *Developmental Psychobiology*, 1974, *7*, 351–358.

Nottebohm, F. A zoologist's view of some language phenomena with particular emphasis on vocal learning. In E. H. Lenneberg & E. Lenneberg (Eds.), *Foundations of language development* (Vol. 1). New York: Academic Press, 1975.

Nottebohm, F. Cerebral lateralization in birds. In H. D. Steklis & M. J. Raleigh (Eds.), *Neurobiology of social communication in primates*. New York: Academic Press, 1979.

Peters, G. Vergleichende Untersuchung zur Lautgebung einiger Feliden. *Spixiana*, 1978 (Suppl. 1).

Ploog, D. Phylogenetic and ontogenetic aspects of vocal behavior. In Language and brain: Developmental aspects. *Neuroscience Research Program Bulletin*, 1974, *12*, 611–618.

Pruitt, C. H., & Burghardt, G. M. Communication in terrestral carnivores, mustelidae, procyonidae, and ursidae. In T. A. Sebeok (Ed.), *How animals communicate*. Bloomington: University of Indiana Press, 1977.

Salzinger, K., & Waller, M. B. The operant control of vocalization in the dog. *Journal of Experimental Analysis of Behavior*, 1962, *5*, 383–389.

Sasaki, C. T., Levine, P. A., Laitman, J. T., & Crelin, E. S. Postnatal descent of the epiglottis in man. *Archives of Otolaryngology*, 1977, *103*, 169–171.

Shaller, G. B. *The Serengeti lion: A study of predator–prey relations*. Chicago: University of Chicago Press, 1972.

Sheppard, W. C., & Lane, H. L. Development of the prosodic features of infant vocalizing. *Journal of Speech and Hearing Research*, 1968, *11*, 94–108.

Shipley, C., Buchwald, J. S., Carterette, E. D., & Strecker, J. Differences in the cries of deaf and hearing kittens. *Society for Neuroscience Abstracts*, 1981, *7*, 774.

Skultety, F. M. The behavioral effects of destructive lesions of the periaqueductal gray matter in adult cats. *Journal of Comparative Neurology*, 1958, *110*, 337–365.

Skultety, F. M. Experimental mutism in dogs. *Archives of Neurology*, 1962, *6*, 235–241.

Skultety, F. M. Mutism in cats with rostral midbrain lesions. *Archives of Neurology*, 1965, *12*, 211–225.

Soltysik, S. S., Nicholas, T., & Wilson, W. J. Postnatal development of respiratory and vocal responses during aversive classical conditioning in cats. *Pavlovian Journal of Biological Science*, 1984, *19*.

Steklis, H. D., & Raleigh, M. J. Behavioral and neurological aspects of primate vocalization and facial expression. In H. D. Steklis & M. J. Raleigh (Eds.), *Neurobiology of social communication in primates*. New York: Academic Press, 1979. (a)

Steklis, H. D., & Raleigh, M. J. Requisites for language: Interspecific and evolutionary aspects. In H. D. Steklis & M. J. Raleigh (Eds.), *Neurobiology of social communication in primates*. New York: Academic Press, 1979. (b)

Sutton, D. Mechanisms and underlying vocal control in nonhuman primates. In H. D. Steklis & M. J. Raleigh (Eds.), *Neurobiology of social communication in primates*. New York: Academic Press, 1979.

Truby, H., & Lind, J. Cry sounds of the newborn infant. In J. Lind (Ed.), Newborn infant cry. *Acta Paediatrica Scandinavica*, 1965, *163* (Suppl.).

Valanne, E. H., Vuorenkoski, V., Partanen, T. J., Lind, J., & Wasz-Höckert, O. The ability of human mothers to identify the hunger cry signals of their own newborn infants during the lying in period. *Experientia*, 1967, *23*, 768–769.

Waldbillig, R. J. Attack, eating, drinking and gnawing elicited by electrical stimulation of rat mesencephalon and pons. *Journal of Comparative Physiology and Psychology*, 1975, *89*, 200–212.

Wasz-Höckert, O., Lind, J., Vuorenkoski, V., Partanen, T., & Valanne, E. The infant cry: A spectrographic and auditory analysis. *Clinics in Developmental Medicine* 29. Philadelphia: Lippincott, 1968.

Winitz, H. *Articulatory acquisition and behavior*. New York: Appleton-Century-Crofts, 1969.

Winter, P., Handley, P., Ploog, D., & Schott, D. Ontogeny of squirrel monkey calls under normal conditions and under acoustic isolation. *Behavior*, 1973, *47*, 230–239.

Zangwill, V. L. The ontogeny of cerebral dominance in man. In E. H. Lenneberg & E. Lenneberg (Eds.), *Foundations of language development. An interdisciplinary approach* (Vol. 1). New York: Academic Press, 1975.

# 14

# The Infant Cry of Primates
## An Evolutionary Perspective

## JOHN D. NEWMAN

## 1. INTRODUCTION

The evolution of the infant cry is essentially a reflection of the evolution of mammals. The origin of suckling behavior and the delivery of milk from the mother gave rise to the intimacy of prolonged contact, a trait that is almost as diagnostic for mammals as the nursing behavior from which it originates. Along with this intimacy came increased possibilities for individual recognition between mother and infant, resulting in the establishment of affiliative bonds that, at least in many primates, extend well beyond the period of infantile dependency into adulthood.

Observation of a variety of primate species indicates that the newborn infant is capable of making sounds clearly recognizable as typical for the species. Primate mothers respond to these sounds with particular urgency. Thus, communication from infant to mother begins at the earliest age.

A biological perspective to the infant cry should consider crying as an identifiable part of a given species' behavioral repertoire. There is substantial documentation for the fact that human infants utter a variety

JOHN D. NEWMAN • Laboratory of Comparative Ethology, National Institute of Child Health and Human Development, National Institutes of Health, Bethesda, Maryland 20205.

of vocalizations, each with definable characteristics and occurring in a limited set of conditions. Even the term *cry* in its commonly used sense refers to a set of structurally and contextually separable utterances. As a biologist concerned with the evolution, causation, development, and adaptive significance of vocalizations, I find it useful to describe and analyze vocal behavior in ways that promote comparisons within and between species. The many parallels between the vocal patterns of human infants and the infants of nonhuman primates suggest a conservative evolutionary history across the entire primate order regarding infant sound production and its underlying neural mechanisms.

## 2. CRYING IN HUMAN INFANTS

Studies of the vocal behavior of human infants have focused mainly on the sounds produced by the hungry, lonely, hurt, or otherwise discomforted infant. This is only natural because the responses of mothers and nursery attendants to infant cries demonstrate that these sounds are effective in eliciting concern and attention from those within hearing range (e.g., Bell & Ainsworth, 1972).

Crying is a complicated motor behavior, and the detailed characteristics of the sounds are worth identifying and describing in some detail, both for the purpose of enhancing their usefulness in clinical diagnosis and in comparing the vocal behavior of human infants with other primates. Fortunately, various authors have analyzed the acoustic structure of infant crying and described some of the significant variables controlling the production of these sounds. Newborns will generally cry when taken from their cribs shortly before feeding and when placed on an examination table (Prechtl, Theorell, Gramsbergen, & Lind, 1969). Even when not disturbed, awake infants begin to cry 3 to 3.5 hours after their last feeding (Stark & Nathanson, 1973). Crying in this general context has been referred to as the *hunger cry*, although it has no unique association with hunger (Wolff, 1969). Another term applied to these sounds is *discomfort crying* (Prechtl *et al.*, 1969). However, the most important triggering stimulus may, in fact, arise from being alone. Infants studied in the home will stop crying immediately when picked up by their mother (Bell & Ainsworth, 1972). Crying, then, may be thought of as "attachment behavior," arising from the need to cling and suckle on the mother and evoking the maternal response of picking up and holding the infant (Bowlby, 1958).

## 2.1. Basic Cry Patterns

During early life, crying by the human infant has been called a *fixed action pattern* (Bell & Ainsworth, 1972) and a *social releaser* (Bowlby, 1958), that is, a relatively stereotyped intraspecific communication signal. Although the mechanisms programming crying behavior are unknown, some authors consider crying to be an innate, genetically determined behavior (Ostwald, Phibbs, & Fox, 1968). That *crying* is relatively stereotyped is apparent in the agreement among various authors as to what is meant by this term. Several efforts to describe the essential attributes of crying have been made.

At birth, the first cry is given after one or two gasping inspirations; it is often voiceless, has a duration of about one second, has a flat or falling melody, and only rarely contains glottal plosives or vocal fry (Wasz-Höckert, Lind, Vuorenkoski, Partanen, & Valanne, 1968). In the very young infant, crying begins with long stressful cries or explosive coughlike sounds. Once fully aroused, crying is sustained, whereas a crying bout frequently ends in a series of low-intensity sounds as the infant pauses to suck its fist or other object in contact with its mouth (Stark & Nathanson, 1973). Crying rate ranges from 50 to 70 utterances per minute, and the duration of each cry unit ranges from 0.4 to 0.9 seconds (Prechtl *et al.*, 1969). A typical cry sequence follows a rhythmic pattern, beginning with a cry, then a break of about .2 seconds, then a short inspiratory whistle, another break, which is followed by another cry (Wolff, 1969). Crying may continue in this manner over a period of 40 seconds to more than 4 minutes (Stark & Nathanson, 1973). This pattern is observable 30 minutes after birth and remains constant until the end of the second month, after which greater variability in several cry parameters appears. Individual cry utterances have a fundamental frequency range of .25 to .45 kHz in both sexes, the frequency changing in a gentle rising, then falling, arc (Wolff, 1969). A cry series with apparently normal structure has been reported in a premature infant less than 1 kg in weight (Truby & Lind, 1965), suggesting that the mechanism underlying the typical cry pattern is operative in all normal term infants.

There is evidence that some cry parameters are distinctive to individual babies. Cry duration and intercry interval appear to be among them (Prechtl *et al.*, 1969). One study provides convincing evidence supporting the long-held belief that a mother can recognize the cries of her own infant. Formby (1967) showed that maternal recognition of an infant's cries requires about 48 hours exposure to the cries under typical nursery conditions. However, because individual differences in cry structure appear not to have been quantitatively assessed as yet, it is not possible to say which acoustic parameters are of greatest importance in conveying individuality. Efforts to document the *changes* in cry structure as individual babies develop are few. Prescott (1975) measured the duration and pitch contour of cries during two age periods, 4 to 6 weeks and 6 to 8 months. Increases in duration were apparent in the early sample, but by 6 months cry durations appeared to have stabilized. On the other hand, pitch contour was more variable in the older sample.

## 2.2. Pain Cry

The cry patterns just described represent observations of vocal behavior spontaneously initiated by the infant and presumably related to diffuse feelings of discomfort or loneliness. However, there are distinctive differences between crying under these circumstances and crying following a painful experience, such as a vaccination. The so-called "pain cries" begin with an inspiration, followed by a long expiratory cry, then another inspiration, then expiratory cries of variable duration (Wolff, 1969). It is on the initial long cry, the least variable in a sequence, that many authors have concentrated their efforts at quantification. A typical pain cry has a duration of about 3 seconds, a maximum pitch averaging .65 kHz, and a falling melody; vocal fry and subharmonic breaks are present in more than half of these cries (Wasz-Höckert *et al.*, 1968). There may be periods where the pitch shifts to a higher frequency (1 to 2 kHz, which is called *hyperphonation;* Truby & Lind, 1965). Interest in the pain cry comes from a desire by investigators to study cry characteristics under standardized conditions. There is also diagnostic value in pain cry analysis; the pain cries of infants with Down's syndrome are longer, lower in pitch, and flatter in melody type compared with normal infants (Wasz-Höckert *et al.*, 1968). However, because the cry patterns following a painful stimulus gradually settle into the basic pattern observed under other conditions (Wolff, 1969), there are likely to be structural transitions between these two distinctive cry types. In support of this idea, Young and Gouin DeCarie (1977) note that crying (*wail* in their terminology) changes to harsher crying (*harsh wail*) with continued distress. Further, Wasz-Höckert *et al.* (1968) mention that the crying of infants left for 7 hours without feeding assumes some of the characteristics of pain cries.

## 3. VOCAL REPERTOIRE OF HUMAN INFANTS

Babies make many sounds besides crying. These include laugh, grunt, whimper, coo, and hum (all terms from Maskarinec, Cairns, Butterfield, & Weamer, 1981). Cooing appears as early as 6 weeks of age

(Stark, 1980), but the equivalent "pleasure signal" (Wasz-Höckert *et al.*, 1968) more commonly occurs first at around 3 months, in the context of being well-fed, held, and reciprocally smiling with the mother or other familiar adult. Cooing is predominantly tonal. Each coo has a duration of about 1 second, a flat or rising/falling melody pattern, and usually lacks glottal plosives. Laughter appears at 4 to 5 weeks (Wolff, 1969). Whimper has not been clearly described structurally, but it is a fussing sound usually associated with crying (Maskarinec *et al.*, 1981). Humming is evidently not a common sound, judging by its general absence in the literature on infant sounds. However, it has been heard from some infants while sucking and swallowing milk (Ostwald, 1972). Stark (1980) has described a number of "vegetative sounds" containing consonantal elements and occurring mainly during nursing. In the newborn period, these consonant elements are predominantly made up of stops, clicks, friction noises, and trills.

## 4. VOCAL BEHAVIOR OF INFANT PRIMATES: AN OVERVIEW

Ethologists and others interested in the evolution of primate communication and its associated physiological mechanisms have provided a wealth of information regarding the vocal behavior of nonhuman primates. This section will provide an overview of the information pertaining to infant vocalizations.

Most primate infants have, at birth, a well-developed grasping reflex that facilitates clinging to the mother's fur as she travels. In species where the infant clings to the mother's ventrum, the mother will often aid her infant's grasp by supporting the baby with one hand or arm. In species where infants are transported on the mother's back this assistance is, of course, not possible, but at the same time it is less necessary. Newborn primate infants share with their human counterparts a rooting reflex to assist in finding the nipple. Communication gestures from newborn primates are generally restricted in number of types or frequency of occurrence, although remarkably adultlike patterns have been recorded within the first few days after birth (e.g., the squirrel monkey; Ploog, Hopf, & Winter, 1967). In the earliest stages of life, primate infants generally do little more than nurse and sleep. Nevertheless, they are as capable as newborn human infants in their vocal abilities. As is the case with humans, infants of other primate species use a range of different sounds in various situations, including searching for the nipple, nursing, or interacting with individuals besides the mother (see, for example,

Winter, 1968). There are apparently no recordings of the "birth cry" of a nonhuman primate infant. Birth cries may not be common, in as much as sounds could attract a predator to mother and infant and would have been selected against in the course of evolution. Crying in hunger is likewise a rare event in nature, inasmuch as the baby and mother are always together in most primate species, and the nipple is therefore always available for nursing. There is one situation that reliably evokes crying, however. That is the physical separation of a baby from its mother.

## 5. THE ISOLATION CALL OF PRIMATES

Occasionally in the wild an infant will accidentally fall off of its mother. Particularly in aboreal species, the two members of the mother–infant dyad may lose visual contact with each other. This event touches off a stream of sound from the infant, providing the mother with the cues necessary to achieve successful retrieval. So rare a situation in nature is unlikely to have human witnesses, which is attested to by the paucity of documentation on this topic in the literature. However, essentially the same conditions of mother–infant separation can be created in captivity, and it is from human intervention with captive animals that we have obtained most of the information about vocalizations of separated infants, the manner in which mothers locate and retrieve their offspring, and the details of mother–infant communication in general.

The structural characteristics of the infant cry, or "isolation call," across a wide range of primate species, is incomplete due to inadequate data. However, based on existing descriptions some general statements about their structure is possible: (1) isolation calls are longer and louder than other sounds made by the infant; (2) the basic structure consists of a continuous tonality, sometimes with an overlay of noise; (3) structural variability in a bout of crying increases with length of time separated or as the mother comes closer; (4) where the isolation call persists into adulthood, there is fixation of a stereotyped structure, providing the possibility for species-, geographic-, and individual-specific markers.

The detailed nature of a species' isolation call is often unclear from behavioral accounts. This is due, in part, to diverse terminology. Infants separated from their mothers are variously said to utter *distress cries*, *lost calls*, *long calls*, or *isolation calls*. Perhaps best of all would be *separation calls*, because these encompass the situation of only partial isolation. However, *isolation call* best describes the context in which these sounds occur.

## 5.1. Prosimians

Andrew (1963) described vocal patterns of several prosimian primates that he considered to represent early stages in the evolution of mammalian vocal behavior. These patterns are evidently derived from typical "protective" responses, in which the eyes and nostrils are closed, the mouth corners are withdrawn, and an expulsion of air is forced through the closed glotti. The full pattern is evident in the infant isolation call of some galagos (*Galago crassicaudatus* and *G. senegalensis*); respiratory movements cease; a low grin develops; at its widest extent, the grin is followed by a violent expiration and abdominal contractions. The resulting vocalization is described as a single loud click. Lemur infants also produce clicks. However, personal experience with three species indicates that long and loud isolation calls occur in the genus *Lemur*, particularly when a familiar adult is calling back to the separated infant. *Lemur catta* infants produce isolation calls that are tonal and rich in harmonics, starting at about 1 kHz. *Lemur fulvus* and *Lemur macaco*, on the other hand, produce isolation calls in which the tonal elements are largely obscured by noise, although the frequency range and duration overlap those of *L. catta* (see Figure 1).

## 5.2. New World Primates

The isolation calls of New World (platyrrhine) primate infants have been described for several species. Marmosets and tamarins (Callitrichidae) produce tonal sounds, like the "long calls" of *Saguinus fuscicollis* (Hodun, Snowdon, & Soini, 1981), the "long whistle" of *Saguinus geoffroyi* (Moynihan, 1970), the "shrilling calls" of *Callithrix jacchus* (Pook, 1977), the "te call" of *Oedipomidas spixi* (Epple, 1968), and the "infant J call" of *Cebuella pygmaea* (Pola & Snowdon, 1975). Oppenheimer (1977) has remarked on the structural similarities in the isolation calls of several platyrrhine species. Members of the Cebidae also produce long tonal isolation calls. In *Callicebus moloch*, most of the acoustic energy in the isolation call is above 8 kHz (Robinson, 1979). In spider monkeys (*Ateles fusciceps robustus*), the "eee-awk" isolation call is long, loud, and ascending in pitch (Eisenberg, 1976). Howler monkey infants (*Alouatta palliata*) produce a "caw" when separated from their mothers (Baldwin & Baldwin, 1976). The infants of squirrel monkeys (*Saimiri sciureus*), about which I shall have more to say, produce a long, tonal isolation call known as the "isolation peep" (Lieblich, Symmes, Newman, & Shapiro, 1980; Winter, Ploog, & Latta, 1966).

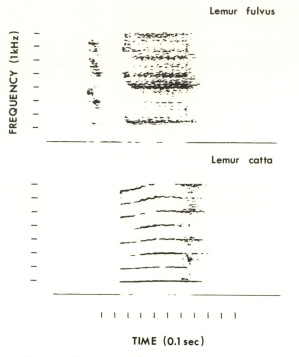

*Figure 1.* Isolation calls of two lemur species recorded at the Duke Primate Center from infants briefly separated from their mothers. The calls are recognizeably different; that of *Lemur catta* is a nasal tone with well-defined harmonics, whereas the raucous isolation call of *Lemur fulvus* has tonal components obscured by noise.

## 5.3. Old World Monkeys

Among Old World monkeys, isolation calls have been described in two major genera, *Macaca* and *Cercopithecus*, with scattered additions from elsewhere in the Catarrhini. The isolation calls of *Cercopithecus* species are predominantly tonal calls with a fundamental under 1 kHz and a duration of .3 second or longer (Figure 16 in Gautier & Gautier, 1977). One species (*Cercopithecus aethiops*) produces two isolation calls, one continuous and one fragmented (Struhsaker, 1967). Macaque isolation calls are similar in general structure to those of *Cercopithecus*. Chevalier-Skolnikoff (1974) found that infant stumptail macaques (*Macaca arctoides*) produce "trilled whistles" beginning around 2 weeks of age, with "clear whistles" appearing around week 4. Older infants produce variations of the "coo" heard from adults. Lillehei and Snowdon (1978)

found that coo variants produced in isolation by this species were structurally equivalent to certain calls described by Green (1975) for the
Japanese macaque (*Macaca fuscata*). Green reported that infants initially
produced coo variants when isolated, but if not retrieved by their mothers, they eventually began making squeals and screeches. Green (1981)
also studied the vocalizations of the lion-tailed macaque (*Macaca silenus*),
where the infant isolation calls are "whistly" tonal calls, frequency modulated over an octave or more. Infant pigtailed macaques (*Macaca nemestrina*) produce a long cry early in infancy, which is a train of harsh sounds
with occasional blurred harmonic episodes (Grimm, 1967). An extended
long cry lasts about 3 seconds and has internal components separated
by .1 to .2 seconds, a temporal pattern similar to that of crying by human
infants. Older separated infant pigtailed macaques make a harsh coo
variant (Simons & Bielert, 1973). Infant calls of the rhesus macaque
(*Macaca mulatta*) have been described by Rowell and Hinde (1962). When
young babies are left by their mother, they make high, rising calls, which
get longer and louder with time. They also make a long, high, plaintive
sound that causes adult females to approach the baby and "mother" it.
Older infants make repeated "clear calls" (coo) when separated from
their mother. Newman and Symmes (1974) described various abnormalities in the isolation calls of rhesus infants deprived of maternal
contact from birth. These abnormalities were not the result of a lack of
auditory experience because the animals were permitted to hear and see
normal adults and infants reared with their mothers (see Figure 2).

## 5.4. Great Apes

And so we arrive at a consideration of ape infants (Hominoidea).
Various persons have had occasion to raise ape infants from soon after
birth and to compare their behavioral development to that of human
infants. Reference to their vocal behavior is rare, however, particularly
spectrographic analyses. There is a suggestion that gorilla infants cry
very much in the same manner as do human babies. Fossey (1972)
described the infant cry in mountain gorillas (*Gorilla gorilla beringei*) as
resembling the cries of human infants. One cry bout lasted 18.9 seconds,
each unit of which ranged from .05 to .15 seconds. Cry units were
predominantly tonal, the lowest frequency component occurring below
1.2 kHz. Crying was heard only from infants (individuals to 3 years of
age), and occurred when left behind or when otherwise needing assistance from their mother. The cries of newborn gorillas are more like

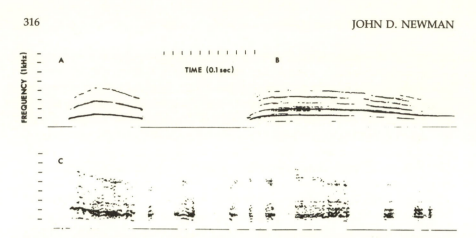

*Figure 2.* (A) Infant isolation call of a mother-reared rhesus macaque; (B) human infant isolation call (first call in a series, after infant is taken from mother); (C) call of a rhesus macaque raised in partial social isolation. The basic tonal structure and smoothly changing frequency of the normal macaque and human infant isolation calls resemble closely the same attributes in prosimian isolation calls (see Figure 1). This suggests a conservative evolution for isolation calls across a wide range of primates. Abnormalities in the cries of neurologically defective human infants include increased duration, fragmentation, and loss of smooth frequency changes (see Wasz-Höckert *et al.*, 1968). As shown in (C), calls of some infant macaques deprived of normal maternal rearing also show these same abnormalities (see Newman & Symmes, 1974).

weak puppy whines (Fossey, 1979). The infants of chimpanzees (*Pan troglodytes*), as described by Lawick-Goodall (1968, 1969), make a "hoo whimper" when trying to reach their mother or her nipple. Mother chimps respond to this call by retrieving the infant and positioning it for suckling. Older infants utter louder hoarse yells and screams after losing contact with their mother. A mother will run to her infant, then cradle and embrace it after such episodes. Andrew (1963, p. 71) relates the description by Ladygina-Kots of chimpanzee crying: At its lowest intensity, the calls are soft interrupted groans, becoming louder, and finally a series of roars; the infant during these intense cries is passive and unresponsive.

## 5.5. Primate Isolation Call Structure: Summary

It is hoped that this brief overview has established that cry patterns across a wide range of primate species share the basic pattern of a gradually frequency-modulated tonality. This widespread similarity suggests that the mechanisms controlling infant cry patterns have had a conservative evolutionary history. Since primate infants and their mothers have essentially the same mutual relationships across the entire primate order, it seems reasonable to assume that patterns of mother–infant communication have been under little selection pressure to change. Hence, where species differences do exist in infant cry structure, the extent of these differences likely represents the extent of genetic relatedness of the species involved. However, where the isolation call persists in adults, it may acquire the secondary role of helping to maintain spatial isolation between closely related sympatric species, thereby reducing the opportunity for interbreeding, and, as a consequence of this function, greater structural differences may have evolved in those species.

## 6. INHERITANCE OF ISOLATION CALL CHARACTERISTICS

A major role for genetic programming of the underlying neural substrate controlling cry patterns appears likely. However, few attempts have been made to document the ontogeny and inheritability of primate infant cry characteristics. At the National Institutes of Health, we have investigated these questions in the squirrel monkey, focusing on isolation calls. The procedure for obtaining these vocalizations in the laboratory involves capturing the mother, gently lifting the infant off of the mother's back, and placing it on a soft surrogate inside a small open mesh cage. Virtually all baby squirrel monkeys cry as soon as they are separated from their mother. During the separation process, the cries are noisy screams. Once alone in the recording studio, however, the infant settles down to a steady stream of cries that have a relatively consistent tonal structure. These calls are the "isolation peeps" (Winter et al., 1966).

Originally described as the isolation call of adults separated from their social companions, it is now clear that the isolation peep (IP) is present at birth. Infant versions have a marked resemblance to the adult call (Lieblich et al., 1980; Winter, 1968; Winter, Handley, Ploog, & Schott, 1973). Some aspects of IP morphology change with maturation, such as a lengthening in duration and a more gradual frequency modulation (Lieblich et al., 1980; Newman & Symmes, 1982). However, there are two attributes ("descriptors") of the IP in newborns that do not change throughout the life of the animal. These are the position in the call where the highest frequency occurs ("peak frequency location," or PFL) and the slope and direction of frequency change at the call terminus ("tail slope," or TL) (Symmes, Newman, Talmage-Riggs, & Lieblich, 1979). There are two types of squirrel monkey, insofar as the IP and these two descriptors are concerned. IPs with a PFL of 90% or more (i.e., the highest frequency is located in the last 10% of the call) and with a positive TL (i.e., frequency direction is upward at the end) are called *Roman*. IPs with an earlier PFL and negative TL are called *Gothic*. The terms *Roman* and *Gothic* are derivations of *Roman arch* and *Gothic arch*, names given to these same two kinds of monkeys based on differences in the shape of the whitish periorbital hair (MacLean, 1964). It is likely that these are really two different species, although the taxonomic status of different squirrel monkey types is presently unclear (see discussion in Newman & Symmes, 1982).

Because the features distinguishing Roman and Gothic IPs are present at birth (Lieblich *et al.*, 1980; Newman & Symmes, 1982), it is probable that these differences in IP morphology are genetically programmed and may, therefore, be investigated as inherited traits. Roman-arch and Gothic-arch monkeys will interbreed and produce viable offspring in captivity, providing the opportunity to determine the inheritance patterns of IP structural differences in "hybrid" offspring. We have found that the Roman trait is expressed more consistently than is the Gothic. This is especially true if the mother is the Roman-arch variety (Newman & Symmes, 1982). Where the mother is of the Gothic-arch type, hybrids are more variable, producing both IP phenotypes.

## 7. ONTOGENY OF ISOLATION CALLS

Although the IP occurs throughout life, there are other calls produced by the isolated individual that are present only during early development. These latter sounds are highly variable in structure, quite unlike the IP in this respect, and are generally characterized by multiple slope reversals (giving the call a quavering quality) and noisy segments. Some begin or end with the tonal structure of an IP but elsewhere break up into a complex sound with closely spaced harmonics superimposed on noise. They are so varied that it is difficult to find a single descriptive term for them. Ploog *et al.* (1967) used the term *Schrei-Piepen*. I will call them *infantile isolation calls* (IIC). They are heard exclusively from infants, being completely absent by the time an infant reaches 1 year of age (Lieblich *et al.*, 1980). This is about the same age that an individual's IP reaches its fully mature, adult dimensions; hence it is possible that the IICs are a reflection of neural circuitry undergoing maturation. If that is the case, it would be of interest to know whether this neural circuitry is replaced or is suppressed by a subsequently developing neural network that comes into play during adult vocal behavior. Experiments conducted on adult squirrel monkeys suggest that the latter hypothesis is the more likely one (Newman & MacLean, 1982; see Figure 3).

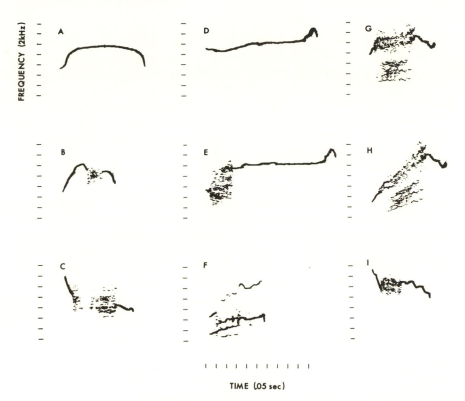

TIME (.05 sec)

*Figure 3.* (A–C) isolation calls of a normal infant Gothic-arch squirrel monkey. (A) Gothic isolation peep; (B) and (C), infantile isolation calls. (D–F), isolation calls of a normal infant Roman-arch squirrel monkey. (D), Roman isolation peep; (E) and (F), infantile isolation calls. (G–I), calls from an adult Gothic-arch squirrel monkey with bilateral lesions in the thalamic tegmentum. The illustrated calls resemble infantile isolation calls (compare G with B, H with F, and I with C) and were given while the subject ranged freely around the monkey holding room.

## 8. NEURAL SUBSTRATES OF ISOLATION CALLS

In the course of investigating the neural substrates underlying the production of isolation calls in squirrel monkeys, we found that two animals with experimental brain lesions produced some isolation calls with infantile characteristics. Both were fully mature adult Gothic-arch males. One individual, with a lesion that spanned the periventricular gray substance to connect the peripeduncular regions on either side of the thalamus, produced both typical adult IPs and infantile fricative sounds. Many of his IPs had abnormal subharmonics along with the typical higher fundamental. The infantile sounds and the abnormal IPs were present for many months aftery surgery but were eventually completely replaced by normal adult IPs. In a second animal, the lesions spared the periventricular gray but destroyed extensive parts of the peripeduncular regions as well as the subthalamic nuclei bilaterally. This animal produced infantile isolation calls only when permitted to move freely about the monkey colony room. When in complete isolation, he uttered typical adult IPs. The histological findings and further description of all the subjects in this study are given in more detail elsewhere (Newman & MacLean, 1982).

Brain damage is often looked upon as removing some function or behavioral capacity. In the case of these squirrel monkeys, however, the lesions resulted in the reappearance of behavior patterns normally absent in adults. It seems likely that this is due to disruption of the neural circuitry normally responsible for the stereotyped and regular tonal quality of adult isolation calls. Presumably, this circuitry is not completely functional in infants, and, as a result, isolation calls with noisy or variable frequency components are occasionally produced.


## 9. CONCLUSIONS

Two themes emerge from this overview that bear directly on the mechanisms and evolution of crying in human infants. One is the widespread occurrence of similar patterns of crying behavior in primate infants, suggesting that the adaptive significance and structural attributes of crying represent ancient and fundamental aspects of primate evolution. That the functional and communicative significance of infant vocalizations in humans has not changed very much from other primate infants appears likely. Because we cannot ask babies directly what they feel or what their sounds mean, the methods used to interpret the meaning of sounds in other primates should have direct applicability in evaluating the meaning of human infant sounds. A second theme addressed in this chapter is that genetic mechanisms play a significant role in programming the neural circuitry underlying the production of infant vocalizations. The clinical descriptions of cry structure in genetically and neurologically abnormal infants suggest that the structural attributes of infant vocalizations may be particularly sensitive monitors of normal neural development. Having found the squirrel monkey to be a useful species for studying both the inheritance patterns and neural control mechanisms of primate isolation calls, it would be worthwhile to look for similar mechanisms in other primate species. This comparative approach should prove to be particularly helpful where questions regarding phylogenetically stable mechanisms are at issue.

## 10. REFERENCES

Andrew, R. J. The origin and evolution of the calls and facial expressions of the primates. *Behaviour*, 1963, *20*, 1–109.

Baldwin, J. D., & Baldwin, J. I. Vocalizations of howler monkeys (*Alouatta palliata*) in southwestern Panama. *Folia Primatologica*, 1976, *26*, 81–108.

Bell, S. M., & Ainsworth, M. D. Infant crying and maternal responsiveness. *Child Development*, 1972, *43*, 1171–1190.

Bowlby, J. The nature of the child's tie to his mother. *International Journal of Pediatrics*, 1958, *39*, 350–373.

Chevalier-Skolnikoff, S. The ontogeny of communication in the stumptail macaque (*Macaca arctoides*). *Contributions to Primatology*, 1974, *2*, 1–174.

Eisenberg, J. R. Communication mechanisms and social integration in the Black Spider Monkey, *Ateles fusciceps robustus*, and related species. *Smithsonian Contributions to Zoology*, 1976, *213*, 1–108.

Epple, G. Comparative studies on vocalization in marmoset monkeys (Hapalidae). *Folia Primatologica*, 1968, *8*, 1–40.

Formby, D. Maternal recognition of infant's cry. *Developmental Medicine and Child Neurology*, 1967, *9*, 293–298.

Fossey, D. Vocalizations of the Mountain Gorilla (*Gorilla gorilla beringei*). *Animal Behaviour*, 1972, *20*, 36–53.

Fossey, D. Development of the Mountain Gorilla (*Gorilla gorilla beringei*): The first thirty-six months. In D. A. Hamburg & E. R. McCown (Eds.), *The great apes*. Menlo Park: Benjamin/Cummins, 1979.

Gautier, J.-P., & Gautier, A. Communication in Old World monkeys. In T. A. Sebeok (Eds.), *How animals communicate*. Bloomington: Indiana University Press, 1977.

Green, S. Variation of vocal pattern with social situation in the Japanese monkey (*Macaca fuscata*): A field study. In L. A. Rosenblum (Ed.), *Primate behavior: Developments in field and laboratory research* (Vol. 4). New York: Academic Press, 1975.

Green, S. Sex differences and age gradations in vocalizations of Japanese and Lion-tailed monkeys. *American Zoologist*, 1981, *21*, 165–184.

Grimm, R. J. Catalogue of sounds of the Pigtailed Macaque (*Macaca nemistrina*). *Journal of Zoology, London*, 1967, *152*, 361–373.

Hodun, A., Snowdon, C. T., & Soini, P. Subspecific variation in the long calls of the tamarin, *Saguinus fuscicollis*. *Zeitschrift für Tierpsychologie*, 1981, *57*, 97–110.

Lawick-Goodall, J. van. A preliminary report on expressive movements and communication in the Gombe Stream chimpanzees. In P. C. Jay (Ed.), *Primates: Studies in adaptation and variability*. New York: Holt, Rinehart & Winston, 1968.

Lawick-Goodall, J. van. Mother–offspring relationships in free-ranging chimpanzees. In D. Morris (Ed.), *Primate ethology*. Garden City: Doubleday, 1969.

Lieblich, A. K., Symmes, D., Newman, J. D., & Shapiro, M. Development of the isolation peep in laboratory bred squirrel monkeys. *Animal Behaviour*, 1980, *28*, 1–9.

Lillehei, R. A., & Snowdon, C. T. Individual and situational differences in the vocalizations of young Stumptail Macaques (*Macaca arctoides*). *Behaviour*, 1978, *65*, 270–281.

MacLean, P. D. Mirror display in the squirrel monkey, *Saimiri sciureus*. *Science*, 1964, *146*, 950–952.

Maskarinec, A. S., Cairns, G. F., Butterfield, E. C., & Weamer, D. K. Longitudinal observations of individual infant's vocalizations. *Journal of Speech and Hearing Disorders*, 1981, *46*, 267–273.

Moynihan, M. Some behavior patterns of platyrrhine monkeys. II. *Saguinus geoffroyi* and some other tamarins. *Smithsonian Contributions to Zoology*, 1970, *28*, 1–77.

Newman, J. D., & MacLean, P. D. Effects of tegmental lesions on the isolation call of squirrel monkeys. *Brain Research*, 1982, *232*, 317–329.

Newman, J. D., & Symmes, D. Vocal pathology in socially deprived monkeys. *Developmental Psychobiology*, 1974, *7*, 351–358.

Newman, J. D., & Symmes, D. Inheritance and experience in the acquisition of primate acoustic behavior. In C. T. Snowdon, C. H. Brown, & M. R. Petersen (Eds.), *Primate communication*. New York: Cambridge University Press, 1982.

Oppenheimer, J. R. Communication in New World monkeys. In T. A. Sebeok (Ed.), *How animals communicate*. Bloomington: Indiana University Press, 1977.

Ostwald, P. The sounds of infancy. *Developmental Medicine and Child Neurology*, 1972, *14*, 350–361.

Ostwald, P. F., Phibbs, R., & Fox, S. Diagnostic use of infant cry. *Biologia Neonatorum*, 1968, *13*, 68–83.

Ploog, D., Hopf, S., & Winter, P. Ontogenese des Verhaltens von Totenkopf-Affen (*Saimiri sciureus*). *Psychologische Forschung*, 1967, *31*, 1–41.

Pola, Y. V., & Snowdon, C. T. The vocalizations of pygmy marmosets (*Cebuella pygmaea*). *Animal Behaviour*, 1975, *23*, 826–842.

Pook, A. G. A comparative study of the use of contact calls in *Saguinus fuscicollis* and *Callithrix jacchus*. In D. G. Kleiman (Ed.), *The biology and conservation of the Callitrichidae*. Washington, D.C.: Smithsonian Institution, 1977.

Prechtl, H. F. R., Theorell, K., Gramsbergen, A., & Lind, J. A statistical analysis of cry patterns in normal and abnormal newborn infants. *Developmental Medicine and Child Neurology*, 1969, *11*, 142–152.

Prescott, R. Infant cry sound developmental features. *Journal of the Acoustical Society of America*, 1975, *57*, 1186–1191.

Robinson, J. G. An analysis of the organization of vocal communication in the titi monkey (*Callicebus moloch*). *Zeitschrift für Tierpsychologie*, 1979, *49*, 381–405.

Rowell, T. E., & Hinde, R. A. Vocal communication by the rhesus monkey (*Macaca mulatta*). *Proceedings of the Zoological Society of London*, 1962, *138*, 279–294.

Simons, R. C., & Bielert, C. F. An experimental study of vocal communication between mother and infant monkeys (*Macaca nemestrina*). *American Journal of Physical Anthropology*, 1973, *28*, 455–462.

Stark, R. E. Stages of speech development in the first year of life. In G. H. Yeni-Komshian, J. F. Kavanagh, & C. A. Ferguson (Eds.), *Child phonology* (Vol. 1). New York: Academic Press, 1980.

Stark, R. E., & Nathanson, S. N. Spontaneous cry in the newborn infant: Sounds and facial gestures. In J. F. Bosma (Ed.), *Development in the fetus and infant, Fourth Symposium on Oral Sensation and Perception*. Bethesda, Md.: U.S. Department of Health, Education and Welfare, 1973.

Struhsaker, T. T. Auditory communication among vervet monkeys. (*Cercopithecus aethiops*). In S. A. Altman (Ed.), *Social communication among primates*. Chicago: University of Chicago Press, 1967.

Symmes, D., Newman, J. D., Talmage-Riggs, G., & Lieblich, A. K. Individuality and stability of isolation peeps in squirrel monkeys. *Animal Behaviour*, 1979, 27, 1142–1152.

Truby, H. M., & Lind, J. Cry sounds of the newborn infant. In J. Lind (Ed.), Newborn infant cry. *Acta Paediatrica Scandinavica*, 1965, 163 (Suppl.).

Wasz-Höckert, O., Lind, J., Vuorenkoski, V., Partanen, T., & Valanne, E. The infant cry: A spectrographic and auditory analysis. *Clinics in Developmental Medicine* 29. Philadelphia: Lippincott, 1968.

Winter, P. Social communication in the squirrel monkey. In L. A. Rosenblum & R. W. Cooper (Eds.), *The squirrel monkey*. New York: Academic Press, 1968.

Winter, P., Ploog, D., & Latta, J. Vocal repertoire of the squirrel monkey (*Saimiri sciureus*), Its analysis and significance. *Experimental Brain Research*, 1966, 1, 359–384.

Winter, P., Handley, P., Ploog, D., & Schott, D. Ontogeny of squirrel monkey calls under normal conditions and under acoustic isolation. *Behaviour*, 1973, 47, 230–239.

Wolff, P. The natural history of crying and other vocalizations in early infancy. In B. M. Foss (Ed.), *Determinants of infant behaviour* (Vol. 4). London: Methuen, 1969.

Young, G., & Gouin DeCarie, T. An ethology-based catalogue of facial/vocal behaviour in infancy. *Animal Behaviour*, 1977, 25, 95–107.

# 15

# Application of Cry Research to Clinical Perspectives

## T. BERRY BRAZELTON

## 1. INTRODUCTION

The first cry of the infant that accompanies his or her entry into the world heralds his or her integrity. If his or her cry is lusty and full bodied, it serves the important purpose of expanding and filling the lungs, and it says to those around, "I'm ready to go." Until recently, a successful delivery was thought of as one in which an actively crying baby was the result. Crying was expected to speed up the baby's pulmonary effectiveness, as he or she made the transition from a passive recipient of oxygenation via the placenta to more active pulmonary oxygenation. As Leboyer (1975) and others have pointed out, the cry of the newborn is not a necessary part of its transition from dependent fetal circulation to independent cardiorespiratory effectiveness, but it does speed it up. Normal, healthy babies can make the transition without crying, but they probably achieve the physiological balance with their new environment more slowly. No research on the relative merits for the infant of either of these conditions—crying or not crying—has been reported, to the best of my knowledge.

T. BERRY BRAZELTON • Division of Child Development, The Children's Hospital, and Department of Pediatrics, Harvard Medical School, Boston, Massachusetts 02115.

The fact that the initial cry of the newborn could carry important diagnostic information was first reported 20 years ago by Karelitz and Fisichelli (1962). On the strength of this, Wasz-Höckert and his associates in Sweden have opened a whole new area of research on the initial cry (Wasz-Höckert, Lind, Vuorenkoski, Partanen, & Valanne, 1968). This has become an exciting window into the early behavioral diagnosis of well-being or pathology of the neonate. At a time when physiological research on sick and premature infants was rapidly expanding, our ability to protect these babies from central nervous system damage and to preserve the integrity of the nervous system was also expanding. Early assessment of these infants has been becoming more critical as a way of monitoring success or nonsuccess of our interventions and of identifying babies who continue to be at risk.

Recently, we have become aware of the importance of identifying at-risk infants for early intervention. The opportunities for salvaging neuromotor, cognitive, and affective function in early infancy has just begun to be tapped (Brazelton, 1982; Brazelton & Lester, 1983). If the impaired infant can be identified early, the opportunities for offering him or her an environment that is appropriate to his or her needs can be addressed. St. James Roberts (1979) identifies five pathways for recovery of an impaired central nervous system (CNS), if the lesion is present in an immature organism: (1) vicarious functioning of other areas of the brain; (2) equipotentiality or redundancy of other pathways; (3) behavioral substitution of other unimpaired systems; (4) regrowth after trauma, which can be impaired or aided by supersensitivity of remaining pathways and their neurotransmitter systems; and (5) diaschisis, or the post-traumatic disruption of systems around the lesion that interfere with function.

Of the five pathways for recovery, one would depend on appropriate input for the development of optimal function and recovery. Hence, an early identification of the impaired infant, coupled with an understanding of his or her level of organization and his or her capacity to receive and organize information from the environment, could be critical to recovery (Brazelton & Lester, 1983). With appropriate input for organizing in spite of CNS or autonomic deviations, the baby's outcome can be expected to be improved significantly (Sell, 1980).

Until recently, assessment of the neonate's neurological integrity was confined to neurological evaluations (Prechtl & Beintema, 1964). These techniques are able to identify groups of severely damaged infants, but they have not been very helpful in predicting recovery from CNS insult or in identifying marginally impaired or depressed newborns. The "gray" areas of identification and prediction to recovery were left wide open to behavioral scientists. Newborn neurological exams were successful in identifying the babies who had severe CNS insults and whose atypical neurological behavior signified an irrecoverable insult, but they were not as successful in predicting to those babies who might recover from their CNS insult. Using the Neonatal Behavioral Assessment Scale (Brazelton, 1973) in the first week, we were able to predict recovery in a number of infants, despite CNS deficits (Tronick & Brazelton, 1975). Their ability to alert and attend to auditory, visual, and other events, to control states of consciousness in order to attend, to have smooth fluid movements in alert state, to shut out disturbing stimuli successfully, and to improve in all these functions over the first few days were the behavioral predictors of recovery. Thus, behavioral organization and responsiveness became a powerful window into future CNS reorganization.

## 2. DIAGNOSTIC USE

The scientists in this book interested in acoustic cry analysis have entered this field of identification and early intervention and have begun to identify important diagnostic information conveyed by the initial cry, by the hunger cry, by the pain cry, and even by the cry of a satisfied state.

The range of cries in normal and in marginal babies is of importance as a baseline and offers us a whole new window into the functional aspects of the central nervous system of prematures (see Chapter 5), of small-for-gestational-age babies (Lester, 1976; Zeskind & Lester, 1981), of postmature babies (Zeskind & Lester, 1981), and even of potential SIDS victims (Golub, 1979).

The acoustical information contained in the cry that pertains to CNS and cardiorespiratory function becomes an important confirmation of the clinician's diagnostic acumen. As the clinician listens, he or she assesses the baby for well-being or for pathology, often at a less-than-conscious level. The parent of a newborn also depends upon his or her own impression about the baby's cry. The parent may well label the baby in the same way as does the clinician, by type of cry (see Chapter 9).

Identification of the normal spectra and of abnormal cries will be of real value to the clinician as a diagnostic tool to help him or her in his or her own observations. The cry can become a predictor for the clinician of the parents' reactions to the baby. By analyzing his or her own reactions, he or she can identify early with the parents. Hence, for the clinician, the cry can become a more meaningful diagnostic window to utilize than he or she dares to rely on at present. The parameters that are being delineated as normal and as abnormal in these chapters are clearly identifiable by the trained and the untrained ear. As the cry patterns are better identified, the clinician will become more sure in his or her use of the cry as a diagnostic entity.

The fact that the variations in cry behavior are correlated with behavioral responsiveness on the Neonatal Behavioral Assessment Scale (Lester, 1979) becomes confirmation that both types of assessments are on the right track of being able to identify at-risk or deviant newborns early.

Clinicians have identified the more severe disorders of cri-du-chat and of hypothyroidism by the cry of the newborn for many years. To extend this area of diagnostic acumen is an exciting prospect. The initial cry could be the first point in a routine noninvasive screening evaluation of the newborn. If the infant's cry is out of the acceptable range of normal, it places him or her in a diagnostic category for further evaluation. Among other screening assessments, the opportunity to assess the cry as the neonate responds to pain, to discomfort, and to hunger might give us the kind of information about range of behavior that other assessment techniques are beginning to give us. Using the Neonatal Behavioral Assessment Scale (Brazelton, 1973), we have found that the range of behaviors as we use states of consciousness from sleep and withdrawn states to involved alert states gives us a comprehensive picture of the neonate. The infant's capacity to respond differentially to positive and negative stimuli within each state reflects his or her range of adaptability. Within acceptable ranges, the wider and richer the range of behavior, the more intact is the CNS. If the baby is under the stress of an acute CNS insult, of being small for gestational age (SGA), of being premature, or of depression from maternal medication, his or her range of responsivity to positive as well as negative experiences is likely to be more limited. But these limits of variability can help us to differentiate at-risk babies from normal babies. Improvement in range and flexibility of responsiveness becomes a reflection of the infant's recovery in the weeks after birth. In the analysis of the "recovery curves" of the behavioral clusters of the NBAS, we have found that the clusters of range and of use of state, as well as of orientation to positive stimuli, are among the most useful predictors of well-being and of recovery (Lester, 1983). If the behavior and the cry are indeed correlated, patterns of acoustic cry features recorded over repeated assessments can become another window into organization of the neonat's CNS as he or she responds over time to the new environment.

As with neonatal behavior, the range of cry features might indicate recovery of the baby and be more important as predictors than would any single cry parameter. Multiple behavioral parameters and repeated assessments would be likely to be the optimal ways to assess deficits and predict to recovery or the need for early intervention.

## 3. PARENTAL ROLE

The fact that parents can identify as early as they do their own baby's cry from others (Weisenfield, Zander Malatesta, DeLoach, 1981) and that they can rapidly identify the meaning behind the different cries (Boukydis, 1979) means to me that there is receptor programming in the new parent that is finely tuned to the significance of different cries as part of the burgeoning attachment process. That the new parent labels his or her baby by the cry has significance (Boukydis & Burgess, 1982) in how he or she categorizes the baby—normal, suspect, or abnormal. The clinician who is concerned with enhancing the parent–infant attachment had best be in tune with this signaling system and its deep significance to parents who are trying to understand their baby. If they claim to the clinician that "the baby's cry gets to us," he or she will do well to understand what they are saying. In order to do so, the clinician must be sensitive to his or her own response to the baby's cry as a diagnostic instrument. This volume will expand his or her view of the significance of the cry as it reflects CNS and autonomic function as well as its "informational" (its meaning to others) and "categorical" (its meaning to the infant) meanings. This research volume carries an opportunity for clinicians to understand the significance of the cry in the baby.

I first became aware of the importance of the cry of the infant when I went into pediatric practice. The telephone hour saved for parents at the beginning of the day used to be almost entirely taken up with parental concerns about their infant's crying. As a pediatrician geared to treating and curing symptoms of distress, I joined parents in their increasingly frantic search for "solutions" to their baby's crying. Day after day, as their tension mounted, so did the duration and the quality of the crying. The fussy crying that they had first reported was now building up into desperate, "colicky" crying in which the whole organism of the baby— gastrointestinal, autonomic, motor—was involved. As we tried unsuccessful remedies, the parents' anxieties mounted, and I realized that my inability to find "the magical cure" for crying that they visualized as part of their search for being adequate parents was playing into the mounting tension in the environment that the baby reflected in his or her colic. I knew I was part of the problem.

## 4. NORMATIVE CRY STUDY

I began to collect "normative" data from a group of 80 healthy, normal infants (Brazelton, 1961) to try to delineate the amount of crying that most parents and infants must share in the first 3 months, for it was an accepted fact that colic lasted only 3 months. The biobehavioral shift that Emde, Gaensbauer, and Harmon (1976) later described was apparent in the parents' reports of the cessation of a baby's regular fussing period at around 10 to 12 weeks. In my own work. I was aware that most crying ceased at 12 weeks as a baby became more responsive in other ways.

As a baby's central nervous system matured, the fussy crying at the end of day seemed to disappear. Benjamin (1959) had helped me understand the start of this regular crying period as he described to me

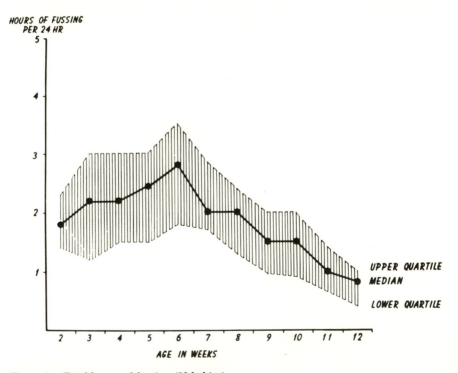

*Figure 1.*   Total hours of fussing (80 babies).

his clinical observation of an earlier biobehavioral shift in a baby's organization around 3 weeks of age. He felt that this shift came at a time when a baby was becoming better organized after the initial adjustment to the new world outside the uterus. It also came at the time when a mother had begun to recover from her own physiological reorganization and was able to look outside herself. Hence, a mother's awareness of the baby increased as the infant became more alert and responsive. Thus Benjamin felt that the fussy crying at the end of the day started at 3 weeks because of a baby's increasing organization and a mother's heightened sensitivity. This first shift in organization coincided with the onset of the regular daily fussy period. Thus, both the beginning and the end of this predictably regular, daily crying was bounded by a maturational shift in the developing central nervous system and in the psychophysiological organization of the baby.

I found that well over half of the 80 babies in my study did cry for predictable periods, usually at the end of the day. The crying was at a regular time of day. It started with a fussy, complaining whimper. If a baby was picked up or his or her diaper was changed, if he or she was talked to or held, the fussing would usually stop for a short period. But, whether a baby was put down or continued to be held, the fussiness resumed in a relatively short time. If the parents continued to search for solutions to stop the infant, each one would work briefly, but a baby would cry again after each new set of stimuli. The fussiness built up to harder and harder crying over the next hour and a half. By the end of the period, the wails were intense, and sobs wracked the baby. It was obviously very difficult for a parent to allow the crying to continue without frequent, repeated attempts at intervention. It was also apparent that almost any intervention that broke through the crying state interfered briefly but not permanently. After the crying period was over, the baby fed actively and well, and slept soundly for a prolonged period.

Parents reported that the crying was heightened at the end of exciting days; usually it came on just as the working father or working mother came home at the end of the day. Increasing tension in the home seemed to carry with it the price of an increase in the duration and intensity of crying in a baby.

As the infants became more and more adept at socializing—at cooing and smiling—the amount of crying decreased. If a baby was adept at sucking on his or her own thumb or could utilize a pacifier or swaddling to help him or her remain calm, there was relatively little crying. Active, intensely driving babies were likely to have long periods of crying, which rapidly built up with more and more activity, startles, and these upset the babies and caused even more crying. High motor activity,

poor consolability, and rapid change of state were predictable characteristics in the newborns to an intense, unreachable crying period at the
end of each day in the first 3 months. These patterns seemed so common
that I began to be convinced that this crying period was probably a
normal part of an active baby's 24-hour sleep/wake cycle. In other words,
the extreme patterns among these babies seemed correlated with an
infant's temperamental type, with other types of activity such as their
abilities to control state shifts, as well as with their self-consoling activity
and with the quality and amount of alert behavior. The quieter, more
easily consolable babies were the only ones who did not cry regularly.
The fussy periods seemed to occur at the end of active efforts to maintain
quiet, alert, responsive states and began to represent to me the "breakdown" that came with exhaustion and represented a discharge phenomenon after the overloading of babies' intake system for receiving and
assimilating information from the environment.

A quiet baby with a high threshold for receiving sensory information from the environment as well as an effectively inexpensive system for shutting it out when he or she was fatigued might not need to
become overloaded and to cry at the end of the day. He or she might
effectively suck the thumb to regulate himself or herself, or he or she
might go to sleep in the face of an exciting environment.

A more active baby whose activity represented a more intense,
driving temperament might also have a lower threshold for receiving
and responding to external stimuli. As the infant received and responded
to auditory, visual, tactile, kinesthetic stimuli, he or she made efforts to
maintain homeostasis of his or her autonomic and central nervous systems throughout the day. As the efforts became more and more expen-
sive and fatigue lent to less effectiveness in controlling his or her
responses, it seemed that a baby's only recourse was to disintegrate in
a period of fussing. This period of active fussing, involving the gastrointestinal, the motor, and the autonomic and central nervous systems,
could then be seen both as a period for discharging overstimulation and
for reorganization toward homeostasis and control over a baby's reactions for the rest of the 24-hour day.

That an immature newborn would make efforts to maintain responsive periods during a 24-hour period seemed obvious as one observed
the infant. Even as a newborn, a well-organized baby made efforts to
hold down his or her interfering motor responses in order to pay prolonged attention to one's face and voice. In a 24-hour day, there were
many such periods of attention, but they seemed to be at some physiological cost to the small babies. The cost to a baby of overloading his
or her receptive and motor central nervous system seemed obvious. The

harder a baby worked, the more he or she seemed to need to disintegrate afterward. Crying at the end of the day began to look to me as if it were a regulatory mechanism that allowed a developing infant to balance the costly but vital mechanisms he or she was mastering as he or she learned to control his or her states of attention (Brazelton, 1961). The babies learned to master their reflex motor activities in order to pay prolonged attention to information from the environment, but it was at some cost to them. After a period of discharge by crying, an infant would sleep more deeply and effectively, and he or she was again available with more prolonged and effective periods of interaction with the environment. Many parents made the association that the fussy period turned into a socially interactive period as the infants developed more and more social competence from the age of 10 to 12 weeks. The reason these crying periods seemed limited to 3 months seemed to coincide with increasing competence of an infant's CNS to respond to and handle sensorimotor responses in other ways. In a period of social interaction, a baby was now able to pay prolonged attention. A baby could smile and gurgle, in long trains of responsive behavior, without overloading his or her systems.

## 5. CRYING AS PART OF NORMAL DEVELOPMENT

By understanding the regular crying of a baby as an important part of his or her day, I could better aid parents toward an understanding of the crying period. No longer need they see it as evidence of pathology or of their failure. If they approached it as a normal part of the day rather than something that demanded a magical cure from them, their approach to a baby could be less frantic, and they could be more objective. No longer need they add their own anxious overreactivity toward quieting an infant, at a time when he or she was already overloaded. By seeing it as a part of an infant's daily activity, I could help them to understand the infant better as a person with the need for both positive and negative reinforcement from the environment at these times. With a look at a baby's total organization of states—from deep to light sleep to alert, then fussy and crying states—rather than at crying as a behavioral symptom, I could become a help for them as they came to understand a baby as parents in the early weeks of a baby's life. Parents who can learn how to anticipate the cycles of state behavior over a 24-hour day are well on their way to an understanding of the basic matrix of their baby. When they cannot understand or work with the whole baby and must concentrate on one aspect, such as crying, their anxiety around such a symptom increases. Then, as they overreact, a baby's crying becomes more intractable and reaches the frantic level of "colic."

A baby seems to pick up his or her parents' anxiety or tension as they handle him or her. A baby is already tired and overloaded, so his or her nervous system is even more sensitive to this tension. As they handle the baby tensely, he or she cries even more, and his or her crying becomes more frantic. I have seen cases in which the 2-hour fussy period became an intractable 8 to 12 hours of insulated, frantic crying. This was called "colic" for the crying simulated the crying of pain. Because a baby's gastrointestinal tract was as hyperactive as was the rest of the body, he or she burped, drew up his or her legs on his or her abdomen as if in pain, passed rectal gas, and it was easy to call this *gastrointestinal* when indeed it had started out as a behavioral discharge of tension. Colic, then, has always appeared to me to be a psychosomatic entity in which a baby and the environment are locked in an ineffective and painful system.

As parents become more upset, and as the baby's crying becomes longer and more entrenched, they feel it as a failure in their parenting. When I cannot reach them to help them deal with it, their failure with their baby's crying becomes an indication for me to become sensitive to the deeper significance of this to them as parents. I then realize that we have more work to do between us to help them toward a successful parent–infant interaction. As Frodi indicates in Chapter 12 (cf. Frodi & Lamb, 1980), crying can become a sign of significant pathology in the parent–child interaction, for in some parents it is a symptom of their own deep-seated disturbance. If it becomes intractable, it can lead to a breakdown as serious as child abuse. Less serious failures in interaction are also indicated by parents who attach too much significance to a baby's crying, and who can not be helped to deal with their anxiety. They are already indicating that they are frightened of the relationship, and a breakdown in it may be anticipated.

## 6. CONSTELLATION OF NEONATAL BEHAVIOR

In attempting to institute anticipatory guidance and to prevent such a breakdown in the developing parent–infant interaction, we utilize the concepts of the Newborn Behavioral Assessment Scale (Brazelton, 1973) as we assess the newborn before discharge. A certain percentage of apparently normal newborns (approximately 10%) will show a combination of the following:

1. Hypersensitivity or overreactivity to stimuli in which

    a. their ability to habituate to stimuli in semisleep states is poor
    b. their reactivity to stimuli throughout the exam shows evidence of overreactivity, such as repeated startling and averting of the eyes, exhaustion after stimulation, and attempting to sleep or cry in order to shut out stimuli

2. Poor state control
    a. An inability to maintain quiet alertness for any relatively long period
    b. Shooting from quiet states to crying and back again to an exhausted state, with either a very short latency or a lag and prolonged latency, or maintenance of insulated crying states in the face of social stimulation

3. Poor consolability when upset either by themselves or by the examiner

4. Increased amount of irritability over the total 20 to 30 minute exam

A combination of any two or all of these findings in the neonate exam seems likely to predict to a baby who could become colicky.


## 7. INTERVENTION AND ANTICIPATORY GUIDANCE

Intervention in the neonatal period can be that of sharing the preceding findings with the parents before discharge. On the third day I take this kind of baby to demonstrate these behaviors to the parents. As I bring him or her from sleep to an alert state, I attempt to get him or her to fix on and follow my face. I try to get the infant to turn to my voice. If he or she overshoots or cannot maintain an alert, steady state, he or she may start crying more quickly than I would expect. A baby ends up by demonstrating a kind of overreactivity to all social stimuli, as well as lability of state behavior. This defines him or her as a labile, hard-to-control baby, and I can predict for myself that he or she will cry often, especially at the end of the day. As I demonstrate the hypersensitivity and the labile state behavior, I describe it to the parents without using perjorative adjectives. A description of this behavior might be "He certainly shoots from sleeping to crying in a hurry." The mother will then say, "I've found that too. What do I do about it?" Because I do not know what to do about it at it that point, I reply that

> I'm not sure yet, but you and I will need to keep in communication so we can help him work it out. As he gets older, he may well learn how to control it himself; if he doesn't, we may have to work to teach him.

In this way, I am trying to ally myself with the mother in "our" work with the baby to help him or her learn smoother state control. The other symptoms of hypersensitivity are handled similarly in order to help the parents to see that these are a part of the baby himself or herself and set the goals for our work to help him or her mature toward a smoother, more comfortable organization. If the parents can see that these mechanisms reside in their baby, they will not be at the mercy of the inevitable feeling that an infant's crying and irritability are symptoms of their own failure as parents. After sharing the baby's behavior during the behaviors elicited by the neonatal assessment, I urge the parents to communicate with me about the progress they are making towards their handling of their infant. I discuss the daily crying that may occur in the second or third week. We speak of it as if it may well become part of a baby's daily cycle and as serving an organizing purpose. I assure them that this kind of crying need not be representative of any other pathology, such as neurological or gastrointestinal pain; or else they will worry about these later, and I shall need to remind them of my having accounted for them in my exam. We discuss other kinds of crying at this time. I anticipate with them the quality of the cries an infant may have that will represent pain, hunger, discomfort, and sleepiness, and we talk briefly about what their own parental responses should be to each of these.

As the regular crying period develops at 2 to 3 weeks, I expect a phone call from the parents. We discuss the way in which to differentiate this predictable crying from one that needs attention. We attempt to rule out a cry of pain and distress. Our differentiating criteria become

1. if the crying period appears at a regular time of day;
2. if the crying stops when the baby is picked up or played with;
3. if it starts as an irritable whimper and only gradually builds up to an intense cry; and
4. if it can be interrupted easily.

In these instances, one can be pretty sure it is not a cry needing serious attention. When I make recommendations about them, they are based on the kind of baby we have shared initially, and they know I know their baby. If I am assured by their description that this does not represent real pain or discomfort and that there is no real pathology behind it, I suggest instituting a routine to help allay their fears and to help the baby with his or her crying period. This routine will consist of

1. trying to find a reason for a baby's cry;
2. if this is unsuccessful, allowing him or her to fuss for 15 minutes at a time;

3. picking the infant up to soothe him or her; afterward
4. feeding him or her water or sweetened water to give him or her a chance at extra sucking; and
5. trying to bring up a bubble.

Afterward, I suggest reducing stimuli at this time of the day. Soft, low-keyed music, swaddling the infant, coupled with other attempts to teach the infant how to calm himself or herself, including a pacifier or thumb sucking, may be of real help. I accompany these suggestions with a repetition of our original observation of the hypersensitivity and state lability of a baby and an understanding of the activity cycle to include the fussing period at the end of the day.

In a small percent (about 8%) of these babies, giving parents an intellectual understanding of this crying does not work. In these cases, I find it is necessary to examine the baby again in order to be sure there are no physical reasons for intractable crying, for example, milk allergies, hernia, or abdominal obstruction. By watching the baby with his or her parents at the time of such a crying period, I can share their anxiety and make observations about the baby's use of crying and inconsolability. I watch the parents' handling and feeding of the baby for clues as to the quality of their interaction. Often, as we watch, I can manipulate the environment and offer simple reassurance as we observe together. If these efforts do not work, I am alerted to the need for even more work toward understanding the distress in the baby and the increasing distress in the parents. Otherwise, I may expect a more serious breakdown in the parent–infant relationship in the future.

## 8. A CLINICAL EXAMPLE

Crying in an infant can be a reflection of an unreachable baby. We (Als, Tronick, Adamson, & Brazelton, 1976) found a group of babies who were small for gestational age by ponderal index (a relationship of length to weight) (Miller & Hassanein, 1971). In these lean babies, the placenta had been inadequate in nurturing the baby at the end of the pregnancy. They were skinny, lean, and worried looking. Their fat and subcutaneous tissue stores were depleted, and they had loose, peeling skin. As neonates, these infants had poor motor tone and low activity levels. They were poor in their responsiveness to social stimuli—to the face and voice and to being cuddled—and were poor in their responses to being consoled. In the first 2 weeks, they preferred to be left alone. We felt that they were already overwhelmed by any stimulation from the environment. Their frowns in response to social stimuli indicated how easily they were overstimulated by usual social cues. They looked exhausted after a short period of interaction. We felt that, as a group, they were hypersensitive babies and were more easily overloaded and exhausted by social interaction. As newborns, their mothers claimed they were quiet, "good, and preferred to be left alone." If their mothers played with them too much, they would frown or go to sleep. If they played with them at feeding time, these babies would spit up. Therefore, their mothers left them alone, and they rarely cried in the first 3 weeks.

Beginning at 3 weeks of age and lasting to 16 weeks, the mothers reported long, unreachable crying periods. We felt that the costly hypersensitivity that accompanied their undernourished state at birth resulted in hypersensitive, crying babies later on. As they became stronger, their "shutting out" of stimuli took the form of crying rather than quiet sleeping. This group of babies may represent one end of a spectrum of normal infants who have a neurophysiological hypersensitivity at birth. Crying may be one of their few ways of dealing with this. We have since recognized other groups of such infants in our clinical work, and there are probably many etiological reasons in addition to poor nutrition for hypersensitivity and of the crying that results from it.

Intractable crying or colic may be a reflection of pathology in the parents, as well. A depressed or an anxious mother may certainly contribute to a breakdown in parenting in which the baby begins to cry for long, inconsolable periods. The emotional state of the parents needs to be a serious consideration in the treatment of "colic."

## 9. CONCLUSIONS

The chapters in this book that address the developmental aspects of crying over time point to these aspects as a combination of innate characteristics of the central nervous system (or of temperament) and an infant's reaction to environmental handling. An infant's ability to respond to stimulation and to calm himself or herself is critical for observations for the clinician to make on each visit over time. The interaction of an infant's characteristics with his or her environment can then be charted on a course that parallels the development of the parent–infant relationship. The symptom of crying then becomes a critical window into the interaction for the clinician who is interested in anticipatory guidance and in the best outcome for parents and infants. This volume will help the clinician and the researcher to understand the important dimensions of crying as a whole, relatively new behavioral window into infants and their interaction with their environment.

## 10. REFERENCES

Als, H., Tronick, E., Adamson, L., & Brazelton, T. B. The behavior of the full term yet underweight newborn. *Developmental Medicine and Child Neurology*, 1976, *18*, 590.

Benjamin, J. D. Prediction and psychopathological theory. In L. Jessner & E. Pavenstedt (Eds.), *Dynamic psychopathology in childhood*. New York: Grune & Stratton, 1959.

Boukydis, C. F. Z. *Adult response to infant cries*. Unpublished doctoral dissertation, Pennsylvania State University, 1979.

Boukydis, C. F. Z., & Burgess, R. Adult physiological response to infant cries: Effects of temperament of infant, parental status, and gender. *Child Development*, 1982, *53*, 1291–1298.

Brazelton, T. B. Psychophysiologic reactions in the neonate. *Journal of Pediatrics*, 1961, *58*, 513.

Brazelton, T. B. Crying in infancy. *Pediatrics*, 1962, *29*, 579.

Brazelton, T. B. Neonate Behavioral Assessment Scale. *National Spastics Foundation Monograph 50*. London: Heinemann, 1973.

Brazelton, T. B. Assessment as a method for enhancing infant development, zero to three. *Bulletin of the National Center for Clinical Infant Programs*, Sept. 1982, 2–8.

Brazelton, T. B., & Lester, B. M. *Infants at risk: Assessment and intervention*. New York: Elsevier–North Holland, 1983.

Emde, R. N., Gaensbauer, T. J., & Harmon, R. J. Emotional expression in infancy: A biobehavioral study. *Psychological Issues Monograph 37*, 1976.

Frodi, A., & Lamb, M. E. Child abusers' responses to infants' smiles and cries. *Child Development*, 1980, *51*.

Golub, H. L. A psychoacoustical model of the infant cry and its use for medical diagnosis and prognosis. In J. J. Wolf & D. H. Klatt (Eds.), *Speech communication*, 1979.

Karelitz, S., & Fisichelli, V. R. The cry thresholds of normal infants and those with brain damage. *Journal of Pediatrics*, 1962, *61*, 679.

LeBoyer, F. *Childbirth without violence*. New York: Alfred Knopf, 1975.

Lester, B. M. Spectrum analysis of the cry sounds of well nourished and malnourished infants. *Child Development*, 1976, *47*, 237.

Lester, B. M. A synergistic process approach to the study of prenatal malnutrition. *International Journal of Behavioral Development*, 1979, *2*, 377–393.

Lester, B. M. Change and stability in the newborn behavior. In T. B. Brazelton, & B. M. Lester (Eds.), *Infants at risk: Assessment and intervention*. New York: Elsevier–North Holland, 1983.

Miller, H. C., & Hassanein, K. Diagnosis of impaired fetal growth in newborn infants. *Pediatrics*, 1971, *48*, 4.

Prechtl, H., & Beintema, O. The neurological examination of the fullterm newborn infant. *National Spastics Foundation Monograph*. London: William Heinemann, 1964.

St. James Roberts, I. Neurological plasticity, recovery from brain insult, and child development. In H. Reese & L. Lipsitt (Eds.), *Advances in child behavior and development* (Vol. 14). New York: Academic Press, 1979.

Sell, E. *Follow-up of the high risk newborn: A practical approach*. Springfield, Ill.: Charles C Thomas, 1980.

Tronick, E., & Brazelton, T. B. Clinical uses of the Brazelton Neonatal Behavioral Assessment. In B. Z. Friedlander (Ed.), *Exceptional infant A3: Assessment and intervention.* New York: Brunner/Mazel, 1975.

Wasz-Höckert, O., Lind, J., Vuorenkoski, V., Partanen, T., & Valanne, E. The infant cry: A spectrographic and auditory analysis. *Clinics in Developmental Medicine 29.* Philadelphia: Lippincott, 1968.

Wiesenfeld, A., Zander Malatesta, C., & DeLoach, L. Differential parental responses to familiar and unfamiliar infant distress signals. *Infant Behavior and Development,* 1981, 4(3), 281.

Zeskind, P. S., & Lester, B. M. Analysis of cry features in newborns with differential fetal growth. *Child Development,* 1981, *52,* 207–212.

# 16

# Crying
## A Clinical Overview

## MARTIN BAX

## 1. INTRODUCTION

Cry studies have been going on for a relatively short period of time, and perhaps it is not surprising that the great majority of cries have either been studied often in the infant, when he or she is "captive" in the hospital, or in the relatively immobile child. If one looks through literature reviews, one finds that it is hard indeed to find much information about crying in older children. This, of course, is because ways of investigating an occasional phenomenon are difficult to devise and because the cry is regarded as a symptom that itself is not of particular significance but that represents a sign of distress. Paradoxically, although in the young infant the cry may actually provide some precise communication about what the infant's needs are, crying in the older child may well represent a breakdown in his or her more sophisticated communication systems, and he or she cries because he or she is unable to talk and communicate about his or her pain and distress. Whereas in the young child, therefore, we can concentrate on the acoustic properties of the cry, in the older child we are looking more to try and understand what underlies or causes him or her to cry.

MARTIN BAX • Community Paediatric Research Unit, St. Mary's Hospital Medical School, London NW3 5RN, England.

341

Very little work taking crying as a straight symptom has been done; yet the cry as a symptom well may have some value in understanding the different personality and psychopathological development of young children. Thus, in any nursery group of children, some children will cry more readily when upset, whereas other children, from an early age, will appear stoical and indifferent to pain and insult. This obviously may represent an interaction with the child's social environment that is ill understood at the moment and is a subject that is very ripe for studying. Crying as a signal of distress in the older school-age child is discussed again later in this chapter, but it has not been the focus of any specific studies; rather, it is related to the diagnosis of antisocial or neurotic behavior. It well might be that a selective study of children who cry would provide us with insight into child psychopathology that we presently lack. The remainder of this chapter is concerned with providing an outline for the clinician who is faced with cry as a symptom, and it is necessarily more anecdotal than in the preceding chapters in this book that deal with the data that we have about crying. This clinical application may seem to some readers as rather limited.

## 2. CRYING IN THE PRESCHOOL CHILD

For the infant and young child, the cry is his or her most obvious way of showing distress when something is wrong with him or her. Although, as the other chapters indicate, there may be acoustical properties of the cry that allow one to hazard some guesses at the reason for a child's crying, in most instances the clinician seeing a child whose parents present with a complaint of crying will not in this day and age have such acoustical studies available to him or her. In general, the cry of the child in trouble will form a more general distress pattern and not be of specific diagnostic value. Although children may sometimes be brought to the doctor with the specific complaint of crying alone as a presenting symptom, this is not very common. We asked parents of children under 2 years of age whether their child cried often or was miserable at four different ages. Although this was a relatively common complaint at 6 weeks, by 6 months it had become uncommon and never occurred in more than 2% of our population. Crying in the very young child was, of course, very commonly associated with colic. On the other hand, in these young children (see Table 1), night waking was a very common symptom, which was virtually always associated with crying, although this was not what the mothers complained of. They were able to stop the crying if they gave the child attention. Over the age of 2,

*Table 1. Number and Percentage of Subjects, by Age, Complaining of Night Waking*

| Night Waking | Age | | | |
|---|---|---|---|---|
| | 6 months | 1 year | 18 months | 4½ years |
| 4 or more nights a week | 43 (13) | 43 (21) | 43 (17) | 28 (10) |
| 2–3 nights a week | 20 (6) | 16 (6) | 25 (9) | 17 (6) |
| Total $n^a$ | 531 | 278 | 251 | 278 |

[a] n for each age is approx 300.

many children present behaviors such as temper tantrums, and these, of course, are virtually always accompanied by crying. We present some figures from our own data at 2, 3, and 4½ years of age where it can be seen that more than 10% of children at all ages were having a temper tantrum nearly every day, and of these, some were having three or more tantrums a day (see Table 2).

## 3. CRYING AT SCHOOL

Crying is an expected behavior in preschool children. By the time a child reaches the age of 5 or 6 and goes to a school, crying is not as common. Children may, however, be tearful on coming to school initially, and this is a quite common phenomenon. We found that about 5% of children might cry in the mornings when they first started school. Most of those children who find school alarming quickly settle in, and, given sympathetic handling, the crying is hardly a worry to the clinician. Crying may continue to occur in the young schoolchild as an occasional phenomenon associated, of course, both with physical and psychological trauma, but it becomes increasingly less common. By the time the child is 8, 9, or 10 years of age, in most Western cultures crying is a behavior that is severely discouraged by the peer group, and reports of frequent distress and crying at this age are a cause for concern. Similarly, during the adolescent years, crying is not a behavior that most young people

*Table 2. Number and Percent of Temper Tantrums by Age[a]*

| Temper Tantrums | Age | | |
|---|---|---|---|
| | 2 years | 3 years | 4½ years |
| 3 or more a day | 18 (6) | 17 (5) | 6 (2) |
| Nearly every day | 39 (13) | 43 (13) | 25 (9) |
| Total $n$ | 302 | 331 | 278 |

[a] Recorded only at age of 2 and over.

in developed countries display. At these ages, boys are not expected to cry, but the behavior is more acceptable in girls, and teenaged girls may be observed weeping in certain situations. A girl who weeps in school may attract the sympathetic attention of her peers, whereas a boy who was seen weeping would be treated negatively by his peers.

This generally descriptive account of crying is not, particularly in the school years, supported by any hard and fast data about crying as a behavior, and the reader must determine for himself or herself how good an impressionistic picture has been painted.

## 4. THE DIAGNOSTIC VALUE OF THE CRY—CRYING UNDER THE AGE OF TWO

In the prelanguage phase, the cry is the only way the child can show distress, and evaluation of the cry is important therefore in assessing many clinical situations. Crying, either as a presenting symptom or as an accompanying symptom in association with some other complaint, needs full assessing. One asks, When does the child cry, how long does the cry persist, and how and why does it stop, or rather, what relieves it? Is the crying accompanied by any other movement, such as the movement of the legs seen in the colicky baby who is crying? I have seen a baby who proved to have an ear infection shaking his head and crying, but I have never been convinced that poking or banging of the ears by a baby is associated with earache. (The baby who cries and pulls at his or her ears usually proves *not* to have an ear infection.)

There are many obvious ways in which both the parent and the clinician can correctly determine the cause of the cry. The response to intervention can confirm that the diagnosis was correct. A baby who is screaming and who immediately stops when offered the breast or bottle and sucks lustily is hungry. The baby who night wakes and cries and stops crying as soon as he or she is picked up, and indeed may even laugh and coo with pleasure, is not in pain and clearly his or her cry is one of distress and boredom at being alone at night. On the other hand, the colicky baby, although his or her crying may ease when he or she is picked up, may still be irritable and restless and cry intermittently. The child who wakes with some infection will continue crying and not be so easy to soothe. In our studies of night waking, we found that children who had had frequent upper respiratory tract infections were more likely to night wake than others. Here the pattern again would be that the child would wake and cry. Presumably he or she may have been remembering the previous occasions when they woke with pain, and the arrival of a reassuring adult will abort the attack. Similarly, a child may start night crying after a hospitalization experience, although in both instances a child may start crying again if he or she is simply returned to his or her own bed or cot.

## 5. THE TODDLER-AGED CHILD

Once a child can talk it becomes possible to ask why he or she is crying. In the 2–3-year-old, of course, it is often not possible to do this during the crying episode when the child is in a temper. People therefore sometimes forget to ask the child to explain his or her symptoms. It is, however, always worth asking the child when he or she is calmer why he or she was crying, and what it was that upset him or her. As in the infant group, the child will, of course, cry with pain if he or she is ill, or if he or she is hurt. The bangs and knocks that the 2-year-old child gets cause instant crying that is usually very quickly soothed. The 2-year-old who trips up and cries often seems not to be crying with pain but with frustration and anger that he or she should have been so clumsy.

The crying of a child in a temper tantrum has a very typical pattern. He or she may, of course, suddenly lose his or her temper and go into a full-blown tantrum at once, but more commonly, irritation builds up more slowly. A tantrum may be set off by a mother's refusing to meet some wish, for example, for a chocolate. The child starts being niggling and then when his or her wishes are persistently thwarted, he or she finally starts full-blown screaming. Once this stage has been reached, the temper tantrum cannot be aborted. Usually a child will scream for 3 to 5 minutes, although he or she can go on longer (and this is particularly true in handicapped children). If a child is left alone, his or her full-blown screaming begins to abate, and he or she then sobs intermittently, finally giving a gasping sob every half minute for some 5 minutes. Attempts to intervene at this stage and comfort the child have the effect of pushing him or her back into the full-blown temper tantrum. An intuitive judgment of the time at which the child is able to accept comfort is needed in such a situation.

As has been well documented by Bowlby and others, a child will cry with distress when he or she is left alone by those with whom he or she has a close affectional bond. Thus, the child deserted in a hospital will sob inconsolably for 10 or 20 minutes. In fact, this distress is reassuring, and a period that causes much more worry is the one that eventually arrives when a child stops crying when his or her mother or father (caretaker) leaves him or her, and, at the same time, fails to cry when his or her mother comes to visit. The absence of the distres signal can also be seen in abused children and is of much more concern than the presence of the distress signal in the normal child.

Crying in the preschool child is common, but persistent crying at this time should alert the pediatrician into thinking about some organic factor that he or she might have missed, which might have caused the child pain. Probably the commonest cause is an otitis media where the young infant will give no indication where the pain is.

## 6. CRYING IN THE SCHOOL-AGED CHILD

The young school-aged child may cry quite often. Crying on arrival at school when a parent leaves him or her is of course common, but usually, providing school and the parents work together (the parent should be encouraged to be present while the child settles in), this sort of upset should be handled easily, and, as the child gets older, parental separations, of course, become easier for him or her to take. Children may cry if they are scolded by the teacher or if they are being bullied by other children, and so on. Here the crying is a useful mechanism that draws attention to the child's problem, which one then hopes will be handled appropriately. Indeed, at these early school ages, the anxious, shy child who does not display emotion may escape attention, which is perhaps a more serious problem. In my experience, crying as a symptom of depression in children is not common, although it may become more common in adolescence. In the older schoolchild during puberty and adolescence, there is a strong sex difference in crying; crying is more common in girls than in boys. Anxiety or rebuff may lead to crying in a girl, and a child who is frequently tearful at school will often prove to have problems at home that make her more vulnerable to the normal rebuffs of social life in the school environment. Cultural patterns may be important here; some societies are more accepting of crying than others.

At all ages, therefore, if crying presents at school, one is going to have to take a careful account of when the crying occurs, what sorts of things trigger it, and then review both the social and emotional situation of the child in the school and at home. Management is rarely directed at the symptom but at the underlying cause of the crying. Mass crying of a very hysterical nature occurs and can be seen, for instance, at rock and pop concerts, the significance of which is beyond the scope of this essay.

## 7. HANDICAPPED CHILDREN

So far, I have been discussing the "ordinary" child with no obvious disorder. There is no doubt that crying is more common in handicapped children. Both the mentally and physically handicapped as well as a severely disturbed child, such as an autistic child, cry more than ordinary children, although I know of no documentation of how often this occurs. I have sat with a child with a severe language disorder, possibly of an autistic nature, who cried for an hour and a half solidly in the clinic, and I could find no way of effectively intervening with this distress. The mother reported that this child frequently cried for hours at home. An indication that he was not usually in pain was that the cry would be abated if his mother took him for a walk. While crying, he would repeatedly drag her by the hand toward the door. He appeared to gain some satisfaction from walking around the streets near their home, and this was the only way she could stop his crying.

Clearly, this account raises more questions than it answers, but the crying attacks were probably related (1) to the mother's depression (the child cried less when the mother was on antidepressants); (2) lack of stimulating and engaging activities in his very restricted home environment; and (3) occasional physical pain (there was some improvement when his gross dental caries were treated).

Crying in the severely handicapped child can be due to a neglected physical cause that must be searched for carefully. A child may cry because he or she is in pain and may be unable to indicate what the pain is. Careful investigations must be carried out to look for the source of pain. Earache and toothache are possibilities, the abdominal pain can be caused by reflex esophagitis or gastritis in the severely handicapped child. Dislocated hip and a restrictive posture associated with skin sores are other examples of pain that causes crying. It is probably true to say that the more one investigates crying in the retarded and handicapped child, the more likely one is to find a physical cause of the crying.

However, the preceding example of the child who needed to walk the streets indicates that there are other reasons for crying that are less easy to identify. Social changes in the child's circumstances may disturb a handicapped child. Thus, a mentally handicapped child became very distressed when his father changed his hours of work and was at home less during the day. The family members failed to identify this and were mystified by the crying. The loss of a particular object that may have had significance to a child can be a cause of crying. If a child is being moved from one residence to another, rituals that have gone on in a previous environment may well need repeating while the child adapts to the new environment. There remain handicapped children in whom it is extremely difficult to locate or understand the cause of their crying, except perhaps as a reflection of the overall sadness of their condition.

## 8. CRYING—ITS SOCIAL ROLE

Crying is a behavior that society says belongs to childhood. It is something the maturing child learns or is taught to leave behind. This may be a mistake. Most clinicians will have observed the relief a client has gained from crying over some deep or genuine distress and recognized an adult who "can't" cry as needing to. Perhaps we should think about teaching our children to cry more often.

## 9. BIBLIOGRAPHY

Bax, M., & Hart, H. Health needs of pre-school children. *Archives of Disability in Childhood*, 1976, *51*(11), 848–852.

Bax, M., Hart, H., & Jenkins, S. Assessment of speech and language development in the young child. *Pediatrics*, 1980, *66*(3), 350–354.

Egan, D. F., Illingworth, R. S., & Mac Keith, R. C. *Developmental screening 0–5 years*. London: Spastics International Medical Publications in association with William Heinemann Medical Books, 1969.

Committee on Child Health Services. *Fit for the future: Report of the Committee on Child Health Services*, Cmnd 6684. London: Her Majesty's Stationery Office, 1976.

Fundudis, T., Kolvin, I., & Garside, R. *Speech retarded and deaf children*. London: Academic Press, 1979.

Haggerty, R. Life stress, illness and social supports. *Developmental Medicine and Child Neurology*, 1978, *20*, 442–452.

Hart, H., Bax, M., & Jenkins, S. The use of the child health clinic. *Archives of Disability in Childhood*, 1976, *51*, 848–852.

Hart, H., Bax, M., & Jenkins, S. The value of a developmental history. *Developmental Medicine and Child Neurology*, 1978, *20*, 442–452.

Hart, H., Bax, M., & Jenkins, S. Community influences on breast feeding. *Childcare, Health and Development*, 1980, *6*, 175–187.

Ingram, T. T. S. Delayed development of speech with special reference to dyslexia. *Proceedings of the Royal Society of Medicine*, 1963, *56*, 199.

Jenkins, S., Bax, M., & Hart, H. Behaviour problems in pre-school children. *Journal of Child Psychology and Psychiatry*, 1980, *21*, 5–17.

Moss, P., & Plewis, I. Mental distress in mothers of pre-school children in Inner London. *Psychological Medicine*, 1977, *7*, 641–652.

Rutter, M., Graham, P., & Yule, W. *A neuropsychiatric study in childhood clinics in developmental medicine*, 35/36. London: Heinemann, 1970.

*Social trends*. London: Her Majesty's Stationery Office, 1980.

Whitmore, K., Bax, M., & Tyrrell, S. Clinical medical officers in a child health service. *British Medical Journal*, 1979, *1*, 242–245.

# Epilogue

PETER H. WOLFF

The 15 essays of this volume present a comprehensive review of current knowledge about the neonatal human cry, its evolutionary origins, diagnostic implications, and effects on the social partner. They also review the technical and theoretical limitations on current objective methods for analyzing cry vocalizations. There is considerable overlap of themes across chapters starting from different theoretical orientations, and there are extensive cross-references to the same body of empirical findings. These convey a sense of closure on the topic that suggests either that most of the essential clinical and theoretical issues have been adequately investigated, or else that a fresh look and new theoretical perspectives are needed if the field is to progress. In these concluding remarks, it may, therefore, be useful to review the primary focus of past research, the major gaps in our current knowledge, and possible directions of future investigations.

Eleven of the 15 essays consider the various diagnostic implications of cry vocalization as a behavioral marker of impaired central nervous system organization or as a communicative signal that may elicit inappropriate and sometimes life-threatening responses from the social partner. The guiding assumption in these essays is that human cries contain much subtle information that cannot be inferred directly from observation and therefore require objective methods of acoustic analysis. Several theoretical chapters provide indirect support for this assumption by

PETER H. WOLFF • Department of Psychiatry, The Children's Hospital, Boston, Massachusetts 02116.

outlining the physiological and neurological substrates of human sound production and by indicating that the production of vocal sounds depends critically on the integration and fine tuning of many neurological and respiratory mechanisms. What appears on the surface to be a "simple" reflex response to physical discomfort is, therefore, in fact, the final common pathway of multiple systems converging on a complex behavior pattern so that distinct pathophysiological variables may influence the quality of cry sound production along different acoustic parameters that are not evident to direct observation but can be identified by computer-assisted analysis.

Chapters on the social communicative function of crying similarly indicate that human cries are not a stable evolutionary guarantee of appropriate social interaction between infant and primary caretaker. Instead, the parents' prior experience with caring for infants, their physiological responses, and idiosyncratic interpretations of the cry as well as the quality of cry sounds themselves may each determine what this species-specific peremptory social signal contributes to the interaction between infant and parent. Therefore, it is reasonable to expect that the objective measurement of cry vocalizations will identify infants at unusual risk for neurological abnormality or deviant behavioral development and will also identify parents who are at greater than usual risk for child abuse and neglect. However, a number of residual theoretical questions and technical difficulties must be resolved before one can safely accept the use of human cries as reliable tools for the diagnosis of brain damage or for the clinical and theoretical prediction of developmental outcome.

Usually the identification of children at high risk for developmental disability from severe behavioral handicaps in the neonatal period is sufficiently straightforward so that it requires no sophisticated technical instrumentation, although even in severe cases long-term outcome is sometimes surprisingly benign. The more challenging and theoretically more interesting problems of diagnosis and prediction stem from subtle transient or variable behavioral abnormalities observed in the young infant. They constitute the greater public health issue and, at the same time, the statistically and theoretically more complex problems of scientific analysis. The urgent need for objective behavioral markers of unusual risk for sudden infant death, child abuse, or deviant intellectual and social development is persuasively argued by the authors of several of the chapters. Yet, previous follow-up studies based on the extended neonatal neurological examination that samples multiple reflexes, behavioral state variations, and the like, as well as detailed observations of mother–child interaction and cry pattern analysis have not been very successful in identifying infants who are at unusual risk for developmental disability or social pathology. At the same time, they may introduce new iatrogenic problems either of overdiagnosis or of unwarranted parental reassurance (Prechtl, 1981). It is, of course, possible that previous methods of behavioral diagnosis were simply inadequate for the task and that computer-assisted methods of acoustic analysis based on deductive models and on knowledge derived from physiology may make it possible to predict long-term behavioral outcome from subtle abnormalities of the neonatal cry without making clinically unacceptable Type I or Type II errors.

Yet, everything we have learned about the ontogenesis of behavior from developmental genetics, embryology, neurobiology, and psychobiology argues against such optimism. Behavioral development invariably involves regressions, deletions, and major transformations in the relation between form and function (Gould, 1977; Oppenheim, 1981). Qualitatively new patterns of behavior are induced during development whose origins cannot be inferred directly from their presumed antecedent behavioral causes (Gottlieb, 1976). Superficially analogous forms serve very different functions in older, as compared to younger, children, whereas qualitatively different forms may fulfill identical functions in the organism at different stages of developmental differentiation (Werner, 1948). What is true for normal development holds equally for deviant development. Rarely, if ever, is there a linear or simple epigenetic link between behavioral abnormalities during the neonatal period and developmental outcome. The qualitative transformations between form and function that characterize behavioral development are also evident in the regressions and deletions of neural mechanisms and in the postnatal emergence of new forms in the central nervous system organization of primates (Goldman & Lewis, 1978). Subtle neurological abnormalities that induce clinically significant delays or disabilities in one social context may have no detectable effect in other circumstances, or they may be entirely overshadowed by the adverse effect of a disorganized social environment (Neligan, Kolvin, Scott, & Garside, 1976; Sameroff & Chandler, 1975).

Such theoretical constraints on the possibility of reliable prediction from neonatal behavior to developmental outcome take on clinical importance in humans because human cultures place a high value on the physical health and optimal mental development of infants so that health professionals are ethically compelled to diagnose as early as possible and to intervene as soon as possible. Yet, current trends in developmental pediatrics and infant psychiatry suggest that a breathless translation from limited data to formal programs of intervention may do infants and parents more harm than good as long as the predictive validity of neonatal marker variables has not been rigorously tested under controlled conditions; as long as there is no strong evidence to indicate that available methods of intervention are of significant benefit to either infant or parent; and as long as there is no sound theoretical basis for predicting development from subtle abnormalities during early infancy. Thus, the detailed study of human cry vocalization has raised ethical problems of risk/benefit ratio that have not been adequately addressed.

In addition, the book reveals a number of important gaps in our knowledge about the functional significance of human cries as mechanisms of behavioral adaptation. Few studies, for example, have examined the developmental history of cry vocalizations, ontogenetic changes in the morphology of cry sounds after the neonatal period, the mechanisms by which infants learn to control their sound productions, the physiological or psychological links between cry vocalization and early speech sounds, or about the differentiation of crying as an expression of emotion. Yet, older infants, children, and even adults do cry, and their causes and motives for crying change dramatically during the growth years (Leach, 1972). As several chapters indicate, there are important functional links between the physiological mechanisms of cry vocalization and of speech production. Some of the mechanisms are adapted exclusively for vegetative regulation, but others are specifically adapted for vocal communication and speech production. The cry signal of nearly all mammalian species can be characterized in terms of its acoustic properties of pitch, intensity, and duration. In humans, the same variables convey semantically important information during vocal communication. Comparative animal studies indicate that experience modifies the sound patterns of vocal communication extensively during development, and similar experiential factors probably transform the cry pattern of humans into more differentiated expressions of emotion and lexically complex forms of prosodic speech. On theoretical grounds, it is unlikely that the mechanisms involved in babbling and early speech sound production should emerge de novo at some stage in development after birth, or that the developing organism should make use of physiological control mechanisms for the production of speech sounds that differ qualitatively from those at their disposal for cry vocalization. Thus, a common set of hierarchically ordered integrative control systems may be involved not only in cry prduction but also in the regulation of prosodic features of human speech; and a detailed developmental analysis of sound production during the first year of life may reveal the process of this transformation (see, for example, Stark, 1980).

By the same token, we know little about changes in the causes and motives of crying as expressions of emotion (Bernal, 1972; Murray, 1979). The traditional classification of neonatal vocalizations as birth cries, hunger cries, and pain cries that is frequently referred to in the volume implies both cause and morphology. However, the range of variations in acoustic signals even within these categories is so extensive that existing taxonomies may not be particularly useful as a point of departure for the developmental analysis of causes and motives for crying. The chapters on vocalization in primates and kittens indicate that isolation, hunger, and fear are nearly universal causes of crying in all vocal mammalian species. In addition, humans acquire new motives for crying as their intellectual grasp of the social world and their psychological needs for emotional interchange differentiate (Leach, 1972; Wolff, 1969). Thus, a developmental analysis of the shift from reflex responses to physical discomfort or social isolation as the principal causes of crying, to the use of cry and noncry vocalizations as instrumentalities for manipulating and communicating with the social partner, should provide important clues concerning the differentiation of emotional expressions and the social basis of sensorimotor intelligence.

This brief review of work that has been accomplished to date on human cry vocalizations and of the major deficiencies in our current knowledge argues against the conclusion that the topic has been exhaustively studied. A considerable effort has been devoted to the use of neonatal cries as diagnostic markers and as predictors of developmental disabilities. Although further work along established lines may be enhanced materially by the introduction of theoretically and technically advanced methods of acoustic analysis, there is some room for skepticism about the possibility of ever making reliable predictions about the long-term developmental outcome on the basis of subtle variations within one discrete behavioral system of the young infant.

On the other hand, there seems to be a significant lack of systematic observational or experimental data concerning the development of crying after early infancy, the transition from cry vocalization to early speech sounds, or the induction of new causes and motives for crying and their behavioral manifestations in differentiated sound patterns. As a fundamental mechanism of sound production that is present in all healthy and most functionally impaired infants and as the most preemptory expression of emotion available to infants during the early months, cry production should from an evolutionary and developmental perspective contain many of the components that will contribute essentially to differentiated forms of social communication and to the expression of complex emotions during later stages of developmental adaptation. As such, the human cry appears to be one ideal candidate for focused developmental investigations.

## 1. REFERENCES

Bernal, J. Crying during the first 10 days of life and maternal response. *Developmental Medicine and Child Neurology*, 1972, *14*, 362–372.

Goldman, P. S. & Lewis, M. E. Developmental biology of brain damage and experience. In C. W. Cotman (Ed.), *Neuronal plasticity*. New York: Raven Press, 1978.

Gottlieb, G. The roles of experiences in the development of behavior and the nervous system. In G. Gottlieb (Ed.), *Development and neural and behavioral specificity*. New York: Academic Press, 1976.

Gould, S. J. *Ontogeny and phylogeny*. Cambridge, Mass.: Belknap Press, 1977.

Leach, E. The influence of cultural context on non-verbal communication in man. In R. A. Hinde (Ed.), *Non-verbal communication*. Cambridge: Cambridge University Press, 1972.

Murray, A. D. Infant crying as an elicitor of perinatal behavior: An examination of two models. *Psychology Bulletin*, 1979, *86*, 191–215.

Neligan, G. A., Kolvin, I., Scott, D. M., & Garside, R. F. *Born too soon or born too small*. London: Heinemann Medical Books, 1976.

Oppenheim, R. W. Ontogenetic adaptations and retrogressive processes in the development of the nervous system and behavior: A neuroembryological perspective. In K. J. Connolly & H. F. R. Prechtl (Eds.), *Maturation and development*. London: Heinemann Medical Books, 1981.

Prechtl, H. F. R. Assessment methods for the newborn infant: A critical evaluation. In P. Stratton (Ed.), *Psychobiology of the human newborn*. New York: Wiley, 1981.

Sameroff, A. J., & Chandler, M. J. Reproductive risk and the continuum of caretaking casualty. In F. D. Horowitz, M. Hetherington, S. Scarr-Salapateck, & G. Siegel (Eds.), *Review of child development research* (Vol. 4). Chicago: University of Chicago Press, 1975.

Stark, R. E. Stages of speech development in the first year of life. In G. H. Yeni-Komshian, J. F. Kavanagh, & C. A. Ferguson (Eds.), *Child phonology* (Vol. 1). New York: Academic Press, 1980.

Werner, H. *Comparative psychology of mental development*. New York: International Universities Press, 1948.

Wolff, P. H. The natural history of crying and other vocalizations in early infancy. In B. Foss (Ed.), *Determinants of infant behaviour* (Vol. 4). London: Methuen, 1969.

# Index